THE COLD WAR

MATCH THE PICTURES

WE STAY IN

SAFE PLACES

Atomic Bombing Care

TURN

MAGILL'S CHOICE

THE COLD WAR

Volume I
1945 — 1955

Edited by
Robert F. Gorman
Texas State University

SALEM PRESS

Pasadena, California   Hackensack, New Jersey

Cover image: The Granger Collection, New York

Frontispiece: Children's educational toy reflecting the pervasive American fear of atomic warfare during the early 1950's, when people of all ages were barraged with instructions on how to prepare for nuclear attack. Using knobs on the lower right side of this box, children moved pictures in the window at the top to match hazardous conditions with appropriate actions. *(Library of Congress)*

The paper used in these volumes conforms to the American National Standard for Permanence of Paper for Printed Library Materials, Z39.48-1992 (R1997).

Most of the essays in this work originally appeared in Salem Press's *Great Events from History: The 20th Century, 1941-1970* (2007) and *Great Events from History: The 20th Century, 1971-2000* (2008). New material has been added.

Library of Congress Cataloging-in-Publication Data
The Cold War / edited by Robert F. Gorman.
    p. cm. – (Magill's choice)
  Most of the essays in this work originally appeared in other Salem Press sets. New material has been added.
  Includes bibliographical references and index.
    ISBN 978-1-58765-730-6 (set : alk. paper) – ISBN 978-1-58765-731-3 (vol. 1 : alk. paper) – ISBN 978-1-58765-732-0 (vol. 2 : alk. paper) – ISBN 978-1-58765-733-7 (vol. 3 : alk. paper) 1. Cold War. 2. History, Modern–1945-1989. 3. World politics–1945-1989. 4. United States–Foreign relations–Soviet Union. 5. Soviet Union–Foreign relations–United States. 6. International relations–History–20th century I. Gorman, Robert F.
  D843.C577242 2011
  909.82–dc22

                                                            2010038864

First Printing

PRINTED IN CANADA

CONTENTS

Contents

PUBLISHER'S NOTE

This fiftieth publication in Salem Press's popular Magill's Choice series offers a comprehensive collection of articles on the individual events and developments that molded one of the most important epochs of modern history—the Cold War. That period is considered to have ended in 1991, but publication of this set comes at a moment when renewed tensions between Russia and the West are evoking memories of the long years during which the entire world was obsessed with the East-West rivalries of the Cold War.

The three volumes of *The Cold War* offer a unique event-by-event history of the full sweep of Cold War history, with 179 up-to-date essays, chronologically arranged, beginning with the early 1945 Yalta Conference and concluding with the December, 1991, dissolution of the Soviet Union. The Introduction by Professor Robert F. Gorman surveys the origins and full history of the Cold War, and his Epilogue reviews post-1991 developments and assesses the legacy of the Cold War through the first decade of the twenty-first century.

COVERAGE

Few eras in modern history have had broader and deeper impacts on the world than the Cold War. It can be said to have begun almost immediately after the conclusion of World War II in 1945 and ended in late 1991 with the virtual collapse of the Soviet Union. At its center, the Cold War was a struggle for economic, military, and ideological supremacy in the world between the United States and the Soviet Union that directly involved most of the nations of North America, Europe, and East Asia and indirectly involved most of the rest of the world at one time or another. Although the Cold War never erupted into a direct military conflict between its two principal adversaries, it raised tensions and aggravated shooting wars all over the globe. Indeed, few armed conflicts among nations between 1945 and 1991 had no Cold War implications.

Drawing on the rich resources of Salem's recently published twentieth century *Great Events from History* sets, *The Cold War* presents 179 essays on specific events and developments. A virtual catalog of the most important world conflicts and crises of nearly a half century, the Table of Contents lists such momentous subjects as Churchill's Iron Curtain speech, the Marshall Plan, formation of the North Atlantic Treaty Organization (NATO) and the Warsaw Pact, Nikita Khrushchev's denunciation of Joseph Stalin's regime, the Hungarian uprising, the space race, the U-2 incident, the Bay of Pigs invasion, the Cuban Missile Crisis, China's Cultural Revolution, the Korean and Vietnam wars, warming U.S.-China relations, the Soviet invasion of Afghanistan, the democratization of communist nations, the fall of the Berlin Wall, and finally, the dissolution of the Warsaw Pact and the Soviet Union.

The events of the Cold War were not confined to political and military strife. They also encompassed economic, cultural, and even athletic conflicts, and they even fostered literary and film genres built around stories of espionage and intrigue that were epitomized in the fictional secret agent James Bond. these subjects are also covered in *The Cold War* in essays on topics such as Olympic Games controversies, George Orwell's dystopian novel *Nineteen Eighty-four,* Arthur Miller's play *The Crucible*, Hollywood blacklisting, the James Bond films, and John le Carré's grimly realistic spy novels.

The Cold War is actually much more than a collection of loosely connected essays, as it can be read as an integrated history of the Cold War. To tie the essays together more thoroughly and make it easier to understand the history and meaning of the Cold War, Professor Gorman's Introduction examines the entire history of the Cold War, from its origins in the rise of American and Russian power during the late nineteenth and early twentieth centuries against the backdrop of the collapse of European international dominance owing to two World Wars, and the emergence of the post-World War II bipolar era. It then goes on to trace each stage in the development of the Cold War up to its end in 1991. Professor Gorman's Epilogue follows the essays on events, reexamining the Cold War in the context of post-1991 developments up to mid-2010.

ORGANIZATION

The first point of entry for users of *The Cold War* is the chronological arrangement of the essays themselves. As in the *Great Events* sets, the essays offer a student-friendly format. With few exceptions, the essays are of approximately uniform length—about 1,900 words each. Almost every essay is illustrated with at least one photograph, map, or textual sidebar.

The top matter of each essay contains these components:
- the most precise date, or date range, of the event
- a descriptive name of the event that highlights its relevance to the Cold War
- a summary paragraph describing the event and encapsulating its significance
- the locale of the event
- a list of subject categories to which the event belongs, such as "Atrocities and War Crimes," "Civil Rights and Liberties," and "Cultural and Intellectual History"

- a list of "Key Figures"—names, vital dates, and a brief descriptions of the major people involved in the event

The text of every essay is divided under these subheadings:

- "Summary of Event" provides a detailed narrative of the event
- "Significance" sums up the event's broader historical impact
- "Further Reading" contains an annotated list of up-to-date sources for further study
- "See also" lists cross-references to other essays on related subjects within *The Cold War*

Additional finding aids in the set include Category, Personage, Photo, and General Subject Indexes at the end of volume 3, and a Table of Contents arranged by keywords in the article titles at the beginning of volume 1. The third volume also contains a Bibliography of general works on the Cold War and a Glossary of Cold War terminology.

ACKNOWLEDGMENTS

Salem Press would again like to thank the more than 135 scholars who wrote or updated the essays in *The Cold War*. We are especially grateful to the set's Editor, Professor Robert F. Gorman of Texas State University, for lending his expertise on the subject to the selection of the set's articles, the updating of individual articles, and the writing of the insightful Introduction and Epilogue.

CONTRIBUTORS

Stanley Archer
Texas A&M University

Paul Ashin
Stanford University

David Barratt
Montreat College

Paul Barton-Kriese
Indiana University East

Iraj Bashiri
University of Minnesota

Richard P. Benton
Trinity College

Milton Berman
University of Rochester

Nicholas Birns
Eugene Lang College, The New School

Arthur Blaser
Chapman University

Kent Blaser
Wayne State University

Steve D. Boilard
Western Kentucky University

Jo-Ellen Lipman Boon
Buena Park, California

Steve Breyman
Rensselaer Polytechnic Institute

Patrick Bridgemon
Fresno, California

John A. Britton
Francis Marion University

William S. Brockington, Jr.
University of South Carolina–Aiken

Michael H. Burchett
Limestone College

Laura M. Calkins
Oglethorpe University

Byron Cannon
University of Utah

R. O'Brian Carter
Berry College

Frederick B. Chary
Indiana University Northwest

Peng-Khuan Chong
Plymouth State College

Eric Howard Christianson
University of Kentucky

Lawrence I. Clark
Delaware, Ohio

Bernard A. Cook
Loyola University

Charles E. Cottle
University of Wisconsin

Mark DeStephano
Saint Peter's College

Dixie Dean Dickinson
Tidewater Community College

Fredrick J. Dobney
St. Louis University

Jack Donnelly
University of North Carolina at Chapel Hill

Victor Manuel Durán
University of South Carolina–Aiken

Loring Emery
Hamburg, Pennsylvania

David G. Fenton
Connecticut College

David G. Fisher
Lycoming College

George J. Fleming
Calumet College

George Q. Flynn
University of Miami

John C. Foltz
University of Idaho

John K. Franklin
Graceland University

Larry N. George
California State University, Long Beach

Mitchel Gerber
Southeast Missouri State University

Nancy M. Gordon
Amherst, Massachusetts

Robert F. Gorman
Texas State University

Hans G. Graetzer
South Dakota State University

Lloyd J. Graybar
Eastern Kentucky University

Johnpeter Horst Grill
Mississippi State University

Manfred Grote
Purdue University–Calumet

Larry Haapanen
Lewis-Clark State College

Michael Haas
California Polytechnic University, Pomona

Celia Hall-Thur
Wenatchee Valley College

P. Graham Hatcher
Shelton State Community College

A. W. R. Hawkins
West Texas A&M University

Peter B. Heller
Manhattan College

Diane Andrews Henningfeld
Adrian College

Samuel B. Hoff
Delaware State University

Ronald K. Huch
Eastern Kentucky University

Raymond Pierre Hylton
Virginia Union University

Mahmood Ibrahim
California Polytechnic State University, Pomona

Yvonne Johnson
Central Missouri State University

Richard C. Jones
Texas Woman's University

Charles L. Kammer III
College of Wooster

Christopher J. Kauffman
Marillac College

Edward P. Keleher
Purdue University, Calumet

Leigh Husband Kimmel
Indianapolis, Indiana

Richard D. King
Ursinus College

Paul W. Knoll
University of Southern California

Gayla Koerting
Nebraska State Historical Society

Ernest H. Latham, Jr.
American Romanian Academy

Joseph Edward Lee
Winthrop University

Ann M. Legreid
Central Missouri State University

Thomas Tandy Lewis
St. Cloud State University

Alar Lipping
Northern Kentucky University

Contributors

Guoli Liu
College of Charleston

R. M. Longyear
University of Kentucky

R. C. Lutz
CII Group

Scott McElwain
University of San Francisco

Paul Madden
Hardin-Simmons University

Robert Franklin Maddox
Marshall University

Paul D. Mageli
Kenmore, New York

Barry Mann
Alliance Theatre

Carl Henry Marcoux
University of California, Riverside

Thomas David Matijasic
Prestonsburg Community College

James I. Matray
California State University, Chico

Laurence W. Mazzeno
Alvernia College

Michael W. Messmer
Virginia Commonwealth University

Christina J. Moose
Pasadena, California

Gordon R. Mork
Purdue University

Maya Muir
Portland, Oregon

Joseph L. Nogee
University of Houston

Cathal J. Nolan
Boston University

Norma C. Noonan
Augsburg College

Deepa Mary Ollapally
Swarthmore College

Robert J. Paradowski
Rochester Institute of Technology

Jerry A. Pattengale
Azusa Pacific University

Thomas R. Peake
King College

William A. Pelz
Institute of Working Class History

Julio César Pino
Kent State University

Kasia Polanska
University of Minnesota

Michael Polley
Columbia College of Missouri

George F. Putnam
University of Missouri, Saint Louis

John Radzilowski
University of Alaska Southeast

Steven J. Ramold
Eastern Michigan University

R. Kent Rasmussen
Thousand Oaks, California

William G. Ratliff
Georgia Southern University

Dennis Reinhartz
University of Texas at Arlington

Charles W. Rogers
Southwestern Oklahoma State University

Jill Rollins
Trafalgar College

Carl Rollyson
City University of New York, Baruch College

Joseph R. Rudolph, Jr.
Towson University

José M. Sánchez
Saint Louis University

Richard H. Sander
Northwestern University School of Law

Richard Sax
Lake Erie College

Larry Schweikart
University of Dayton

Heather L. Shaffer
Temple University

Martha A. Sherwood
Eugene, Oregon

Michael S. Smith
University of South Carolina

Ira Smolensky
Monmouth College

Marjorie Smolensky
Carl Sandburg College

Barry M. Stentiford
Grambling State University

Taylor Stults
Muskingum College

Emory M. Thomas
University of Georgia

Jack Ray Thomas
Bowling Green State University

Stephen C. Thomas
University of Colorado at Denver

Ryan M. Touhey
University of Waterloo, Canada

Marcella Bush Trevino
Barry University

William M. Tuttle
University of Kansas

Robert D. Ubriaco, Jr.
Illinois Wesleyan University

Charles F. Urbanowicz
California State University, Chico

William T. Walker
Chestnut Hill College

Donald A. Watt
Dakota Wesleyan University

Martha Ellen Webb
University of Nebraska–Lincoln

Gregory Weeks
Webster University, Vienna

Ivan Weinel
Kansas City, Missouri

Theodore A. Wilson
University of Kansas

Clifton K. Yearley
State University of New York, Buffalo

Edward A. Zivich
Calumet College

COMPLETE LIST OF CONTENTS

VOLUME I

VOLUME II

VOLUME III

KEYWORD LIST

Pact Is Signed by Three Pacific Nations Against Communist Encroachment, Security (Sept. 1, 1951), 234

Pact Is Signed, Warsaw (May 14, 1955), 358

Pact, Dissolution of the Warsaw (July 1, 1991), 1033

Pact, Stalin and Mao Pen a Defense (Feb. 14, 1950), 192

Pasternak's *Doctor Zhivago* Is Published (Oct., 1957), 424

Payments Union Is Formed, European (July 1, 1950), 203

Peace with Japan Is Signed in San Francisco, Treaty of (Sept. 8, 1951), 237

Peacekeeping Expenses, Crisis in U.N. Financing Emerges Over (1963-1965), 547

People's Republic of China Is Seated at the United Nations (Oct. 25, 1971), 674

Persecution of Jews, Soviets Escalate (1948), 115

Peruvian Guerrilla War Begins (1976), 752

Pipeline, Soviets Begin Construction of Siberian Gas (Nov. 20, 1981), 856

Poland Forms a Noncommunist Government (June-Sept., 1989), 951

Poland Imposes Martial Law and Bans Solidarity (Dec. 13, 1981), 862

Polish Communist Government Arrests the Primate of Poland (Sept. 25, 1953-Oct. 26, 1956), 286

Political Abuses of Psychiatry, Soviet Citizen Group Investigates (1977-1981), 768

Political Order, French Students and Workers Rebel Against the (May-June, 1968), 631

Politics Mar the Melbourne Summer Olympics, Cold War (Nov. 22-Dec. 8, 1956), 408

Politics, Morgenthau Advances Realist School of Power (1948), 111

Pope, John Paul II Becomes (Oct. 16, 1978), 787

Potsdam Conference (July 17-Aug. 2, 1945), 34

Power Plant, Soviet Union Completes Its First Nuclear (June 27, 1954), 314

Primate of Poland, Polish Communist Government Arrests the (Sept. 25, 1953-Oct. 26, 1956), 286

Prisoners of War are Forced into Repatriation, Soviet Exiles and (Feb. 11, 1945), 25

Private Ownership, Soviet Parliament Allows (Mar. 6, 1990), 1009

Prodemocracy Demonstration in Tiananmen Square, China Crushes (June 4, 1989), 958

Psychiatry, Soviet Citizen Group Investigates Political Abuses of (1977-1981), 768

Pueblo, North Korea Seizes the USS (Jan. 23, 1968), 626

Reagan Proposes the Strategic Defense Initiative (Mar. 23, 1983), 870

Realist School of Power Politics, Morgenthau Advances (1948), 111

Red Scare Era, *The Crucible* Allegorizes the (Jan. 22, 1953), 267

Reforms in China, Death of Mao Zedong Leads to (Sept. 9, 1976), 756

Refugee Crisis, Arab-Israeli War Creates (Nov. 29, 1947-July, 1949), 104

Refugees from North Vietnam, Operation Passage to Freedom Evacuates (Aug., 1954-May, 1955), 326

Refugees Statute Is Approved, United Nations High Commissioner for (Dec. 14, 1950), 220

Repatriation, Soviet Exiles and Prisoners of War are Forced into (Feb. 11, 1945), 25

Republics, Germany Splits Into Two (Sept. 21-Oct. 7, 1949), 185

Revolution Begins in China, Cultural (May, 1966), 610

Revolution in Czechoslovakia, Velvet (Nov. 17-Dec. 29, 1989), 980

Revolution, Cuban (July 26, 1956-Jan. 8, 1959), 393

Rights Abuses, China Promises to Correct Human (Spring, 1978), 782

Rights Committee Is Founded, Moscow Human (Nov. 11, 1970), 667

Rights, United Nations Adopts the Universal Declaration of Human (Dec. 10, 1948), 150

Riot Against Russians, Kazakhstan Muslims (Dec. 17-19, 1986), 916

THE COLD WAR

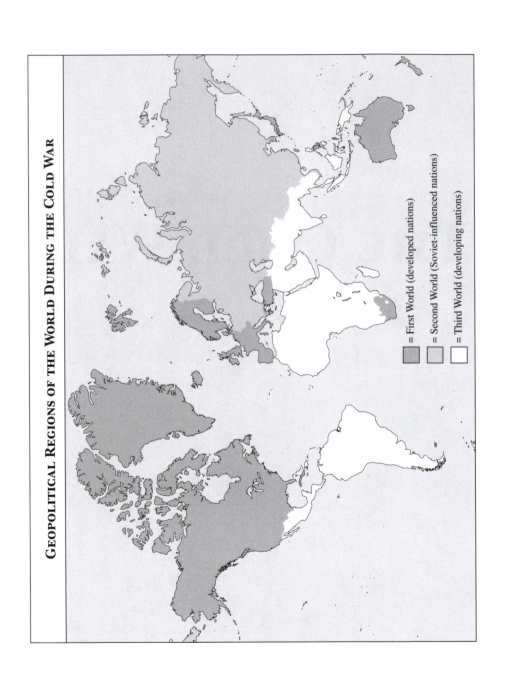

GEOPOLITICAL REGIONS OF THE WORLD DURING THE COLD WAR

= First World (developed nations)

= Second World (Soviet-influenced nations)

= Third World (developing nations)

■ EDITOR'S INTRODUCTION

AN OVERVIEW OF THE COLD WAR

The latter half of the twentieth century was dominated by a colossal ideological struggle known as the Cold War that permeated almost every aspect of international and domestic politics, economics, and culture throughout the world. This Cold War took its name from the growing international realization that the United States and the Soviet Union, the two major superpower protagonists, should, under the threat of global nuclear annihilation, avoid engagement in a direct or "hot" war. However, the contest between two opposing political and economic systems—the Western free world capitalist system led by the United States, and the Soviet-led Eastern bloc communist system—was an all-embracing contest that dominated international politics for almost a half century, from the end of World War II in 1945 to the fall of communism in 1991. Many hot wars and civil conflicts took place during this period of heightened international tension, often among proxies of the two superpowers. Fortunately, however, the two superpowers themselves avoided direct military confrontation.

ROOTS OF THE COLD WAR

In future centuries, as historians muse over the causes of the Cold War from the distance of time, they will probably notice that the late twentieth century was essentially a period of great power adjustment and realignment that was similar to other transitional periods of international relations in history. The ideological intensity of the contest will still be noticed, as will its intellectual, spiritual, and cultural dimensions. At the heart of the contest, it will be hard not to notice that two nations were the chief contestants. Both were two sleeping giants that arose during the late nineteenth century amid an international system still dominated by European colonial powers. These two new powers, the United States and Russia (later the core of the Soviet Union), would emerge as the dominant competing powers of the late twentieth century, after the old European powers had exhausted their imperial energies in two world wars.

The rise of these two superpowers will be seen as abetted by astounding technological advances in transportation, communication, and military weaponry that made their global reach possible in a relatively short time. It will be hard not to notice that the majority of the advances in science and technology originated in the United States, which emerged not only as one of two dominant military powers, but also as by far the most economically productive country yet seen in human history. However, this American advantage, which is clear even at our current distance from the twentieth century, was not always so visible during the midst of the Cold War, which more than one expert believed would end with the victory of Soviet communism.

Compared to European colonial powers, the United States and Russia both enjoyed direct control over large and expanding contiguous territories, with large national populations and substantial natural resources. By contrast, the old European powers relied increasingly on distant and often balky colonial territories and populations as sources of their wealth and power. After the U.S. Civil War ended in 1864, the United States advanced so rapidly that it ranked as the world's leading industrial nation by the early twentieth century. Russia's development was far more problematic, as its humiliating loss to the Japanese in a 1905 war illustrated. However, in terms of raw statistics such as the size of its population and extent of its territory, the Russian state was potentially a force to be reckoned with by European powers. The two devastating world wars of the twentieth century, coupled with a Marxist revolution and an often brutal internal restructuring of Russia, would eventually transform Russia into a centralized Soviet Empire with substantial military clout.

Ideology, then, cannot be ignored in any appreciation of the Cold War. During the nineteenth century, Karl Marx, the great German critic of European capitalism, had asserted with confidence that the internal contradictions of capitalism would lead inevitably to revolution and a socialist restructuring of economic life that would culminate in the ultimate victory of the communist state of materialist well being. His practical successors, such as the Russian revolutionary leader Vladimir I. Lenin and the Chinese revolutionary leader Mao Zedong, would ultimately emphasize power politics as the driving force behind economic restructuring, after they had led successful socialist revolutions in their nations in which free enterprise, individual liberty, autonomous family life and religious freedom would all give way to the centralized dominance and the power of the state.

The first great historical opportunity to experiment with the construction of the socialist state came during World War I (1914-1918), when the government of Germany smuggled Lenin back into Russia, hoping that his success in destabilizing Russia and removing it from the war would allow Germany to focus its efforts on winning victory on its western front. Lenin did succeed in toppling Russia's czarist regime, as Germany had hoped. However, around the same time, the other sleeping giant, the United States, entered the war against Germany on the side of the Allied Powers, which then won the war. The importance of the two sleeping giants was made visible, but both in certain respects both entered into another period of national introversion: Russia to build socialism in one country; the United

Vladimir Ilich Lenin, principal founder of the Soviet state.
(Library of Congress)

States to enjoy the Roaring Twenties and enter a period of isolation from international affairs.

The victory of Lenin's Bolshevik Revolution in Russia aroused opposition from Western powers, many of which openly undermined Russia's new regime during its three-year struggle to eliminate the czarist supporters. Although this opposition did not prevent the extension of substantial humanitarian aid to what became the Soviet Union during its famine of the early 1920's, a pervasive fear of the Bolshevik regime's subversive character persisted in the West. Most Western governments refused to recognize its legal existence, including the United States, which did not officially recognize the Soviet Union until 1933—the same year in which the Soviet Union finally won admission into the League of Nations.

The Soviet Union's Stalinist era began in 1924, when Joseph Stalin took power after Lenin's death. It lay the groundwork for the industrialization of the Soviet Union and its emergence as a major military power, but it was also a brutal period marked by purges, famines, and human rights abuses on a massive scale. Internationally, the Soviet Union was increasingly regarded as a dangerous regime because of the rise of communist parties across the globe that showed deference to the Soviet Union as the only existent communist state.

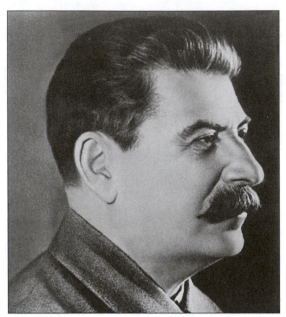

Joseph Stalin, Lenin's successor and the architect of the Soviet communist system. (Library of Congress)

Meanwhile, issues in European great-power politics left unresolved after World War I were producing an increasingly unstable political situation. The rise of the Adolf Hitler's Nazi Party in Germany in 1933 posed a threat to the whole of Europe, particularly as the Nazis initially pursued a strategy of cooperation with the Soviet Union. The 1939 nonaggression pact between Germany and the Soviet Union, coupled with their shared invasion of Poland that same year, precipitated World War II (1939-1945) in Europe and gave evidence of Soviet premier Joseph Stalin's willingness to use force to advance his own imperial aims. However, Hitler turned on his Soviet ally only a few years later, forcing Western powers—as unsavory as the prospect of alliance with Stalin was—to come to the assistance of the Soviet Union as a mutual ally against Nazi aggression.

Although Western assistance to the Soviet Union during World War II ensured its survival, mutual distrust pervaded the Three-Power Alliance led by U.S. president Franklin D. Roosevelt, British prime minister Winston Churchill, and Soviet premier Joseph Stalin. Although the three leaders would lay the groundwork for the United Nations (U.N.) as a new global organization for international peace and cooperation, strains within the Allied alliance and their competing interests doomed hopes for postwar cooperation. Stalin expected the Western capitalist countries to begin immediately competing and bickering amongst themselves, eventually allowing him to dominate Europe. The iron-fisted approach he took in Eastern Europe under Red Army occupation signaled to the West that Stalin was no democrat and that Soviet interests would for the most part prevail wherever Soviet armies held sway. At the close of World War II, the stage was already set for the Cold War to emerge.

THE COLD WAR EMERGES

By the late summer of 1945, the most global and cataclysmic of all the wars in human history was over, after claiming as many as 40 million lives. Europe lay largely in ruins, and Japan, the great power of East Asia, had suffered two atomic bomb attacks that left Hiroshima and Nagasaki covered with radioactive ash. Japan was soon occupied by American forces. The Soviet Union controlled most of Eastern Europe and the eastern part of Germany, including Germany's capital city, Berlin. China was struggling to survive after years of war and Japanese occupation, followed by its own civil war. Allied forces controlled all of Western Europe including most of Germany, with the exception of Austria. A tentative compromise between Soviet Russia and its capitalist allies prevailed, but within a climate of mutual suspicion. Hope for a better, more stable, and more peaceful world surrounded the establishment of the United Nations organization. The international body first met in London, England, in January of 1946, but within weeks of this meeting, Iran charged the Soviet Union with interfering in its internal affairs in Azerbaijan, thereby serving notice of the Soviet Union's imperial heavy-handedness. East-West controversy also marred the selection of the first U.N. secretary-general, Trygve Lie.

As the old world order of Western European domination crumbled, two anticolonialist powers, the United States and the Soviet Union, stood above amid the general ruin, although only the territory of the United States was left largely unscathed by the war. As the United States prepared to take the lead in rebuilding the world, the Soviet Union began a systematic reduction of East Germany, in reparation for the damage done to Russia. Austria, Hungary, Poland, and Romania also suffered extensively from Soviet reparations. The Western Allies also initially exacted reparations, but quickly realized that West Germany would be ruined if they continued. Followed by its allies, the United States ceased the reparations and instead began to invest in Germany's economic recovery. By contrast, the Soviet Union removed complete industries from its East German occupation zone.

As early as 1944, before World War II ended, the United States, in cooperation with other Western powers, had reconstituted the international monetary system on the foundation of the strength of the U.S. dollar, established the International Bank for Reconstruction and Development and the International Monetary Fund. Then, after the war ended, the United States embarked on the long and arduous process of rebuilding the devastated infrastructure of Europe. The Soviet Union was invited to participate in the Bretton Woods system, but it opted out of this capitalist system of reconstruction in favor of its own centrally planned communist economic system. The capitalist world of free enterprise economies and Western democratic political systems proved too free and too democratic for Soviet communism. Ideology emerged as an embedded feature of East and West bloc relations. Western European powers cleaved closely to the United States as the dominant free world power, even as the Soviet capital, Moscow, asserted ever more stringent control over the peoples of Eastern Europe.

Despite the hopefulness in the immediate postwar period, the years 1946 and 1947 proved instead to be harsh and difficult. In February, 1946, Stalin announced that international peace was impossible, putting the Soviet Union on a footing of ongoing industrial armament. U.S. policy makers recognized this development as a challenge to American leadership in the West. Within a month, former British prime minister Winston Churchill gave his famous "Iron Curtain" speech, signaling the realization of a long impending Cold War. Everywhere, retribution was in the air, with war crimes tribunals actively punishing war criminals in Europe and the Far East. Soviet prisoners of war were forcibly repatriated by Western forces to face nearly certain death in the Soviet Union. Proposals at the United Nations to put the atomic genie back into the bottle were urged, unsuccessfully, even as the new global bodies addressed the plights of refugees, children, and displaced persons.

To make matters even worse, two of Europe's coldest winters intervened while millions of displaced persons were struggling to find permanent homes. During those years, every Eastern European country was placed under the command of local communist governments answerable to Moscow, and communist parties within Western Europe also made advances. In India, revolts against British rule emerged, and Ho Chi Minh returned to Vietnam to direct communist opposition to French colonial rule. The Philippines gained independence from the United States. Mao Zedong's communist party tenaciously opposed Chang Kai-shek's Kuomintang government in China as a civil war in that devastated country deepened. Rankling under European colonial rule, many other nations began to claim their right to self-determination, as symbolized in the Indian sub-continent, which finally birthed two nations from British control with the bloody partition of India and Pakistan in 1948. In the Middle East, the Jewish state of Israel was born in conflict and spawned the Arab-Israeli dispute.

SEEDS OF THE COLD WAR

On February 9, 1946, Joseph Stalin delivered a speech in Moscow arguing that the world wars were the result of capitalism and that communism, especially as it played out in Eastern Europe, was a superior system and would eventually prevail. The speech, which alarmed Western leaders, was part of the newly emerging Cold War propaganda:

Marxists have more than once stated that the capitalist system of world economy contains the elements of a general crisis and military conflicts, that, in view of that, the development of world capitalism in our times does not proceed smoothly and evenly, but through crises and catastrophic wars. The point is that the uneven development of capitalist countries usually leads, in the course of time, to a sharp disturbance of the equilibrium within the world system of capitalism, and that group of capitalist countries which regards itself as being less securely provided with raw materials and markets usually attempts to change the situation and to redistribute "spheres of influence" in its own favor—by employing armed force. As a result of this, the capitalist world is split into two hostile camps, and war breaks out between them. . . .

The issue now is not whether the Soviet social system is viable or not, because after the object lessons of the war, no skeptic now dares to express doubt concerning the viability of the Soviet social system. Now the issue is that the Soviet social system has proved to be more viable and stable than the non-Soviet social system, that the Soviet social system is a better form of organization of society than any non-Soviet social system.

One of the leaders alarmed by Stalin's speech was British prime minister Winston Churchill, who warned in a speech of his own that Stalin's plan was expansion for Russia. Angered, Stalin struck back, and the Cold War was under way:

In substance, Mr. Churchill now stands in the position of a firebrand of war. And Mr. Churchill is not alone here. He has friends not only in England but also in the United States of America.

In this respect, one is reminded remarkably of Hitler and his friends. . . . Mr. Churchill begins to set war loose, also by a racial theory, maintaining that only nations speaking the English language are fully valuable nations, called upon to decide the destinies of the entire world.

Sources: Joseph Stalin, *Speeches Delivered at Meetings of Voters of the Stalin Electoral District* (Moscow: Foreign Language Publishing, 1950). "Stalin's Reply to Churchill." *The New York Times*, March 14, 1946, p. 4.

By 1947, nationalist anger and resentment roiled across the world, and human hardship and ideological contest sharpened. In the spring of that year, U.S. president Harry S. Truman announced American economic support for Greece to help it regain stability to stave off its own communist rebellion. The Truman Doctrine, as it came to be known, extended support to other countries similarly situated, and under the Truman administration's evolving Marshall Plan, American aid would bolster economic production and allow nations to strengthen their local military capacities to confront seditious activity. Moscow rejected involvement in the Marshall Plan and forbade its East European satellites from participating. When Czechoslovakia voted to participate in the plan, Moscow called its leaders to account, and Czech foreign minister Jan Masaryk died under suspicious circumstances. In Hungary, the Communist Party moved against the Roman Catholic hierarchy, and Cardinal József Mindszenty took refuge in the U.S. embassy in Budapest.

Meanwhile, Americans were urged to evacuate China, as that country's communist rebellion gained steam in advance of its victory in 1949. Inside communist countries, repression of human rights was common, and Western governments fearing communist subversion began investigations that touched their foreign services, their educational systems, and even their institutions of popular culture, such as the Hollywood movie industry. In the Soviet Union, even music was subjected to repression and control. In 1949, the Cold War intensified when the Soviet Union imposed a blockade on Berlin to prevent ground supplies from reaching the city's Western occupation zones. The West responded by resupplying the city by air, and the North Atlantic Treaty Organization (NATO) took form as the means by which to contain communist expansionism. The Cold War was in full bloom, and it was about to grow hot.

CONFRONTATION, CONFLICT, AND PEACEFUL COEXISTENCE

The success of the Maoist rebellion in China in 1949 signaled that communism was a global threat, intent on expansion and domination, and thus requiring the establishment on the part of the noncommunist world of strenuous efforts at regional alliance building and containment. As announced by President Truman's secretary of state, Dean Acheson, Korea seemed beyond the line of Western concern. In the summer of 1950, the Korean War began when North Korean troops, with tacit Soviet support, invaded South Korea, occupying most of the Korean peninsula before U.N. forces were deployed under American leadership. A U.N. counterattack repelled North Korean forces and subsequently occupied most of the North. The deployment of U.N. forces was possible because the Soviet Union had boycotted U.N. meetings owing to that body's failure to accept the credentials of the new communist government in China. In the Soviet Union's absence, the Security Council took swift action to oppose North Korean aggression. Realizing its error, the Soviet delegation returned to the United Nations to limit the damage. As American forces approached the Yalu River, China entered the fray. The Korean War mired down into a bloody war of attrition until both sides agreed in 1953 to a cease-fire that essentially placed the border between North and South Korea where it had been before the war.

Meanwhile, China had invaded and subdued Tibet in 1950. This action was a further indication of its willingness to dominate neighboring states. These developments showed that the Cold War was capable of growing very hot and very deadly, but the scale of the conflicts had remained limited. During the 1950's, confrontations and hot spots would develop with communist China and the West over the Taiwan (Formosa) Strait, with Soviet intervention in Hungary in 1956, and with the Suez crisis of the same year. New refugee flows kept the office of U.N. High Commissioner for Refugees (UNHCR) busy as it faced a rising tide of humanitarian crises, many of which concerned exiles escaping from behind the Iron Curtain.

During the 1950's, the United States continued its policy of containment implied in its establishment of the Rio Pact in 1947 with Latin American Countries and in the formation of NATO in 1949. In 1951, the United States established the Australia, New Zealand, United States alliance (ANZUS), in 1954 the Southeast Asia Treaty Organization (SEATO), and in 1955 the Central Treaty Organization (Baghdad Pact) to protect Central Asia. The American containment policy also included bilateral security pacts with a number of key countries, including Taiwan and South Korea.

The Soviet Union regarded Western containment as "capitalist encirclement" and responded in 1955 by establishing the Warsaw Pact to serve as its own regional security agreement with East European communist states. In Western Europe, the move toward economic cooperation was intensified under the perception of a potential threat from the Soviet military presence in Eastern Europe. In 1950, the European Payments Union was established to coordinate Marshall Plan resources, and an even more intense experiment at economic integration, the European Coal and Steel Community, was formed by six European countries. The success of this organization led to the establishment of the European Common Market in 1956. Global and regional alliance politics remained a constant feature of the Cold War.

An ominous feature of Cold War competition included the emergence nuclear weapons in the arsenals of the competing blocs. The United States developed the first atomic bomb in 1945. Attempts to eliminate this class of weapons foundered within the United Nations, as the Soviet Union quietly developed its own atomic bomb, which it tested in August, 1949. In November, 1952, the United States countered by testing its first, and far more deadly, thermonuclear hydrogen bomb, which the Soviet Union matched only nine months later. The nuclear arms race was in full career as both sides developed increasingly deadly hydrogen bombs and methods of delivering them, such as long-distance bombers, intercontinental ballistic missiles, and nuclear submarines capable of launching missiles from under water.

The threat of global nuclear annihilation cast a terrible pall over the Cold War years. Defensive actions and technology emerged for advance detection of potential nuclear attacks. The United States and Canada established the Distant Early Warning (DEW) Line in 1954, and the North American Aerospace Defense Command (NORAD) in 1958. When the United States had enjoyed sole nuclear status or superior nuclear status during the late 1940's and early 1950's, it had threatened Moscow with massive retaliation should the Soviet Union attack its Western European allies. However, as the Soviets gained substantial nuclear weapons capacity, the Western military doctrine shifted to a strategy of flexible response. With the death of Stalin in 1953 and the rise of Nikita Khrushchev as his successor, the Cold War settled down into a period of "peaceful coexistence."

Peaceful coexistence did not imply the cessation of competition, which pervaded nearly all aspects of life. It affected cultural life and domestic politics. In the United States, Joseph McCarthy's hearings on government subversion in the Senate raised the specter of Soviet espionage inside the United States. In Eastern Europe, communist powers attacked bishops of the Catholic Church, arresting and incarcerating Poland's Cardinal Stefan Wyszyński from 1953 to 1956—a replay of Hungary's arrest of Cardinal Mindszenty in 1948. After Mindszenty's release from prison in 1956, he took shelter in the U.S. embassy in Budapest when the Soviet Union invaded Hungary in November of that year. He remained sequestered there through fifteen years.

Communist hostility to basic religious freedom and expression was pervasive, with churches placed under direct communist control, harassed or in some cases, as with the Catholic Church in Romania, officially dissolved. Even the world of sports was marred by Cold War hostility, notably the Melbourne Olympic Games of 1956. Indeed the Olympics became a kind of scorecard of free world versus communist superiority, even to the point of boycotts of the Moscow Olympics in 1980, and the Los Angeles Olympics of 1984. East-West competition also extended to space technology, with the Soviet Union successfully launching the first space satellite in 1957—an event that sparked the space race in subsequent years. During the following year, the United States established its National Aeronautical and Space Administration (NASA), and the space programs that eventually led to the United States landing men on the moon in 1969.

During the 1950's and 1960's, another aspect of Cold War competition and confrontation centered on nations of the developing world that won independence from European rulers by the dozens as the colonial era came to a rapid close. As new countries gained independence, the Soviet Union competed for their support and favor. Although many new nations preferred a policy of neutrality or nonalignment—as evidenced in the 1955 Afro-Asian Conference on Non-Alignment held in Bandung, Indonesia—in reality many of them perceived socialist forms of government and economic life as preferable to Western capitalism and democracy.

Meanwhile, the United Nations, once firmly under Western control, changed dramatically as the Soviet Union and China competed successfully for foreign policy allies in the international body. National liberation movements in many parts of the developing world relied on communist support, or at least on socialist principles of opposition and organization. During the

A famous moment in Cold War history that would become known as the "Kitchen Debate" occurred in 1959, when Soviet premier Nikita Khrushchev (center left) and U.S. vice president Richard M. Nixon (center right) were caught on camera arguing the relative merits of capitalism and socialism at the American National Exhibition in Moscow, Russia. In response to Nixon's invitation, Khrushchev visited the United States later the same year. (Library of Congress)

1950's, this was especially apparent with Ho Chi Minh's successful opposition to French rule in Indochina. In 1954, Vietnamese communists defeated the French at Dien Bien Phu, precipitating a massive flow of refugees from North to South Vietnam the following year. The stage was then set for a divided Vietnamese state and an even more deadly civil war in subsequent decades.

Fearing communist influences in Central America, the United States supported the toppling of a pro-socialist government in Guatemala in 1954. In Cuba, the seeds of civil war had been planted in 1953 with an unsuccessful military rebellion in which the young revolutionary leader Fidel Castro had been captured. His release in 1955 and return to Cuba in December, 1956, led to three years of increasingly successful resistance to the dictatorship of Fulgencio Batista, whom Castro finally brought down in January, 1959. Although his government was recognized by the United States, Castro soon announced his full support for communism, and Cuba became ground zero of the Cold War in the Western Hemisphere. Meanwhile, in Asia, in Latin America—where U.S. vice president Richard Nixon confronted rioters during his 1958 tour of the region—and in the Middle East and Africa where new nations were rising, the specter of the Cold War reared its head, and the developing world became a battleground of Cold War competition.

During the early 1960's, Cold War confrontation became especially tense. In Africa, an appeal to the United Nations by the newly independent government of the former Belgian Congo to keep its country from falling apart initially produced cooperation by the great powers on the Security Council. However, as the U.N. operation in the Congo proceeded, deep ideological fissures opened up between Western and Soviet interests allied with the contending forces inside the Congo. Soviet vetoes threw the matter into the U.N. General Assembly, which authorized expanded military operations that bogged down into an expensive and controversial four-year operation. The Soviet Union opposed and resented the Congo operation and refused to pay any of its expenses.

In 1961, East Germany began raising the Berlin wall to prevent its citizens from fleeing to the West as refugees. Meanwhile, refugees were streaming out of Cuba, where Castro's regime repressed business elites, treating them as enemies of the state. The United States demonstrated its hostility toward the regime through its support of the Bay of Pigs invasion. That attempt to topple Castro was easily crushed by the Cuban government, but it left an impression of indelible hostility between Havana and Washington. Shortly thereafter, Castro secretly invited Moscow to begin erecting missile silos on Cuban soil to give the Soviet Union a nuclear beachhead in the Western Hemisphere. When this development was discovered by the United States in

October of 1962, it precipitated the Cuban Missile Crisis, during which the world appeared to hover on the brink of nuclear war. In the showdown that followed, it was Soviet premier Nikita Khrushchev who blinked and agreed to dismantle Soviet missile silos in Cuba. The Soviet Union was not then in a position to force a successful conventional or nuclear confrontation with the United States. This Soviet humiliation led to Khrushchev's downfall in 1964, but it also prompted a more determined effort by his successor, Leonid Brezhnev, to seek nuclear parity with the United States. The first serious attempts to step back from open nuclear confrontation also took place, as the United States and the Soviet Union negotiated the Hotline Agreement and the Limited Nuclear Test Ban Treaty in 1963. After China joined the nuclear club in 1964, further progress was made by the superpowers to negotiate a nuclear nonproliferation treaty in an effort to staunch the spread of nuclear weapons.

During the years that followed the Cuban Missile Crisis, the Cold War moved into a phase of limited cooperation, along with ongoing competition, as the United States sank deeper into the mire of the Vietnam War, and the Soviet Union explored a much more robust foreign policy of expansionism. Indeed, during the 1960's and 1970's circumstances appeared to shift decisively in favor of global communist forces, as the United States and the West experienced a crisis of confidence.

RISING SOVIET INFLUENCE AND THE AGE OF DÉTENTE

In retrospect, the Cuban missile crisis seems to have demarcated a shift in Cold War behavior and strategy. On one hand, it revealed the military superiority of the West. On the other hand, it revealed how closely Washington and Moscow had flirted with possible nuclear cataclysm. While the crisis led to a more sober exploration of policies that would stabilize the nuclear arms race, it also moved Soviet leaders to redouble their efforts to strengthen their military capacity, to court more allies in the developing world, and to expand their influence in the United Nations. This could be accomplished, as Brezhnev showed, while seeking a generally friendlier relationship with Washington.

As for the United States, its expensive intervention in Vietnam during the 1960's had a number of deleterious effects that forced it eventually to reconsider its containment policy and its role as global policeman. As war casualties mounted in Southeast Asia and domestic and foreign opposition to the Vietnam War increased during the late 1960's, the United States began to explore ways to extricate itself from this increasingly expensive and destabilizing conflict. During the 1960's, the Civil Rights and antiwar movements produced riots in American cities and on university campuses. President Lyndon B. Johnson's domestic spending on his Great Society program coupled with military spending on the Vietnam War without raising taxes, sent U.S. budget deficits soaring and foreign trade imbalances rising. Even U.S. allies began to voice opposition to the Vietnam War and its adverse effects on the international economy. Foreign confidence in the American economy, the American dollar, and American leadership waned as a domestic crisis in leadership and authority increased. During the spring of 1968, Johnson announced that he would not seek another term as president, paving the way for Richard Nixon's electoral victory in 1968. That same year was marked by the communists' Tet Offensive in Vietnam that seemed to challenge optimistic military claims that American troops would "be home by Christmas." The assassination of presidential candidate Robert F. Kennedy and violent clashes between police and antiwar demonstrators at the Democratic National Convention in the summer of 1968, gave Nixon, the Republican "law-and-order" candidate the edge over Democrat Hubert H. Humphrey, even as Alabama governor George Wallace's third-party campaign attracted the support of conservative southern Democrats, signaling a major realignment in American party politics.

Meanwhile, a more confident Soviet Union crushed a political uprising in Czechoslovakia in September of 1968, even as the United States was exploring peace talks with North Vietnam. In November, 1968, as Nixon celebrated his electoral victory, Brezhnev asserted that the Soviet Union had a right to intervene in the affairs of socialist states when forces hostile to socialism threatened them. The Brezhnev Doctrine, as it came to be known, asserted Soviet supremacy in the Warsaw Pact, and its aggressive intention to prevent any socialist state from withdrawing from the socialist bloc. By contrast, President Nixon unveiled his own weakened version of the containment policy less than a year later in July, 1969, when he announced that U.S. allies facing internal threats would be obliged to undertake the primary responsibility for their own military defense. Under this Nixon Doctrine, the United States would honor its treaty agreements with its allies and provide general nuclear defense, but no longer would it deploy military forces to meet every civil war.

With Henry Kissinger as his secretary of state, Nixon also began to explore ways to cooperate with both the Soviet Union and China in a policy known as détente. Brezhnev reciprocated Nixon's offer of cooperation, and this new-found détente resulted in arms control treaties, such as the 1969 Strategic Arms Limitations Talks (SALT), along with cultural and trade exchanges and technological agreements. After China emerged from the scars of its Cultural Revolution, it, too, was receptive to peace overtures from Washington during the early 1970's. Its receptivity was partly motivated by its own disputes with the Soviet Union that had included armed clashes along the Ussuri River in 1969. Although Nixon's détente policy promoted greater superpower cooperation during the 1970's, it masked the fact that the Soviet Union was steadily spending to strengthen its conventional military capacity and gradually gaining nuclear superiority over the United States. Moreover, a confident and global assertion of Soviet power advanced deepening ties with allies in Southeast Asia, Africa, and Latin America, even as American confidence sank in the wake of the Watergate Scandal that forced President Nixon's resignation coupled with the general humiliation of military failure in Vietnam.

By contrast, Soviet fortunes seemed to rise as Moscow backed the successful victory of communists in South Vietnam in 1975. Marxist forces, with Soviet and Cuban help, triumphed in Angola, even as the U.S. Congress refused to authorize support for pro-Western factions there. In 1976, the Soviets, again with Cuban help, backed a new Marxist government in Ethiopia that severed ties with the United States. During the late 1970's, the Soviet Union began to supply substantial support to the new Marxist regime in Nicaragua and to leftist guerrillas in El Salvador, even as U.S. president Jimmy Carter chastised friend and foe alike for human rights violations. In 1979, the Soviets invaded Afghanistan to install a Marxist government to Brezhnev's liking there. Détente had reached its limits. Soviet power was confidently being asserted throughout the globe. Even before the Soviet invasion, Jimmy Carter, assessing the general condition of his country in June, 1979, asserted that the United States was experiencing a "crisis of confidence," in what came to be known as his "malaise" speech. After the invasion, he took stock of the situation again. Finding a more determined voice, he increased U.S. military expenditures, slapped a grain embargo on the Soviet Union and announced an American boycott of the Moscow Olympics as punishment for the Soviet invasion of Afghanistan. Despite Carter's bold moves, a demoralized American public looked elsewhere for a leader to restore public confidence and found him in the form of Ronald Reagan, who resoundingly defeated Carter in the 1980 elections.

TOWARD THE COLLAPSE OF COMMUNISM AND THE COLD WAR

By 1980, a new cast of characters was emerging on the global stage with a world vision that went beyond the parameters of out-worn Yalta agreements of the 1940's. As historian John Lewis Gaddis has observed, these new leaders, coupled with millions of anonymous freedom seekers, established the basis for the ultimate collapse of the stifling and increasingly desiccated communist system. The notable personages included Pope John Paul II, British prime minister Margaret Thatcher, and U.S. president Ronald Reagan, who would establish in the West a new sense of confidence and hope. During the early 1980's, they faced a succession of aging Soviet leaders. After Brezhnev, the architect of Soviet resurgence, died in 1982, he was followed in rapid succession by Yuri Andropov, who died in 1984, and Konstantin Chernenko who died in 1985. These deaths opened the way for the younger and reform-minded Mikhail Gorbachev to lead the Soviet Union. Although Gorbachev is credited by many as the star performer in the eventual end of the Cold War, it is pertinent to note that Gorbachev essentially failed to achieve his goal of reforming the communist system while preserving the Soviet Union's general position of leadership in the global communist system. This proved to be impossible in light of the over-extension of Soviet power, the bankruptcy of its economic situation, and its inability to address the deepest desires of the human spirit for freedom and dignity. In China, another "new leader," Deng Xiaoping, whose more liberal views on ideology had won him demotion under Mao, emerged paramount leader of China in 1978, when he began ushering in a new era of flexibility to Chinese foreign and economic policy.

When a little known Polish bishop, Karol Josef Wojtyła, was elevated to the papacy as Pope John Paul II in 1978, Poles, who had suffered under communist repression for decades, rejoiced. Within a year, the communist state would find itself powerless to prevent millions from flocking to his papal masses during his first papal visit to Poland. The new pope preached a message of human rights, religious liberty, and peace. After his visit, workers in the Gdansk shipyard were led by Lech Wałesa, a little-known electrician, to form the worker's trade union called Solidarity. This bold assertion formed a direct challenge to the communist claim of being a worker's paradise. In May, 1981, an assassination attempt against the pope, traceable through Bulgaria to Moscow, indicated how threatening he was to the communist system. Meanwhile, the Polish worker's rebellion continued throughout the year, ending with the imposition of martial law in December. During this crisis the Soviet Union decided that it dare not invade in the face of such widespread popular opposition that had been inspired by John Paul II, despite the Brezhnev Doctrine. Over the next decade, the pope made many more trips to Poland and other parts of Eastern Europe, always to enthusiastic public responses. His clarion call to respect human rights and to seek religious liberty through peaceful change, offered new hope to millions who had lived under repression, thus planting a revolutionary seed that would later blossom into direct challenges to communist governments. However, even more would be needed to effect political changes.

In 1978, Margaret Thatcher assumed office as prime minister of Great Britain, and in January, 1981, Ronald Reagan became president of the

United States. Their shared support for liberty and their condemnation of the repressive nature of the communist system was often met with scorn both in domestic and international settings. Nevertheless, both leaders presided over substantial economic recoveries within their two countries. Both restored a sense of national confidence, even as they both attacked the evils of communist repression and took steps directly to confront it. Reagan doubled U.S. defense spending by 1985 and declared American support for freedom fighters around the globe and direct military support in the new Reagan Doctrine. He also announced a new Strategic Defense Initiative (SDI) to replace the mutually assured destruction policy of earlier Cold War origins and called the Soviet Union an "Evil Empire."

Although many critics deplored and opposed Reagan's moves, a majority of Americans applauded this new sense of American confidence. After Gorbachev took power in the Soviet Union in 1985, it seemed that the Soviets finally had a leader who could fence with Reagan. However, even Gorbachev, though pursuing policies of glasnost (openness) and perestroika (restructuring), was ultimately no match for Reagan, who insisted not on arms control talks, but on arms reductions talks, even as SDI would proceed to put nuclear deterrence on a defensive rather than offensive footing. As Reagan outspent Gorbachev and as the U.S. economy soared in the wake of tax cuts, the Soviet Union found itself in a position of economic stagnation and international overreach. The Soviet war in Afghanistan was going badly, as American aid supplied Afghan guerrillas with missiles capable of denying air superiority to Soviet forces. Soviet client states around the world drained Soviet resources. Riots by minority populations in Kazakhstan in 1986 and in Armenia in 1988 served notice of the impending collapse of the Soviet Union's vaunted multicultural empire. Under all these pressures, Gorbachev reluctantly bowed to the American challenge, eventually agreeing to participate in Reagan's Strategic Arms Reduction Treaty initiative and to negotiations on conventional force reductions, which began in 1987, and to the complete removal of intermediate nuclear weapons from Europe in the same year.

By 1989, the winds of political change were blowing irresistibly. During that year, both Hungary and Poland adopted democratic systems of government without a whimper of protest from Moscow. Soviet troops withdrew from Afghanistan. East Germans flooded into West Germany, and even the Berlin Wall came tumbling down. Czechoslovakia began its Velvet Revolution and in one of the few violent transitions, Romanian president Nicolae Ceauşescu was overthrown. Within a single decade, the paper tiger of Soviet communist power had been starkly revealed.

Also during 1989, however, China's Communist Party crushed prodemocracy demonstrations in Tiananmen Square, showing its reluctance to promote political reform in tandem with liberalization of the economic sphere. Gorbachev, ever the flexible reformer, rolled with the punches, reducing the Soviet military profile, gradually releasing Eastern Europe from Soviet control, and even permitting private ownership of property inside the Soviet Union. By the end of 1989, Europe's communist regimes had largely disappeared. In 1990, the two Germanys would be united. The end of Soviet control in Eastern Europe would soon be followed by the internal collapse of the Soviet Union itself, as peoples from the Baltic states to the Caucasus demanded their right to self-determination.

The pace of the changes was astounding, even to U.S. president George H. W. Bush's administration, which had come to regard Gorbachev as a figure of stability with whom a new international order could be devised to spread the benefits of liberty and to resolve long-standing regional conflicts through cooperation in the U.N. collective security system. However, Gorbachev was no longer in control of the forces of change he had fostered, and his vision of a smaller but stronger Soviet communist state was no longer possible, if it ever had been. On Christmas Day, 1991, five months after he had signed the Strategic Arms Reduction Treaty with Bush in Moscow, Gorbachev resigned from office. The Soviet Union ceased to exist as he fixed his signature on a decree formally dissolving the union that had been born in and bred by so much blood. In his farewell address, he noted that an end had been put to the Cold War, the arms race, and the insane militarization of his country that had crippled its economy, "distorted our thinking and undermined our morals." That frank admission might well have been composed by John Paul II, who had lived under communist repression and well understood its contradiction of the human spirit.

The Cold War was a surely a struggle between global powers seeking to advance their competing interests as well as a struggle of contradictory ideologies concerning political and economic philosophy. However, as Gorbachev himself admitted, it was also a struggle over different conceptions of the moral order and ultimately of the very nature of the human person. This spiritual dimension of the Cold War, though often hidden in the mutual and competing propaganda, was no less important than the more visible events making up the history of the Cold War.

Robert F. Gorman

■ FEBRUARY 4-11, 1945

YALTA CONFERENCE

The Yalta Conference among British, American, and Soviet representatives provided a controversial blueprint designed to guide how major geopolitical issues would be addressed in the postwar world. The problems that surfaced at the conference both influenced and presaged the advent of the Cold War.

LOCALE: Yalta, Soviet Union (now in Ukraine)
CATEGORIES: Diplomacy and international relations; World War II; wars, uprisings, and civil unrest

KEY FIGURES

Winston Churchill (1874-1965), prime minister of Great Britain, 1940-1945 and 1951-1955
Anthony Eden (1897-1977), British foreign secretary, 1940-1945
Harry Hopkins (1890-1946), special assistant to President Roosevelt
Vyacheslav Mikhailovich Molotov (Vyacheslav Mikhailovich Skryabin; 1890-1986), Soviet commissar of foreign affairs, 1939-1949 and 1953-1956
Franklin D. Roosevelt (1882-1945), president of the United States, 1933-1945
Joseph Stalin (Joseph Vissarionovich Dzhugashvili; 1878-1953), general secretary of the Central Committee of the Communist Party of the Soviet Union, 1922-1953, and premier, 1941-1953
Edward Reilly Stettinius, Jr. (1900-1949), U.S. secretary of state, 1944-1945

SUMMARY OF EVENT

Early in 1945, as Russian armies were advancing on Germany through Eastern Europe and American and British armies were entering western Germany, the leaders of the Allied nations met at Yalta, in the Russian Crimea, to consider the political problems arising out of the approaching defeat of Germany, to plan an occupation policy for the conquered nations, and to discuss the problems of the United Nations, Eastern Europe, and the Far East.

The Yalta Conference lasted from February 4 to February 11, 1945. The United States was represented by President Franklin D. Roosevelt, his closest civilian adviser, Harry Hopkins, and Edward Reilly Stettinius, Jr., the U.S. secretary of state. The British were represented by Prime Minister Winston Churchill and Anthony Eden, the British foreign secretary. As host country, the Soviet Union was represented by Joseph Stalin, the Soviet leader, and Vyacheslav Mikhailovich Molotov, the Soviet commissar of foreign affairs. The three Allied leaders had met once before, at Tehran in 1943, but had postponed many of their decisions to be discussed later or to be worked out by their foreign ministers for presentation at Yalta. Generally, the atmosphere at Yalta was cordial. Churchill and Stalin, however, were suspicious of each other's motives, and Roosevelt, who died two months later, was in failing health.

Many of the decisions made at Yalta were ratifications of earlier accords worked out by the foreign ministers; some agreements were reached only after much bargaining. The United Nations, for example, had been proposed as far back as 1941. In 1944, the foreign ministers of the Allied nations had established an organizational structure for the new organization. The Russians had insisted upon a Security Council veto on all matters, even procedural ones, and had demanded sixteen seats in the General Assembly on the grounds that each of the Soviet Republics was autonomous. These demands were intended to offset the Pan-American and British Commonwealth blocs that would likely emerge in the future organization.

Viewing the establishment of the United Nations on terms favorable to the United States as a prime objective, Roosevelt believed that it "was the only device that could keep the United States from slipping back into isolationism" after the war. Thus, when Stalin agreed to drop his demands for an unlimited veto in the Security Council, Roosevelt agreed to the Soviet Un-

Winston Churchill, Franklin D. Roosevelt, and Joseph Stalin at the Yalta Conference. (NARA)

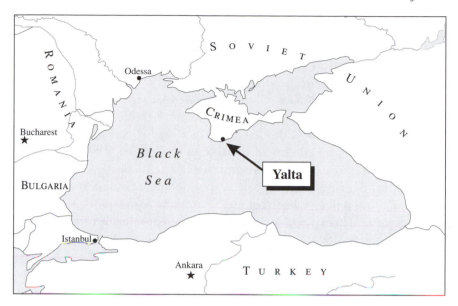

ion's request for membership in the General Assembly for the Soviet Ukrainian and Byelorussian republics. After all, members of the British Commonwealth would have six votes in the assembly. Stalin agreed to send Molotov to the founding meeting of the United Nations, to be held in San Francisco in April, 1945.

Poland presented two problems for the Allies: its frontiers and its government. When Poland had been conquered by the Germans and the Russians in 1939, a Polish government-in-exile had been established in London. After the Soviet Union joined the Allies in 1941 and began liberating Poland from Nazi rule in 1944, Stalin had formed the Polish Committee of National Liberation, essentially a communist government-in-exile, which was known as the Lüblin government.

Stalin wanted the communist government to be recognized as the legitimate government by the Allies. Furthermore, he wanted the Curzon line—an ethnically based boundary—to be the frontier between the Soviet Union and Poland, with Poland's western frontier moved farther west into Germany. Stalin stood in a strong position, since Russia's Red Army was moving through Poland, and he argued that he needed a Polish security buffer between Germany and the Soviet Union.

Stalin, dealing mostly with Churchill, won the concession that Poland's eastern boundary would basically follow the Curzon line and that Poland would receive substantial territories in the north and west. The final boundary was to be decided at a peace conference at war's end. Stalin did, however, agree that the Polish provisional government should be reorganized on a broader, democratic basis to include democratic leaders from within Poland and from abroad. Moreover, he agreed the elections for this united Polish government would occur "as soon as possible."

As for the other countries of newly liberated Eastern Europe, the Allies agreed to support all interim governments until free elections could be held. Specific problems in the Balkans had already been settled by Stalin and Churchill at a meeting held in Moscow in October, 1944, when they agreed that spheres of temporary influence would be established. The Americans and the British were to be preponderant in Greece, the Russians, in Romania and Bulgaria. Each country was to have equal shares in Hungary and Yugoslavia. This agreement was not discussed at Yalta, nor was there discussion on the future of Czechoslovakia, Finland, or the Baltic states, all of which later came under Russian influence or control.

The future of Germany was the most divisive problem taken up at Yalta. Most of the decisions were based on recommendations made by the foreign ministers, who had been discussing the problem since 1943. Stalin favored a partition of Germany in order to keep it under control, and Churchill toyed with the idea of a dismembered Germany. Since Roosevelt was vague, they decided to refer the matter to the ministers of foreign affairs. Ironically, the Soviets would abandon their position by late March.

The Allies approved a temporary military occupation; Germany was to be divided into four zones of military occupation, with France (whose section would be carved out of the Anglo-American part) being included as an occupying power. Policy decisions pertaining to the administration of the occupation were to be made by a four-power Allied control commission in Berlin. Berlin itself was to be divided and occupied by all four powers, and the Allies agreed that common occupation policies were to be imposed, by mutual agreement, on the whole of Germany.

As for German reparations and the German economy, Stalin favored a plan proposed earlier by U.S. secretary of the Treasury Henry Morgenthau, Jr. Morgenthau's plan favored complete deindustrialization of Germany: All of Germany's industry was to be given to the Allies as reparations, and Germany would be allowed to maintain only an agrarian economy. At Yalta, neither Churchill nor Roosevelt favored this plan, nor could they agree with Stalin on the exact amount of reparations to demand from Germany. Roosevelt did agree in principle, to a ten-billion-dollar figure for reparations to the Soviet Union as a "basis for discussion." The only agreement made, however, was the appointment of a reparations commission to study the problem and to make recommendations.

Apart from the military occupation, there was no agreement as to whether

Germany should be dismembered, kept intact, or given new boundaries, other than that Poland would be given compensation in Germany and that East Prussia would be divided between the Soviet Union and Poland. The Allies agreed to appoint another commission to make recommendations on these questions.

The question of the Far East loomed as a major priority for Roosevelt and to some degree for Churchill. Even though the British prime minister did not participate in the discussions about the Far East, he did sign off on the resulting understanding. At the time of the Yalta Conference, the Japanese seemed a long way from surrender. The atomic bomb had not yet been tested, and Allied forces in the Pacific were a long way from closing in on the homeland of Japan. Likewise, Japanese troops had proved to be able fighters who were not inclined to surrender easily. Thus, Roosevelt wanted Stalin to commit to a Russian entry into the war against Japan in order to save hundreds of thousands of American lives.

Earlier, at Tehran, Roosevelt and Stalin had reached substantial agreements concerning the Far East, and at Yalta, by secret accords, their agreement was formalized. Thus, the Soviet Union would declare war on Japan within three months after the surrender of Germany. In return, the Soviets would be given control over certain areas in the Far East, including the Kuril Islands and the southern portion of Sakhalin, as well as receiving concessions in Manchuria and a lease on Lüshun (Port Arthur), on China's Liaodong Peninsula. These concessions were granted without the knowledge or agreement of the Chinese government. It was also agreed that Dalian, another Liaodong port, would be internationalized.

SIGNIFICANCE

Most of the agreements made at Yalta were considered to be temporary in nature. Nevertheless, when World War II ended and the Cold War began, these temporary agreements quickly became permanent. As the globe was divided between East and West, the boundaries and apportionments tentatively agreed to at Yalta came to define the points of contact between the Soviet bloc and the Western democracies, up to and including the 1961 construction of the Berlin Wall that would symbolize the height of the conflict.

José M. Sánchez and Robert Franklin Maddox

FURTHER READING

Buhite, Russell D. *Decisions at Yalta: An Appraisal of Summit Diplomacy.* Wilmington, Del.: Scholarly Resources, 1986. The author concludes that Roosevelt pursued a policy of détente with cooperation with the Soviets as his main goal.

Churchill, Winston S. *The Second World War.* Vol. 6: *Triumph and Tragedy.* Boston: Houghton Mifflin, 1953. This memoir deals with the events of the conference from the British perspective.

Feis, Herbert. *Churchill, Roosevelt, Stalin.* Princeton, N.J.: Princeton University Press, 1967. This volume evaluates each decision made at the Yalta Conference and concludes that the conference was a victory for the West in that it limited Russian aims.

Freidel, Frank. *Franklin D. Roosevelt: A Rendezvous with Destiny.* Boston: Little, Brown, 1990. Written after four decades of research, this definitive political biography deals with the major issues surrounding Yalta.

Gaddis, John Lewis. *We Now Know: Rethinking Cold War History.* New York: Council on Foreign Relations, 1995. Focuses on the period from the end of World War II to the Cuban Missile Crisis. Incorporates extensive research from American archives as well as archives in the former Soviet Union, Eastern Europe, and China.

Hughes, Matthew, and Matthew S. Seligmann. *Does Peace Lead to War? Peace Settlements and Conflict in the Modern Age.* Stroud, Gloucestershire, England: Sutton, 2002. Includes a chapter on the Chinese Civil War of 1946-1949, arguing that the Yalta accords were responsible for the conflict. Bibliographic references and index.

Laloy, Jean. *Yalta: Yesterday, Today, Tomorrow.* New York: Harper & Row, 1988. Written by a French historian, this work places Yalta's impact in the perspective of the European community.

Perlmutter, Amos. *FDR and Stalin: A Not So Grand Alliance, 1943-1945.* Columbia: University of Missouri Press, 1993. A study of the relationship between Roosevelt and Stalin during World War II.

Senarclens, Pierre de. *From Yalta to the Iron Curtain: The Great Powers and the Origins of the Cold War.* Translated by Amanda Pingree. Washington, D.C.: Berg, 1995. Traces the history of the Cold War, beginning with the decisions made at Yalta. Bibliographic references and index.

Sherwood, Robert E. *Roosevelt and Hopkins.* New York: Harper & Row, 1948. This revealing work is written from the perspective of the key Roosevelt adviser.

Snell, John L., ed. *The Meaning of Yalta.* Baton Rouge: Louisiana State University Press, 1956. This group of essays by noted historians treats the various issues that dominated the Yalta Conference.

SEE ALSO: Apr. 25-June 26, 1945: United Nations Charter Convention; July 17-August 2, 1945: Potsdam Conference; Aug. 6 and 9, 1945: Atomic Bombs Destroy Hiroshima and Nagasaki; Mar. 5, 1946: Churchill Delivers His Iron Curtain Speech; Apr. 3, 1948: Marshall Plan Provides Aid to Europe; June 24, 1948-May 11, 1949: Berlin Blockade and Airlift; Sept. 21-Oct. 7, 1949: Germany Splits into Two Republics; Aug. 13, 1961: Communists Raise the Berlin Wall; June 21, 1973: East and West Germany Establish Diplomatic Relations; Nov. 9, 1989: Fall of the Berlin Wall.

FEBRUARY 11, 1945

SOVIET EXILES AND PRISONERS OF WAR ARE FORCED INTO REPATRIATION

Tens of thousands of mostly Soviet citizens who were left in Western hands after World War II as prisoners of war, along with Cossack soldiers and others fleeing Eastern Europe and communism, were forced to return to the Soviet Union after the signing of a postwar repatriation agreement among the Allies. On return, however, the refugees were imprisoned or executed, because Stalin had condemned them as traitors.

ALSO KNOWN AS: Agreement Relating to Prisoners of War and Civilians Liberated by Forces Operating Under Soviet Command and Forces Operating Under United States of America Command; Operation Keelhaul
LOCALE: Eastern Europe; Soviet Union
CATEGORIES: Atrocities and war crimes; human rights; immigration, emigration, and relocation; World War II; military history; wars, uprisings, and civil unrest

KEY FIGURES

Joseph Stalin (Joseph Vissarionovich Dzhugashvili; 1878-1953), general secretary of the Central Committee of the Communist Party of the Soviet Union, 1922-1953, and premier, 1941-1953
Franklin D. Roosevelt (1882-1945), president of the United States, 1933-1945
Andrey Vlasov (1900-1946), leader of the Russian Liberation Army

SUMMARY OF EVENT

Among the agreements made by the Allied leaders at the Yalta Conference near the close of World War II was one for the repatriation of persons displaced by the war, particularly prisoners of war. On the surface the agreement, called the Agreement Relating to Prisoners of War and Civilians Liberated by Forces Operating Under Soviet Command and Forces Operating Under United States of America Command (February 11, 1945), seemed innocent enough, a humanitarian effort to get people safely back to their homeland now that the war was near its end. However, the Allies failed to comprehend the suspicious and cruel mind of their ally from the east, Joseph Stalin. The leader of the Soviet Union had mastered the technique of presenting himself as a wise and gentle visionary leader, the father of his people, while at the same time committing atrocities against those very people. The Western press praised his Moscow Trials of 1936 and 1937 as models of Soviet justice, when in fact they were rigged from the very beginning. Thus it was easy to convince U.S. president Franklin D. Roosevelt and British prime minister Winston Churchill that Stalin would welcome home Soviet citizens stranded abroad by the depredations of the Nazis.

To Stalin, many of the refugees were dangerous because they had been exposed to foreigners and foreign influence, including new ideas and new possibilities. Thus, Stalin decreed that all Soviet citizens who were former prisoners of war were also traitors because they "failed" to hold their ground to the very death. He called for their execution or for their perpetual exile to Siberia. Stalin's actions in this regrettable affair were prelude to the Soviet regime's later widespread violations of human rights during the Cold War which soon broke out as the tenuous Allied alliance collapsed. This disregard would extend not only to Soviet citizens, but also to subject peoples, serving as one of the great contrasts between the regard for human persons as practiced in the Communist and Free Worlds.

The number of Soviet prisoners of war was great because whole divisions had been encircled and captured in the chaotic early days of the war, largely because of the incompetence of the top-level leadership. The final purges of the Great Terror had gutted the army, for Stalin believed that Mikhail Tukhachevsky and the other truly talented leaders intended to conduct a coup against him. The leaders he kept alive were largely his old friends from the Russian civil war, who proved utterly inadequate fighting the Germans.

The large numbers of returning prisoners of war, even allowing for the vast numbers who had died as a result of mistreatment by the Nazis, could be considered a silent indictment of the quality of the Red Army's leadership, something Stalin could not tolerate. When the mass repatriations of prisoners of war began, about one hundred processing stations were created along the borders of the Soviet Union. Agents of the Soviet secret police determined which returnees were to be shot on the spot as traitors and which were merely to be shipped to Siberia.

Prisoners of war were not the only repatriates. In addition to the soldiers who had been captured in those first catastrophic weeks of the invasion of the Soviet Union, there were large numbers of people who had fled the Soviet Union before the war and who had become enmeshed in the Nazi system. Also, thousands of people were fleeing Soviet-occupied Eastern Europe. These exiles included whole communities of Cossacks previously loyal to the czar who had fled into Eastern Europe early in the war and subsequently fought for the Nazis. The Cossack fighters believed that aiding the Nazis was the lesser of two evils, and they hoped for a chance to destroy the Soviet system that had destroyed their old way of life. When it was announced that the Cossacks had to return to the Soviet Union under the terms of the repatriation agreements, they resisted, often violently. Others went on hunger strikes to protest the prospect of being handed over to Stalin. Their plight attracted the attention of such luminaries as British king George VI and Geoffrey Francis Fisher, the archbishop of Canterbury. However, these pleas for a humanitarian exception went mostly unnoticed, and the Cossacks were returned to the Soviet Union by force. Even British troops fired on those who attempted to escape through the woods.

The returning former prisoners then had to face the Russian Liberation Army. During the early hopeless months of the Nazi invasion of the Soviet Union, many captives considered the Nazis not as enemies but as liberators who would free them from Stalin's tyranny. Among them was General Andrey Vlasov, a capable young officer who had been catapulted into high position by the purges that had murdered older, more senior officers. He was painfully aware of how Stalin had gutted the Red Army, and when the Nazis offered him an opportunity to fight against Stalin, he accepted the leadership of the Russian forces in the Wehrmacht. It is difficult to determine how many of the soldiers under him joined the Russian Liberation Army because they held a deep and burning desire to destroy Stalin or how many joined because doing so got them out of the hellish conditions of the prisoner-of-war camps. These questions did not matter either to the Allies or to Stalin. The Allies saw them as treacherous enemies and Stalin saw them as traitors because they had fought for the Nazis. Thousands of them were shot immediately on entering Soviet territory. Vlasov was given a secret trial sometime in July of 1946. Although some accounts claim that he was shot, others claim that the "honorable" penalty of being shot was considered too good for a turncoat and he was instead hanged, with the drop being made deliberately short so that he would endure a slow and painful death by strangulation.

SIGNIFICANCE

As the full implications of the prisoners of war agreement became known in the West, it became a matter of great contention, particularly for the conservative elements who considered Roosevelt to have betrayed Eastern Europe to Stalin. Others considered the agreement a great shame to the U.S. military, who obeyed the orders to send the refugees back to their homeland, particularly given that the refugees themselves were so clearly opposed to their repatriation. All involved believed that the U.S. leadership should have suspected that something was amiss, that Stalin's intention regarding the repatriation of prisoners were not motivated by benign humanitarianism. In fact, there is some evidence that a number of U.S. and British leaders knew what Stalin really intended but did not wish to put their own prisoners of war, stranded in Soviet-held territory, at risk by playing political hardball.

Leigh Husband Kimmel

FURTHER READING

Montefiore, Simon Sebag. *Stalin: The Court of the Red Tsar.* New York: Knopf, 2004. An examination of the workings of Stalin's inner circle, particularly the way in which Stalin frequently used his followers to deflect blame for his atrocities away from himself.

Perlmutter, Amos. *FDR and Stalin: A Not So Grand Alliance, 1943-1945.* Columbia: University of Missouri Press, 1993. A study of the relationship between Roosevelt and Stalin during World War II.

Polian, Pavel. *Against Their Will: The History and Geography of Forced Migrations in the USSR.* Translated by Anna Yastrzhembska. New York: Central European University Press, 2004. First published in 2001, this comprehensive study of forced migration and repatriation to and from the Soviet Union includes discussion of the repatriations following World War II. Highly recommended.

Seaton, Albert. *The Horsemen of the Steppes: The Story of the Cossacks.* New York: Hippocrene Books, 1985. A history of the Cossacks, from their origins in the cultural collision between the Tatars and the Russians, through the great peasant rebellions, to the post-revolution flights west, to the attempts to forcibly repatriate those who had fought for the Nazis.

Tolstoy, Nikolai. *The Secret Betrayal.* New York: Scribner, 1978. The most extensive account available in English of the forced repatriations. A highly controversial work that presents the story of the deaths of the repatriates to the Western world. Published as *Victims of Yalta* in 1977.

Ure, John. *The Cossacks: An Illustrated History.* New York: Penguin Books, 2002. An accessible history of the Cossacks, their explorations, and their rebellions, particularly of interest since it includes material only available since the fall of the Soviet Union, which gave Western scholars access to previously secret archives.

SEE ALSO: Mar. 5, 1946: Churchill Delivers His Iron Curtain Speech; 1948: Soviets Escalate Persecution of Jews; 1949-1961: East Germans Flee to West to Escape Communist Regime; Dec. 14, 1950: United Nations High Commissioner for Refugees Statute Is Approved; Mar. 5, 1953: Death of Stalin.

■ **APRIL 25-JUNE 26, 1945**

UNITED NATIONS CHARTER CONVENTION

The birth of the United Nations established a global international organization for conflict resolution and maintenance of world peace originally attempted after World War I with the League of Nations.

LOCALE: San Francisco, California

CATEGORIES: United Nations; organizations and institutions; diplomacy and international relations

KEY FIGURES

Winston Churchill (1874-1965), prime minister of Great Britain, 1940-1945 and 1951-1955

Joseph Stalin (Joseph Vissarionovich Dzhugashvili; 1878-1953), general secretary of the Central Committee of the Communist Party of the Soviet Union, 1922-1953, and premier, 1941-1953

Franklin D. Roosevelt (1882-1945), president of the United States, 1933-1945

Harry S. Truman (1884-1972), president of the United States, 1945-1953

Edward Reilly Stettinius, Jr. (1900-1949), U.S. secretary of state, 1944-1945, and chairman of the U.S. delegation to the Charter Convention

Tom Connally (1877-1963), chairman of the Senate Committee on Foreign Relations and member of the U.S. delegation to the Charter Convention

Arthur Hendrick Vandenberg (1884-1951), U.S. senator from Michigan and member of the U.S. delegation

Vyacheslav Mikhailovich Molotov (Vyacheslav Mikhailovich Skryabin; 1890-1986), Soviet commissar of foreign affairs, 1939-1949 and 1953-1956

Cordell Hull (1871-1955), U.S. secretary of state, 1933-1944

SUMMARY OF EVENT

On January 1, 1942, Franklin D. Roosevelt, Winston Churchill, Maksim Maksimovich Litvinov (Russian ambassador to the United States), and representatives of twenty-three other nations signed the Declaration of the United Nations, pledging themselves to a continued alliance in the struggle against the Axis and to uphold the principles enunciated in the Atlantic Charter. This latter document was a joint statement made by Roosevelt and Churchill on August 14, 1941, that spoke of the need to establish a permanent organization for collective security. Eventually, this commitment to permanent collective security led to the establishment of the United Nations on June 26, 1945, in San Francisco, as a successor to the League of Nations, which had rested on similar principles but had failed to achieve consensus from all the Great Powers.

Throughout the evolution of the United Nations, initiative came from the Western powers, particularly the United States. From its inception, the United Nations was a Western idea, but the United States believed that Soviet participation was essential to its success. It was not until the October, 1943, Moscow Declaration, however, that the Soviet Union made a firm commitment to establish a general international organization. In August, 1944, the Big Four—the United States, the Soviet Union, China, and Great Britain—at last met to discuss the actual structure of the postwar security organization. At the invitation of President Roosevelt, the delegates assembled at a suburban Washington, D.C., estate, Dumbarton Oaks, to review proposals.

By October 7, the conferees at Dumbarton Oaks had reached agreement on a number of vital points. There were a number of outstanding problems after the convention adjourned, however, the most notable of which was a disagreement between the United States and the Soviet Union over the functioning of veto power in the new organization. The Soviet Union insisted that each Big Four country be permitted an absolute veto over issues in which they were involved. Roosevelt appealed directly to Joseph Stalin in the hope of modifying this position but without success. The president decided to accept the progress that had been made and reserve a final decision on the veto question until after he had an opportunity to discuss the matter with the Soviet leader in person.

The next major diplomatic conference between the major powers was at Yalta in February, 1945. On paper, Roosevelt had every reason to feel that he had achieved his goal after the conclusion of the Yalta Conference. Although concerned with many different topics of far-reaching implications, the Yalta meeting of Stalin, Roosevelt, and Churchill did produce a temporary accord on the United Nations veto question. Stalin accepted the U.S. proposition that those issues that were defined as procedural could not be vetoed by any member of the organization; such issues would instead require a majority vote of the Security Council. It was further agreed that in certain cases a disputant to an issue—even one of the Big Four—must abstain from voting. Finally, it was decided that all nations that declared war on the Axis by March 1, 1945, would be considered charter members of the United Nations.

At the invitation of the Big Four, forty-six other nations assembled in San Francisco on April 25, 1945, to establish the United Nations. President Roosevelt had chosen the U.S. delegation with great care. Recalling the unfortunate experiences of Woodrow Wilson and the Paris convention, Roosevelt picked a bipartisan delegation. At the head of the group was Edward R. Stettinius, Jr., newly appointed secretary of state. He was joined by a number of other delegates, the most notable of whom were Senator Arthur Hendrick Vandenberg, a Michigan Republican who had moved from an isolationist position to one of full support of the president, and Senator Tom Connally, a Texas Democrat who was chairman of the Senate Foreign Relations Committee. The president did not live to see the convention open: He died of a stroke on April 12, 1945, two months before World War II ended.

Harry S. Truman, Roosevelt's successor, was firmly committed to the same sort of program Roosevelt had supported, and he endorsed the delegation. At the convention, the U.S. representatives immediately became bogged down in a number of disputes. Russia already was creating tensions within the Allied coalition by its supposed intransigence regarding Poland. It was only at Truman's insistence that Stalin, who viewed the entire San Francisco affair as a Western production, permitted Vyacheslav Mikhailovich Molotov, the Soviet foreign minister, to attend the convention in place of a lower-ranking official. In San Francisco, the United States and Russia again disagreed over voting procedure. Seeking to revoke the decision made at Yalta, Molotov now insisted that each Great Power be granted the veto over any attempt by the Security Council to discuss an issue. Truman appealed to Stalin personally and finally was able to persuade him that a decision to discuss an issue was a procedural question and therefore not subject to a simple veto.

On another issue, however, the United States found itself in complete agreement with the Soviet Union. As conceived by the Big Four in pre-San Francisco meetings, the United Nations was to operate through the domination of the five major powers, which now included France. It was agreed by all major powers that only unanimity among themselves could keep the peace. This agreement, however, met stiff resistance from the smaller powers, both before and during the U.N. Conference at San Francisco. Latin American representatives met at Mexico City in early 1945 and called for a more powerful general assembly and an international court, and they insisted on a greater role for regional organizations in the maintenance of peace. Small powers expressed resentment at San Francisco concerning the veto provisions insisted upon by the major powers, but the latter held firmly to their dominant role in the Security Council.

On a host of other points, concessions were made to the smaller powers that resulted in a strengthening of provisions for regional collective security in cooperation with the Security Council and in the elaboration of an extensive set of articles dealing with decolonization and trusteeship arrangements for non-self-governing territories. The Dumbarton Oaks proposals developed by the Great Powers had been largely silent on these issues, so the details of these initiatives had to be sketched out at San Francisco. The result was a U.N. structure with six major organs instead of the four anticipated at Dumbarton Oaks. To the Security Council, the General Assembly, the Secretariat, and the International Court of Justice were added the Economic and Social Council (ECOSOC) and the Trusteeship Council.

While the Security Council was created to deal with the major U.N. goal of maintaining global peace and security and punishing acts of aggression under chapters 6 and 7 of the charter, the General Assembly was granted even broader authority not only to discuss peace and security matters (although it could make no recommendations on such matters while the Security Council was engaged in deliberations concerning them) but also to coordinate U.N. efforts to eliminate the underlying causes of conflict. ECOSOC and the Trusteeship Council, as well as mechanisms established to promote decolonization under General Assembly oversight, were established to address these underlying causes of conflict, which were attributed to the lack of self-determination, poverty, violations of human rights, and other social pathologies. The General Assembly, unlike the Security Council, was open to all member states, with equal voting rights for each state. The General Assembly could make recommendations only with regard to areas under its purview, while the Security Council could bind U.N. members under the provisions of chapter 7 for enforcement of international peace and security.

The United Nations Charter was signed on June 26, 1945. By October 24, the five permanent members of the Security Council and a majority of the other charter member-nations had ratified the charter, and on that day, the United Nations officially came into existence.

SIGNIFICANCE

Almost immediately after the creation of the United Nations, the Cold War deepened and the Allied consensus Roosevelt had hoped would furnish the basis for effective global management of conflict evaporated. Security Council action was often frustrated by the threat or use of the veto. Apart from the Korean War—during which the Soviet Union was boycotting Security Council sessions, thus enabling the latter to deploy forces to resist North Korean aggression—the Security Council was unable to invoke its collective enforcement powers. This led to the development of roles for the General Assembly and the Secretariat in pursuing peacekeeping initiatives that the Security Council itself eventually adopted, short of using economic sanctions or military force. Over time, with the development of the United Nations Educational, Scientific, and Cultural Organization (UNESCO) and the United Nations International Children's Emergency Fund (UNICEF; later the United Nations Children's Fund), the organization became associated more with philanthropic endeavors than with the maintenance of peace or the enforcement of social justice, goals in the pursuit of which it tended to be relatively powerless.

George Q. Flynn and Robert F. Gorman

FURTHER READING

Bennett, A. LeRoy. *International Organizations: Principles and Issues.* 6th ed. Englewood Cliffs, N.J.: Prentice Hall, 1995. A comprehensive treatment of the origins, genesis, and historical development of the United Nations in the context of wider developments in international organization.

Claude, Inis L., Jr. *Swords into Plowshares: The Problem and Progress of International Organization.* 3d rev. ed. New York: Random House, 1964. A standard history of the early development of the United Nations.

Goodrich, Leland M., Edvard Hambro, and Anne P. Simons. *Charter of the United Nations: Commentary and Documents.* 3d ed. New York: Columbia University Press, 1969. Although dated, an invaluable, article-by-article analysis of the actual practice of the United Nations in its first two decades of implementing charter provisions.

Lee, Roy S., ed. *Swords into Plowshares: Building Peace Through the United Nations.* Boston: Martinus Nijhoff, 2006. Anthology of essays evaluating the United Nations' history and progress from the point of view of the early twenty-first century.

Mingst, Karen A., and Margaret P. Karns. *The United Nations in the Post-Cold War Era.* Boulder, Colo.: Westview Press, 1995. Traces the development of the United Nations and its prospects for renewed activity in global peacekeeping and economic development.

The United Nations Conference on International Organization, San Francisco, California, April 25 to June 26, 1945. Selected Documents. U.S. Department of State Conference Series 83. Washington, D.C.: Government Printing Office, 1946. Contains a wealth of documents, reports, verbatim records, and summaries of meetings leading up to and including the U.N. Conference in San Francisco.

Weiss, Thomas, David P. Forsythe, and Roger A. Coate. *The United Nations and Changing World Politics.* Boulder, Colo.: Westview Press, 1994. Examines the theory of collective security and its applicability to U.N. efforts at peacekeeping and the protection of human rights in the late twentieth century.

Westad, Odd Arne. *The Global Cold War: Third World Interventions and the Makings of Our Times.* Cambridge, U.K.: Cambridge University Press, 2007. Examines the aftermath of the Cold War in terms of globalization and American interventionism in developing nations. Illustrated.

SEE ALSO: Feb. 4-11, 1945: Yalta Conference; Feb. 1, 1946: First U.N. Secretary-General Is Selected; Nov. 9-Dec. 15, 1946: United Nations Admits Its First New Member States; Dec. 14, 1950: United Nations High Commissioner for Refugees Statute Is Approved; Apr. 10, 1953: Hammarskjöld Is Elected U.N. Secretary-General; Dec. 14, 1955: United Nations Admits Sixteen New Members; July, 1960: United Nations Intervenes in the Congolese Civil War; 1963-1965: Crisis in U.N. Financing Emerges Over Peacekeeping Expenses; Oct. 25, 1971: People's Republic of China Is Seated at the United Nations; 1990-1994: United Nations Admits Many New Members.

JULY 17-AUGUST 2, 1945

POTSDAM CONFERENCE

The Potsdam Conference was intended to settle unresolved issues between the three major Allied Powers as to the ending of World War II. It helped shape relations between those powers after the war, beginning the foreign policies that would lead to the Cold War and shaping the map of Europe for the next few decades.

LOCALE: Potsdam, Germany

CATEGORIES: Diplomacy and international relations; World War II; wars, uprisings, and civil unrest

KEY FIGURES

Winston Churchill (1874-1965), prime minister of Great Britain, 1940-1945 and 1951-1955

Joseph Stalin (Joseph Vissarionovich Dzhugashvili, 1878-1953), general secretary of the Central Committee of the Communist Party of the Soviet Union, 1922-1953, and premier, 1941-1953

Harry S. Truman (1884-1972), president of the United States, 1945-1953

Harry Hopkins (1890-1946), special assistant to President Franklin D.
  Roosevelt

Clement Attlee (1883-1967), prime minister of Great Britain, 1945-1951

Charles de Gaulle (1890-1970), head of the provisional government of
  France, 1944-1946

SUMMARY OF EVENT

At the close of the Yalta Conference in February of 1945, the leaders of the United States, Great Britain, and the Soviet Union had agreed that they would meet again to settle remaining European problems resulting from the defeat of Germany. These problems concerned peace treaties with the former Axis nations and satellites. For the Western Allies, the problems included the Soviet Union's violation of its agreement to allow the establishment of free governments in Eastern Europe.

When Germany surrendered in May, 1945, the Allied leaders began preparations for another conference. Prime Minister Winston Churchill was particularly eager for the meeting to be held as soon as possible, not only to forestall further Soviet gains in Europe but also because of the possibility that upcoming British elections to be held in July might vote him out of office before he could participate in these important foreign policy decisions. Harry S. Truman, who had taken office as president of the United States in April after the death of Franklin D. Roosevelt, wanted to delay the meeting long enough to familiarize himself with the issues to be discussed. Soviet leader Joseph Stalin had no apparent preference regarding the scheduling of the meeting. It was finally agreed that the conference would open on July 17 and be held in Potsdam, Germany.

Two other problems had to be solved. One involved the provisional president of France, Charles de Gaulle. France had been allotted an occupational zone in Germany, but past relations between the Allies and de Gaulle had been so trying that no one wanted him at the Potsdam Conference, and he was not invited. The other problem concerned the occupation armies in Germany. During the course of the war, both Western Allied troops and Soviet troops had occupied German areas not included in their agreed occupational zones. In addition, there were no American troops in Berlin, and the American military commanders wanted soldiers there to protect the president on his trip to Potsdam. The Soviet Union refused to allow troops into Berlin until Western soldiers left the Russian zone. Despite Churchill's misgivings, Truman ordered a retreat, and the British and Americans were allowed into Berlin.

The Potsdam Conference began on July 17, 1945, and lasted for two weeks. In the middle of the conference, British election returns proclaimed the defeat of Churchill and the triumph of the Labour Party. Churchill was replaced as prime minister by Labour Party leader Clement Attlee. Since Attlee had attended the conference earlier, however, there was no change in British policy.

Recalling the hasty decisions and mistakes made at the Paris Peace Conference of 1919, Truman proposed that the Council of Foreign Ministers meet at their leisure to draft peace treaties for the defeated Axis nations. This proposal was accepted by all. Within two years, the foreign ministers produced acceptable treaties.

Eastern Europe, however, was a much more complicated matter. Stalin wanted Western diplomatic recognition for the procommunist governments there, but Truman and Churchill refused. As for Poland, the Allies had agreed at Yalta that free elections would be held "as soon as possible"; since the Yalta Conference, however, the communist-controlled Warsaw government had taken over Poland and had made no plans for free elections. Furthermore, members of the anticommunist Polish government-in-exile had been arrested when they had returned from London to Poland after the German surrender.

Truman had sent Harry Hopkins, formerly President Roosevelt's top civilian adviser, on a diplomatic mission to Moscow in May to inquire into the Polish situation. Hopkins had arranged a compromise between the London and Warsaw Poles on a coalition government, despite the fact that the communists held fourteen out of twenty-one of Poland's cabinet seats, and the Polish government had agreed to hold free elections. At Potsdam, this agreement was ratified with the stipulation that the Allied press be admitted and allowed to report on the elections. The Polish interim government was granted Western diplomatic recognition.

As for the Polish-German frontier, when Soviet troops had liberated Poland, they had turned over all German lands east of the Oder-Western Neisse River line to the Poles. The southern half of East Prussia had also been turned over to the Poles. Stalin proposed that the Allies recognize these boundaries permanently. Truman and Churchill accepted them only as temporary borders pending a final peace treaty with Germany.

The German problem was the central issue at Potsdam. The main dispute was between the Soviet desire for harsh reparations and a weak Germany to act as a buffer against future invasion and the Western Allied aim of a restored and pacified Germany to act as a buffer against Soviet expansion. So intense was this dispute that the leaders could agree only on noncontroversial issues. Thus, the Allies agreed to abolish Nazi institutions and prohibit arms manufacturing. They also agreed that Germany was to be treated as a single economic entity and that the Control Council in Berlin was to make unanimous decisions for Germany as a whole. Within each occupation zone, however, each military commander was to have sovereign authority. Local self-government was to be encouraged, and the German economy was to be geared toward peaceful pursuits.

On the question of reparations, the conference members agreed that each power could take what it wanted from its occupation zone. The Soviets, however, wanted industrial equipment from the Ruhr complex, which was located in the British zone, in order to compensate for the meager resources in their zone. The Soviets finally agreed to accept a percentage of the Ruhr industrial machinery in return for food products that they were to ship from their zone to the zones of the Western Allies. These Western zones needed food supplies, because they had become heavily crowded with refugees who had fled the Russian zone in the last days of the war. All other reparations were renounced.

In other matters, the Potsdam Conference members agreed on an occupational zone arrangement for Austria similar to that in Germany. They condemned Spain for having supported the Axis Powers during the war and forbade Spain's entry into the United Nations. Finally, they agreed upon the orderly and humane transfer to Germany of nine million displaced German

Winston Churchill, Harry S. Truman, and Joseph Stalin at the Potsdam Conference. (National Archives)

civilians living in areas outside Germany. They also established a mechanism to deal with the details of the peace treaties in the postwar period. In a final gesture, the Potsdam Declaration was issued to the Japanese government, calling upon it to surrender unconditionally or face total destruction. On August 2, a statement of the agreements, known as the Potsdam Protocol, was signed, and the participants went home.

SIGNIFICANCE

The Potsdam Conference thus helped to draw the map of the postwar world—the map that would constitute the arena of the Cold War. As a result, the issue of atomic weapons has loomed in retrospect as a major backdrop to this conference, causing much historical debate. Some scholars argue that the United States helped bring about the Cold War by taking a tough stance with the Soviets as a result of U.S. possession of an atomic bomb. Some have even argued that the exact date of the beginning of the nuclear arms race can be traced to Truman's conversation with Stalin on July 24, 1945, in which he revealed that the United States had a weapon of "unusual de-structive force."

Other scholars point out that the United States no longer needed Soviet intervention in the Pacific war after they had successfully tested the bomb, so it had no reason to court Soviet favor or to appease Soviet desires. Many conservative historians see Potsdam as part of an overall acquiescence to the communists. Nevertheless, given the military strength and strategic location of Soviet troops at the time of the conference, the agreements reached at Potsdam generally have been accepted as being motivated by political real-ism. The Soviets, who had lost tens of millions of people in the war, were ab-solutely committed to protecting their borders. The Western Allies' motives for resisting the Soviet will were not equally compelling at the time, given that the Soviets could not have been dislodged from Eastern Europe with-out beginning another all-out war—something neither the United States nor Britain was prepared to do.

José M. Sánchez and Robert Franklin Maddox

FURTHER READING

Alperovitz, Gar. *Atomic Diplomacy: Hiroshima and Potsdam.* New York: Simon & Schuster, 1965. This revisionist historian blames American bellicosity at Potsdam on the fact that Truman knew about the successful explosion of the atomic bomb.

Feis, Herbert. *Between War and Peace: The Potsdam Conference.* Princeton, N.J.: Princeton University Press, 1960. The author maintains that compromise was necessary since the Russian army stood in a strong European position, which placed it in control of Eastern Europe in 1945, and since the war against Japan was still in progress.

Ferrell, Robert H. *Harry S. Truman: A Life.* Columbia: University of Missouri Press, 1994. Written by a premier Truman scholar, this work argues that no Western figure could allow the status quo to be defined by the presence of Soviet troops in the eastern part of Europe.

Hasegawa, Tsuyoshi. *Racing the Enemy: Stalin, Truman, and the Surrender of Japan.* Cambridge, Mass.: Belknap Press, 2005. Details the role of Potsdam (which it calls "the turning point") in the campaign against Japan after Germany's surrender, as well as discussing the broader implications of Stalin's interactions with Truman.

Maddox, Robert James. *From War to Cold War: The Education of Harry S. Truman.* Boulder, Colo.: Westview Press, 1988. Maddox analyzes the Potsdam Conference in the overall context of Truman's coming to grips with the problems of the ending of the war and the subsequent unraveling of the coalition.

Mee, Charles L., Jr. *Meeting at Potsdam.* Reprint. New York: Franklin Square Press, 1996. This volume argues that the victorious leaders acted in a Machiavellian fashion to achieve their goals, and that the origins of the Cold War and nuclear arms race can be found in this conference.

Robertson, David. *Sly and Able: A Political Biography of James F. Byrnes.* New York: W. W. Norton, 1994. Critical of revisionists, the author concludes that Byrnes's primary motivation for use of the atomic bomb was to end the war with Japan and not to impress the Russians.

Woods, Randall, and Howard Jones. *Dawning of the Cold War: The United States' Quest for Order.* Athens: University of Georgia Press, 1991. This work, which is based on a synthesis of scholarship, concludes that the potential impact the atomic bomb would have on Russia was "not decisive" in Truman's decision.

SEE ALSO: Feb. 4-11, 1945: Yalta Conference; Apr. 3, 1948: Marshall Plan Provides Aid to Europe; June 24, 1948-May 11, 1949: Berlin Blockade and Airlift; Sept. 21-Oct. 7, 1949: Germany Splits into Two Republics; Sept. 25, 1953-Oct. 26, 1956: Polish Communist Government Arrests the Primate of Poland; Aug. 13, 1961: Communists Raise the Berlin Wall; June 21, 1973: East and West Germany Establish Diplomatic Relations; Dec. 13, 1981: Poland Imposes Martial Law and Bans Solidarity; June-Sept., 1989: Poland Forms a Noncommunist Government; Nov. 9, 1989: Fall of the Berlin Wall.

■ August 6 and 9, 1945

Atomic Bombs Destroy Hiroshima and Nagasaki

U.S. military planes dropped atomic bombs on two Japanese cities with consequences both human and environmental that were of unprecedented proportions. Japan surrendered on August 14, leading to the end of World War II and signaling the start of an age of nuclear weaponry.

Also known as: Fat Man and Little Boy
Locale: Hiroshima and Nagasaki, Japan
Categories: World War II; wars, uprisings, and civil unrest

Key Figures

Harry S. Truman (1884-1972), president of the United States, 1945-1953, who gave final approval for the dropping of the bombs
Henry L. Stimson (1867-1950), U.S. secretary of war under Truman
James Francis Byrnes (1879-1972), U.S. secretary of state under Truman
Leslie Richard Groves (1896-1970), head of the Manhattan Project
Leo Szilard (1898-1964), Hungarian-born physicist who first considered the possibility of a nuclear chain reaction

Summary of Event

At 8:15 A.M. on August 6, 1945, the first atomic weapon ever released over a human population exploded in the air above Hiroshima, Japan. The blast energy and destruction were on a scale hitherto unknown and heralded the beginning of the atomic age. Three days later, on August 9, a second atom bomb was released over the city of Nagasaki at about 11:00 A.M.

That weapon, originally planned for the city of Kokura—a strategically important location that housed a Japanese army base located only 100 miles west of Hiroshima—was delivered to Nagasaki instead. The weather observation aircraft accompanying the bomber directed the attack toward Nagasaki because of heavy clouds over Kokura. Nagasaki might have escaped destruction on that day had it not been for a small break in the clouds that permitted the crew to release the weapon over a munitions plant.

It has been estimated that the total explosive power of the weapon released over Hiroshima by the B-29 bomber *Enola Gay* was equivalent to 12.5 thousand tons of trinitrotoluene (TNT). Its explosive power was derived from the fission of uranium 235. The bomb delivered to Nagasaki was al-

The Japanese city of Hiroshima after it was leveled by the atomic bomb blast. (Library of Congress)

most twice as powerful; its energy came from the fission of the element plutonium. Each of the weapons was equivalent in destructive power to the explosives that might have been carried at that time by a fully loaded fleet of several thousand of the world's largest bomber planes—an unprecedented release of energy.

Many of those who fell victim to the Hiroshima weapon were engaged on that fateful day in the open air, demolishing structures to provide adequate firebreaks in the event that the city was struck by conventional weapons. Some were volunteer students; others had been drafted by the army for a variety of jobs within the city. It has been estimated that there were about 350,000 individuals in Hiroshima on the morning when the *Enola Gay* dropped its bomb. Released from an initial altitude of six miles, the weapon exploded about one-third of a mile above the ground, at a point judged to cause maximum damage on the ground below. Both the detonation altitude and the point directly beneath it were later determined from the lengths of shadows cast by standing objects; the shadows were seared into the ground by the intense heat of the explosion.

Seen as an isolated historical event, the release of these two weapons over predominantly civilian populations is almost impossible to comprehend. In 1945, however, following the defeat of Germany by the Allies, the Japanese military was in retreat throughout the Pacific theater. Returning to its homeland, where civilian morale, food, and strategic supplies were already at paralyzingly low levels, the Japanese army was determined to fight to the last soldier, even if it led to the destruction of the entire country and its people.

It was during the meetings in Potsdam, Germany, between the leaders of Russia, Great Britain, and the United States, that news of the first successful nuclear detonation at Alamogordo, New Mexico, was conveyed to President Harry S. Truman. That was in July, 1945, just one month before the bombings. There had been, throughout the preceding months, intense discussions among scientists and between government officials concerning the best strategy for concluding the war in the quickest way.

In 1939, the year in which World War II began in Europe, Hungarian-born physicist Leo Szilard met with Albert Einstein, the most prestigious scientific figure in the world. Szilard was persuasive in expressing his concerns that Germany should not be allowed to be the first to create an atomic weapon, and he enlisted Einstein's assistance to persuade U.S. president Franklin D. Roosevelt to support a vigorous program of nuclear research. This ultimately led to the formation of the Manhattan Project, the U.S. effort to build an atomic weapon for the United States before the Germans or Japanese, who were known to be vigorously engaged in nuclear research, could build their own.

SIGNIFICANCE

No other event in recorded history can be compared with the impact of the first uncontrolled release of the energy of the atom. In terms of psychological, social, human, and potential environmental consequences, there were no precedents. People began to come to terms with a force that possessed the potential for the destruction of all life on Earth, including the extinction of the human species itself.

There exist many firsthand accounts by individuals who survived the Hiroshima and Nagasaki bombings. One student recalled that she felt as though she had been struck on the back by a hammer, then thrown into boiling oil, then blown away by the force of the ensuing wind. A five-year-old child who had escaped from entrapment under his house attempted to flee the city and later reported seeing naked people with skin so badly damaged it was hanging from their bodies like rags. Others likened the scene to a painting of Hell. It has been estimated that nearly 50 percent of those who happened to be within a three-quarter-mile radius of the burst point died that day; many more would die subsequently as a result of direct wounds or severe radiation exposure.

Prior to the dropping of the atomic bombs, the most severe wartime casualties on Japanese soil had occurred earlier that year in Tokyo, when approximately 10 percent of the city's population of one million had died of firebombing-related injuries. It has been estimated that nearly 200,000 lives ultimately were lost in Hiroshima within five years of the bombing, and about 74,000 in a similar period in Nagasaki.

The Japanese military was unsure of the nature of the deadly weapon that had been released. Many people believed that everyone would die. Others believed that all natural life in Hiroshima—once regarded as among the most beautiful of all Japanese cities—would perish. During that five-year span, evidence of increased incidences of leukemia, together with dramatic increases in the rates of other cancers, served to confirm suspicions of delayed effects of nuclear radiation on humans. Survivors of Hiroshima

---

"THE MOST TERRIBLE THING EVER DISCOVERED"

U.S. president Harry S. Truman wrote in his diary of July 25, 1945, about the decision to drop atomic bombs on Japan.

We have discovered the most terrible bomb in the history of the world. It may be the fire destruction prophesied in the Euphrates Valley Era, after Noah and his fabulous Ark.

Anyway we "think" we have found the way to cause a disintegration of the atom. An experiment in the New Mexican desert was startling—to put it mildly. Thirteen pounds of the explosive caused the complete disintegration of a steel tower 60 feet high, created a crater 6 feet deep and 1,200 feet in diameter, knocked over a steel tower ½ mile away and knocked men down 10,000 yards away. The explosion was visible for more than 200 miles and audible for 40 miles and more.

This weapon is to be used against Japan between now and August 10th. I have told the Sec. of War, Mr. [Henry L.] Stimson, to use it so that military objectives and soldiers and sailors are the target and not women and children. Even if the Japs [sic] are savages, ruthless, merciless and fanatic, we as the leader of the world for the common welfare cannot drop that terrible bomb on the old Capitol or the new.

He and I are in accord. The target will be a purely military one and we will issue a warning statement asking the Japs to surrender and save lives. I'm sure they will not do that, but we will have given them the chance. It is certainly a good thing for the world that Hitler's crowd or Stalin's did not discover this atomic bomb. It seems to be the most terrible thing ever discovered, but it can be made the most useful.

showed a death rate from leukemia seven times higher than the nation's average, and the incidence of human and animal cancers of all types—breast, lung, thyroid—continued to rise in the following years. Long-term genetic effects were also issues of deep concern for future generations of the survivors of Hiroshima and Nagasaki. The immediate combined losses of life in this brief span of time can be compared to the total loss of U.S. military personnel—about 300,000—in World War II.

In addition to the immediate thermal and blast effects created by the enormous fireball, the fires ignited on the ground gave rise to smoke plumes containing soot and radioactive debris; these rose into the atmosphere, where they were absorbed by thunderclouds. This produced the "black rain" that fell in the hours following the explosion. With a sticky, oil-like consistency, it quickly poisoned fish in the local river and deposited its lethal radioactivity onto the skin of the survivors. The black rain suggested that in a large-scale nuclear exchange, dense smoke clouds in the atmosphere could hold the potential for dramatic climate changes. Such sooty smoke would absorb the light of the sun, heating the atmosphere and allowing the surface of the earth to cool. This could have disastrous effects on the earth's ability to produce crops, and it could also dramatically reduce normal summer temperatures. In Hiroshima, survivors shivered in the middle of summer.

By the spring of 1945, on the verge of successfully achieving and testing the bomb, many atomic scientists, including Szilard, had urged that it not be used against Japan. The war in Europe was ending, and there were increasing concerns that a first-use strategy against a country that was so close to defeat would have serious consequences for the United States in the postwar world. Truman, however, received the advice of an interim committee to drop the bomb as soon as possible. His secretary of state, James Francis Byrnes, seconded that opinion, believing that an unprecedented show of U.S. power would serve to control the postwar expansion of the Soviet Union in Eastern Europe. That view was shared by Secretary of War Henry L. Stimson, who believed further that a postwar sharing of atomic secrets with the Soviets would tend to ensure their good behavior in the postwar world.

Another point of view held that a demonstration of the bomb on some neutral territory might in itself induce the Japanese to surrender. Fears that the still-experimental weapon would fail to detonate, along with concerns that the Japanese military might sabotage the weapon, prevailed when the decision was finally made. The added sense that the United States had within its grasp a tool that could end the war quickly, and so avoid any further losses of the lives of its service personnel, made a compelling argument in favor of the bomb's use.

Within a few years of the surrender of Japan, several more of the world's technologically advanced nations had their own atom bombs. In 1954, the United States exploded an entirely different type of weapon, a hydrogen bomb, the energy of which was almost a thousand times that of the Hiroshima device. The postwar years saw the birth of numerous efforts to control the spread and proliferation of nuclear arsenals, which rapidly increased during the Cold War. With the end of the Cold War in the 1990's, however, genuine nuclear disarmament began to take place, reducing fears of nuclear confrontation and war.

Nuclear proliferation continued to be a threat, however, gaining renewed attention with the growth of terrorist movements with potential access to nuclear materials and the capacity to produce smaller "dirty" bombs. The peaceful exploitation of nuclear energy also expanded greatly, producing about 17 percent of global energy sixty years after the use of atomic weapons against Japan.

David G. Fenton

FURTHER READING

Bird, Kai, and Lawrence Lifschultz, eds. *Hiroshima's Shadow.* Stony Creek, Conn.: Pamphleteer's Press, 1998. An excellent resource that explores the moral and ethical aspects of the United States' decision to drop the atomic bomb on Japan. Also discusses the controversies concerning how to remember this part of U.S. and Japanese history, including the ethics of memorializing the destruction in the *Enola Gay* exhibition at the Smithsonian in 1995.

Fogelman, Edwin. *Hiroshima: The Decision to Use the A-Bomb.* New York: Charles Scribner's Sons, 1964. A compilation of contemporary works excerpted from the writings of those involved in the events that led to the bombing. The principal scientists, the decision makers in government, and writers in Japan report on their own perspectives.

Hersey, John. *Hiroshima.* New York: Alfred A. Knopf, 2002. This classic work, written in 1946, adds a chapter written nearly forty years after the original and recounts the author's search for the six original survivors of Hiroshima whose stories were documented in the first edition of the book. Widely read in its original form (except in Japan, where U.S. authorities blocked its publication until 1949), this work is probably the most moving story of individual human responses to the tragedy.

Hogan, Michael J., ed. *Hiroshima in History and Memory.* New York: Cambridge University Press, 1999. A work of memory and remembrance that focuses on how Hiroshima and Nagasaki have remained as poignant symbols in the national consciousness not only of Japan but also of the United States.

Ishikawa, Eisei, and David L. Swain, trans. *Hiroshima and Nagasaki.* New York: Basic Books, 1981. Prepared by a committee of Japanese commissioned by the two cities to report on the physical, medical, and social effects of the bombings. Contains an extensive bibliography as well as photographs, maps, charts, and tables.

Kurzman, Dan. *Day of the Bomb: Countdown to Hiroshima.* New York: McGraw-Hill, 1986. Written by a former journalist and foreign correspondent, this is a highly readable work with citations from personal interviews, unpublished documents, and papers. Contains an extensive bibliography, including periodical and broadcast materials.

Lifton, Robert Jay. *Death in Life: Survivors of Hiroshima.* 1967. New ed. Chapel Hill: University of North Carolina Press, 1991. Perhaps more than any other writer, Lifton has succeeded in conveying the psychological ramifications of the disastrous events. The research that led to the present work was undertaken in Japan by way of many interviews with survivors and their relatives. Includes an updated preface.

Selden, Kyoko, and Mark Selden, eds. *The Atomic Bomb: Voices from Hiroshima and Nagasaki.* Armonk, N.Y.: M. E. Sharpe, 1989. Mark Selden's opening chapter reviews, and is highly critical of, the U.S. decision to employ the weapons against Japan. The balance of the book contains four short novels, as well as many poems and drawings, some by authors who were children in Hiroshima at the time of the bombing. Essential reading for an understanding of the events and their impact on the people of the two cities.

Walker, Samuel J. *Prompt and Utter Destruction: Truman and the Use of Atomic Bombs Against Japan.* Rev. ed. Chapel Hill: University of North Carolina Press, 2004. An analysis of President Truman's decision to drop the atomic bombs. Highly recommended for general readers and students of American and Asian history, World War II, and the atomic age.

See also: 1951-1952: Teller and Ulam Develop the First Hydrogen Bomb; Mar. 1, 1954: Nuclear Bombing of Bikini Atoll; June 27, 1954: Soviet Union Completes Its First Nuclear Power Plant; July 9, 1955-early 1960's: Scientists Campaign Against Nuclear Testing; Aug. 5, 1963: Nuclear Powers Sign the Limited Test Ban Treaty; Oct. 16, 1964: China Explodes Its First Nuclear Bomb; Mar. 5, 1970: Nuclear Non-Proliferation Treaty Goes into Effect; May 26, 1972: SALT I Is Signed; June 18, 1979: SALT II Is Signed; Aug. 10, 1981: United States Announces Production of Neutron Bombs.

■ **FEBRUARY 1, 1946**

FIRST U.N. SECRETARY-GENERAL IS SELECTED

Norwegian diplomat Trygve Lie was selected the first proper secretary-general of the United Nations. His tenure was both rocky and diplomatically successful. His most enduring contributions include a ten-point program for lasting peace and his work in building U.N. headquarters in New York City.

LOCALE: New York, New York
CATEGORIES: United Nations; diplomacy and international relations; organizations and institutions; government and politics

KEY FIGURES

Trygve Lie (1896-1968), Norwegian politician and diplomat who served as the first proper secretary-general of the United Nations, 1946-1952
Andrei Andreyevich Gromyko (1909-1989), Soviet politician and diplomat who served as Soviet minister of foreign affairs
Paul-Henri Spaak (1899-1972), Belgian socialist politician who served as Belgian minister of foreign affairs

SUMMARY OF EVENT

Norwegian diplomat Trygve Lie was forty-nine years old when he was selected unanimously by the eleven-member U.N. Security Council and General Assembly as the first secretary-general of the United Nations. A Norwegian candidate was to everyone's liking, given that Norway was a neutral country and not powerful enough militarily to be a threat to any global superpower. American representatives had not supported Lie's candidacy, however, preferring instead Canada's ambassador to the United States, Lester B. Pearson. In turn, the Soviet Union openly opposed Pearson as a candidate, because Canada was a close ally of both the United Kingdom and the United States.

Lie, who was experienced in Norwegian politics but not well known in world political circles, was accepted by all sides as a compromise candidate. He was also a war hero. During World War II he served as Norway's foreign minister in London and is credited with bringing the Norwegian merchant fleet to England in 1940, away from Nazi control and into active resistance for the Allies. Active in the Norwegian Labor Party for years, Lie had a range of experience in Norwegian political life that served as a prelude to work at the United Nations. He served as minister of justice (1935-1939), minister of trade and industries (July-September, 1939), and, with the outbreak of World War II, as minister of supply and shipping.

Lie's selection as secretary-general placed him in the spotlight of global politics and it established the five-year term as the standard period of service for the position. He had originally been interested in the presidency of the General Assembly, which had held its election two weeks earlier, and was disappointed with his selection as secretary-general. In the last days of 1945 he was led to believe that he had solid American support and that he would be approved universally as the assembly president. Adlai E. Stevenson, acting head of the U.S. delegation to the United Nations, had a telegram delivered to Lie on Christmas Day, 1945. The telegram asked Lie if he intended to run for the assembly presidency, to which Lie responded affirmatively. Stevenson made clear to Lie that the Americans were supportive and, in fact, that the United States would present his name to the United Nations for consideration.

At the General Assembly meeting in London a few weeks later, however, the U.S. contingent did not express solid support for Lie and was unclear in its position. To complicate things, Great Britain and Belgium promoted Belgian foreign minister Paul-Henri Spaak for the assembly presidency and encouraged the Americans to support their choice. The British and the Americans did not plan nominating speeches and anticipated a vote by secret ballot. Soviet ambassador Andrei Andreyevich Gromyko, however, surprised the participants by speaking to the issue, first to laud Norway's wartime performance and, second, formally to nominate Lie for the presidency. The head of the U.S. delegation, Secretary of State James Francis Byrnes, did not speak openly in support of Lie, making it appear that Lie was the candidate of the Soviet Union only. The Ukrainian representatives called for approval by acclamation, but the effort failed. The General Assembly proceeded with a secret ballot election as planned. The vote was 28 for Spaak and 23 for Lie, with U.S. support reportedly for Lie.

Article 99 of the U.N. charter accords the secretary-general power to bring matters to the attention of the Security Council that may threaten the peace and security of the world. Lie did not intend to follow in the footsteps of James Eric Drummond, first secretary-general of the League of Nations. Drummond had been characterized as a quiet, invisible leader. Lie preferred to express his views publicly, engage the opposition in debate, and stay at the forefront of U.N. affairs by making regular statements on political and substantive matters. As secretary-general, he struggled with the question of the proper power and procedure of the position, that is, he was not clear how far his position could reach into the realm of global politics. In essence, Lie believed that the office of secretary-general should evolve slowly. He was not a prolific speechwriter, nor did he issue an extraordinary number of memoranda.

SIGNIFICANCE

Lie led the United Nations during the difficult first years of the Cold War, a time when tensions were heightened by the paranoia of McCarthyism. He was opposed to the employment of American communists at the United Nations and cooperated with the Federal Bureau of Investigation (FBI) looking into the lives of American citizens working at the United Nations during the McCarthy years.

Shortly after Lie's election as secretary-general, Joseph Stalin set forth a new five-year plan for the Soviet Union and announced that military preparedness would have priority over consumer production. The Cold War became even more tense. Acrimony between the United States and the Soviet Union took the spotlight in discussions at the United Nations. Throughout his tenure there, Lie was criticized both by the Americans, who accused him of communist sympathies, and by the Soviets, who regarded him as a puppet of the Americans.

His most ambitious and enduring contribution was the preparation of a program for lasting peace, a ten-point program that was carried to the capital cities of the chief member states and subsequently considered by the General Assembly. By many accounts, Lie built a reputation as a pragmatic and capable diplomat who was outspoken and temperamental; at times he misjudged situations. His intervention in the Iranian case, insisting on the evacuation of Soviet troops, was not well received by the United States or by Britain. The U.S. government strongly opposed his belief that communist China should be seated in the United Nations. He opposed North Korea's invasion of South Korea in 1950, a position that drew the wrath of the Soviet Union and ultimately led to his downfall as the Soviets became intent on blocking his reelection as secretary-general.

The Cold War was manifest in these reelection proceedings, with the United States staunchly supporting him and the Soviets leading the charge to oust him. By U.N. charter, the Security Council is required to recommend a candidate to the General Assembly for final approval. The assembly voted 46-5 (8 abstentions) to extend Lie's tenure as secretary-general. The Soviets refused to work with him, however, and set in place an uncompromising political and social boycott. This circumstance greatly reduced Lie's political authority with the global community. Lie realized his political position, and so, to the delight of Moscow, resigned in November, 1952. The Lie era at the United Nations was a tense, uncertain time that set the stage for many more years of Cold War acrimony. His tenure also helped foster a dangerous perspective among Americans that the United Nations was strongest when the United States was in the lead.

Largely because of Lie's initiative, the United Nations found a new home in New York City. Lie had approached New York mayor William O'Dwyer and city planner Robert Moses about using New York land as the site for a new U.N. headquarters. After John D. Rockefeller, Jr., offered to buy land in the Turtle Bay neighborhood of midtown Manhattan, the General Assembly accepted the New York plan. The United Nations opened its new headquarters on the site in 1952.

Ann M. Legreid

FURTHER READING

Barrows, James. *Trygve Lie and the Cold War: The U.N. Secretary-General Pursues Peace, 1946-1953*. De Kalb: Northern Illinois University Press, 1989. An analysis of Lie's strengths and shortcomings in presiding over the United Nations.

Browne, Marjorie Ann. *United Nations Secretary-General: The Appointment Process*. Washington, D.C.: Congressional Research Service, Library of Congress, 1996. A brief twelve-page document covering the selection and appointment of the secretary-general of the United Nations.

Gaglione, Anthony. *The United Nations Under Trygve Lie, 1945-1953*. Lanham, Md.: Scarecrow Press, 2001. Discusses the events and personalities associated with the creation of the United Nations during Lie's tenure.

Gordenker, Leon. *The U.N. Secretary-General and Secretariat*. New York: Routledge, 2005. Outlines the roles and responsibilities of secretary-general and secretariat of the United Nations. Part of the Global Institutions series.

Meisler, Stanley. *United Nations: The First Fifty Years*. New York: Atlantic Monthly Press, 1995. Includes a chapter on Lie's efforts to evacuate Soviet forces from Iran in the early stages of his career as secretary-general.

Thakur, Ramesh. "The Political Role of the United Nations Secretary-General." In *The United Nations, Peace, and Security: From Collective Security to the Responsibility to Protect*. New York: Cambridge University Press, 2006. Examines the secretary-general's responsibilities in the theater of world politics.

SEE ALSO: Feb. 1, 1946: First U.N. Secretary-General Is Selected; Nov. 9-Dec. 15, 1946: United Nations Admits Its First New Member States; Dec. 14, 1950: United Nations High Commissioner for Refugees Statute Is Approved; Apr. 10, 1953: Hammarskjöld Is Elected U.N. Secretary-General;

Dec. 14, 1955: United Nations Admits Sixteen New Members; July, 1960: United Nations Intervenes in the Congolese Civil War; 1963-1965: Crisis in U.N. Financing Emerges Over Peacekeeping Expenses; Oct. 25, 1971: People's Republic of China Is Seated at the United Nations; 1990-1994: United Nations Admits Many New Members.

■ MARCH 5, 1946

CHURCHILL DELIVERS HIS IRON CURTAIN SPEECH

Winston Churchill's Iron Curtain speech was one of the inaugural moments of the Cold War. In it, the former prime minister sounded an alarm to Great Britain about Soviet encroachments in Eastern Europe and the Middle East. The speech reflected a simultaneous change in U.S. foreign policy toward the Soviet Union.

ALSO KNOWN AS: 1946 John Findley Green Foundation Lecture; "The Sinews of Peace"
LOCALE: Fulton, Missouri
CATEGORY: Diplomacy and international relations

KEY FIGURES
Winston Churchill (1874-1965), prime minister of Great Britain, 1940-1945 and 1951-1955
Harry S. Truman (1884-1972), president of the United States, 1945-1953
James Francis Byrnes (1879-1972), U.S. secretary of state, 1945-1947

SUMMARY OF EVENT
When Winston Churchill delivered his historic Iron Curtain speech, he uttered a phrase that may be considered the first rhetorical shot of the Cold War. The Soviet Union's postwar posture was condemned, and the former ally of the West was portrayed as the arch-aggressor. The dramatic character of the speech is intensified when one recalls that the United States, fresh from victory, was sighing with profound relief; war-torn Western Europe was on the brink of economic collapse; and Great Britain had recently rejected its wartime prime minister, Churchill, preferring instead Clement Attlee's Labour Party with its bold social democratic schemes.

The phrase "Iron Curtain" was first used by Joseph Goebbels, Adolf Hit-

---

"AN IRON CURTAIN HAS DESCENDED ACROSS THE CONTINENT"

British prime minister Winston Churchill's "Iron Curtain speech" denounced the Soviet Union and marked the beginning of the Cold War:

From Stettin in the Baltic to Trieste in the Adriatic, an iron curtain has descended across the Continent. Behind that line lie all the capitals of the ancient states of Central and Eastern Europe. Warsaw, Berlin, Prague, Vienna, Budapest, Belgrade, Bucharest, and Sofia . . . lie in what I must call the Soviet sphere and all are subject in one form or another, not only to Soviet influence but to a very high and increasing measure of control from Moscow.

---

ler's propaganda minister, but Churchill had also used it in a dispatch sent to President Harry S. Truman on May 12, 1945, exactly one month after President Franklin D. Roosevelt's death. With Germany's defeat imminent, Churchill tried to persuade Truman to disregard the occupation zones arranged at the Quebec Conference in August of 1943 and to continue to hold firmly the Anglo-American positions in Yugoslavia, Austria, Czechoslovakia, Germany, and Denmark. Churchill concluded his message by advising Truman not to move his armies until the three chiefs of state had met and the Western Allies had reached agreement about their Eastern partner's occupation policy.

Although Great Britain's primary enemy, Germany, was virtually defeated at the time of Churchill's dispatch, the United States was still fighting Japan in the Pacific. Truman was suspicious of the Soviet Union, but he was advised to hope for a settlement by exercising restraint. If he had pursued a hard line, the Soviet Union might have responded with an equally tough line and shut the West out of Berlin and Vienna. Since the atomic bomb had not yet been tested, Truman's advisers stressed the need for cooperation with the Russians to ensure that the Russians would keep the promises they had made at Yalta to enter the Pacific war and to work toward the establishment of a world organization (the United Nations). Thus, Churchill's top-level wartime dispatch was rejected in Washington. When Churchill used the phrase "Iron Curtain" publicly a year later, the context had greatly changed.

In the winter of 1946, Churchill was visiting Washington, D.C., and was invited to deliver the John Findley Green Foundation Lecture at Westminster College in Fulton, Missouri. Since Truman assured Churchill that he would preside at the lecture, the occasion assumed an official character. U.S. foreign policy still reflected confidence in the United Nations, faith in the cooperation of the Soviet Union, and a belief in the idea that power politics was an obsolete diplomatic procedure. Although traditional American isolationism supported this policy of restraint and hope, the State Department was actually experiencing the severe limitations of the policy, particularly in Poland and Iran.

Secretary of State James Francis Byrnes's agreement with the content of Churchill's preparatory notes for the speech seems to indicate that the Truman administration was groping for new directions in foreign policy. Indeed, the transition in the United States' foreign policy toward the Soviet Union actually began in mid-February of 1946, as it moved from a position of accommodation to a position of firmness. On February 12, 1946, Byrnes initiated a reorientation of U.S. foreign policy by taking firmer actions in Eastern Europe. The secretary refused to recognize a Soviet-inspired accommodation in Bulgaria, and he took the position that the Soviet-dominated Romanian government was not in compliance with earlier Allied agreements. Moreover, he formally complained of harassment of U.S. officials in Albania, and he threatened to withhold U.S. recognition of their government. Likewise, he charged the Russians with holding up economic recovery in Hungary, and he complained vigorously about noncompliance with the Potsdam Declaration in Eastern Europe.

Winston Churchill delivering the "Iron Curtain" speech at Missouri's Westminster College on March 5, 1946. U.S. president Harry S. Truman (wearing cap) is seated to his left. (Winston Churchill Memorial, Westminster College)

As part of this reorientation, Byrnes went to Miami for a February 17 meeting with Churchill, where the former prime minister's upcoming speech was discussed. On February 22, Byrnes initiated a change in policy toward Iran, which encouraged that government to resist Soviet pressure, a move that thrust the United States into confrontation with the Soviet Union in the eastern Mediterranean and the Middle East. In a speech delivered on February 28 in New York, Byrnes announced a new policy of "patience and firmness" toward the Soviet Union. He even called for universal military training in the United States. Finally, he appointed Bernard Baruch to the United Nations Atomic Energy Commission to preserve the atomic monopoly for the United States. A columnist for the *New York Post* wrote on March 1, "A stiffening American attitude toward Russia is in prospect. . . . evidence will soon be forthcoming." Prior to the Churchill speech, President Truman read it with approval. Beginning in late 1945, *The New York Times* had buttressed support for a change along these lines by stepping up its own anti-Soviet stance.

Churchill's speech, titled "The Sinews of Peace," was delivered on March 5, 1946, to an audience of forty thousand people. He opened with an urgent reminder to the American people that victory in war had left them at the pinnacle of power, where they must be sensitive to the demands of peace. He urged all nations to cooperate with the United Nations and to add to its effectiveness by establishing an "International Armed Force." Churchill argued that the secrets of atomic weaponry, still restricted to the United States, Canada, and Great Britain, must remain safely guarded in their hands until "the essential brotherhood of men is truly embodied and expressed in a world organization."

Speaking again in general terms, he warned the American people that, while they must be vigilant against any threat of war, they should beware of another "world marauder"—tyranny—and join with all liberty-loving people, particularly their British cousins, in proclaiming "in fearless tones the great principles of freedom and the rights of man." As a complement to the United Nations, Churchill specifically called for a "fraternal association of English-speaking peoples," which would include a permanent defense agreement whereby British and American military forces would pursue a mutual security policy. A strong Anglo-American pact was needed to stabilize the foundations of peace.

Before the rising action of this dramatic speech reached its climax, Churchill eased into his attack upon the Soviet Union's bellicose behavior by stating his admiration for the Russian people and his wartime comrade, Joseph Stalin. As if he were talking directly to the Kremlin, Churchill acknowledged their right to be secure on their western frontiers against the possibility of

German aggression and assured them of the Anglo-American resolve to establish lasting friendship with the Soviet Union in spite of "the many differences and rebuffs." He noted, however, that it was his duty "not to misstate the facts . . . about the present position in Europe." Churchill then uttered his famous warning against the "Iron Curtain" that threatened to separate central and Eastern Europe from the West.

Churchill was convinced that while the Soviet Union did not want war, it did aim at the indefinite expansion of its power and doctrine. Because Churchill contended that the Soviet Union admired strength and scoffed at military weakness, his response to the descent of the Iron Curtain was to propose the establishment of Western military and moral unity. The first step toward such unity was to cement an Anglo-American defense pact. As a sign of solidarity, on the day of Churchill's speech, Byrnes sent three strong messages to the Soviet Union, questioning their actions in Eastern Europe, China, and Iran.

In a United States seeking postwar tranquillity, the Soviet Union's military occupation of Eastern Europe did not clearly reveal its political design. Confidence in the United Nations bolstered American hopes for a cooperative policy with the Soviet Union. In general, Churchill's speech was considered shocking in its bold references to Russian bellicosity. Although Churchill recalled that Truman and Byrnes indicated their approval of his remarks immediately following the speech, Eleanor Roosevelt, Henry Wallace (a former vice president under Roosevelt and Truman's secretary of commerce), and the *New York Herald Tribune* openly disagreed with the tone and content of Churchill's Fulton address. Eight days after the speech, *Pravda* published a bitter condemnation of the speech, expressing Stalin's indignation that Churchill's remarks were sowing discord among the Allied governments. When Prime Minister Clement Attlee of Great Britain was asked to comment on the speech, he diplomatically retreated with a "no comment" response to Churchill's warnings.

Despite Truman and Byrnes's earlier reorientation of their Soviet policies, the Truman administration publicly greeted Churchill's speech with ambivalence. Although privately respecting the former prime minister's vision, both Truman and Byrnes publicly responded to the Russian rejoinder and the rift in public opinion by dissociating American policy from Churchill's belligerence toward the Soviet Union. Iran, Manchuria, and the Balkans were points of conflict in U.S.-Soviet relations, but the Truman administration continued to pursue a cooperative policy. During the transition from "cooperation" to "containment," public opinion appeared to be capricious in the extreme. The public opinion polls indicated a shift from a rejection of Churchill's attitude to agreement with it in a matter of a few weeks.

SIGNIFICANCE

Churchill's dramatic Iron Curtain speech set forth the rhetorical terms that would guide Western foreign policy for decades. By 1947, Churchill's Fulton utterances had worked their way into diplomatic realities when certain Cold War facts became clearly visible. The Soviet Union was exerting greater political pressure in Central and Eastern Europe, was uncooperative in the joint occupation of Berlin, was threatening to secure bases in Turkey, and was interfering in a guerrilla war in Greece. When Great Britain announced its withdrawal from Greece, President Truman responded in March, 1947, with his Truman Doctrine, promising military and economic aid to Greece and Turkey. The development of the Marshall Plan in 1948 and the North Atlantic Treaty Organization (NATO) in 1949 further cemented the American commitment to European stability. By that time, the phrase "Iron Curtain" was a common term in the diplomatic rhetoric of the day, as American foreign policy gradually emphasized containment of the Soviet Union, which was increasingly perceived as a global menace to freedom in the West.

Christopher J. Kauffman and Robert Franklin Maddox

FURTHER READING

Churchill, Winston S. *Memoirs of the Second World War.* Boston: Houghton Mifflin, 1959. This volume is an abridgment of the six-volume *The Second World War.* In this work, Churchill recalls events surrounding his famous speech.

Ferrell, Robert H. *Harry S. Truman: A Life.* Columbia: University of Missouri Press, 1994. Ferrell concludes that Churchill's speech "embarrassed" the president, who backed away from it.

Halle, Louis J. *The Cold War as History.* London: Chatto & Windus, 1967. Halle views the Fulton speech as a lesson in the foreign policy education of the American people.

Harburt, Fraser J. *The Iron Curtain: Churchill, America, and the Origins of the Cold War.* New York: Oxford University Press, 1986. This work focuses attention on the role of Winston Churchill as "the most active protagonist of a joint Anglo-American political front against the Soviet Union" during and after World War II.

Muller, James W., ed. *Churchill's "Iron Curtain" Speech Fifty Years Later.* Columbia: University of Missouri Press, 1999. Anthology of essays reconsidering the speech from a post-Cold War perspective. Bibliographic references and index.

Robertson, David. *Sly and Able: A Political Biography of James F. Byrnes.* New York: W. W. Norton, 1994. This work places the Iron Curtain speech and Byrnes's role in context.

Taylor, A. J. P., ed. *Churchill Revised: A Critical Assessment.* New York: Dial Press, 1969. This collection of essays from four historians and one psychiatrist attempts to bring into focus one of the major figures of the period.

Tropp, Sandra Fehl, and Ann Pierson-D'Angelo, eds. *Essays in Context.* New York: Oxford University Press, 2001. Reprints the text of Churchill's speech, "The Sinews of Peace."

Truman, Harry S. *Memoirs of Harry S. Truman.* Vol. 2: *The Years of Trial and Hope.* New York: Doubleday, 1956. Truman's account of his administration provides an interesting contrast to Churchill's vision.

Winkler, Allan. *The Cold War: A History in Documents.* New York: Oxford University Press, 2000. Includes excerpts from Arthur Miller's *The Crucible* among speeches by Winston Churchill, Harry S. Truman, Joseph Stalin, and other major Cold War figures. Also contains a collection of photos and cartoons related to nuclear weapons.

SEE ALSO: Mar. 12, 1947: Truman Doctrine; Apr. 3, 1948: Marshall Plan Provides Aid to Europe; Jan. 25, 1949: Soviet Bloc States Establish Council for Mutual Economic Assistance; Apr. 4, 1949: North Atlantic Treaty Organization Is Formed; Oct. 22, 1951: United States Inaugurates Mutual Security Program; Oct. 23, 1954: Western European Union Is Established; May 14, 1955: Warsaw Pact Is Signed; Nov. 12, 1968-Dec., 1989: Brezhnev Doctrine Mandates Soviet Control of Satellite Nations; Mar. 11, 1985: Gorbachev Initiates a Policy of Glasnost.

■ AUGUST 1, 1946

ATOMIC ENERGY COMMISSION IS ESTABLISHED

President Harry S. Truman signed a law establishing the Atomic Energy Commission as the nation's primary policy-making agency for the development of nuclear energy.

ALSO KNOWN AS: Atomic Energy Act of 1946; McMahon Act
LOCALE: Washington, D.C.
CATEGORIES: Organizations and institutions; laws, acts, and legal history; energy; government and politics

KEY FIGURES

Leslie Richard Groves (1896-1970), chief of the Manhattan Project, who remained involved with nuclear weaponry after the founding of the AEC

Brien McMahon (1903-1952), U.S. senator from Connecticut, who was the prime mover in shaping the bill that established the AEC

Andrew Jackson May (fl. mid-twentieth century), U.S. representative from Kentucky who cosponsored the original bill providing for postwar management of nuclear facilities

Edwin C. Johnson (1884-1970), U.S. senator from Colorado who was the Senate sponsor of what was known as the May-Johnson Bill

Harry S. Truman (1884-1972), president of the United States, 1945-1953, who signed the bill establishing the AEC

SUMMARY OF EVENT

Prior to 1942, the U.S. government, acting primarily through the Office of Scientific Research and Development (OSRD), had spent modest sums in underwriting some of the nuclear research being carried on at various colleges, including Princeton University, Columbia University, the University of Chicago, and the University of California, Berkeley. Since the actual production of atomic weapons would require dedicated research labs and large facilities where uranium of weapons-grade quality could be separated from uranium ore, construction would be a major element in the development of nuclear weapons.

In 1942, the U.S. Army was therefore given the authority to build the necessary facilities and direct the nuclear program that became known as the Manhattan Engineer District, or simply the Manhattan Project. To head it, the Army appointed General Leslie Richard Groves, a hard-driving engineer and expert in construction. Groves remained in command until the Atomic Energy Commission officially began operations.

Although the results of the wartime nuclear program are well known, the development of an atomic bomb was only one aspect of the new field of nuclear energy. Eminent scientists believed that the United States needed to be prepared to maintain leadership in nuclear research, to develop the potential of nuclear energy as a source of industrial power, and, if necessary, to stockpile fissionable materials for both military and industrial use. Executives of corporations such as Union Carbide, Tennessee Eastman (a subsidiary of Eastman Kodak), Du Pont, and Westinghouse also participated in discussions about the future uses of nuclear energy.

When World War II ended, scientists and others who perceived the unique nature of nuclear energy rallied to the idea that efforts should be made to secure mechanisms for the international control of atomic energy. The failure of the resulting negotiations guaranteed that the United States and the Soviet Union would become rivals in atomic energy. With Cold War tensions already growing, the Soviet Union made every effort to move rapidly ahead in the field. The United Kingdom already had the capability to progress in applications of nuclear energy, and other nations were sure to become involved. Although disputes over priorities and timing were inevitable, there was considerable agreement among military, scientific, and industrial leaders that the United States needed to remain preeminent in nuclear energy.

As early as 1944, officials in the OSRD drafted a bill establishing guidelines for postwar government control of nuclear energy. The OSRD proposal envisioned a twelve-member commission appointed by the president. The commission would have the power to regulate transfers of fissionable materials and to oversee the construction and operations of all production plants and experiments involving significant amounts of fissionable material, such as uranium 235 and plutonium. The issue of postwar government involvement, however, was by no means cut and dried; questions remained about numerous issues, including security procedures, patents resulting from government-funded research, and the extent of government control needed.

On October 3, 1945, President Harry S. Truman sent a message to Congress setting forth the broad principles that the administration wished to pursue in its quest for the domestic and international control of the atom. The ideas in Truman's message were based on the plans prepared by the OSRD and modified in important ways by Kenneth Royall and William Marbury, War Department lawyers. Following Truman's announcement, the bill that the two attorneys drafted was directed to the military affairs committees of the House and the Senate, chaired by Representative Andrew Jackson May of Kentucky and Senator Edwin C. Johnson of Colorado, both Democrats. The enabling legislation that the two men agreed to sponsor became known as the May-Johnson Bill.

Speedy passage of the bill was not forthcoming, however, for nuclear scientists and concerned members of the media convinced Congress to hold careful hearings on a matter of such consequence. Much of the testimony called for limitations on military involvement in the control and direction of nuclear energy. Scientists who had chafed under wartime regulations imposed by Groves labored to see security restrictions kept to a minimum, for they agreed that the free exchange of ideas was vital to progress in their disciplines. Within Congress, opponents of the May-Johnson Bill succeeded in transferring the hearings to the newly established Senate special committee

"A Problem More of Ethics
than of Physics"

Before the founding of the Atomic Energy Commission, U.S. president Harry S. Truman asked American financier Bernard Baruch to address the United Nations on how atomic energy—namely its potential to effect both good and bad outcomes—must be controlled by all nations. Baruch spoke before the United Nations on June 14, 1946:

We are here to make a choice between the quick and the dead. That is our business.

Behind the black portent of the new atomic age lies a hope which, seized upon with faith, can work our salvation. If we fail, then we have damned every man to be a slave of fear. Let us not deceive ourselves, we must elect world peace or world destruction.

Science has torn from nature a secret so vast in its potentialities that our minds cower from the terror it creates. The terror is not enough to inhibit the use of the atomic bomb. The terror created by weapons has never stopped man from employing them. . . .

Science, which gave us this dread power, shows that it can be made a giant help to humanity, but science does not show us how to prevent its baleful use. So we have been appointed to obviate that peril by finding a meeting of the minds and the hearts of our people. Only in the will of mankind lies the answer. . . .

Science has taught us how to put the atom to work. But to make it work for good instead of evil lies in the domain dealing with the principles of human duty. We are now facing a problem more of ethics than of physics.

chaired by Brien McMahon of Connecticut. Under McMahon, who sympathized with the opponents of May-Johnson in important ways, the hearings continued for several months. In response to mounting criticism of the May-Johnson Bill, Truman quietly withdrew his support of it and some months later endorsed the McMahon Bill instead.

Compromises began to be made. The May-Johnson Bill tilted toward military control, while the McMahon Bill favored civilian control but was amended to allow the military ample influence in shaping weapons development. There was, however, substantial agreement that the government should be authorized to control nuclear facilities and to set nuclear policy in its civilian as well as military aspects. Paradoxically, as historians George Mazuzan and J. Samuel Walker have pointed out, many of the most unyielding advocates of government monopoly during the congressional hearings were political conservatives who had spent years railing against the New Deal and government involvement in the economy.

Both bills therefore envisioned the establishment of a government agency to continue in peacetime what the Manhattan Project had begun in wartime. The new agency, which was named the Atomic Energy Commission (AEC), would also chart the future course of nuclear policy.

As differences were narrowed, the bill that took shape in the summer of 1946 gave the AEC exclusive authority over the development and applications of atomic energy, ownership of all fissionable materials (amended by the 1954 Atomic Energy Act) and the facilities for producing them, and control of patents already owned by the government, in addition to any that might be developed during research funded by the government. There were also provisions for security checks on all individuals who worked for the AEC and its civilian contractors.

Five commissioners appointed by the president for two-year terms (later changed to staggered five-year terms) would determine AEC policy, while daily operations would be directed by a general manager, also a presidential appointee. To ensure the military's continued involvement in policy decisions, the bill called for a Military Liaison Committee that would have direct access to the civilian heads of the armed services. In addition, eminent scientists and engineers were to serve on the General Advisory Council (in practice, the AEC itself had one seat for a scientist). To maintain legislative oversight of the powerful new executive agency, the bill established an eighteen-member Joint Committee on Atomic Energy. Each house of Congress would receive nine seats on the committee. No more than five seats in each house could go to members of one party.

SIGNIFICANCE

Although President Truman signed the enabling legislation for the AEC on August 1, 1946, the commission did not begin operations until midnight of December 31, when it received from the Manhattan Project control of the principal facilities developed during World War II. Weeks, however, had already been devoted to preparing for the official transfer. The inherited facilities included the bomb lab at Los Alamos, New Mexico, and large sites and plants at Oak Ridge, Tennessee, and Hanford, Washington. The principal activity at Oak Ridge was the separation of uranium so that U-235 (the fissionable isotope of uranium) could be made available for weapons research and manufacture. Plutonium (an artificially processed fissionable material) was produced at Hanford.

The AEC began operations with about four thousand civilian employees, two thousand military personnel, and thirty-eight thousand civilians working for it through its prime contractors. Union Carbide and General Electric would manage the production plants at Oak Ridge and Hanford, respectively, while the University of California continued to direct the laboratory at Los Alamos.

Although the Manhattan Project had lost momentum in the demobilization that followed World War II, Groves had kept the project functioning and had even committed funds to develop still more facilities, including laboratories at Argonne, Illinois, and Brookhaven, New York. The AEC decided that Argonne would concentrate on the development of reactors for the generation of electricity and for submarine propulsion, while Brookhaven's mandate would be limited to peaceful uses of the atom and to basic research in such fields as radiation biology and medicine.

Both Argonne and Brookhaven were designated as national laboratories. Several northeastern universities were authorized to form a consortium to manage Brookhaven, while the University of Chicago managed Argonne. The AEC also funded research done at individual campuses. The actual testing and construction of reactors would soon lead to the opening of a national reactor testing site near Idaho Falls, Idaho.

The AEC empire would grow even larger as the 1940's drew to a close, for Cold War anxieties helped bring about U.S. determination to expand its nuclear arsenal. A fourfold increase in the AEC's budget between 1947 and 1952 revealed the extent of the nation's alarm. Truman's decision to authorize development of a hydrogen bomb further increased the demand for fissionable materials and led to the building of additional AEC facilities. A second weapons lab was constructed at Livermore, California. Moreover, hundreds of private corporations were subcontracted to join the nuclear weapons program.

In 1950, the AEC and the Department of Defense jointly selected a site in Nevada as the proving grounds for the many tests that would be held as new types of nuclear weapons were readied. (Thermonuclear weapons were tested at a Pacific Ocean site.) The magnitude of the AEC operations was described in 1952 by *Time* magazine as a "land area half again as big as Delaware, growing more rapidly than any great U.S. business ever did. Its investment in plant and equipment . . . makes it bigger than General Motors." Radioactive wastes were produced at all the AEC sites; while it was AEC policy to dispose of these wastes in accordance with the safety standards that existed at the time, there was always the possibility that new findings would reveal these standards to be inadequate or that something unforeseen could occur while wastes were being handled.

From its beginning, the AEC had a complex and often contradictory mission. Originating at the dawn of the Cold War, the agency emphasized research in nuclear weaponry, testing of new designs, and production of fissionable materials for the military. The agency's charter also addressed the development of commercial applications of nuclear power and dealt with the funding of research into the health and environmental effects of radiation. By the early 1950's, the growing output of nuclear warheads and the testing of new designs demonstrated that the AEC was fulfilling its mandate to design and help produce weaponry. Whether it could fulfill its other roles equally well remained to be seen, but such progress would not be an unmixed blessing. The development of commercial nuclear power meant that more reactors would be constructed and placed at new locations throughout the United States. Once commercial nuclear power plants became a reality, contractors would be charged with handling fissionable materials and nuclear wastes.

These developments and an increasing awareness that the regulatory and promotional aspects of the AEC's work ought to be separated led to initiatives for legislative reform. In 1974, pursuant to the passage by Congress of the Energy Reorganization Act, the AEC ceased to exist, as the regulatory functions of the AEC were vested in a new Nuclear Regulatory Commission and its promotional functions given to a new Energy Research and Development Administration, which was later absorbed into the U.S. Department of Energy.

Lloyd J. Graybar

Further Reading

Anders, Roger M., ed. *Forging the Atomic Shield: Excerpts from the Office Diary of Gordon E. Dean.* Chapel Hill: University of North Carolina Press, 1987. A former law partner of Brien McMahon, Dean became the AEC's second chairman in 1950. The Cold War was then at its height, and Dean's diary provides insight into the concerns of the AEC.

Duffy, Robert J. *Nuclear Politics in America: A History and Theory of Government Regulation.* Lawrence: University Press of Kansas, 1997. A study of government policy and regulation of the nuclear power industry in the United States. Chapters include "Subgovernment Dominance, 1945-65," "Redefining Nuclear Power," and "The Demise of the AEC."

Hewlett, Richard G., and Oscar E. Anderson, Jr. *The New World, 1939-1946.* Vol. 1 in *A History of the United States Atomic Energy Commission.* University Park: Pennsylvania State University Press, 1962. Based on research in archives, published sources, and numerous interviews, this book provides a reliable study of the wartime development of the Manhattan Project as well as the congressional maneuvers that resulted in the establishment of the AEC.

Hewlett, Richard G., and Francis Duncan. *Atomic Shield, 1947-1952.* Vol. 2 in *A History of the United States Atomic Energy Commission.* University Park: Pennsylvania State University Press, 1969. Begins with the confirmation hearings of the original five appointees to the AEC and concludes with the detonation of the world's first thermonuclear device at Eniwetok in the Pacific late in 1952.

————. *Nuclear Navy, 1946-1962.* Chicago: University of Chicago Press, 1974. Provides a reliable overview of the U.S. Navy's efforts to develop and utilize nuclear reactors as a source of propulsion. Surveys the people involved in the Navy's efforts.

Hewlett, Richard G., and Jack M. Holl. *Atoms for Peace and War, 1953-1961: Eisenhower and the Atomic Energy Commission.* Berkeley: University of California Press, 1989. Much more concerned with safety issues than the two previous volumes listed above. An "Essay on Sources" by Roger M. Anders will point the way to many books dealing with nuclear topics.

Lilienthal, David Eli. *Change, Hope, and the Bomb.* Princeton, N.J.: Princeton University Press, 1963. A distinguished public servant, Lilienthal was the first chairman of the AEC. This extended essay presents his thoughts on issues such as nuclear disarmament, nuclear fuels versus fossil fuels, and peaceful uses of the atom.

————. *The Journals of David E. Lilienthal.* Vol. 2 in *The Atomic Energy Years, 1946-1950.* New York: Harper & Row, 1964. Lilienthal's journal describes the pressures he felt from the military, the media, and congressional critics as the AEC's first chairman.

Mazuzan, George T., and J. Samuel Walker. *Controlling the Atom: The Beginnings of Nuclear Regulation, 1946-1962.* Berkeley: University of California Press, 1985. Complements the official history of the AEC by analyzing government efforts to define radiation hazards and to provide safeguards.

Pfau, Richard F. *No Sacrifice Too Great: The Life of Lewis L. Strauss.* Charlottesville: University Press of Virginia, 1984. A hard-driving, successful, and opinionated businessman, Strauss worked in the Navy Department during World War II and later became involved in nuclear affairs as a member of the AEC and, later, as its chairman. He often disagreed with Lilienthal.

Walker, J. Samuel. *Containing the Atom: Nuclear Regulation in a Changing Environment, 1963-1971.* Berkeley: University of California Press, 1992. Continues the story of government-sponsored research in radiation hazards and efforts to provide controls.

————. *A Short History of Nuclear Regulation, 1946-1999.* Washington, D.C.: U.S. Nuclear Regulatory Commission, 2000. Seventy-page history of the Atomic Energy Commission and the Nuclear Regulatory Commission.

SEE ALSO: Aug. 6 and 9, 1945: Atomic Bombs Destroy Hiroshima and Naga-saki; Mar. 1, 1954: Nuclear Bombing of Bikini Atoll; June 27, 1954: Soviet Union Completes Its First Nuclear Power Plant; July 9, 1955-early 1960's: Scientists Campaign Against Nuclear Testing; Aug. 5, 1963: Nuclear Powers Sign the Limited Test Ban Treaty; Oct. 16, 1964: China Explodes Its First Nuclear Bomb; Mar. 5, 1970: Nuclear Non-Proliferation Treaty Goes into Effect; Oct. 16, 1980: China Conducts Atmospheric Nuclear Test; Oct., 1983: Europeans Demonstrate Against Nuclear Weapons; Sept. 27, 1991: George H. W. Bush Announces Nuclear Arms Reductions.

NOVEMBER, 1946-JULY, 1954

NATIONALIST VIETNAMESE FIGHT FRENCH CONTROL OF INDOCHINA

Viet Minh forces defended the independence of Vietnam against French forces that were seen as a vestige of colonial influence.

ALSO KNOWN AS: First Indochina War; French-Indochina War
LOCALE: North Vietnam
CATEGORIES: Colonialism and occupation; independence movements; wars, uprisings, and civil unrest

KEY FIGURES

Ho Chi Minh (1890-1969), the president of the Republic of Vietnam, committed to the idea of Vietnamese independence
Vo Nguyen Giap (b. 1912), a Vietnamese patriot and the commander of Ho Chi Minh's military arm, the Viet Minh
Sir Douglas David Gracey (1894-1964), commander of the Allied Land Forces in French Indochina, 1945-1946, who led 20,000 Indian troops to occupy Saigon
Jean Sainteny (1907-1978), a French negotiator, who developed the blueprint for the recognition of the Republic of Vietnam
Georges Thierry d'Argenlieu (1889-1964), the French high commissioner for Indochina at the end of World War II
Henri Navarre (1898-1983), commander of the French forces in Indochina, 1953-1954

Summary of Event

In September of 1945, while the eyes of the world were focused on the Japanese surrender in the Pacific following World War II, Vietnamese nationalist leader Ho Chi Minh proclaimed the Republic of Vietnam. After nearly one hundred years of oppressive French domination, Ho believed that the United States would enforce the ideals articulated in the Atlantic Charter of 1941: the return of self-government to nations that had been forcibly denied this right. Ho and other Vietnamese nationalists did not realize that Vietnam had been used as a bargaining chip by the United States in several wartime political maneuvers. In 1942, President Roosevelt had guaranteed the Free French that they would be able to retain all of their overseas possessions, including Vietnam. This promise had been offered as an inducement to encourage greater efforts by the French military forces. In 1943, Roosevelt had countered this promise and proposed a trusteeship for postwar Indochina, claiming that the French had mismanaged the people and resources of the area. Still later in the war, in 1945, Roosevelt tried to bargain with the leader of the Nationalist Chinese, Chiang Kai-shek, by offering him control of Vietnam and any other countries in Indochina. The Chinese turned down the offer because of the difficulty of trying to govern a nation that would not conform to Chinese rule.

In 1945, therefore, the fate of Vietnam was still undecided. During the war, Vietnam had been occupied by the Japanese with French approval. France's credibility concerning Japan was called into question as a result of this, and at the Potsdam Conference (1945) the decision was made to allow neutral allied nations to oversee Japanese disarmament in Vietnam. The British were to supervise in the south and the Chinese were in charge of northern disarmament. The French high commissioner (governor) for Indochina, Admiral Georges Thierry d'Argenlieu, was to coordinate between the areas. The new Republic of Vietnam had no military institutions to protect its claim of independence and no political organization that represented the nation as a whole. In 1945, the new republic was led by communist-styled cadres known as Viet Minh. These cadres were organized politically by Ho Chi Minh and militarily by Vo Nguyen Giap, Ho's trusted assistant.

Within days of the landing of the British forces, conflict broke out between the Viet Minh and the French and British. The British officer in charge, General Sir Douglas David Gracey, ordered to remain neutral, was unquestionably in favor of French rule in the area. A product of the British colonial system, Gracey did not believe that the Vietnamese were capable of self-government, nor that they should ever be allowed to threaten the control of their masters. As soon as rioting broke out in Saigon, he released French legionnaires from their Japanese prisons and armed them with Brit-

Vietnamese nationalist leader Ho Chi Minh. (National Archives)

ish weapons. Fearing the return of French rule, the Viet Minh continued rioting and increased attacks against French units as well as against the British. In Saigon, the fighting was fierce at times and atrocities against civilians were committed by both sides. The British, fearing increased involvement, turned over their weapons and supplies to the French and left the country.

In the north, Vietnamese-Chinese relations went somewhat more smoothly. General Lu Han's troops were not of the caliber of the British units. The soldiers were starving, ill-equipped, and often tubercular, more interested in ransacking the towns and countryside of Vietnam for food, clothing, and medicine than in French-Vietnamese politics. Ho feared the incursion of Chinese troops more than he feared the French and British, as China had been attempting to overrun Vietnam for one thousand years. He feared that the Potsdam Agreement had given China political gains in Southeast Asia that it had been unable to attain militarily. Because of this fear, Ho made no effort to prevent French attempts to negotiate a deal with China to override the Potsdam design and give France the control of all of Vietnam. On February 28, 1946, a French-Chinese agreement was reached. The Chinese would remove their troops from North Vietnam, to be replaced by an equal number of French. In return, France gave up all claims to the Kwangchowan region of China (held by France since the late nineteenth century). France also agreed to sell the Yunnan railroad to Chiang Kai-shek's nationalist government and to designate Haiphong as a free trade port for China.

Ho, glad to be rid of the Chinese, was not yet ready to settle for the return of French domination. Vietnam, to Ho and his followers, was now an independent republic, and he encouraged Vo Nguyen Giap to step up recruitment and training of more cadres of Viet Minh to ensure the protection of the country. The French, unable to stabilize both halves of the country, allowed a French diplomat, Jean Sainteny, to attempt negotiations with Ho. The Sainteny-Ho Agreement was completed on March 6. France guaranteed the recognition of Vietnam as an independent state within the French Union (Laos, Cambodia, and Vietnam). In return, Ho agreed to allow twenty-five thousand French troops to remain in the country for a period of five years to protect French interests.

As each side stepped up its attempts to control the area, one situation became clear. The key to success was going to be in the countryside. The rural villages and peasant farm holdings were going to be needed as base camps. The average villager, desiring neutrality, was caught between the two opposing forces. By day, the villagers were victims of French recruitment and commissary officers. Fear for their lives or those of their families and the threat of losing the family farm, more than a committed belief in the right of the French to control Vietnam, caused peasant farmers to join the French forces. The French began to control the countryside around the major cities of Vietnam. By night, the countryside of Vietnam belonged to the cadres of the Viet Minh. The cadres were small, self-sufficient units that survived alone in the jungle. Usually without adequate weapons or supplies, they depended on local villages for support as well as additional recruits for Vo Nguyen Giap's army. Several nights a week, they moved into the villages and conducted classes in nationalism, communism, anti-French tactics, and basic reading and writing skills. They targeted the youth of these villages as the source of future independence guerrillas and a present spy network against the French. Most of the peasants philosophically believed in independence, but they had no stomach for more warfare. Laboring to feed their families and to preserve their small plots of land, they became trapped in an untenable position. Harangued, threatened, beaten, and sometimes tortured and killed, the peasants of Vietnam were pulled into a conflict that the Sainteny-Ho Agreement was supposed to prevent.

Before the agreement could be signed officially in Paris, French president Charles de Gaulle sent one thousand additional troops to Saigon. Ho Chi Minh appealed to Vo Nguyen Giap to redouble his military recruiting and training efforts. Colonial businesspeople, planters, and state officials published strong complaints against the agreement. They cabled Paris with their complaints and turned to the local governor, Admiral d'Argenlieu, with their fears. D'Argenlieu, committed to the policy of French colonialism in Vietnam, did not wait for orders from Paris. He violated the March agreement and declared the Republic of Cochin China (South Vietnam), in the name of France.

Ho, who was then in Paris for the official signing of the Sainteny Accords, was discredited as an impotent political upstart by d'Argenlieu's actions and returned to Vietnam having failed to achieve recognition of Vietnam's independence. Complaints from colonists in Vietnam put political pressure on the French cabinet to claim economic rights to both the north and south of Vietnam. Fearing the loss of what little recognition he had gained for his country's right to political autonomy, Ho returned to Paris in October. Pressured by French intransigence, Ho agreed to and signed a draft of an accord known as the Fontainebleau Agreement, a vague attempt to give joint rule over North Vietnam to both the French and the Vietnamese. Because of unstated lines of authority concerning the policing of cities and collection of customs, the draft led to frustration and dissatisfaction for both sides.

The confusion caused by the Fontainebleau Agreement can be argued as the direct cause of the French-Indochina War. Fighting broke out Novem-

Vietnamese military commander Vo Nguyen Giap. (Library of Congress)

ber 20, 1946, when a French patrol boat apprehended Chinese smugglers in the waterways of Haiphong Harbor. A Vietnamese patrol, observing the French apprehension of the Chinese smugglers and unsure of exact lines of authority, considered the act as one more indication of French unwillingness to allow the republic to control itself. The Vietnamese approached and overtook the French boat and arrested the three crewmen. Fighting broke out in the city of Haiphong as soon as the French became aware of the arrests. Throughout the day of November 20, French tanks entered the city of Haiphong and overran Vietnamese barricades. The Viet Minh cadres responded with mortar fire. A cease-fire was called the next day, and both sides began appealing to Paris for direction. Ho appealed to the French government to honor the signed accords. He was ordered to cede French control of the city and ports of Haiphong. When he refused, the battle resumed.

The French attack on Haiphong utilized the gamut of military technology of the day: infantry, tanks, artillery, air strikes, and naval bombardment. The underequipped Viet Minh responded with mortar fire and guerrilla raids. Entire neighborhoods of flimsy houses in the poorest sections of town were demolished, and thousands of Vietnamese refugees poured out of the city. The official French reports at the time stated that six thousand civilians had been killed as they fled the area. Later, the figures were reduced to read that no more than several hundred had died. The fighting spread to the city of Hanoi and lasted through most of December. On December 19, at 9:00 P.M., Vo Nguyen Giap declared virtual war on the country of France and Ho called on the people of Vietnam to rise up and to defend Vietnamese independence and unification. Ho continued to appeal to the Western powers to stop French aggression throughout the month of December. While not agreeing with the French policies, Europe and the United States refused to step in.

The war between France and Vietnam lasted eight years and did not go well for the French. A succession of commanders—Philippe Leclerc de Hauteclocque, Jean-Étienne Valluy, d'Argenlieu, Jean de Lattre de Tassigny, and Raoul Salan—could not overcome the guerrilla forces of the Viet Minh and their peasant support. The war finally ended with a devastating rout of the French at the Battle of Dien Bien Phu (March-May, 1954). This decisive conflict—in which French commander Henri Navarre attempted to defend Laos and overwhelm the Viet Minh from an air base near the village of Dien Bien Phu, located in a ten-mile-long valley in a remote portion of northwestern Vietnam—failed in the face of Vo Nguyen Giap's unexpectedly strong and sophisticated two-month siege.

Navarre assumed command after de Lattre, in the spring of 1953, and was shocked by the lack of an overall plan and the deterioration of French morale. His mandate at this point in the war, although still the subject of controversy, was primarily to consolidate southern support and, in the north, create conditions that would allow an "honorable political solution" to the Indochina problem in preparation for peace talks in Geneva. The strategy was to consolidate southern support and conduct offensives in the north in order to negotiate from a position of strength. The issue of whether Navarre's mandate included the defense of Laos, which had been overrun by Viet Minh, is still debated but was understood by Navarre to be part of his mandate. Navarre's task was overwhelming and his options few, and he settled on a strategy he hoped would reproduce an earlier French victory at Nan Sanh. He did not, however, expect the Viet Minh to succeed in hauling heavy artillery into the remote region, and he did not bank on Vo Nguyen Giap's willingness to wait until March, when his Viet Minh were entrenched with their weapons assembled and well hidden in the hills above the French base and its seven satellite fortresses. After a two-month siege, the satellites were defeated and, despite heavy casualties, the Viet Minh had won. In this battle alone, the French suffered more than 2,200 dead, nearly 5,200 wounded, and 11,800 captured (most of whom died on the 250-mile march to the prison camps or of disease or brutal treatment at the camps). The Viet Minh suffered more than three times the number of dead, 7,950, and 15,000 wounded, but these numbers paled against their moral victory.

SIGNIFICANCE

The victory at Dien Bien Phu, as British historian Martin Windrow put it, represented "the first time that a non-European colonial independence movement had evolved . . . to defeat a modern Western occupier in a pitched battle." The victory not only put an end to French Indochina; it remains a milestone today in the minds of people in all so-called Third World nations, a symbol of colonialism's demise and the potential of developing nations. As one World Bank official from India put it, "A small Asian nation had defeated a colonial power, convincingly. It changed history."

After Dien Bien Phu, the 1954 Geneva Accords divided Vietnam into communist North Vietnam and French-administered South Vietnam. The United States, which had supplied significant equipment and technological support to the French during the First Indochina War, supported South Vietnam after the French withdrew and after the failure of the two countries to reunite in 1956, as mandated by the Geneva Accords. Accusations that Ho's forces were terrorizing both northerners and southerners led the South's Emperor Bao Dai and his prime minister, Ngo Dinh Diem, to break with the accords. Thus began another long engagement, the Second Indochina War, which eventually involved U.S. forces on the ground in the Vietnam War (1959-1975).

French colonialism thus had widespread effects not only in Southeast Asia but throughout Europe, China, and the United States also. Unable to receive the aid and support needed to break French control of Vietnam, Ho Chi Minh reverted to seeking assistance from communist China and Russia. This action placed Vietnam in the middle of Cold War politics and on a direct line of confrontation with the United States. Vietnam paid a heavy price for Ho Chi Minh's dream of independence. More than three million Vietnamese were killed between 1946 and 1976, as fighting shifted from the First Indochina War to the Second Indochina War, the latter now known as the Vietnam War. Civil War in Vietnam was a harbinger of the inimical effects that the Cold War competition would later wreak throughout the developing world as colonial areas sought independence, often in the context of wars of national liberation in which Western and Eastern bloc countries would contend during the Cold War.

Thousands of children, along with women and soldiers, were burned and maimed as a result of bombings, mines, and enemy raids on villages. The civilians of Vietnam were all soldiers in the eyes of their enemies, and their elimination was often condoned as a way to prevent future generations of resistance fighters. Without sufficient medical supplies or technology, the Vietnamese victims were condemned to a lifetime of suffering and nonproductivity. The use of defoliant and other chemicals imparted the ongoing legacy of fear—fear of cancer and birth defects.

The physical human damage to the Vietnamese people was tremendous, but so was the fiscal damage. Thirty years of war not only prevented industrialization from occurring but also devastated the agricultural base, leaving the country at times unable to feed its citizens adequately. An economically devastated and war-torn land, Vietnam would continue to struggle for acceptance in world trade and for economic assistance to rebuild industry, farmland, and educational institutions into the 1990's.

Celia Hall-Thur, updated by Christina J. Moose

FURTHER READING

Asselin, Pierre. "New Perspectives on Dien Bien Phu." *Explorations in Southeast Asian Studies* 1, no. 2 (Fall, 1997). Identifies the Battle of Dien Bien Phu as more historically significant than previously recognized, and aims "to clarify the historical record by highlighting some of the main misconceptions about the engagement and providing more accurate descriptions of its origins and implications." Chief among these were Vo Nguyen Giap's decision to delay engagement from January 26 to March 13, when his troops and their artillery were well entrenched in the highlands above the valley, and the timing of the Geneva talks.

Boettcher, Thomas D. *Vietnam: The Valor and the Sorrow.* Boston: Little, Brown, 1985. One of the basic overviews of the Vietnam war. While the emphasis is on American political and military involvement in the area, there is a cursory overview of the French colonial period and the French war. There is no consideration given to the history of Vietnam prior to the late eighteenth century. Contains pictures, chapter notes, and an index.

Davidson, Phillip B. *Vietnam at War: The History 1946-1975.* Novato, Calif.: Presidio Press, 1988. Presents a comprehensive history of the Vietnam War from a military perspective.

Fairbank, John King, Edwin O. Reischauer, and Albert M. Craig. *East Asia.* Boston: Houghton Mifflin, 1983. Possibly the best text for an overview of the entire Vietnamese-Chinese-European experience prior to 1950. The emphasis is on political, social, and military developments in specified periods. Contains a complete list of references and an index.

Fall, Bernard B. *Hell in a Very Small Place: The Siege of Dien Bien Phu.* Philadelphia: J. B. Lippincott, 1967. Analysis both of the Battle of Dien Bien Phu and of its global geopolitical consequences.

Hayslip, Le Ly, and Charles Jay Wurts. *When Heaven and Earth Changed Places.* New York: Doubleday, 1989. A personal account of what it was like to live in Vietnam under the rule of both the French and the American armies. The emphasis is on the peasant families and how they were controlled by the Viet Cong. Offers no references.

Karnow, Stanley. *Vietnam, a History: The First Complete Account of Vietnam at War.* New York: Viking Press, 1983. Possibly the definitive history of both the French and the American involvements in Vietnam. The book, while highly researched and detailed, does not relate the history of the country prior to the eighteenth century. Excellent photographs. Provides chapter notes, sources, and an index.

Troung, Tang Nhu, with David Chanoff and Doan Van Toai. *A Vietcong Memoir: An Inside Account of the Vietnam War and Its Aftermath.* San Diego, Calif.: Harcourt Brace Jovanovich, 1985. A personal account of how and why Ho Chi Minh gained the hearts of the Vietnamese people. Emphasis is on the author's experiences with French rule and why many Vietnamese were willing to work against it. Contains a glossary of names and an appendix of Vietcong documents. No other reference material is listed.

Windrow, Martin. *The Last Valley.* Cambridge, Mass.: Da Capo Press, 2004. Examines the French military strategy at the Battle of Dien Bien Phu, which was based on the successful one used at Nan Sanh but which failed to take differences into account and which did not anticipate the superior strategy of Viet Minh commander Vo Nguyen Giap. A detailed account of the siege that also examines the historical impact of the event.

SEE ALSO: Nov. 9, 1953: Cambodia Gains Independence from France; Aug., 1954-May, 1955: Operation Passage to Freedom Evacuates Refugees from North Vietnam; Sept. 8, 1954: SEATO Is Founded; Nov. 14, 1961: Kennedy Expands U.S. Involvement in Vietnam; Aug. 7, 1964-Jan. 27, 1973: United States Enters the Vietnam War; Mar., 1973: U.S. Troops Leave Vietnam; May, 1975: Indo-Chinese Boat People Begin Fleeing Vietnam; Feb. 17-Mar. 16, 1979: China Invades Vietnam; Sept., 1989: Vietnamese Troops Withdraw from Cambodia.

■ **NOVEMBER 9-DECEMBER 15, 1946**

UNITED NATIONS ADMITS ITS FIRST NEW MEMBER STATES

The United Nations admitted Sweden, Iceland, Afghanistan, and Thailand to membership in the world organization, even as Albania, Mongolia, Ireland, Transjordan, and Portugal faced delays in their acceptance because of objections from members of the Security Council. Admitting new members tested the admissions process and exposed its political character, including the tensions between two superpowers: the United States and the Soviet Union.

LOCALE: New York, New York
CATEGORIES: United Nations; organizations and institutions; diplomacy and international relations; government and politics

KEY FIGURES
Andrei Andreyevich Gromyko (1909-1989), Soviet politician, diplomat, and representative to the United Nations and Security Council
Hershel V. Johnson (fl. mid-twentieth century), American politician, diplomat, and acting representative to the United Nations and Security Council
Trygve Lie (1896-1968), Norwegian politician and diplomat, who was the first secretary general of the United Nations, 1946-1952
Paul-Henri Spaak (1899-1972), Belgian politician and diplomat, who was the first president of the U.N. General Assembly

SUMMARY OF EVENT

At the forty-seventh plenary meeting of November 9, 1946, under the leadership of Secretary Trygve Lie and General Assembly president Paul-Henri Spaak, the General Assembly adopted a resolution admitting Afghanistan, the Republic of Iceland, and Sweden to membership in the United Nations. At the sixty-seventh plenary meeting of December 15, the General Assembly adopted a resolution admitting Siam (now Thailand) to membership in the United Nations. These new members were only four out of the nine that had applied for membership.

Their admission was a result of recommendations made by the U.N. Security Council to the General Assembly. In 1946, the Security Council was composed of five permanent members (China, France, the Union of Soviet Socialist Republics, the United Kingdom of Great Britain and Northern Ireland, and the United States of America) and six nonpermanent members (Australia, Brazil, Egypt, Mexico, the Netherlands, and Poland).

The Security Council members had discussed and debated applications for membership in the United Nations submitted by Albania, Mongolia, Afghanistan, Transjordan, Ireland, Portugal, Iceland, Siam, and Sweden in August. During the discussion, the American representative, Hershel V. Johnson, expressed the United States' reservations about admitting Albania and Mongolia (then both under communist control) but proposed that all applicants be admitted, in keeping with the United Nations' principles of universality and the goal to admit as many states as possible. This proposal was supported by China, Brazil, Egypt, Mexico, and the Netherlands. The Soviet Union's representative, Ambassador Andrei Andreyevich Gromyko, opposed the en bloc admission of states and eventually asked for the withdrawal of the U.S. proposal. In response, the United States requested a delay in deciding about the admission of Albania and Mongolia. Gromyko also opposed the admission of Ireland, Portugal, and Transjordan on the grounds that these states had no formal relationship with the Soviet Union.

The recommendation to the General Assembly to admit Afghanistan, Iceland, and Sweden was made on August 29, with ten Security Council member votes in support and one member abstaining (Australia). The recommendation to admit Siam was made unanimously on December 12.

SIGNIFICANCE

Sweden, Iceland, Afghanistan, and Siam became the first members of the United Nations admitted after the founding of the influential international body. Prior to their admission, the United Nations comprised the original

U.N. Assembly president Paul-Henri Spaak. (Library of Congress)

fifty-one member states. These nations had participated in the San Francisco conference in 1945 or had signed the Declaration of the United Nations in January of 1942.

The process of admitting new members was important because it tested the procedure for admission and exposed the political character of the process. States wishing to join the United Nations first needed to secure a recommendation from the Security Council, which required seven affirmative votes. Any permanent member, however, could veto admission in cases of substantive issues. The Security Council's recommendation was to be followed by a two-thirds vote of the General Assembly.

The process of admission also exposed the emerging Cold War tension between the world's two ideological blocs, led by the two superpowers: the communist states under the leadership of the Soviet Union and the noncommunist states, led by the United States. The process of admission revealed that the permanent Security Council members used veto power as a political tool despite the fact that there were no substantive grounds to use it. For example, the Soviet Union hindered admission of Italy, which enjoyed support of the United States and other Western members, even though the Italian government had met all the conditions to be admitted. The United States did not use its veto power during these proceedings, in part because initially it was able to secure a majority of countries on the Security Council to vote for pro-Western candidates.

Kasia Polanska

FURTHER READING

Bailey, Sydney D., and Sam Daws. *The Procedure of the U.N. Security Council.* 3d ed. Oxford, England: Clarendon Press, 1998. Examines the procedures of the U.N. Security Council, including examples of discussions about specific membership applications.

Bishop, William W., Jr. "Conditions of Admission of a State to Membership in the United Nations." *American Journal of International Law* 42, no. 4 (October, 1948): 927-934. The text of the advisory opinion by the International Court of Justice dated May 28, 1948.

Chamberlin, Waldo, Thomas Hovet, Jr., and Erica Hovet. *A Chronology and Fact Book of the United Nations, 1941-1976.* Dobbs Ferry, N.Y.: Oceana, 1976. Details U.N. events and activities, including those surrounding the 1946 membership debates. Lists members, presidents of U.N. bodies, and dates of member states' application for U.N. membership along with dates of admission.

Lee, Roy S., ed. *Swords into Plowshares: Building Peace Through the United Nations.* Boston: Martinus Nijhoff, 2006. Anthology of essays evaluating the United Nations' history and progress from the point of view of the early twenty-first century.

Malone, David M., ed. *The U.N. Security Council: From the Cold War to the Twenty-First Century.* Boulder, Colo.: Lynne Rienner, 2004. A thorough history of the U.N. Security Council and its powers within the international organization.

Rudzinski, Aleksander W. *The Admission of New Members.* New York: Carnegie Endowment for International Peace, 1952. Discusses the process of admitting new member states to the United Nations.

_____. "The So-Called Double Veto." *American Journal of International Law* 45, no. 3 (July, 1951): 443-461. Explores the application of the veto power in the Security Council. Gives examples of how the veto has been used in cases of application for membership.

SEE ALSO: Feb. 1, 1946: First U.N. Secretary-General Is Selected; Nov. 9-Dec. 15, 1946: United Nations Admits Its First New Member States; Dec. 14, 1950: United Nations High Commissioner for Refugees Statute Is Approved; Apr. 10, 1953: Hammarskjöld Is Elected U.N. Secretary-General; Dec. 14, 1955: United Nations Admits Sixteen New Members; July, 1960: United Nations Intervenes in the Congolese Civil War; 1963-1965: Crisis in U.N. Financing Emerges Over Peacekeeping Expenses; Oct. 25, 1971: People's Republic of China Is Seated at the United Nations; 1990-1994: United Nations Admits Many New Members.

■ **1947-1951**

BLACKLISTING DEPLETES HOLLYWOOD'S TALENT POOL

Amid the early days of the Cold War and growing hysteria about communists in the United States, the House Committee on Un-American Activities launched an investigation of communist influence in the motion picture industry. The resulting blacklist, or ban on employment of alleged communists, hurt both individual careers and the morale of the film community as a whole.

LOCALE: Hollywood, California; Washington, D.C.
CATEGORIES: Motion pictures and video; social issues and reform; business and labor

KEY FIGURES

J. Parnell Thomas (1895-1970), U.S. congressman from New Jersey, 1937-1950, and chair of HUAC, 1947-1948

John S. Wood (1885-1968), U.S. congressman from Georgia, 1931-1935 and 1945-1953, and chair of HUAC, 1945-1946 and 1949-1952

Dalton Trumbo (1905-1976), American screenwriter and one of the Hollywood Ten

Ring Lardner, Jr. (1915-2000), American screenwriter and one of the Hollywood Ten

Elia Kazan (1909-2003), Turkish-born stage and film director

Carl Foreman (1914-1984), American screenwriter and blacklist victim

SUMMARY OF EVENT

During World War II, the Soviet Union and the United States were allies against Nazi Germany. When the war ended in 1945, a rapid worsening of

Soviet-American relations turned the American Communist Party, advocating the Soviet model of socialism, from a tolerated political sect into a band of persecuted political outcasts. As Soviet dictator Joseph Stalin installed puppet governments in one Eastern European country after another, blockaded Berlin, and acquired the atomic bomb, American communists came to be seen as actual or potential traitors, who, for the safety of the country, needed to be purged from trade-union leadership, government employment, the teaching profession, and even the entertainment industry. American anxiety about domestic communists later was heightened by the Korean War.

The American Communist Party had been more popular in the 1930's, when massive unemployment at home contrasted with apparently full employment in Stalin's Soviet Union, and when Stalin opposed German expansion and helped the Spanish Republic battle fascist rebels. The party's respectability, diminished by the German-Soviet Pact of August, 1939, was restored when Germany invaded the Soviet Union in June, 1941.

Communism had special appeal for writers, who found Hollywood to be an oasis of good pay in the economic desert of Depression-era America. After talking pictures were introduced, journalists, playwrights involved in New York City's struggling left-wing theater, short-story writers, and even some who had never written before found scriptwriting jobs in the film industry. Many of them joined the Hollywood branch of the Communist Party, which helped organize the Screen Writers Guild. The industry's profit orientation, however, left communist writers little chance, except during World War II, to give films an ideological slant.

The House Committee on Un-American Activities (HUAC) was created in 1938. In 1947, Committee Chairman J. Parnell Thomas demanded that individuals in the film industry answer questions about their own and their colleagues' past or present communist affiliations. That October, ten of those subpoenaed—the so-called Hollywood Ten—refused to answer questions, basing their refusal not on the Fifth Amendment's guarantee against self-incrimination but on the First Amendment's protection of freedom of speech and association. Five of the Hollywood Ten—Lester Cole, Ring Lardner, Jr., Dalton Trumbo, Edward Dmytryk, and Adrian Scott—were then under contract to major studios. The House of Representatives voted the Hollywood Ten to be in contempt of Congress.

When the rude behavior of some of the Hollywood Ten at the hearings turned public opinion against them, the heads of the major studios became frightened. In November, 1947, the Motion Picture Association of America announced that the Hollywood Ten would be dismissed from their jobs at the various studios and that no known member of the Communist Party would be hired in the future. This ban on employment, the blacklist, later was extended to all who refused to cooperate with HUAC, whether they were proven to be communists or not. The American Legion exerted pressure on motion-picture studios to maintain the blacklist; other private organizations and individuals smoked out communists, publishing lists of supposedly subversive entertainers and writers.

Liberal actors and directors who once had vocally opposed the HUAC investigation now stopped doing so, fearing for their careers. The president of the Screen Actors Guild, a young actor named Ronald Reagan, cooperated with the blacklisters. On April 10, 1950, the U.S. Supreme Court, after a long legal battle, upheld the Hollywood Ten's lower court conviction on contempt charges; in June, nine of them went to prison. Adrian Scott was sentenced in September.

In 1951, HUAC, with John S. Wood of Georgia now its chairman, resumed its investigation of Hollywood communism. This probe continued through 1951. Some of those summoned refused to cooperate, citing the Fifth Amendment; others, including stage and motion-picture director Elia Kazan, cooperated willingly, naming past associates who had been communists. Either because of eagerness to leave prison and resume his career or because of a genuine change of heart, Dmytryk publicly renounced communism, giving the names of past associates who were communists. He was the only one of the Hollywood Ten to do so.

In the late 1950's, HUAC suffered some setbacks, and its investigatory zeal began to flag. In 1958, Arthur Miller, a gifted playwright whose entry into film work had been blocked by his reputation as a leftist, rejected the HUAC demand that he name past associates who were communists. Miller's conviction on contempt of Congress charges in 1957 was overturned by a higher court decision in 1958. In 1956, Carl Foreman, who had been blacklisted for refusing to cooperate with HUAC, finally offered, in a closed session with Chairman Francis Walter, to cooperate. This time, however, the chairman did not ask Foreman to name names. Foreman's name was removed from the blacklist. In 1975, after public tolerance toward dissent had been increased considerably by the national turmoil over civil rights and the Vietnam War, HUAC was abolished.

Many blacklisted writers continued to write screenplays under assumed names. Indeed, the screenplay for *The Brave One* (1956)—written under the fictitious name Robert Rich—won the Academy Award for Best Original Story. That award went unclaimed until 1975, when Dalton Trumbo stepped forward to claim that he had written the script. In 1960, Frank Sinatra was forced to renege on a promise to hire Albert Maltz, another of the Hollywood Ten. Also in 1960, however, director Otto Preminger announced that Dalton Trumbo had written the script for *Exodus* (1960). Actor and pro-

---

COUNTERING RED FASCISM

Red Channels: The Report of Communist Influence in Radio and Television (1950) was published by the antifascist and anticommunist journal Counterattack, *based in New York City. The introduction to the report is reminiscent of the anticommunist paranoia of the time. The report also listed a number of well-known individuals—namely entertainers, actors, and writers—suspected of being communists, producing, in effect, its own "blacklist."*

The Communist party has made intensive efforts to infiltrate every phase of our life, and because of its great propaganda value has concentrated on radio and television. Networks, individual stations, advertising agencies, "package producers," radio-TV unions and even the trade press have been more and more "colonized" by the Party. The "colonists" need not be members or even deliberate cooperators. It is sufficient if they advance Communist objectives with complete unconsciousness.

. . . The hour is not too late for those of the patriotic and intelligent majority to immediately undertake a suitable counter-attack. No time is to be lost. As one former head of a Soviet espionage ring commented bitterly, after breaking with Red Fascism: "What American businessmen and the American public do not seem to realize is that these people are playing for keeps, with no holds barred. They don't lose time just making resolutions or having meetings. They're *activists!* Until we Americans learn to take prompt, effective action, too, they'll win every round!"

---

ducer Kirk Douglas stated that Trumbo had also written the script for *Spartacus* (1960). Neither film's box-office success was hurt seriously by airing Trumbo's contribution. Nevertheless, it was not until the late 1960's, when Ring Lardner, Jr., was hired under his own name to write the screenplay for the antiwar black comedy *M*A*S*H* (1970), that the blacklist era really ended.

SIGNIFICANCE

The effects of the blacklist and of the era of suspicion that it exemplified were many. The blacklist is estimated to have claimed about three hundred victims. It certainly harmed individual careers, although not all blacklistees were hurt equally. Scriptwriters could keep working in several ways: by leaving the United States and working for foreign film studios; by arranging to have someone else, a "front," pretend to be the author of scripts that they had written, while still receiving at least some of the monetary reward; or by writing under a pseudonym. Some blacklisted scriptwriters ultimately regained their careers in the American film industry, but many did not.

Actors who refused to cooperate with HUAC or who were revealed by informers or professional communist hunters to have had past associations with Communist Party causes usually saw their livelihoods ruined. Working under pseudonyms was impossible, as their faces would appear on screen. The film industry shunned them; the nascent television industry, dependent on corporate sponsors for advertising revenue, was even more determined to steer clear of politically tainted performers. One actor committed suicide, possibly because of problems caused by the blacklist. Left-leaning African American singer and actor Paul Robeson was stripped of his passport and was shunned even by black civil rights leaders.

Playwrights, such as Lillian Hellman (who had written Hollywood scripts in the 1930's and 1940's) and Arthur Miller, did not suffer as much financially from their refusal to cooperate with HUAC as did other creative professionals. Playwrights had an outlet for their work on Broadway, which the blacklist never affected as completely as it did cinema and television.

The damage done to the film industry by the blacklist was ameliorated by the extent to which the blacklist could be circumvented. The practice of writing under a pseudonym not only allowed some blacklisted screenwriters to keep writing; it also allowed motion-picture companies to take advantage of the blacklistees' skills at reduced rates of pay. The Hollywood studios sometimes were permanently deprived of the services of blacklisted writers who found employment in foreign film industries; Joseph Losey, who carved out a career for himself in Great Britain, is an example. Similarly, the stigmatization of playwrights Arthur Miller and Lillian Hellman as communist sympathizers meant that Hollywood studios deprived themselves of the talents of these two first-rate dramatists, even as their careers continued on Broadway. The banishment of actors for past political actions did cost the film industry some talent. In an industry with a surplus of fresh new faces always eager to break in, however, the loss was small.

One sometimes overlooked effect of the blacklist was the loss of foreign-born talent. Some of the German refugees who had been living and working in Hollywood during World War II went back to Europe to escape harassment for their political views. These included dramatist Bertolt Brecht, who had coauthored a screenplay, novelist Thomas Mann, and composer Hanns Eisler. Charlie Chaplin, the once-beloved British-born film comedian, was hounded out of the United States for a while because of revulsion against both his left-wing political views and his romantic peccadilloes.

Not only the employees but also the bosses of the Hollywood film empire were frightened by the specter of anticommunist vigilantism. The type of films produced, therefore, was to some extent affected. The trend toward daring films of social realism that had been evident in the late 1940's was halted, at least for a while. There was a spate of pointedly anticommunist films, generally of poor artistic quality and almost all box-office failures. They probably were produced to appease congressional investigators and anticommunist vigilante organizations. Examples include *The Red Menace* (1949), *I Married a Communist* (1950), *I Was a Communist for the FBI* (1951), and *My Son John* (1952).

The first Hollywood films to discuss the blacklist explicitly, *The Way We Were* (1973) and *The Front* (1976), were released after the era was safely over. Two films made during the blacklist era, however, dealt in a disguised form with the issues involved in the blacklist and the anticommunist witchhunt. *High Noon* (1952), the story of a Western marshal who is forced to face a band of outlaws alone without the aid of the townsmen, is often regarded by film critics as a veiled criticism of Hollywood's timidity in the face of congressional investigating committees. Carl Foreman wrote the script shortly before he was blacklisted for his noncooperative stand at a HUAC hearing and was forced to seek work in Great Britain. Elia Kazan's *On the Waterfront* (1954), in which a longshoreman works up the courage to inform on corrupt union bosses, is often seen as a veiled justification for Kazan's decision, during the HUAC hearings of 1952, to inform on past communist associates from his days in the New York City theater in the 1930's.

The decision of some Hollywood figures to cooperate with congressional investigators by naming names, thereby exposing others to the blacklist and perhaps even destroying such people's careers, created rifts in the Hollywood community, and in the entertainment world in general, that lasted for years. Elia Kazan, for example, would spend the rest of his life defending his decision to "name names."

Paul D. Mageli

FURTHER READING

Buhle, Paul, and Dave Wagner. *Hide in Plain Sight: The Hollywood Blacklistees in Film and Television, 1950-2002.* New York: Palgrave Macmillan, 2003. Extensive discussion of every significant work of film and television worked on by a blacklistee in the second half of the twentieth century. Bibliographic references and index.

Ceplair, Larry, and Steven Englund. *The Inquisition in Hollywood: Politics in the Film Community, 1930-1960.* Garden City, N.Y.: Anchor Press/Doubleday, 1980. An exhaustive study of the Hollywood Ten, the investigation of 1951-1952, and the fate of the blacklistees. Especially informative on the pre-1947 Hollywood communist subculture. The authors view Hollywood's communists with a mixture of criticism and admiration. Bibliography, endnotes, index, and photographs. Relies heavily on interviews.

Cole, Lester. *Hollywood Red: The Autobiography of Lester Cole.* Palo Alto, Calif.: Ramparts Press, 1981. The life story of a screenwriter who never beat the blacklist and who never recanted his faith in communism. Although obviously biased, it provides a good victim's-eye view of the post-World War II purge of the film world. Filmography, photographs, and index.

Kanfer, Stefan. *A Journal of the Plague Years.* New York: Atheneum, 1973. A film critic's chronicle of blacklisting from 1947 to 1958, showing its effects on radio, television, and Broadway as well as Hollywood. Especially informative on the private individuals and organizations that helped HUAC by ferreting out show-business communists. Sympathetic to blacklistees. Photographs, annotated bibliography, index, no notes.

Kazan, Elia. *Elia Kazan: A Life.* New York: Alfred A. Knopf, 1988. In this lengthy but briskly written autobiography, covering everything from childhood to professional life to love life, Kazan vigorously defends his decision to cooperate with HUAC in 1952. Provides some insights into communism in the 1930's New York City theater. Photographs and index. For the general reader.

Lardner, Kate. *Shut Up He Explained: The Memoir of a Blacklisted Kid.* New York: Ballantine Books, 2004. Ring Lardner's daughter provides a personal account of the effects of blacklisting on her father and her family.

Navasky, Victor S. *Naming Names.* Reprint. New York: Hill & Wang, 2003. A journalist examines the ethical dilemma faced by those who named names for HUAC, thus avoiding their own blacklisting but causing others to be blacklisted. Excellent chapter, based on interviews, on informers' motives. Rejects anticommunism as a morally valid rationale for naming names. Endnotes, list of interviewees, index. For the general reader.

Schwartz, Nancy Lynn. *The Hollywood Writers' Wars.* New York: Alfred A. Knopf, 1982. A history of the Hollywood communist screenwriters' subculture during the 1930's and 1940's. The author expresses nearly undiluted admiration for that subculture. Supplements but does not supplant the book by Ceplair and Englund. Endnotes, photographs, index, and filmographies of more than thirty blacklisted and investigated actors and writers. For scholars.

Whitfield, Stephen J. *The Culture of the Cold War.* Baltimore: Johns Hopkins University Press, 1991. Views the blacklist as part of a general trend toward conformity in the United States during the 1940's and 1950's. Especially useful for its examination of how blacklist-era anxieties affected the kind of films made. Excellent bibliographical essay. Index; no notes.

SEE ALSO: Oct. 20, 1947: HUAC Investigates Hollywood; Jan. 15, 1953-Dec. 2, 1954: McCarthy Hearings; Jan. 22, 1953: *The Crucible* Allegorizes the Red Scare Era; 1962: *Dr. No* Launches the Hugely Popular James Bond Series; 1963: Le Carré Rejects the Fantasy World of Secret Agents.

■ **MARCH 12, 1947**

TRUMAN DOCTRINE

Following World War II, President Harry S. Truman declared that the United States would use its resources to aid nations resisting Soviet encroachment and to contain Soviet expansion. He thus articulated the cornerstone of the next forty years of U.S. foreign policy, setting the terms of U.S. participation in the Cold War.

LOCALE: Washington, D.C.
CATEGORY: Diplomacy and international relations

KEY FIGURES

Harry S. Truman (1884-1972), president of the United States, 1945-1953
George F. Kennan (1904-2005), U.S. State Department's director of policy planning, 1947-1949
George C. Marshall (1880-1959), U.S. secretary of state, 1947-1949
Joseph Stalin (Joseph Vissarionovich Dzhugashvili; 1878-1953), general secretary of the Central Committee of the Communist Party of the Soviet Union, 1922-1953, and premier, 1941-1953
James Francis Byrnes (1879-1972), U.S. secretary of state, 1945-1947
Winston Churchill (1874-1965), prime minister of Great Britain, 1940-1945 and 1951-1955
Henry A. Wallace (1888-1965), vice president of the United States, 1941-1945, secretary of commerce, 1945-1946, and editor of the *New Republic*, 1946-1947

SUMMARY OF EVENT

Soon after the conclusion of World War II, the United States was faced with the necessity of finding a new principle to guide its foreign policy. Franklin D. Roosevelt's concept of a global postwar peace based on cooperation between the United States and the Soviet Union had proven to be ineffective. The Soviet army occupied most of eastern and central Europe and made it clear that the Soviet Union would not tolerate independent regimes there.

Despite the agreements made at the Yalta Conference, Joseph Stalin, the Soviet dictator, unilaterally imposed communist regimes on Poland, Hungary, Bulgaria, Czechoslovakia, and Romania. The protests of the United States and Great Britain did not alter this policy of Soviet control. Furthermore, the Soviet government attempted to expand into areas where it had no military control, including Greece, Turkey, and Iran.

In confronting these emergencies, the United States at first attempted ad hoc measures that, although essentially successful in achieving their immediate objectives, failed to establish policy guidelines for the postwar world. In Iran, for example, the Soviet Union refused to withdraw its occupation forces and made demands through diplomatic channels for exclusive oil and mineral rights. The United States and Great Britain joined in a strong protest, which implied the threat of Western military assistance to counter Soviet pressure. In March, 1946, Soviet troops began a complete withdrawal, and the Iranian government succeeded in stabilizing its rule.

In the case of Turkey, the Soviet Union sent several diplomatic notes in 1945 and 1946 that demanded the cession of border territory and a joint administration of the Dardanelles. These demands were to be ratified in a treaty that also would provide for the leasing of navy and army bases in the Dardanelles to the Soviets to implement joint control. Following a second Soviet note, the United States sent a strong naval fleet into the Mediterranean, the first U.S. warships to be sent into those waters during peacetime since 1803. A week later, Great Britain joined the United States in rejecting Soviet demands on Turkey. Meanwhile, in Greece, only extensive British military and economic aid prevented a complete collapse of the war-torn country and a coup d'état by communist guerrillas.

Following extensive domestic debate, the United States formally abandoned its traditional peacetime isolationist approach to world affairs and adopted a long-range policy intended to deal with Soviet expansionism. One position in the debate was dramatized by Winston Churchill, the former prime minister of Great Britain, in a speech at Fulton, Missouri, in early 1946. There, with President Harry S. Truman on the platform, Churchill characterized the Soviet Union as an expansionist state that would react only to a strong counterforce. Soviet expansion, Churchill believed, could be prevented only by a collaboration between the United States and Great Britain to preserve the independence of Europe and to prevent the extension of what came to be called the "Iron Curtain."

A contrasting attitude was expressed by Secretary of Commerce Henry A. Wallace, who declared that only U.S.-Soviet cooperation could prevent another war. He pointed out that the Soviet desire for control of areas on its borders was understandable and reasonable, and that the United States had

TRUMAN DOCTRINE

U.S. president Harry S. Truman addressed Congress on the topic of the security and autonomy of Greece and Turkey in the face of an encroaching Soviet Union in the region following World War II. The speech is now known as the Truman Doctrine.

One of the primary objectives of the foreign policy of the United States is the creation of conditions in which we and other nations will be able to work out a way of life free from coercion. This was a fundamental issue in the war with Germany and Japan. Our victory was won over countries which sought to impose their will, and their way of life, upon other nations.

To ensure the peaceful development of nations, free from coercion, the United States has taken a leading part in establishing the United Nations. The United Nations is designed to make possible lasting freedom and independence for all its members. We shall not realize our objectives, however, unless we are willing to help free peoples to maintain their free institutions and their national integrity against aggressive movements that seek to impose upon them totalitarian regimes. This is no more than a frank recognition that totalitarian regimes imposed on free peoples, by direct or indirect aggression, undermine the foundations of international peace and hence the security of the United States. . . .

The seeds of totalitarian regimes are nurtured by misery and want. They spread and grow in the evil soil of poverty and strife. They reach their full growth when the hope of a people for a better life has died. We must keep that hope alive.

The free peoples of the world look to us for support in maintaining their freedoms. If we falter in our leadership, we may endanger the peace of the world—and we shall surely endanger the welfare of our own nation.

Great responsibilities have been placed upon us by the swift movement of events. I am confident that the Congress will face these responsibilities squarely.

long acted to secure its own hemispheric security. Substantial segments of U.S. public opinion supported either Churchill or Wallace. However, the State Department sought a middle ground. Rejecting both the Soviet-expansion position of Churchill and the sphere-of-influence concept of Wallace, Secretary of State James Francis Byrnes urged that the Soviet Union adopt a more cooperative diplomatic policy. The United States, he said, should pursue a policy of firmness and patience and wait for the Soviets to see the reasonableness of negotiation. It appeared to many, including President Truman, that the United States was the one that was always being

U.S. State Department officer George F. Kennan, the author of an anonymous magazine article articulating the Truman Doctrine. (National Archives)

reasonable, not the Soviet Union. By 1947, the administration had adopted the position that the revolutionary postulates of the Soviet regime made traditional diplomacy impossible.

The first step in the development of the new policy toward the Soviet Union came in response to the continuing Soviet threat to Greece and Turkey. In February, 1947, Great Britain informed the U.S. State Department that the British government could no longer continue to support the regime in Greece. Great Britain, like all of Western Europe, was suffering from grave economic problems. As the British Empire retreated, the United States stepped forward. Within the next few weeks, President Truman decided that the independence of Greece and the recovery of Europe were crucial to the security of the United States.

On March 12, 1947, the president appeared before a joint session of Congress and presented what became known as the Truman Doctrine. He outlined the desperate situation in both Greece and Turkey and called upon the American people to "help free peoples to maintain their free institutions and their national integrity against aggressive movements that seek to impose upon them totalitarian regimes." Most important, he pointed out, was the fact that such totalitarian aggression was a direct threat to the security of the United States. In response, Congress appropriated $400 million for economic aid to both Greece and Turkey. Additionally, the president was authorized to dispatch civilian and military advisers to help both nations defend their sovereignty.

The next step in this new policy was to bring the same consideration to bear upon Western Europe, an even more critical area. There is debate over the degree to which U.S. economic aid to postwar Europe was motivated by the desire to contain Soviet influence in Western Europe. Nevertheless, to proponents of the new internationalism in U.S. foreign policy, it seemed axiomatic that if aid to Greece and Turkey could be justified by their strategic importance, the United States must aid other European countries where the situation was equally desperate. Great Britain was suffering from the wartime destruction of its factories and the loss of its capability to export manufactured goods. Germany was in ruins and virtually incapable of feeding its population. In France and Italy, the Communist Party had wide support within the industrial laboring class and was working by both overt and covert means for a radical change in the government of both countries. A further difficulty was that the winter of 1946-1947 was the most severe experienced by Europeans for generations.

From a military viewpoint, new weaponry made it essential that European control of the Atlantic gateways be in friendly hands. In terms of trained technicians, industrial capacity, and raw materials, Western Europe was a potential giant worth keeping in the U.S. camp. These factors led to an announcement by the new secretary of state, George C. Marshall, at Harvard University in June, 1947, of what came to be known as the Marshall Plan: If the European countries could develop a cooperative approach to their economic problems, Marshall said, the United States would assist in their recovery.

Congress eventually authorized a grant of $17 billion to the Organization for European Economic Cooperation over a four-year period. A total of about $13 billion was actually spent. Although aid was offered to all European nations, including the Soviet Union, the Soviet-dominated areas were not permitted to cooperate, because doing so would have required revealing Soviet economic secrets and sacrificing Soviet economic control. Success of the Marshall Plan emerged quickly; in 1952, Europe exceeded its prewar production figures by some 200 percent.

A discussion of the theory behind the policy embodied in the Truman Doctrine and the Marshall Plan appeared in an unsigned article on the subject of containment in the July, 1947, issue of *Foreign Affairs*. The author, it was later disclosed, was George F. Kennan, a high-ranking member of the

State Department. Kennan's essay proposed that the antagonism that existed between the United States and the Soviet Union was merely the logical extension of certain basic Soviet assumptions. The United States, Kennan maintained, could count on Soviet hostility, because the rhetoric of the Bolshevik Revolution demanded war against capitalist states. World War II had submerged this antagonism only temporarily. "These characteristics of Soviet policy," he wrote, "like the postulates from which they flow, are basic to the internal nature of Soviet power, and will be with us . . . until the nature of Soviet power is changed."

The immediate question, Kennan insisted, was how the United States should counter this new ideological crusade that threatened to engulf Europe. In Kennan's view, the United States should adopt a policy of "long-term, patient, but firm and vigilant containment." To counter the Soviet policy, the United States should adopt a long-range course of diplomacy toward the Soviet Union and pursue it consistently. This containment, or the counterapplication of force wherever Soviet expansion threatened, had a negative aspect, because it put a tremendous burden on U.S. consistency and steadfastness. On the positive side, through containment, the United States could help work changes within the Soviet system and help modify the revolutionary zeal of the regime. If expansionist dynamics were constantly frustrated, Kennan reasoned, the forces must be expended within the system itself, and this would mean some modification of totalitarian control.

SIGNIFICANCE

Although the Truman Doctrine, strictly speaking, applied only to Greece and Turkey, its importance went well beyond the fate of those two countries. Truman's speech of March 12, 1947, represented the first tentative articulation of the policy of containment later placed in print by Kennan. The doctrine was a commitment to utilize the economic resources of the United States—as well as its military expertise in the form of advisers and trainers—to resist Soviet expansion and aggression in Europe. The Truman Doctrine thus represented the first proactive statement made by a U.S. president of the principles that guided the United States during the Cold War. Combined with Churchill's Iron Curtain speech, it represents one of the founding Western foreign policy statements of that war. The principles enunciated by Truman were followed for decades thereafter, shaping the history of the second half of the twentieth century.

George Q. Flynn and Joseph R. Rudolph, Jr.

FURTHER READING

Acheson, Dean. *Present at the Creation: My Years in the State Department.* New York: Norton, 1969. Written by Truman's last secretary of state, an often poignant, immensely interesting accounting of the years during which United States foreign policy shaped the postwar world.

Gaddis, John Lewis. *The United States and the Origins of the Cold War, 1941-1947.* New ed. New York: Columbia University Press, 2000. History of U.S.-Soviet relations during World War II and the postwar period, up to and including the announcement of the Truman Doctrine. Bibliographic references and index.

Jeffery, Judith S. *Ambiguous Commitments and Uncertain Policies: The Truman Doctrine in Greece, 1947-1952.* Lanham, Md.: Lexington Books, 2000. Study focused on Greece of the effects of the Truman Doctrine upon the nation it was originally designed to help. Bibliographic references and index.

Jones, Howard. *"A New Kind of War": America's Global Strategy and the Truman Doctrine in Greece.* New York: Oxford University Press, 1989. A detailed analysis of the effect of the containment policy on politics in its first beneficiary.

Jones, Joseph M. *The Fifteen Weeks (February 21-June 5, 1947).* New York: Viking Press, 1955. A good account of the crucial weeks during which the Truman administration committed itself to first the containment doctrine and then the Marshall Plan.

Judge, Edward H., and John Langdon. *The Cold War: A History through Documents.* Upper Saddle River, N.J.: Prentice Hall, 1999. Collection of more than 130 primary sources including speeches, agreements, and declarations, arranged chronologically.

Lieberman, Sanford R., et al., eds. *The Soviet Empire Reconsidered.* Boulder, Colo.: Westview Press, 1994. Many of the generally excellent essays address the impact of the containment policy on postwar Soviet foreign policy.

McGhee, George Crews. *The U.S.-Turkish-NATO Middle East Connection: How the Truman Doctrine Contained the Soviets in the Middle East.* New York: St. Martin's Press, 1990. An excellent regional study of containment at work.

Powaski, Ronald E. *The Cold War: The United States and the Soviet Union, 1917-1991.* New York: Oxford University Press, 1998. Traces the roots of the Cold War to czarist Russia and early America and contends that each nation's psychology led to the decades-long conflict.

Rees, David. *The Age of Containment: The Cold War, 1945-1965.* New York: St. Martin's Press, 1967. A view of the coldest days of the Cold War from a British perspective.

SEE ALSO: Feb. 4-11, 1945: Yalta Conference; Mar. 5, 1946: Churchill Delivers His Iron Curtain Speech; Apr. 3, 1948: Marshall Plan Provides Aid to Europe; Apr. 4, 1949: North Atlantic Treaty Organization Is Formed; Oct. 22, 1951: United States Inaugurates Mutual Security Program; Jan. 5, 1957: Eisenhower Doctrine; July 25, 1969: Nixon Doctrine Is Unveiled.

■ JULY 26, 1947

NATIONAL SECURITY ACT

The National Security Act created the modern governmental bureaucratic structure responsible for the defense of the United States. It created the Department of Defense and the cabinet-level post of secretary of defense, as well as the National Security Council, the Central Intelligence Agency, and the Joint Chiefs of Staff.

ALSO KNOWN AS: U.S. Code Title 50, sections 401 et seq.
LOCALE: Washington, D.C.
CATEGORIES: Laws, acts, and legal history; government and politics

KEY FIGURES
Harry S. Truman (1884-1972), president of the United States, 1945-1953
James Vincent Forrestal (1892-1949), U.S. secretary of the Navy, 1944-1947, and the first secretary of defense, 1947-1949
Robert Porter Patterson (1891-1952), secretary of war, 1945-1947
Louis A. Johnson (1891-1966), U.S. secretary of defense, 1949-1950
Omar N. Bradley (1893-1981), chairman of the Joint Chiefs of Staff, 1949-1953
George C. Marshall (1880-1959), chief of staff of the U.S. Army, 1939-1945, secretary of state, 1947-1949, and secretary of defense, 1950-1951
Richard M. Nixon (1913-1994), president of the United States, 1969-1974

SUMMARY OF EVENT
As steps were taken to strengthen the U.S. commitment to European security by means of the Truman Doctrine and the Marshall Plan, it became increasingly clear that measures were needed at home to increase the efficiency of the United States' military establishment. A major impetus to the reorganization of the U.S. defense system had come from the obvious weaknesses revealed during World War II. One prime example of such weaknesses was the military disaster at Pearl Harbor. The war also had revealed

numerous cases of duplication of effort among the various services. Another new factor that needed to be considered was that Cold War diplomacy required close collaboration between military and diplomatic elements, a condition that had hardly existed during the war. Therefore, many officials, including President Harry S. Truman, thought that the need for a more efficient system of defense was obvious.

On July 26, 1947, Truman signed the National Security Act, responding to this need, but reaching an agreement on the exact details of the reorganization and centralization of the military establishment had not been an easy task. As early as 1945, President Truman had submitted a plan for reorganization to Congress, but it took two years to settle the differences of opinion among the three branches of the armed forces. The Navy was especially reluctant to sacrifice its independence to what it feared would be a defense establishment dominated by the Army. In particular, the Navy feared that the new system might mean the abolishment of the Marines, or at least their transferral to the Army.

Another sensitive area of dispute centered on the Navy's newly acquired air capability. Having become firmly convinced of the value of aircraft carriers during World War II, the Navy wanted to expand its air arm, which would include the construction of super-carriers able to accommodate the newly

From left: Chairman of the Joint Chiefs of Staff General Omar N. Bradley, Secretary of Defense Louis A. Johnson, President Harry S. Truman, and an unidentified official watching an Army Day parade in 1949. (National Archives)

designed jet planes. Many admirals feared that an Army-dominated defense system might mean an emphasis on land-based, long-distance bombers. During 1946 and 1947, President Truman worked to bring together the Army, represented by Secretary of War Robert Porter Patterson, and the Navy, represented by Secretary of the Navy James Vincent Forrestal. In this campaign, Truman was assisted especially by Forrestal, who, although entirely sympathetic to the Navy's point of view, did work for a reasonable compromise.

As a result of these meetings, agreements were reached that culminated in the National Security Act of 1947. The act created the Department of Defense (called the National Military Establishment until 1949) with a secretary holding cabinet rank. The Department of the Army, the Department of the Navy, and a new Department of the Air Force were made into separate subcabinet agencies within the Department of Defense. The act also gave legal recognition to the Joint Chiefs of Staff, with a rotating chairman. Each of the three services would be represented on this committee, which was to be responsible for providing close military coordination, preparing defense plans, and making strategy recommendations to another new agency, the National Security Council, which was to be chaired by the president of the United States.

The other members of the National Security Council were to include the vice president, the secretary of state, the secretary of defense, the secretaries of the three services, and the chairman of another new agency, the National Security Resources Board. The president could designate additional persons to serve on the council; under Truman, the council had twenty members. Critics labeled the council "Mr. Truman's Politburo," because it attempted to blend diplomatic and military considerations at the highest level of national interest. Finally, the act created the Central Intelligence Agency as an independent source of security information.

This impressive reorganization plan had barely gotten under way when serious problems arose. In some instances, these problems were merely continuations of the traditional competition between the Army and the Navy; the new system did little to eliminate interservice rivalry, despite the outstanding work of Forrestal as the first secretary of defense. Some opponents asserted that the new system merely created one more contending party, the Air Force. The three services soon were engaged in conducting separate, elaborate publicity and congressional lobbying campaigns to gain increased shares of the defense budget. The Navy championed the merits of its supercarrier program, while the Air Force pointed to the new B-36 bomber as the best defense investment. Secretary Forrestal tried to mediate this struggle, but the issues seemed to be beyond the capacity of any one person to control. In failing health, the secretary resigned on March 3, 1949. Although interservice rivalry still existed, Forrestal had reported prior to his resignation that the new defense system had already saved U.S. taxpayers more than $56 million.

The new secretary of defense appointed by President Truman was Louis A. Johnson of West Virginia, who approached his job with a pugnacious attitude that may have been a result of his lack of administrative experience at a comparably high level of government employment. He soon plunged into the interservice rivalry by favoring the Air Force. The building of new naval aircraft carriers was suspended, and considerable amounts of money went into expanding the strength of the Air Force. Although this executive policy saved money, some critics claimed that it weakened national defense. The State Department joined in the growing criticism of Johnson, because it resented the new secretary's unilateral approach to national security. Apparently, it was not long before Truman had reason to regret his appointment of Johnson, as in September, 1950, he turned to General George C. Marshall, former secretary of state, to take over the Department of Defense. The simultaneous appointment of Marshall's service colleague, General Omar N. Bradley, as chairman of the Joint Chiefs of Staff helped make operations smoother within the Defense Department.

SIGNIFICANCE

The full implications of the new diplomatic and military structures created by the National Security Act did not become evident until the administration of President Richard M. Nixon. Nixon's national security adviser and secretary of state, Henry Kissinger, established the supremacy of those two positions over the rest of the foreign policy apparatus. Although efforts were made to decentralize that apparatus after Kissinger's departure, his legacy continued into subsequent administrations.

The overall result of the National Security Act was to create a U.S. foreign policy system that fit the country's new and unprecedented role as a global superpower and leader of the Western bloc in the emerging Cold War. The law also created a system in which the national security adviser became a major player in foreign policy decisions, enjoying daily direct access to the president as an integral member of the executive branch of the government. More than one secretary of state would complain about having to do battle with influential national security advisers who had the president's ear. Finally, the legal requirement that the secretary of defense not be an active member of the military cemented the tradition of the U.S. military being commanded at its highest levels by civilians, a policy that would have far-reaching effects throughout the twentieth and early twenty-first centuries.

George Q. Flynn and Steve D. Boilard

FURTHER READING

Destler, I. M. "National Security Advice to U.S. Presidents: Some Lessons from Thirty Years." *World Politics* 29, no. 2 (January, 1977): 143-176. An analysis and critique of the foreign policy advisory system created by the National Security Act. Although thorough and based on three decades of experience, the analysis is now somewhat dated.

Hoffman. David. *The Dead Hand: The Untold Story of the Cold War Arms Race and Its Dangerous Legacy.* New York: Doubleday, 2009. Describes American and Soviet strategies and decision making related to the superpowers' nuclear arsenals. Includes discussion of the continued threat posed by these weapons after the breakup of the Soviet Union. The title refers to a Soviet plan to create a system to automatically retaliate after a nuclear attack. Contains illustrations and maps.

Hoxie, R. Gordon. "James V. Forrestal and the National Security Act of 1947." In *Command Decision and the Presidency: A Study in National Security Policy and Organization.* New York: Readers Digest Press, 1977. Discusses the origins and provisions of the National Security Act; provides particular detail on the 1949 amendment to the act. Written in a narrative style. Notes and bibliography.

Leffler, Melvyn P. *A Preponderance of Power: National Security, the Truman Administration, and the Cold War.* Stanford, Calif.: Stanford University Press, 1992. Places the National Security Act within the context of the Cold War. See especially chapter 4, "From the Truman Doctrine to the National Security Act, November 1946-July 1947." Notes and bibliography.

Rosati, Jerel A. "Presidential Management and the NSC Process." In *Politics of United States Foreign Policy.* Fort Worth, Tex.: Harcourt Brace Jovanovich, 1993. Discusses the foreign-policy-making system created by the National Security Act. Clear and well organized. Tables, charts, and bibliographic essay.

Stuart, Douglas T. "Present at the Legislation: The 1947 National Security Act." In *Organizing for National Security,* edited by Douglas T. Stuart. Carlisle Barracks, Pa.: Strategic Studies Institute, U.S. Army War College, 2000. Essay detailing the 1947 act and its importance to U.S. national security structures. Also examines changes in that structure throughout the rest of the twentieth century. Bibliographic references.

Theoharis, Athan G., ed. *The Truman Presidency: The Origins of the Imperial Presidency and the National Security State.* Stanfordville, N.Y.: Earl M. Coleman Enterprises, 1979. A compilation of extracts from declassified memos, addresses, letters, and analyses, with commentary by the editor. The chapter on the political and legislative history of the National Security Act and its amendments is especially useful. Notes and bibliography.

SEE ALSO: Mar. 12, 1947: Truman Doctrine; Apr. 3, 1948: Marshall Plan Provides Aid to Europe; Feb. 15, 1954: Canada and the United States Establish the DEW Line; May 12, 1958: Canada and the United States Create NORAD; May 1, 1960: U-2 Incident; Jan. 17, 1961: Eisenhower Warns of the Military-Industrial Complex; Apr. 17-19, 1961: Bay of Pigs Invasion; Nov. 14, 1961: Kennedy Expands U.S. Involvement in Vietnam; Apr. 28, 1965: U.S. Troops Occupy the Dominican Republic; Nov. 7, 1973: U.S. Congress Overrides Presidential Veto to Pass the War Powers Act.

■ **OCTOBER 20, 1947**

HUAC INVESTIGATES HOLLYWOOD

The House Committee on Un-American Activities investigated communist influence in Hollywood, calling members of the entertainment industry to testify before it. A group of ten writers and directors who refused to cooperate with HUAC on First Amendment grounds was imprisoned for contempt of Congress, and the major motion picture studios announced that they would no longer employ any known communist.

ALSO KNOWN AS: House Special Committee to Investigate Un-American Activities; House Committee on Un-American Activities; House Un-American Activities Committee
LOCALE: Washington, D.C.
CATEGORIES: Government and politics; motion pictures and video; civil rights and liberties

KEY FIGURES

J. Parnell Thomas (1895-1970), U.S. congressman from New Jersey, 1937-1950, and chair of HUAC, 1947-1948
Martin Dies, Jr. (1900-1972), U.S. congressman from Texas, 1931-1944, 1953-1958, and chair of HUAC, 1938-1944
Harry S. Truman (1884-1972), president of the United States, 1945-1953

SUMMARY OF EVENT

In 1938, nine-year-old film star Shirley Temple was accused of being a dupe of the Communist Party, because she had waved at a group of communist journalists while in France. This accusation was not an aberration; it was a logical outcome of the right- and left-wing extremism that infected the United States at the time. During times of intense crisis, Americans have been prone to hunt for scapegoats to explain their troubles. Having correct ideas is used as a measure to prove that a person is indeed "100 percent American." Extremists on both the right and left vie to have their ideas become the moral law of the land. Purges ("witch hunts"), flag-waving, and a decreased tolerance for dissent are symptoms of such epochs.

Anticommunist and general antiforeign sentiment increased during World War I in the United States, and it continued to find support into the 1920's. This sentiment was expressed in legal action against foreigners, such as the raids conducted by U.S. attorney general Alexander Palmer against people suspected of socialist beliefs, as well as the passage of several acts limiting immigration into the United States. Hate groups such as the Ku Klux Klan, with their message of intolerance of "foreign" or different peoples and ideas, flourished.

In 1934, Representatives John W. McCormack and Samuel Dickstein formed a committee to investigate what they called "un-American activities." Given the rise to power of Adolf Hitler in Germany the previous year, the McCormack-Dickstein Committee (officially the Special Committee on Un-American Activities Authorized to Investigate Nazi Propaganda and Certain Other Propaganda Activities) focused primarily on fascist, rather than communist, activities in the United States. The committee is most famous for investigating the so-called Business Plot, in which fascists allegedly conspired to overthrow President Franklin D. Roosevelt and seize the White House. Ironically, Congressman Dickstein was revealed in the 1990's to have been on the payroll of a Soviet intelligence agency in the late 1930's, although there is some dispute as to how much of the information he promised to the Soviets he actually delivered.

On May 26, 1938, the U.S. House of Representatives authorized another Special Committee to Investigate Un-American Activities. The committee was commonly known as the Dies Committee, after Martin Dies, Jr., its chair. Dies was assisted by his former clerk, Robert E. Stripling, as counsel, and by Representative J. Parnell Thomas and others. Although it, too, was meant to investigate Nazi infiltration, the committee quickly focused its efforts on communism instead.

During the first days of the committee's existence, 640 organizations, 483 newspapers, and 280 labor unions were accused of un-American activities. The patriotism of the Boy Scouts, the Camp Fire Girls, and Shirley Temple was questioned. When the committee could find no communists more substantial than such long-dead playwrights as Christopher Marlowe and Euripides, it quickly lost credibility. Nevertheless, a similar lack of knowledge about Marxism and communism continued to underlie later inquests.

The Dies Committee contributed heavily to Congress's June 1, 1939, elimination of the proposed Federal Theatre from President Roosevelt's New Deal agenda. The committee's lessons were not forgotten: Show-business people were easy targets, and targeting Hollywood brought instant media attention. The Dies Committee established the tactics that would be used by its own later incarnation, by Senator Joseph McCarthy, and by others after World War II. These tactics included sensational press releases, secret, fabricated lists of "known" communists, attacks on anything liberal, and "proof" in the form of gossip, illogic, and association with a touch of truth.

Attacks on communism diminished once the Soviet Union entered World War II on the side of the Allied Powers. As part of the war effort, *Song of Russia* (1944) and other pro-Soviet films were made at the War Department's request. *Song of Russia* would be denounced in 1947 hearings, because it showed happy, smiling people in the Soviet Union.

After World War II, the U.S.-Soviet alliance dissolved. Republicans and ultraconservative groups assaulted communism anew. The House Committee on Un-American Activities, or House Un-American Activities Committee (HUAC), became a permanent, standing committee of the U.S. House of Representatives in 1946. On March 12, 1947, President Harry S. Truman announced the Truman Doctrine, an anticommunist foreign-aid effort designed to blunt Republican charges that he was soft on communism. The State Department was purged of alleged communists, and Truman established a peacetime security and loyalty program. U.S. attorney general Tom C. Clark compiled a list of organizations espousing communist, fascist, totalitarian, or subversive ideas, which was to be used internally to determine which government employees should be investigated. The list was published and quickly became HUAC's primary source document.

On October 20, 1947, a subcommittee of HUAC opened its first postwar hearings. Because of prehearing publicity, more than one hundred news agencies were present, along with three major radio networks and eleven newsreel and television cameras stationed above the witness table. The committee was chaired by J. Parnell Thomas, and Robert E. Stripling served as its chief counsel. Other members of note were Richard M. Nixon and John S. Wood, who became HUAC's chair in 1950.

Friendly witnesses, mainly studio executives, were called to testify before the committee during its first week of hearings. During the second week, nineteen witnesses, mainly writers, were subpoenaed. Ten witnesses said that the proceedings themselves were un-American and unconstitutional. They refused to cooperate with the committee. These ten, who became known as the Hollywood Ten or the Unfriendly Ten, were writers Alvah Bessie, Lester Cole, Ring Lardner, Jr., John Howard Lawson, Albert Maltz, Sam Ornitz, and Dalton Trumbo, as well as directors Herbert Biberman and

Edward Dmytryk and writer-producer Robert Adrian Scott. The Hollywood Ten asserted their right to the freedoms of speech and assembly under the First Amendment. Hollywood's entertainment community loudly supported the ten's First Amendment rights. The ten were liberal, and all had some affiliation, however cursory, with the Communist Party.

On November 24, 1947, Congress voted to cite the Hollywood Ten for contempt. Immediately, fifty top studio executives met at the Waldorf-Astoria Hotel in New York City to determine their position regarding the ten. Eric Johnson, the president of the Motion Picture Association of America, read the Waldorf Declaration: The Hollywood Ten would be suspended without pay, and from that point forward, no studio would "knowingly" employ anyone associated with the Communist Party.

Traditionally, a congressional investigatory committee has two primary functions: to secure information needed to create legislation and to oversee the executive branch's activities. These committees have no direct legislative or judicial functions. HUAC, however, performed both those functions, and in so doing it violated both the constitutional separation of powers and the civil rights of subpoenaed witnesses. Witnesses were not allowed to meet

Screen Actors Guild president Ronald Reagan listening to testimony at a hearing of the House Committee on Un-American Activities on October, 23, 1947, a week before he was scheduled to testify. (AP/Wide World Photos)

or cross-examine their accusers, no exclusionary rules regarding hearsay evidence were used, and witnesses were not allowed due process. Eight of the ten were writers, but the committee produced no evidence that they had written anything that was subversive or that called for the violent overthrow of the U.S. government. The committee never documented any evidence of communist infiltration of the movie industry, and even if it had, membership in the Communist Party was not illegal. Nevertheless, without judge or jury, the Hollywood Ten were tried and sentenced.

If the committee had been serious about its attempt to root communism out of the film industry, it could have succeeded. The contributions of highly paid Hollywood artists to Communist Party causes were known but not investigated. Thomas contended that he had a list of seventy-nine prominent communists in his files, but only the Hollywood Ten were prosecuted. The subpoenaing of entertainment-industry figures was not done to support legislation (none was ever proposed). None of the witnesses were government employees, so the attorney general's list was not relevant. The Hollywood Ten were judged guilty because their thoughts were improper. They were convicted of contempt of Congress, because they refused to answer the committee's questions the way the committee wanted them to.

In 1950, after the Supreme Court refused their last appeals, the Hollywood Ten went to jail for at least a year apiece. Ring Lardner, Jr., and Lester Cole were sent to the federal prison in Danbury, Connecticut—as was J. Parnell Thomas, who in 1948 had been convicted of fraud in a payroll scam. Lardner was made a stenographer in the classification and parole office; Thomas was made caretaker of the prison's chicken yard.

SIGNIFICANCE

Between March, 1947, and December, 1952, some 6.6 million people were investigated by Truman's security program. No espionage was discovered, but some five hundred people were dismissed from government-related jobs. Alger Hiss was convicted in January, 1950, of perjury in a highly publicized and sensational trial. In February, the British uncovered massive espionage that eventually led to the execution of American spies Julius and Ethel Rosenberg. Senator Joseph McCarthy began his campaign for reelection by using his attack on communism as a stepping stone to power. In June, the Korean War began, and three former Federal Bureau of Investigation agents published *Red Channels: The Report of Communist Influence in Radio and Television* (1950), which became the bible of blacklisting.

HUAC's Hollywood investigation began again in 1951. Blacklisting—for ridiculing HUAC, for being subpoenaed, or for unknowingly being on the list that Hollywood studios and professional guilds claimed did not exist—

became institutionalized. A suspected communist could not get work without publically naming names of other communists and recanting supposed sins, thereby receiving absolution from the committee. Not only did Hollywood not support its own, but no one else did either. No one questioned the right of the committee to exist or to do what it was doing—not the press, not the American Civil Liberties Union, and not the Anti-Defamation League of B'nai B'rith or the Hollywood-based American Jewish Committee. Ten of the nineteen subpoenaed were Jewish, as were six of the ten who were indicted.

The blacklisted went underground and set up their own networks. The names of "clean" writers who were willing to act as "fronts" were put on scripts. Fictional names were also used. Only the Hollywood community knew that Maltz wrote *The Bridge on the River Kwai* (1957) and *The Robe* (1953) or that Trumbo wrote *Roman Holiday* (1953), *Cowboy* (1958), and—by his own claim—*The Brave One* (1956). *The Brave One* won an Oscar that no one claimed until 1975. A mystique developed around the blacklisted writers. As a result, more work gradually came to them.

The blacklist had a chilling effect on social criticism. In 1947, 28 percent of Hollywood studio movies dealt with social issues; in 1949, only 18 percent did. By 1954, only about 9 percent of Hollywood films dealt with social problems. In 1953 and 1954, the U.S. Supreme Court made two rulings that finally protected witnesses from the abuses experienced by the Hollywood Ten and others caught up in the anticommunist sweep.

Dixie Dean Dickinson

FURTHER READING

Bentley, Eric. *Are You Now or Have You Ever Been: The Investigation of Show Business by the Un-American Activities Committee, 1947-1958.* New York: Harper & Row, 1972. Abridged testimonies of eighteen witnesses appearing before HUAC, 1947-1958. Testimonies of Edward Dmytryk (1947, 1951), Ring Lardner, Jr. (1947), Larry Parks (1951), Lillian Hellman (letter, 1952), and Paul Robeson (1956) are of particular interest. No references; easy to read. Photographs.

Dmytryk, Edward. *Odd Man Out: A Memoir of the Hollywood Ten.* Carbondale, Ill.: Southern Illinois University Press, 1996. A personal account of the director's experience during the "witch hunts."

Miller, Douglas T., and Marion Nowak. *The Fifties: The Way We Really Were.* Garden City, N.Y.: Doubleday, 1977. Written by a historian and a journalist. Documented and informative and still very readable. See in particular Chapter 1 on McCarthy and Chapter 12 on Hollywood. College-level reading.

Navasky, Victor S. *Naming Names*. New York: Penguin Books, 1982. Navasky was trained as a lawyer and a journalist; he gives a factual, informative study of the era and explains why so many people became informers. Excellent source. References provided. College-level reading.

Redish, Martin H. *The Logic of Persecution: Free Expression and the McCarthy Era*. Stanford, Calif.: Stanford University Press, 2005. An examination of the anticommunist hysteria of the 1940's and 1950's. Includes a chapter on HUAC and the Hollywood Ten. Bibliographic references and index.

Schlesinger, Arthur M., Jr., and Roger Burns, eds. *Congress Investigates, 1792-1974*. New York: Chelsea House, 1975. Of particular interest here are Schlesinger's introduction, which discusses Supreme Court cases related to congressional hearings, and the article by H. Lew Wallace, "The McCarthy Era." Good background material on the era, and bibliography.

Schrecker, Ellen. *Many Are the Crimes: McCarthyism in America*. Boston: Little, Brown, 1998. Presents an account of Joseph McCarthy, the Hollywood blacklist, and the impact of McCarthyism on American history.

Schumach, Murray. *The Face on the Cutting Room Floor*. New York: William Morrow, 1964. Enlightening book on censorship in Hollywood from the silent film era through the 1960's. Appendix gives samples of censorship rules in other countries and Hollywood's motion-picture code. Photographs. No references. Good source on the gray list, the Hollywood underground, and the American Legion.

Vaughn, Robert F. *Only Victims: A Study of Show Business Blacklisting*. New York: G. P. Putnam's Sons, 1972. This book is based on the actor's doctoral dissertation, covering the time period 1938-1958. Well documented and informative. Introduction by Senator George McGovern. Focuses on the sociological and psychological underpinnings of the radical right and left that fueled HUAC. Good documents in appendixes.

Whiffield, Stephen. *The Culture of the Cold War*. 2d ed. Baltimore: Johns Hopkins University Press, 1996. Describes and analyzes the anticommunist rhetoric that flourished in the popular culture of the 1940's and 1950's, including films, television, and literature. Includes bibliography and index.

SEE ALSO: 1947-1951: Blacklisting Depletes Hollywood's Talent Pool; Jan. 15, 1953-Dec. 2, 1954: McCarthy Hearings; Jan. 22, 1953: *The Crucible* Allegorizes the Red Scare Era.

■ November 29, 1947-July, 1949

Arab-Israeli War Creates Refugee Crisis

More than 400,000 Palestinians were driven from their homeland after the Arab-Israeli War of 1948, joining those who fled to safety after the United Nations initially voted to create Israel as a Jewish state.

Also known as: First Arab-Israeli War
Locale: Palestine (now Israel)
Categories: Immigration, emigration, and relocation; wars, uprisings, and civil unrest; expansion and land acquisition; geography

Key Figures

Arthur Balfour (1848-1930), British prime minister, 1902-1905, and foreign secretary, 1916-1919
Folke Bernadotte (1895-1948), Swedish diplomat and U.N. mediator
Haj Amin al-Husseini (1893/1895-1974), mufti of Jerusalem, 1921-1936, and leader of the Arab Higher Committee
Chaim Weizmann (1874-1952), chief Zionist delegate to the Paris Peace Conference and first president of Israel, 1949-1952
David Ben-Gurion (1886-1973), prime minister of Israel, 1948-1953 and 1955-1963

Summary of Event

As World War I raged in the Middle East, Great Britain and France signed the Sykes-Picot Agreement in 1916 to divide the region into British and French zones of influence. Meanwhile, the British high commissioner of Egypt, Sir Henry McMahon, carried out diplomatic contacts with Hussein ibn Abdallah, emir of the Hijaz, whereby the British promised the Arabs independence if they joined the Allies against the Turks. On November 2, 1917, however, British foreign minister Arthur Balfour issued a declaration favoring the idea of establishing a Jewish national home in Palestine.

The Balfour Declaration stipulated that nothing would be done to harm the rights of the indigenous Arab population, at the time numbering nearly 575,000, or 92 percent of the population. Subsequent events proved otherwise. Violence was already foretold by the King-Crane Commission, dispatched by U.S. president Woodrow Wilson in the summer of 1919 to investigate conditions of the region in preparation for the Paris Peace Conference.

The Zionist delegates at the conference argued that Great Britain, not

France, should be given the League of Nations' mandate to rule Palestine. Having been supported by the Balfour Declaration, the Zionists were handed their second victory when the British were given the mandate to govern Palestine and when the preamble of the mandate contained a copy of the Balfour Declaration. Article 2 of the mandate gave the British responsibility "to place the country under such political, administrative and economic conditions as will secure the establishment of the Jewish national home."

Article 4 called for the establishment of a Jewish agency "as a public body for the purpose of advising and cooperating with the Administration of Palestine in such economic, social and other matters as may affect the establishment of the Jewish national home." The agency was allowed "to construct or operate, upon fair and equitable terms, any public works, services and utilities, and to develop any of the natural resources of the country." Thus, the British were constrained by their commitment to the idea of a Jewish homeland in Palestine from protecting the civil rights and nurturing the national aspirations of the indigenous population, as mandate powers were supposed to do.

A rural, largely peasant, society long ruled by the Ottoman Turks, the Palestinians entered the twentieth century ill-equipped to cope with the problems presented by the modern world. The traditional Palestinian leadership consisted mostly of urban notables, who failed to unite and to form an effective response either to the British or to the Zionists. Palestinian political parties were divided according to family or local, rather than national, interests. Furthermore, the Palestinians found themselves isolated as the Sykes-Picot Agreement took effect and the new Arab states fell under British and French colonial rule.

The imbalance in the benefits of the British mandate became manifest in the growing ability of the Zionist movement and the Jewish Agency to create an infrastructure for a future state, especially as Jewish immigration increased in the 1930's. Palestinians and their political parties became gravely alarmed as the institutional gap between the two communities widened. The parties set aside their differences and, in 1935, formed the Palestine Arab Higher Committee, headed by Haj Amin al-Husseini. The Palestinians resisted the British and the Zionist program with a long general strike, followed by the 1936-1939 revolt. The weakness of the Palestinians, the might of the British troops, and the pressure applied by surrounding Arab governments combined to defeat the revolt.

The Zionist drive to establish a Jewish state in Palestine began to bear fruit. Already the Peel Commission, sent in 1937 to investigate the sources of Palestinian unrest, had recommended partition of the country. The United Nations authorized the creation of the United Nations Special Committee on Palestine (UNSCOP) to investigate all questions and issues relevant to the Palestine problem and to make its recommendations to the United Nations by September, 1947.

When UNSCOP finally submitted its findings to the U.N. General Assembly, it recommended partition of the country into a Jewish state and an Arab state and that Jerusalem become an international city. The Palestinians rejected partition on the grounds that it violated their rights, as it violated the provisions of the U.N. Charter. They pointed out that the proposed Jewish state included 56 percent of Palestine, even though Jews were not in the majority. Also, Jews owned only 10 percent of the land in the proposed Jewish state. Despite the misgivings of some and the total rejection by others, the partition was passed on November 29, 1947.

The partition resolution guaranteed, in theory, the civil, political, economic, religious, and property rights of the Arabs who were to be included in the Jewish state. It stipulated, among other things, that no discrimination of any kind would be made among the inhabitants on the grounds of race, religion, language, or sex. Palestinians and Arabs, however, rejected even the right of the existence of the Jewish state and indeed sought immediately after the partition to exterminate it. Small numbers of Arab forces entered Israel to support local Palestinian resistance almost immediately after the approval of the partition plan, and were resisted by Israeli army and irregular forces such as the Irgun, in small-scale actions. British forces eventually abandoned the mandate.

The Arab Liberation Army formed by the Arab League undertook largely ineffective attacks in northern Israel, but elsewhere irregular Arab forces had greater success in cutting off the road from Tel Aviv to Jerusalem. Waves of violence resulted throughout the winter and spring months of 1948 and nearly 300,000 Palestinians fled their homes to safer areas before May 14, 1948, the date the state of Israel was proclaimed. A significant event in this period was the April 9 attack on the Arab village of Deir Yassin, on the outskirts of Jerusalem, where about 120 men, women, and children were massacred. News of the massacre spread, raising the level of fear and panic among the population. This Israeli attack was followed four days later by an Arab attack on a Jewish medical convoy in which 77 Jewish personnel were killed in what seems to have been a retaliatory action. Having already lost its leadership and having no institutional support, the Palestinian civil and political authority quickly collapsed. Villagers felt defenseless, and the numbers of those fleeing to safety grew. The exodus left some areas with no resistance to approaching Zionist forces. Tiberias fell on April 18, Safad on May 10, and Jaffa on May 13, 1948.

Neighboring Arab states alternatively supported Palestinian guerrilla action, but also at times encouraged Palestinians to flee on the theory that they would crush the fledgling Jewish state, making room for Palestinians to reclaim all of their land. King Abdullah of Jordan quietly opposed the establishment of a Palestinian state and eventually claimed areas that came under the control of the Transjordanian Army. The full-scale invasion by about thirty thousand regular Arab forces occurred on May 15, after Israel's declaration of independence, which was rapidly recognized by both the United States and the Soviet Union.

During the ensuing war, in which Israel steadily consolidated and expanded its territory at the expense of Arab forces, thousands more villagers fled to safety, hoping to return soon, but the Arab armies failed to destroy Israel, and so the Palestinians who fled awoke to the hard reality of indefinite exile. On May 22, the United Nations ordered a cease-fire, which was affirmed on May 29. Intermittent truce violations and outbreaks of fighting led to another U.N. Security Council-sponsored cease-fire on July 15. Count Folke Bernadotte, the U.N. special mediator, was charged with the supervision of truce arrangements. In his attempt to reconcile the two sides, Bernadotte submitted plans for a settlement advocating the refugees' right to return home. He argued that "It would be an offense against the prin-

David Ben-Gurion announcing the independence of the state of Israel on May 14, 1948. (Library of Congress)

ciples of elemental justice if those innocent victims of the conflict were denied the right to return to their homes while Jewish immigrants flow into Palestine."

On November 16, with no peace in sight and with more refugees being forced out of their homes, the United Nations ordered the establishment of an armistice in Palestine. Armistice agreements between Israel and its Arab neighbors were negotiated between February and July of 1949 with the mediation of Ralph Bunche, who became U.N. special mediator after Bernadotte's assassination. By then, Israel controlled 77 percent of Palestine, and neighboring Arab governments controlled the rest, leaving Palestinians without any territory of their own. Estimates of the total number of refugees range from 750,000 to 900,000. Most of them were placed under the care of the United Nations Relief and Works Agency for Palestine Refugees in the Near East (UNRWA), established on December 9, 1949.

SIGNIFICANCE

The war of 1948 is regarded by the Palestinians as a catastrophe. They had become a shattered nation. Palestinians who remained under Israeli rule suddenly found themselves a defeated minority in their own land. Palestinian national authority was destroyed. The majority of Palestinians became stateless refugees, even when living in areas originally intended to be part of the new Palestinian state but now occupied by neighboring Arab countries. To add insult to injury, many of these lived in makeshift camps and depended on rations issued by the United Nations.

The Arab host countries were poor and underdeveloped, and were often reluctant hosts. Their fledgling, and largely agrarian, economies were unable to absorb the sudden influx of refugees. The UNRWA offered food and health care, started development programs, and built schools, among other assistance programs. Once education and vocational training became available to the Palestinians, their social, economic, and political role in the region improved. Many moved to Saudi Arabia and to the Gulf emirates when these began to develop their oil economies. Palestinians served in a variety of roles, such as educators and skilled laborers. Many became wealthy, but they remained stateless, except for those who acquired Jordanian citizenship.

Their presence throughout most of the Arab world was a reminder to the Arab people as well as to various governments of the plight of the Palestinians. To the Arab people, the Palestinians became a symbol of their own lack of power and the backward conditions of the region after years of misrule. A bond would be established between the forces for social change. To the majority of Arab governments, for whom realization of the Palestinians' right to return became a humanitarian duty and a political necessity, their presence was viewed as a radicalizing factor. This shaped the relationship of the Palestinians to the Arab governments: sometimes championed, at other times barely tolerated because of their influence, and sometimes even expelled, as the Palestine Liberation Organization (PLO) was from both Jordan and Syria, when those governments believed the PLO to be a threat to their national stability. For the most part, Palestinians' civil rights were neglected whether they were living in refugee camps in the surrounding Arab countries or were under Israeli rule.

The region experienced revolutionary upheavals after the creation of Israel in 1948, changing the nature of the ruling groups and radicalizing the domestic and international policies of the Arab states. The Arab-Israeli conflict remained alive and led to major wars in 1956, in 1967 (when Israel took over the West Bank and the Gaza Strip), and in 1973. Two major Israeli military operations against the Palestinians in Lebanon were carried out in 1978 and in 1982. In 1979 Egyptian president Anwar el-Sadat agreed to the Camp David Peace Accords, by which Egypt recognized Israel, removing Egypt as a threat to its security and drastically reducing Arab hopes of any future military victory.

The Palestinian question had global repercussions as the United States and the Soviet Union supplied arms and extended, to their respective allies, economic assistance and diplomatic backing. During the era of the Cold War, the Arab-Israeli conflict remained a dangerous issue for the two superpowers. The PLO, formed in 1964, represented the Palestinians after 1967. Arab and non-Arab governments gradually recognized the position of the PLO, which was eventually granted observer status at the United Nations in the continuing effort to find a just solution to the Palestine question and to redress the loss of Palestinian national rights.

Mahmood Ibrahim

FURTHER READING

Abu-Lughod, Ibrahim, ed. *The Transformation of Palestine.* Evanston, Ill.: Northwestern University Press, 1971. Written by a host of scholars, this book contains valuable articles on the demography of Palestine, land alienation, resistance to the British mandate, and regional and international perspectives on the Arab-Israeli conflict.

Flapan, Simha. *Zionism and the Palestinians.* New York: Barnes & Noble Books, 1979. A valuable account of the relationship of the Zionist movement to the Palestinians before 1948 by a well-known Israeli author. The details that Flapan provides will challenge the myths of the Arab-Israeli conflict and the creation of the refugee problem.

Heller, Joseph L. *The Birth of Israel, 1945-1949: Ben-Gurion and His Critics.* Gainesville: University Press of Florida, 2000. Details the events that led to the founding of Israel and features a study of the many contenders fighting for leadership of this new state. Included are a bibliography and an index.

Hourani, Albert. *A History of the Arab People.* Cambridge, Mass.: Harvard University Press, 1991. A comprehensive history of the Arab people from the rise of Islam to the present. Places the political developments in the region and their international implications in historical perspective.

Khouri, Fred. *The Arab-Israeli Dilemma.* 3d ed. Syracuse, N.Y.: Syracuse University Press, 1985. An excellent, well-documented account of the Arab-Israeli conflict from 1947 through the 1980's, with chapters on the refugee problem, Jerusalem, and the American administrations' involvement. This book has been described as a model of objectivity.

Laqueur, Walter, ed. *The Israel-Arab Reader: A Documentary History of the Middle East Conflict.* New York: Citadel Press, 1969. An important sourcebook for students of the modern Middle East and the Arab-Israeli conflict. It contains excerpts from major works on Zionism, Israel, the Palestinians, Arab-Israeli relations, Pan-Arabism, and other topics.

Morris, Benny. *The Birth of the Palestinian Refugee Problem: 1947-1949.* New York: Cambridge University Press, 1987. A controversial issue regarding Palestinian refugees is whether they left on their own accord or as a result of their leaders' urging. Benny Morris, one of few Israeli scholars to challenge official claims and Zionist propaganda, shows in this well-documented account that Palestinians were forced out of their homes.

Reich, Bernard, ed. *An Historical Encyclopedia of the Arab-Israeli Conflict.* Westport, Conn.: Greenwood Press, 1996. Invaluable research tool for examining many aspects of the Arab-Israeli conflict. Includes a chronology and extensive bibliographical information.

Rouhana, Nadim N. *Palestinian Citizens in an Ethnic Jewish State: Identities in Conflict.* New Haven, Conn.: Yale University Press, 1997. The author, who grew up in Palestine, provides a psychological and sociological account of the influences of Israel on its Arab minority. Includes appendixes and a bibliography.

Westad, Odd Arne. *The Global Cold War: Third World Interventions and the Makings of Our Times.* Cambridge, U.K.: Cambridge University Press, 2007. Examines the aftermath of the Cold War in terms of globalization and American interventionism in developing nations. Illustrated.

SEE ALSO: 1948: Soviets Escalate Persecution of Jews; Dec. 14, 1950: United Nations High Commissioner for Refugees Statute Is Approved; 1960's: Soviet Jews Demand Cultural and Religious Rights; Oct. 6-26, 1973: Yom Kippur War.

■ **1948**

MORGENTHAU ADVANCES REALIST SCHOOL OF POWER POLITICS

After World War II, scholars in the field of international relations sought a better theoretical basis for understanding conflict and diplomacy. Hans Joachim Morgenthau argued in Politics Among Nations *that political realism provided the best account of these areas.*

ALSO KNOWN AS: *Politics Among Nations: The Struggle for Power and Peace*
LOCALE: New York, New York
CATEGORIES: Government and politics; diplomacy and international relations

KEY FIGURES
Hans Joachim Morgenthau (1904-1980), German-born American political theorist
George F. Kennan (1904-2005), American political theorist and diplomat
Kenneth N. Waltz (b. 1924), American political theorist
Reinhold Niebuhr (1892-1971), American theologian

SUMMARY OF EVENT
The publication of Hans Joachim Morgenthau's book *Politics Among Nations: The Struggle for Power and Peace* (1948) was a watershed in the twentieth century theory of international relations. While not the first expression of what is called the realist school of political theory, Morgenthau's work caught the attention of scholars and politicians. The solid intellectual foundation and the clearly defined principles of political realism made it impossible to disregard. It was the basis for future discussions, whether one agreed or disagreed with Morgenthau. The text was widely used in international relations classes for decades.

Western analysis of international relations is often seen as beginning with

> ### SIX PRINCIPLES OF POLITICAL REALISM
>
> *Hans J. Morgenthau, in* Politics Among Nations: The Struggle for Power and Peace *(1948), outlines the six main points of political realism:*
>
> 1. Political realism believes that politics, like society in general, is governed by objective laws that have their roots in human nature. . . .
> 2. The main signpost that helps political realism to find its way through the landscape of international politics is the concept of interest defined in terms of power. . . .
> 3. Realism assumes that its key concept of interest defined as power is an objective category which is universally valid, but it does not endow that concept with a meaning that is fixed once and for all. . . .
> 4. Political realism is aware of the moral significance of political action. It is also aware of the ineluctable tension between the moral command and the requirements of successful political action. . . .
> 5. Political realism refuses to identify the moral aspirations of a particular nation with the moral laws that govern the universe. As it distinguishes between truth and opinion, so it distinguishes between truth and idolatry. . . .
> 6. . . . Intellectually, the political realist maintains the autonomy of the political sphere. . . .

the ancient Greek historian Thucydides, who wrote about the Peloponnesian War (431-404 B.C.E.). Writing about and practicing diplomacy during the early sixteenth century, Niccolò Machiavelli is often seen as a forerunner of the modern power-politics approach to international relations. In the seventeenth century, Thomas Hobbes also espoused a power approach to international relations, while Hugo Grotius put forward an organizational theory as being the best way to deal with international uncertainty. Within Europe, the nineteenth century opened with the Napoleonic Wars (1793-1815) and the Prussian unification of the German states (1815-1871), and it closed with the British and Germans vying for dominance. The intellectual response to this situation was to seek an end to warfare through organizations such as the Permanent International Peace Bureau.

Although organizations such as the bureau did not prevent World War I, it was believed by many that a stronger international organization might more effectively promote peace. A basic tenet of this idealistic school of thought was that an outmoded international system or corrupt individuals were the cause of international conflict. This was the foundation for the League of Nations, through which many sought to change or control the condition that had led to the so-called War to End All Wars. When the league was unable to prevent World War II, many looked for a new theory to explain what had happened and to give political leaders a guide for the future.

Morgenthau moved into this void, offering an understandable if pessimistic analysis. He assumed that anarchy was the norm for the international system, which could be made orderly only through the use of power. He saw the nation-state as the principal international entity, with organizations and other entities playing secondary roles. He assumed each nation-state followed its own self-interest; thus, competition was to be expected, with conflict occurring more often than cooperation.

From this foundation, Morgenthau developed "Six Principles of Political Realism," the first chapter of *Politics Among Nations*. The six principles put forward in that chapter include the idea that human nature does not change, which allows rational theories of politics to be developed. Self-interest, moreover, can be viewed in terms of power, which allows the development of political thought. Power is the ability to control others and is seen by Morgenthau as a universal goal. While morality is still seen as a part of life, realism understands it to be expendable in the pursuit of political success. The goals or morals of one group cannot be assumed to be those of all groups. Even though other dimensions of life exist, politics takes place within its own sphere and must be seen within this light and not judged by a set of rules that might apply only to other aspects of life.

Politics Among Nations was seen by many as a guide for the emerging Cold War between the United States and the Soviet Union. The creation of the United Nations at the end of World War II gave some hope to the idealists. However, events such as the communist victory in China and the invasion of South Korea by North Korea made many doubt the ability of this organization to be effective in world politics. Morgenthau's contention that international relations could be understood rationally gave leaders what seemed to be an approach that would allow them to deal with real events. He also rejected the proposition of those who thought that technology made the post-World War II era different from previous eras. His study of European political history was the reason he believed that the power politics of previous centuries remained intact.

One individual who is believed by many to have helped pave the way for Morgenthau was the Protestant theologian Reinhold Niebuhr. Basing his writing on the New Testament assertion of humankind's sinful nature, he saw a desire for power, both individually and collectively, as the normal state of affairs. Although differing significantly from Morgenthau's position on morality in politics, Niebuhr taught that countries must understand international power politics. Thus, when Morgenthau put forward what might

113

seem to be a pessimistic view of world politics, many saw it in the light of the religious teachings of Niebuhr.

If Niebuhr was an important precursor of Morgenthau, George F. Kennan was his intellectual follower, developing the realist school of political theory in a slightly different way than did Morgenthau. While Morgenthau was from Europe (he immigrated from Germany in 1937), Kennan's analysis of the international situation was based upon an American point of view. He believed that the errors of American idealists were due to their belief that the American system of government had created a relatively peaceful region of the world. He asserted that it was power politics that had created the relative peace of the Western Hemisphere. Thus, plans for a peaceful future should be based on a realist approach to international relations, not an idealistic one that based its hopes on international organizations.

Another individual who built upon the realist school of thought was Kenneth N. Waltz. Waltz did not focus on human nature as the primary cause for power politics; rather, his focus was on the anarchy of the international system. Thus, the structured international system plays the most important role in Waltz's system in determining whether or not countries can achieve their goals given the specific balance of power between them and their rivals.

SIGNIFICANCE

Hans Morgenthau's expression of political realism occurred when leaders were searching for a new way to understand international relations. The structural solutions that had been tried in the first half of the twentieth century had failed. The most costly war in history had just ended, and a new rivalry was heating up. Morgenthau's assertion that there was a rational approach to understanding these issues fit well with the modern mind-set. The fact that military power had just defeated the aggressive Axis Powers in a world war seemed to confirm Morgenthau's ideas. In the minds of many Americans, the ideology of the Soviet Union could be contained only through the use of power.

Thus, unlike the works of some scholars, Morgenthau's book directly affected the outlook of the American government and helped shape world events. For most of the time since the publication of *Politics Among Nations*, American foreign policy has been shaped by those who accept many of its basic tenets. In addition, Morgenthau shaped the way in which the theory of international relations was discussed during the latter half of the twentieth century. It was impossible for scholars to ignore the realist school of thought. Whether their theories supported or opposed those put forward by Morgenthau, others had to respond to the ideas he presented.

Donald A. Watt

FURTHER READING

Bucklin, Steven J. *Realism and American Foreign Policy: Wilsonians and the Kennan-Morgenthau Thesis.* Westport, Conn.: Praeger, 2001. Monograph on the opposed realist and idealistic approaches to foreign policy of Woodrow Wilson and the post-World War II realists. Bibliographic references and index.

Craig, Campbell. *Glimmer of a New Leviathan: Total War in the Realism of Niebuhr, Morgenthau, and Waltz.* New York: Columbia University Press, 2003. Compares Morgenthau's work to that of Waltz and Niebuhr using the concept of "total war" to discuss international relations in the nuclear age. Bibliographic references and index.

Frei, Christopher. *Hans J. Morgenthau: An Intellectual Biography.* Baton Rouge: Louisiana State University Press, 2001. Initially a standard biography, the latter portion of the book treats its topic more in terms of philosophical development and Morgenthau's developing realist position.

Lang, Anthony F., ed. *Political Theory and International Affairs: Hans J. Morgenthau on Aristotle's "The Politics."* Westport, Conn.: Praeger, 2004. Allows the reader to gain a fuller understanding of Morgenthau's political theory, as it is taken from lectures on the application of Aristotle's ideas, which he gave over a three-year period.

SEE ALSO: Mar. 12, 1947: Truman Doctrine; Apr. 4, 1949: North Atlantic Treaty Organization Is Formed; June 25, 1950-July 27, 1953: Korean War; Jan. 5, 1957: Eisenhower Doctrine; Nov. 14, 1961: Kennedy Expands U.S. Involvement in Vietnam; July 25, 1969: Nixon Doctrine Is Unveiled.

■ **1948**

SOVIETS ESCALATE PERSECUTION OF JEWS

Soviet Jews, accused of being disloyal to the Soviet state, were driven from positions of power and responsibility and were imprisoned and executed en masse by Premier Joseph Stalin's regime.

LOCALE: Soviet Union
CATEGORIES: Atrocities and war crimes; human rights; cultural and intellectual history

KEY FIGURES

Joseph Stalin (Joseph Vissarionovich Dzhugashvili; 1878-1953), general
    secretary of the Central Committee of the Communist Party of the
    Soviet Union, 1922-1953, and premier, 1941-1953
Andrei Zhdanov (1896-1948), Politburo member
Solomon Mikhoels (1890-1948), Jewish playwright and director of the
    Moscow State Jewish Theater

SUMMARY OF EVENT

Although anti-Semitism in twentieth century dictatorships is generally associated with Nazi Germany, the Soviet Union also regularly persecuted its Jewish population and frequently executed significant numbers of Jews. While the anti-Semitism of Adolf Hitler and his henchmen was based on various pseudoscientific theories of the biological origins of race and of pure and impure races, Soviet anti-Semitism was the straightforward political and economic hostility to a people who had a strong loyalty to an outside entity and who tended to do well even in adversity.

Many of the original Bolshevik leaders were Jewish, although a number of them adopted Russian-sounding pseudonyms in part to disguise their ethnic origins, as well as to keep themselves one step ahead of the Okhrana, the czarist secret police. When Vladimir Ilich Lenin died in 1924 and Joseph Stalin emerged as the winner of the resulting power struggle, many of these Old Bolsheviks fell victim to Stalin's purges. The Great Terror, however, was primarily directed at eliminating all possible alternative power bases from the country, and overt anti-Semitism was not part of its rhetoric, although suspicion of Jews was already an important part of Stalin's character. Nikita S. Khrushchev noted this character in his memoirs.

It was only after the close of World War II that Stalin began specifically to target Jews for being Jewish. The establishment of the modern state of Israel in 1948 was a powerful trigger for the suspicion that was such a fundamental part of Stalin's personality. Having hundreds of thousands of Soviet Jews requesting permission to emigrate only confirmed in his mind that he was dealing with a threat of worldwide proportions.

The immediate object of suspicion was the Jewish Anti-Fascist Committee, which was established in 1942 as an organization to encourage Jewish support around the world for the Soviet war effort. During the Soviet Union's life-and-death struggle with Hitler, Stalin had accepted the need for the committee to have connections with Jews abroad, particularly in the United States, in order to drum up much-needed Western support for the war on the Eastern Front. Now that the war was won, those connections with the capitalist West quickly became conduits of subversion in Stalin's mind, and he ordered the committee dissolved.

With Hitler's anti-Semitism, promulgated through the propaganda of Joseph Goebbels and the crude caricatures of Julius Streicher's newspaper *Der Stürmer* (1923-1945), Stalin did not dare to say that he was attacking the Jewish people. Instead, he disguised his attacks with various euphemistic catchphrases, the most prominent of which was "rootless cosmopolitanism," referring to the Jewish people having existed without a land to call their own for nearly two millennia (the Romans destroyed the Temple of Jerusalem in the year 70) and having thus lived among the various Gentile nations. Stalin also condemned "Zionism," focusing his attacks on questions of the loyalty of Jews to the Soviet Union rather than to their Jewishness. While "rootless cosmopolitans" were considered to be not loyal to anyone, Zionists were considered traitors: loyal to Israel while remaining in the Soviet Union.

Jewish artists and organizations felt the wrath of anti-Semitism during the Zhdanovshchina (Zhdanov Doctrine, a policy instituted in 1946 by Andrei Zhdanov that called for Soviet writers, artists, and the intelligentsia to conform to the Communist Party line). The comprehensive attack, which peaked in 1948, was aimed at alleged decadence in the arts and culture in general. The famous Moscow Jewish Theater, directed by playwright Solomon Mikhoels, was a special target. Yiddish-language newspapers were shut down because they were believed to represent the persistence of a cultural viewpoint not firmly rooted in the Soviet Union. Harsh quotas were placed on the admission of Jews into a number of intellectual pursuits in which they had historically flourished—particularly law, diplomatic services, and academia—making life very difficult for the Jewish communities of Moscow and Leningrad (now St. Petersburg).

Many prominent Jews were arrested, exiled, and even executed during this period. Politician and diplomat Vyacheslav Mikhailovich Molotov's wife Polina Semyonovna Zhemchuzhina was arrested for meeting with Israeli prime minister Golda Meir and for having spoken Yiddish with her during Meir's September, 1948, visit to the Soviet Union. Molotov was then ordered to divorce his wife, and they would not see one another again until after Stalin's death.

Furthermore, the intellectual attack on Jewish "cosmopolitanism" spread into a general denial that "foreigners" could produce anything of value. This campaign soon descended into the depths of absurdity, with Soviet propagandists claiming that many technological and other significant inventions were made by Russians, and not by those who had been credited through professional agreement. For example, the Soviets claimed that it was not Scottish inventor James Watt who invented the steam engine but instead a Siberian mechanic. Other Russians were credited with the first pow-

Joseph Stalin. (Library of Congress.)

ered flight and with inventing the light bulb and the radio. Although some of these claims were based on some evidence behind them—such as Boris Rosing's early experiments in using a cathode-ray tube to display images, work that was inflated into "the invention of electronic television" well before Philo Farnsworth's 1927 transmissions—most were so patently absurd as to merit nothing but derision. This "we invented it first" line soon became a staple of satirical humor in the West.

In the Soviet Union, this was no laughing matter, for it was becoming increasingly important to anticipate these intellectual attacks. Doctoral students were instructed to remove all references to foreign scientists and inventors in their work, replacing the names with vague phrases such as "scientists have shown." Soviet scientists and inventors were celebrated as patriots and heros—unless one of them should be discovered to have been an enemy of the people, at which time his or her name would vanish altogether from the dissertation or other work.

By 1950, a new theme began to emerge after the "discovery" of a "conspiracy" among doctors at the clinic of the Stalin Automotive Works; also implicated were executives and other officials. Interestingly, every one of them was Jewish. Although the trial and subsequent executions attracted little attention in the government-controlled press, they were a dress rehearsal for a much larger drama Stalin was planning. It was revealed that in 1948 a medical technician by the name of Lidia Timashuk had reported that an ailing Andrei Zhdanov was not receiving proper treatment. His subsequent death under mysterious circumstances was seized on as evidence of a vast, sinister conspiracy among the doctors entrusted with the care of the Soviet Union's leaders. Again, all of the doctors and other caretakers were Jewish.

SIGNIFICANCE

Anti-Semitism remained a central theme of Soviet politics, with many of the same catchphrases first introduced by Stalin in 1948 being tossed about by new leaders, even those leaders who claimed to disavow Stalin. It is often hypothesized that the so-called Doctors' Plot, which was derailed by Stalin's death in 1953, was in fact intended to be the opening act in a massive pogrom against the Jews on a scale to rival the Holocaust.

In the 1970's, the plight of the refuseniks, Jews who were persistently denied exit visas, became a major issue for international human rights organizations during the Cold War, while in the 1980's during perestroika, openly anti-Semitic and quasi-fascist organizations such as Pamyat (memory) began to appear among the disaffected youth. After the 1991 fall of the Soviet Union, anti-Semitism cropped up repeatedly in post-Soviet Russia, particularly among reactionaries such as the Stalinist bloc, a group that looked back with nostalgia on the time when their country was still feared on the world stage.

Leigh Husband Kimmel

FURTHER READING

Brent, Jonathan, and Vladimir Namurov. *Stalin's Last Crime.* New York: HarperCollins, 2003. A study of the events leading up to Stalin's death, particularly the "Doctors' Plot" and the apparent preparations for a major pogrom against the Soviet Jewish population.

Khrushchev, Nikita S. *Khrushchev Remembers.* Translated by Strobe Talbott. Boston: Little, Brown, 1970. A revealing primary source, although with certain predictable blind spots regarding Khrushchev's own complicity in many of the crimes he describes.

Kostyrchenko, Gennadi. *Out of the Red Shadows: Anti-Semitism in Stalin's Russia.* Amherst, N.Y.: Prometheus Books, 1995. A study of the lives of Jewish intellectuals in Stalinist Russia. Chapters include "Ethnocide," "Arrests of the Intellectuals," "The Closing of the Theaters," "Attacking the 'Cosmopolitans'" and "Escalation of the Anti-Jewish Purges." Chapters also look at Jews working in journalism, the arts, the humanities, and industry.

Lustiger, Arno. *Stalin and the Jews: The Red Book.* New York: Enigma, 2003. A unique book by a survivor of a Nazi death camp that explores Stalin's desire to eliminate Soviet Jews. Focuses especially on the Jewish Anti-Fascist Committee. The book's introduction notes the work is "the most exhaustive, indeed encyclopedic, account of the monumental tragedy that befell the Soviet Jews during the rule of Joseph Stalin."

Montefore, Simon Sebag. *Stalin: The Court of the Red Tsar.* New York: Alfred A. Knopf, 2003. Includes information on Stalin's henchmen and how the dictator used them to deflect attention from himself during the bloody purges.

Rayfield, Donald. *Stalin and His Hangmen: The Tyrant and Those Who Killed for Him.* New York: Random House, 2004. A study of the relationship of Stalin and his chief henchmen.

SEE ALSO: Feb. 11, 1945: Soviet Exiles and Prisoners of War Are Forced into Repatriation; Mar. 5, 1946: Churchill Delivers His Iron Curtain Speech; Nov. 29, 1947-July, 1949: Arab-Israeli War Creates Refugee Crisis; Feb. 10, 1948: Zhdanov Denounces "Formalism" in Music; 1949-1961: East Germans Flee to West to Escape Communist Regime; Mar. 5, 1953: Death of Stalin; Feb. 25, 1956: Khrushchev Denounces Stalinist Regime; Nov. 11, 1970: Moscow Human Rights Committee Is Founded; Feb.-Mar., 1977: Soviets Crack Down on Moscow's Helsinki Watch Group.

■ **FEBRUARY 10, 1948**

ZHDANOV DENOUNCES "FORMALISM" IN MUSIC

The Central Committee of the Communist Party of the Soviet Union published a decree opposing "antidemocratic formalism" in the music of the country's leading composers.

LOCALE: Moscow, Soviet Union
CATEGORIES: Civil rights and liberties; government and politics

KEY FIGURES
Andrei Zhdanov (1896-1948), Soviet politician
Joseph Stalin (Joseph Vissarionovich Dzhugashvili; 1878-1953), general secretary of the Central Committee of the Communist Party of the Soviet Union, 1922-1953, and premier, 1941-1953
Sergei Prokofiev (1891-1953), Soviet composer

Dmitri Shostakovich (1906-1975), Soviet composer
Aram Khachaturian (1903-1978), Armenian Soviet composer
Nikolai Miaskovski (1881-1950), Soviet composer
Tikhon Khrennikov (1913-2007), president of the Union of Soviet Composers
Vano Muradeli (1908-1970), Georgian Soviet composer

SUMMARY OF EVENT

On February 10, 1948, the newspapers of the Soviet Union published a decree on music by the Central Committee of the Soviet Communist Party. The decree was preceded by a three-day conference presided over by Andrei Zhdanov, Joseph Stalin's heir apparent, even though both Zhdanov's health and his power were in decline. At that conference, the works of internationally famous Soviet composers—Sergei Prokofiev, Dmitri Shostakovich, Aram Khachaturian, and Nikolai Miaskovski in particular—were denounced and musical modernism or formalism was condemned explicitly.

The Soviet Union emerged from World War II considerably enlarged in territory but suffering from the immense destruction of four years of intense, total war with Nazi Germany and its allies. Attempts to subvert the governments of neighboring countries to increase Soviet dominance led to a reaction by the Western countries, in particular the Truman Doctrine (1947) to prevent further Soviet expansion through subversion in Turkey and Greece and the formation of the North Atlantic Treaty Organization in 1949. Western reaction against Soviet expansionism, poor harvests in the devastated western parts of the Soviet Union, and fear of popular disaffection resulted in an intensification of dictatorial controls after an initial relaxation of wartime stringencies. As the Cold War deepened, Stalin cut the Soviet Union and its client states off from contact with the West, encouraged Russian nationalism, and proclaimed hostility to all foreign influences, and even culture was not spared from the bracing winds of Cold War.

Stalin's actions usually took place behind the scenes and were revealed only obliquely by others, whose role was to take public initiatives in denouncing trends to which Stalin was hostile. Andrei Zhdanov was assigned to this role. The period of control over the arts, sciences, and philosophy between 1946 and 1948 has been called the Zhdanovshchina, or Zhdanov's purge. Zhdanov at this time was engaged in a power struggle with Georgi M. Malenkov, minister for heavy industry, and Lavrenty Beria, head of the secret police, to succeed Stalin, who was in his late sixties.

Music actually was one of the last areas to be placed under tight state control. By early 1948, Zhdanov was in poor health, with a heart condition exacerbated by years of heavy drinking. His political influence had waned; his chief claim to influence was the marriage of his son to Stalin's daughter.

The Soviet people, however, did not know about Zhdanov's eclipse, and his very appearance before the Union of Soviet Composers as a senior member of the governing Politburo signaled official government sanction of his decrees.

Zhdanov's speech opening the general assembly of Soviet composers in January, 1948, began, as did the attack by the Central Committee, with denunciation of the opera *Great Friendship* by Vano Muradeli, a Georgian composer of limited gifts, for its lack of melody, misuse of the orchestra, dissonant harmonies, and lack of folk music to characterize the North Georgian peoples. He compared portions of the work to "noise on a building lot, at the moment when excavators, stone crushers and cement mixers go into action."

Zhdanov did not attack any other composers by name. This was left to Tikhon Khrennikov, the new president of the Union of Soviet Composers. He referred to an article in *Pravda* in 1936 condemning Shostakovich's excesses and attacked the "formalistic distortions and anti-democratic tendencies" in the postwar music of the leading Soviet composers, whose works were well known and popular in the West as well—Prokofiev, Khachaturian, Shostakovich, and others. He also denounced the overemphasis on abstract music at the expense of program music on subjects of Soviet life, and the "anti-realistic decadent influences . . . peculiar to the bourgeois movement of the era of imperialism." His speech closed with attacks on Igor Stravinsky, Paul Hindemith, Arnold Schoenberg, Olivier Messiaen, and such younger composers as Benjamin Britten and Gian Carlo Menotti.

One composer of popular music asked whether the workers in factories and on collective farms loved the symphonies of Shostakovich and Prokofiev. Others attacked the ultraindividualist conception of life, derived from bourgeois idealism, artistic snobbishness, neoclassicism as musical escapism, a desire to startle with spicy and scratchy harmonies, and a cult of form and technique, the latter described by many as "bourgeois formalism."

Examination of individual works criticized reveals the grounds for these criticisms. Prokofiev's Sixth Symphony (1945-1947) is not an optimistic and accessible work like the wartime Fifth Symphony; it is grim, with moments of horror in the first two movements and with a barely concealed menace in the seemingly lighthearted finale, which ends with the sad theme of the first movement. The symphony seems to be not a celebration of victory but a portrait of the horrors of war. Shostakovich's symphonies of the 1940's displayed even sharper contrasts. The Seventh ("Leningrad") Symphony of 1941 is a textbook example of Socialist Realism (although denounced in 1948 as doing a better job of depicting the advancing Nazis than of showing the resistance of the Soviets), whereas his Eighth Symphony of 1943 is a gloomy, austere work with inner movements that almost graphically depict the terrors of war. The Ninth Symphony of 1945, lightheartedly neoclassical in tone, was criticized three years later as frivolously mocking the victory of the Soviet people (there are amusing parodies of military march idioms in some movements), though the second movement did receive praise for its lyricism.

Prokofiev, Shostakovich, Muradeli, Khachaturian, and the other composers made dutiful obeisance in published statements in which they repented their errors. The congress summed up its work in a letter to Stalin in which its members acknowledged the justness of the Communist Party's criticism of Soviet music and apologized for forgetting the traditions of Russian musical realism.

Significance

For two months in 1948, none of the music of any of the denounced composers was performed publicly in Moscow, a most effective way of showing what government control could mean to composers suspected of the slightest dissidence. Prokofiev's first wife (Spanish by birth) was even arrested as a spy and sentenced to eight years in the labor camps of the gulag.

A few of Prokofiev's works subsequently were performed that year. He devoted most of his time, limited because of his declining health, to writing vocal works on topics fitting the Communist Party line, such as his oratorio *On Guard for Peace* (1950). The main work of his final period is a reworking of an earlier cello concerto as the *Sinfonia Concerto for Cello and Orchestra* (1950-1952), written for the young Russian cellist Mstislav Rostropovich. Prokofiev's death from a cerebral hemorrhage on March 5, 1953, ironically was on the same day as Stalin's death.

Miaskovski turned to a simpler style in his last piano sonatas, teaching pieces for children, and his twenty-seventh and last symphony. Khachaturian continued to compose, but none of his subsequent works achieved the popularity of his colorful scores of the 1940's such as the piano and violin concertos of the *Gayaneh* ballet, from which the "Saber Dance" remains his most popular composition.

Shostakovich, after a duly submissive letter to Stalin, composed film music and Party-line works such as the oratorio *Song of the Forests* and extremely simple and accessible works such as the Fourth String Quartet, very placid in contrast to the grotesqueries of the preceding quartet. He was sent to the United States in 1949 as part of a peace delegation but withheld his Tenth Symphony from performance until after Stalin's death. The tone of this work is darkly brooding, with a sense of forced gaiety in the finale. One frightening portion is said to be a musical portrait of Stalin.

The thaw of the Nikita S. Khrushchev years permitted Shostakovich to re-write his earlier controversial opera that had gotten him into trouble with Stalin in 1936, *Lady MacBeth of the Mtsensk District*, as *Katerina Izmailova*. His two epic symphonies on the genesis of the communist revolution, the Eleventh ("The Year 1905") and Twelfth ("The Year 1917"), were followed by the controversial Thirteenth, which includes a setting of Yevgeny Yevtushenko's poem "Babiy Yar," in which the poet condemned not only the Nazis but their local accomplices as well. Such a condemnation angered the Leonid Brezhnev regime, and the poet was compelled to change the text. The Fourteenth Symphony is a chamber symphony with solo voices; the Fifteenth, one of the composer's farewell works, contains quotations from Gioacchino Rossini's *William Tell Overture* and the "Fate" motive from Richard Wagner's *Die Walküre* (1856; the Valkyrie).

Shostakovich's greatest postwar works are his string quartets. Only two of these were written before 1945. The most frequently performed is the Eighth, written during a visit to Dresden (in what was then the German Democratic Republic); the sight of the ruins left by the Allied bombardments in 1945 provoked the composer to dedicate the quartet to the victims of war and Fascism. The quartet includes citations from several of his earlier works, including the First and Fifth symphonies, the Violin Concerto, and the E Minor Piano Trio, which Shostakovich wrote in 1944 after reading about the atrocities in the Majdanek extermination camp. Its opening movement and especially the last two movements have been compared to a lunar landscape, whereas the second movement is an intensely terrifying war piece (like the third movement of the Eighth Symphony) and the third is a nightmare waltz. Other important quartets include the Twelfth, with its experimentation with serial techniques, and the last, the Fifteenth, composed of six slow movements with no fast movement to relieve the prevailingly gloomy atmosphere.

The decree on music from the Central Committee was not rescinded until 1958. Stalin, and secondarily Malenkov and Beria, were blamed for the 1948 resolution, with its harsh judgments cited as examples of the negative traits that marked the period of the cult of personality, a code phrase for Stalinism. The composers once condemned were officially rehabilitated.

Khrennikov continued to serve as president of the Union of Soviet Composers, surviving under the regimes from Joseph Stalin through Mikhail Gorbachev and able to tell composers what and how they had to write if they wanted their music played. Many of the younger composers emigrated as a result. In 1992, after the breakup of the Soviet Union, the Union of Soviet Composers was dissolved. Khrennikov reportedly found a position teaching composition part time at the Moscow Conservatory.

The decree of 1948 did much damage to Soviet music and also to the reputation of the Soviet Union abroad. Although the Red Army had stopped Adolf Hitler and contributed markedly to his eventual defeat, the Cold War crackdowns on literature, art, science (especially genetics), philosophy, and finally music repelled many intellectuals in the West who originally had been grateful to the Soviets for the defeat of fascism and were attracted to communism for its alleged support of the arts, as opposed to the commercial orientation of the West.

R. M. Longyear

FURTHER READING

Edmunds, Neil. *The Soviet Proletarian Music Movement.* New York: Peter Lang, 2000. Study of Soviet proletarian composers, official state policy, and the evolution of music under the Communist Party. Bibliographic references, discography, index.

Hahn, Werner G. *Postwar Soviet Politics: The Fall of Zhdanov and the Defeat of Moderation, 1946-1953.* Ithaca, N.Y.: Cornell University Press, 1982. The author advances the thesis that Zhdanov was a moderate, locked in a power struggle with such hard-liners as Malenkov and Beria, and that the attack on music came after Zhdanov had been stripped of most of his influence.

Kuhn, Laura. *Music Since 1900.* 6th ed. New York: Schirmer Reference, 2001. Contains the texts of the resolutions, speeches, and letters of Soviet musical policy in 1948 and the document of rescission in 1958.

MacDonald, Ian. *The New Shostakovich.* Boston: Northeastern University Press, 1990. Emphasizes Shostakovich as a dissident who used a covert musical language of dissent against communism.

Moor, Paul. "A Reply to Tikhon Khrennikov." *High Fidelity/Musical America* 36 (August, 1986): 52-54, 79. Shows the control that Khrennikov continued to exercise over Soviet music even into the years of Gorbachev's glasnost.

Norris, Christopher. "Shostakovich: Politics and Musical Language." In *Shostakovich: The Man and His Music.* Boston: Marion Boyars, 1982. The author suggests that a new form of artistic biography is necessary for this composer, wherein the central themes are impulse and commitment.

Robinson, Harlow. *Sergei Prokofiev: A Biography.* New York: Viking Press, 1987. A discussion of the composer's life more than of his music, this very readable biography places him in the Soviet context during the various changes of government.

Schwarz, Boris. *Music and Musical Life in Soviet Russia, 1917-1970.* New York: W. W. Norton, 1972. An excellent study that shows the impact of Zhdanov's purges in all areas of Soviet musical life.

Volkov, Solomon. *Testimony: The Memoirs of Dmitri Shostakovich.* New York: Harper & Row, 1979. These memoirs have been attacked as an ideological anticommunist tract, but many passages give a strong feeling of the paranoia of the Soviet Union in 1948. Prokofiev, Muradeli, and other composers are assailed.

Werth, Alexander. *Musical Uproar in Moscow.* London: Turnstile Press, 1949. Reprint. Westport, Conn.: Greenwood Press, 1973. Contains a valuable discussion of Zhdanov by the Moscow correspondent of *The New Statesman* and the speeches of attack and defense made at the January, 1948, meeting preceding Zhdanov's denunciation.

SEE ALSO: Mar. 12, 1947: Truman Doctrine; Apr. 4, 1949: North Atlantic Treaty Organization Is Formed; Mar. 5, 1953: Death of Stalin; Oct., 1957: Pasternak's *Doctor Zhivago* Is Published; Feb. 13, 1974: Soviet Union Expels Solzhenitsyn.

■ **FEBRUARY 25, 1948**

COMMUNISTS SEIZE POWER IN CZECHOSLOVAKIA

A coalition government set up under President Edvard Beneš after World War II was undermined by Communist Party members under Prime Minister Klement Gottwald, who seized the chance to transform the Czechoslovak Republic into a communist state modeled on the Soviet Union. The Soviets held great influence in Eastern and Central Europe after the region was designated a Soviet "sphere of interest" after World War II.

LOCALE: Prague, Czechoslovakia (now Czech Republic)
CATEGORIES: Wars, uprisings, and civil unrest; government and politics

KEY FIGURES

Edvard Beneš (1884-1948), president of Czechoslovakia, 1935-1938, 1940-1945, and 1945-1948

Klement Gottwald (1896-1953), secretary general of the Communist Party of Czechoslovakia, 1929-1945, first post-World War II premier, 1946-1948, and president of Czechoslovakia, 1948-1953

Jan Masaryk (1886-1948), a leading noncommunist, son of the founder of Czechoslovakia, and foreign minister in Gottwald's cabinet

SUMMARY OF EVENT

At the end of World War I, the Treaty of Versailles of 1919 created a number of new countries in Central Europe out of the remains of the Austro-Hungarian Empire. One of these new countries was Czechoslovakia, formed out of the Czech lands previously incorporated into the German-speaking Austrian part of the empire, and Slovakia, previously part of the Hungarian part of the empire. The Czechs and the Slovaks were racially and linguistically similar, but the Czechs had more experience in self-rule and in the democratic process. Also, Czech lands—the provinces of Bohemia and Moravia—were more industrialized. In drawing the country's new boundaries, the Allied Powers included several sizable minority groupings, such as the Sudeten Germans, who were living along the borders with Germany.

Czechoslovakia's new constitution established it as a democracy, using the system of proportional representation in voting, which led to a series of coalition governments. The first president was Tomáš Masaryk, whose drive had persuaded the Allied leaders to agree to the new country. In the 1920's, the new democracy flourished both politically and economically. Czech light industrial goods found ready markets in the West, and Masaryk's statesmanship kept the center and moderate left coalition stable.

In 1921, the Social Democrats split and a Czech Communist Party (the

Young Czechs parading through Prague carrying banners depicting Czech premier Klement Gottwald (left) alongside Soviet leader Joseph Stalin. (National Archives)

Tomás Masaryk. (Library of Congress)

KSČ) was formed. Although the KSČ never became part of the ruling coalition, it nevertheless participated in parliamentary procedures and enjoyed a large membership. In 1929, Klement Gottwald became the party's secretary-general, and under him the party began to model itself more on the model of the Soviets.

In the 1930's the worldwide economic depression led to unrest. The rise of Nazi Germany, however, was much more of a threat to the stability of the small country, as the Sudeten Germans became increasingly Nazified. They had suffered economically in the various social land reforms in the 1920's, and this was used by Adolf Hitler to accuse the Czech government of oppression. In the end, Hitler demanded the incorporation of the Sudeten German lands into Germany, to which the leaders of France and Britain agreed at Munich on September 29, 1938. This capitulation disenchanted the Czechoslovaks with the Western powers.

In March, 1939, German troops occupied the remaining Czech lands, despite Masaryk's desperate attempts at diplomacy. The Slovaks, increasingly restless under the Czech majority, asked for autonomy, and the Nazis allowed them a puppet state. From this point on, the democratic republic of Czechoslovakia ceased to exist. Edvard Beneš, Masaryk's deputy, fled to London and was soon joined by other refugees and by air force officers, forming a government in exile recognized by the Allied Powers. The Communist Party leadership fled to Moscow, while a number of Czechs formed an army brigade that would fight in the Soviet Red Army.

In December, 1943, Beneš, realizing that any future government for a newly constituted Czechoslovakia would need to include communists, flew to Moscow and held talks with Gottwald. They agreed on the continuation of the democratic system that had worked well in the 1920's, except that any party that had collaborated with the Nazis was to be excluded. In effect, this eliminated all right-wing parties, reducing eligible parties in Slovakia to only two. In 1944, the Allied Powers held a summit at Yalta, in the Russian Crimea, to discuss the future of a postwar Europe. "Spheres of interest" were established, and the Soviets were allocated Eastern and Central Europe. In effect, this sealed Czechoslovakia's fate and dealt a deathblow to Masaryk's original vision of the country becoming a bridge between East and West.

The Russian army was the first to reoccupy Czechoslovak territory, advancing from the east in early 1945. Although the U.S. army reached western Czechoslovakia soon after, the Soviet armies entered Prague first and were greeted as liberators. The Czechoslovak Republic was founded April 4, 1945, and a provisional government was installed.

Political activities soon resumed. In the 1946 elections, the Communist Party did well in the Czech lands, receiving some 40 percent of the votes and emerging as the largest party, though in Slovakia, the communists were soundly defeated by the Nationalists. However, as the Slovak communists supported central government from Prague, as did all the Czech parties, a centralized government took office, with Gottwald as prime minister. His cabinet consisted of representatives of all the parties, with eight posts going to the communists. There was now effectively no opposition to the new coalition. Gottwald appointed communists to the key interior ministry, which included the police, and the information ministry, which included control of radio.

A generally socialist policy was promulgated, including land redistribution, wage equality, and nationalization of the larger industries and businesses. The new policy was beneficial to the working class, as it increased its wage level and helped it acquire land. Many working-class people joined the Communist Party, whose membership rose rapidly. A crisis soon developed between the communists and non-communists, however. The Marshall Plan was being instituted to provide U.S. aid to a devastated Europe, and Czechoslovakia was invited to send a delegation to discuss its inclusion in the plan. On orders from Moscow, though, Gottwald had to refuse the invitation, and instead, he demanded further nationalization and land reform.

The non-communist cabinet ministers tried to withstand Gottwald's demands, but by this time the trade unions were under communist control, and large-scale demonstrations were organized. "Local committees," demanded by the communists in 1945, had effectively replaced many local non-communist officials and bureaucrats with communists, so that the non-communist power base was relegated to the ballot box alone. New elections were due in May, 1948, and the non-communist ministers, hoping the party was losing popularity among the middle class, took the calculated risk of resigning en masse, hoping to force President Beneš to call elections early. Beneš, however, knew nothing of this and refused to accept their resignations or to declare early elections.

Instead, various local committee members, aided by factory-based militias, took over the ministries of those ministers who had resigned. The police, under communist leadership, made it clear they would suppress further demonstrations, and the army's general, a communist sympathizer, confined all non-communist officers to barracks. Gottwald declared a state of emergency and mobilized police forces. Beneš felt he had no option but to ask Gottwald to appoint new cabinet ministers. The list Gottwald submitted consisted almost entirely of communists. He declared on February 25, at a town square in Prague, that the Communist Party was now in charge of the government.

SIGNIFICANCE

The May, 1948, elections did take place, but voters were offered only a limited choice of candidates, all vetted by the Communist Party. However, the mood of the country was still largely sympathetic to communism and the party. The Soviets were considered liberators, and the Red Army had quickly withdrawn from the country in 1946. Memories of Western betrayal in 1938 were strong, and throughout Europe there was a strong left-wing surge, in the hope of a more just society. A new constitution was passed May 9, 1948, making Czechoslovakia a one-party state.

Beneš resigned in June and Gottwald was immediately voted in as new president by the National Assembly. In March, Jan Masaryk, the former foreign secretary and the leading noncommunist (who was also the son of Tomáš Masaryk), reportedly committed suicide, though many suspected he was assassinated. In September, Beneš died after falling ill.

Moscow soon exercised its control over Gottwald, and in the new Cold War atmosphere, compliance was absolute. Further nationalization followed, as did land reform, so that effectively the vast majority of the population was employed by the government. The army and security forces were purged of noncommunists, as was the Communist Party itself, especially whose socialist tradition was not Soviet in nature. Also purged from the party were many people who had fought with the resistance in World War II. Before the purge, the resistance made up a privileged cadre.

A five-year economic plan was implemented that shifted the economy to one of heavy industry, and all trade was directed away from the West to the Soviet Union and its satellites. Independent political opinion was suppressed, as were the independent voices of church leaders and academics, already devastated under the Nazis. The Czechoslovak experience of democracy died, and it would not be revived for another generation. In 1993, the nation divided into the Czech Republic and Slovakia.

David Barratt

FURTHER READING

Abrams, Bradley F. *The Struggle for the Soul of the Nation: Czech Culture and the Rise of Communism.* Lanham, Md.: Rowman & Littlefield, 2004. A study of the political thought that accompanied Czechoslovakia's transformation from a democratic republic to a communist state. Includes the chapters "The Reorientation of National Identity: Czechs Between East and West" and "Socialism and Communist Intellectuals: the 'Czechoslovak Road to Socialism.'"

Dowling, Maria. *Czechoslovakia.* New York: Oxford University Press, 2002. Part of the Brief Histories series, this work forms a good updated overview of Czechoslovakia's history as a nation. Includes maps, a bibliography, and an index.

Fowkes, Ben. *Eastern Europe, 1945-1969: From Stalinism to Stagnation.* New York: Longman, 2000. Provides a detailed history of Eastern Europe after World War II. Discusses the profound influence of the Soviets and of socialism on the region. Examines the formation of Czechoslovakia as a communist nation.

Gaddis, John Lewis. *We Now Know: Rethinking Cold War History.* New York: Council on Foreign Relations, 1995. Focuses on the period from the end of World War II to the Cuban Missile Crisis. Incorporates extensive research from American archives as well as archives in the former Soviet Union, Eastern Europe, and China.

Held, Joseph, ed. *The Columbia History of Eastern Europe in the Twentieth Century.* New York: Columbia University Press, 1992. Chapter four discusses Czechoslovakia in the context of twentieth-century European history. An excellent overview.

Krejí, Jaroslav, and Paul Machonin. *Czechoslovakia, 1918-1992: A Laboratory of Social Change.* New York: St. Martin's Press, 1996. Examines Czechoslovakia's attempts to solve the political and social problems endemic to Central Europe after World War I.

Leff, Carol Skalnik. *National Conflict in Czechoslovakia: The Making and Remaking of a State, 1918-1987.* Princeton, N.J.: Princeton University Press, 1988.

Discusses particularly the Czech-Slovak conflicts and how these conflicts shaped the course of Czechoslovakian history.

McMahon, Robert J. *The Cold War: A Very Short Introduction.* New York: Oxford University Press, 2003. Broad, accessible overview of the Cold War that covers key events and themes. Contains illustrations, maps, and index.

Stone, Norman, and Eduard Strouhal, eds. *Czechoslovakia: Crossroads and Crises, 1918-88.* New York: St. Martin's Press, 1989. Chapters nine through eleven examine the transformation of Czechoslovakia into a communist nation in 1948. Written by leading Czech historians under the editorship of a respected modern historian of Europe.

SEE ALSO: Feb. 4-11, 1945: Yalta Conference; July 17-Aug. 2, 1945: Potsdam Conference; May 14, 1955: Warsaw Pact Is Signed; Oct. 23-Nov. 10, 1956: Soviets Crush Hungarian Uprising; Dec. 3, 1963: Havel's *The Garden Party* Satirizes Life Under Communism; Aug. 20-21, 1968: Soviet Union Invades Czechoslovakia; Nov. 12, 1968-Dec., 1989: Brezhnev Doctrine Mandates Soviet Control of Satellite Nations; Nov. 17-Dec. 29, 1989: Velvet Revolution in Czechoslovakia; Feb. 26, 1990: Soviet Troops Withdraw from Czechoslovakia.

■ **APRIL 3, 1948**

MARSHALL PLAN PROVIDES AID TO EUROPE

The Marshall Plan was an American economic aid program for Europe. Meant both to relieve suffering resulting from World War II's economic devastation and to contain the Soviet Union by strengthening Western Europe's ability to resist Soviet expansion, the plan was largely successful on both counts.

ALSO KNOWN AS: European Recovery Program; European Recovery Act of 1948

LOCALE: United States; Western Europe

CATEGORIES: Diplomacy and international relations; economics; banking and finance

KEY FIGURES

George C. Marshall (1880-1959), U.S. secretary of state, 1947-1949

George F. Kennan (1904-2005), U.S. State Department's director of policy planning, 1947-1949

Harry S. Truman (1884-1972), president of the United States, 1945-1953
Ernest Bevin (1881-1951), British foreign minister, 1945-1951
Joseph Stalin (Joseph Vissarionovich Dzhugashvili; 1878-1953), general
    secretary of the Central Committee of the Communist Party of the
    Soviet Union, 1922-1953, and premier, 1941-1953
Vyacheslav Mikhailovich Molotov (Vyacheslav Mikhailovich Skryabin; 1890-
    1986), Soviet commissar of foreign affairs, 1939-1949 and 1953-1956

SUMMARY OF EVENT

In the winter of 1946-1947, European nations struggled to recover from the widespread devastation of World War II. The conflict had leveled cities, destroyed thousands of factories, disrupted transportation and communication systems, and rendered machinery for extracting raw materials useless. The European standard of living had fallen drastically below prewar levels, even in nations that had not borne the brunt of the fighting. In the spring of 1947, two million British industrial workers were unemployed, and many others were underemployed because of shortages in raw materials. In Italy, industrial production stood at 20 percent of prewar levels. In Germany's Ruhr region, coal production had dropped to 45 percent of its previous level, and similar declines elsewhere affected industrial production and transportation systems throughout Europe. Millions of homeless and displaced citizens strained the existing social services beyond their limits.

The unusually severe European winter of 1946-1947 exacerbated the hardships brought through war. Food shortages existed in most nations and, consequently, food rationing was widely instituted. Politically, France and Italy faced growing leftist movements whose popularity increased as a result of these economic hardships. European governments that had managed vast colonial regions before the war could no longer adequately manage even their internal affairs. These harsh conditions produced despondency that only increased the nations' economic problems.

European industrial workers witnessed a diminished standard of living, as postwar inflation significantly outpaced wage increases. Worker productivity declined. Farmers, unable to purchase fertilizer and farm equipment, converted their fields to pastureland, resulting in a sharp decrease in agricultural productivity. Meanwhile, although the United States had lost many soldiers and much wartime equipment, the land and its civilian population had been left untouched by the destruction of World War II. The U.S. economic picture was therefore one of prosperity and rapid growth. Despite a large postwar debt, the economy quickly responded to the release of pent-up demand for goods and services following the war. There was, however, concern within the government about the postwar settlement in Europe and particularly about the Soviet role and influence in Europe.

Soviet positions on the withdrawal of their forces from countries such as Iran, on the nature of Eastern European governments, and on war reparations from Germany created apprehension within the administration of President Harry S. Truman. Political unrest on the fringes of Europe, especially in Greece and Turkey, became America's concern after the United Kingdom took the position that it could no longer afford to aid those countries' governments against communist-backed guerrilla insurgencies. Truman addressed Congress on March 12, 1947, in an appeal for more than $300 million in aid to these nations. The occasion marked the inauguration of what became known as the Truman Doctrine, which committed the United States to defend governments throughout the world when they were threatened with communist subversion.

The open-ended nature of Truman's commitment to fight communist insurgency internationally left many in Congress and the State Department bewildered, since militarily the United States had demobilized and was in no position to make such a global military commitment. Within the State Department, moreover, diplomats had already begun to formulate the concept that in the looming East-West conflict, American economic power would prove to be the decisive factor. In the same month Truman made his speech, the newly appointed secretary of state, General George C. Marshall, led an American delegation to the Moscow Conference of Allied Leaders to negotiate the future of Germany. After weeks of futile discussions, Marshall on April 15 took the American proposals directly to Joseph Stalin, the Soviet premier.

Since he had known Stalin during the war and had earned the premier's respect, Marshall believed that personal diplomacy had a reasonable chance of success. He found Stalin polite but vague and noncommittal, however, and he left the meeting with the view that Stalin saw no need for compromise. The Soviet leader seemed to think that time was on his side in Europe. After returning to the United States, Marshall established a strategic think tank within the State Department called the Policy Planning Staff. The staff was headed by George F. Kennan, who had recently earned recognition in the inner circles of government as an expert on the Soviet Union. Within eight weeks, the staff produced a general policy statement that addressed the economic crisis in Europe.

Kennan's policy statement proposed to return the European standard of living to its prewar level and to ensure that the European economic system would be capable of sustained growth. The idea was to work in cooperation with existing European governments by offering aid that would restore a measure of prosperity—not by providing direct relief to suffering people but by attacking the problems of those people through improving their national economies. Not content to require government-to-government cooperation between the United States and other nations, moreover, the policy makers devised a procedure that would require a measure of cooperation among the European nations themselves.

On June 5, General Marshall, in a commencement address at Harvard University, delivered the essence of the Marshall Plan. Since he had the complete confidence of the president, Marshall made the proposal on his own without prior clearance. After describing the effects of war on European economies—pointing out that food and fuel shortages in European cities

---

TRUMAN CALLS FOR THE MARSHALL PLAN

U.S. president Harry S. Truman signed the European Recovery Act, better known as the Marshall Plan, in 1948. In a message to Congress on December 19, 1947, Truman outlined his rationale for the plan.

In considering the requirements for the rehabilitation of Europe, the physical loss of life, the visible destruction of cities, factories, mines, and railroads was correctly estimated, but it has become obvious during recent months that this visible destruction was probably less serious than the dislocation of the entire fabric of European economy. For the past 10 years conditions have been highly abnormal. The feverish maintenance of the war effort engulfed all aspects of national economics. Machinery has fallen into disrepair or is entirely obsolete. Under the arbitrary and destructive Nazi rule, virtually every possible enterprise was geared into the German war machine. Long-standing commercial ties, private institutions, banks, insurance companies and shipping companies disappeared, through the loss of capital, absorption through nationalization or by simple destruction. In many countries, confidence in the local currency has been severely shaken. The breakdown of the business structure of Europe during the war was complete. . . .

Aside from the demoralizing effect on the world at large and the possibilities of disturbances arising as a result of the desperation of the people concerned, the consequences to the economy of the United States should be apparent to all. It is logical that the United States should do whatever it is able to do to assist in the return of normal economic health in the world, without which there can be no political stability and no assured peace. Our policy is directed not against any country or doctrine but against hunger, poverty, desperation, and chaos. Its purpose should be the revival of working economy in the world so as to permit the emergence of political and social conditions in which free institutions can exist.

General George C. Marshall. (Library of Congress)

were severe and people there were badly undernourished—he proposed that the United States should aid all European nations, even those in Eastern Europe, provided that they presented a joint plan clarifying their needs and explaining their priorities. From the American standpoint, this proposal had the advantage of avoiding a piecemeal economic solution that evaluated the needs of each nation on an ad hoc basis. It also required a degree of cooperation among European nations that Americans believed essential to Europe's long-term economic health.

In response to Marshall's proposal, Ernest Bevin, the British foreign minister, arranged a meeting of European ministers to plan a response. Nothing in Marshall's speech excluded the Soviet Union or its satellites, and at the first European planning session in June the Soviets were represented by Vyacheslav Mikhailovich Molotov, the Soviet foreign minister. However, rather than disclose details of their national economic condition and needs, the Soviets quickly withdrew from the meeting, as the Americans, British, and French had hoped they would. After long negotiations, which were made more difficult by the concerns of France over the inclusion of aid to West Germany, the European nations presented a plan to the United States. Following revisions suggested by American officials, the plan became the basis for the European Recovery Act of 1948.

The act created the European Recovery Program (ERP), popularly known as the Marshall Plan, providing approximately $13.3 billion over a period of four years for European economic relief in seventeen nations. Since the American federal budget was less than $100 billion at the time, this sum represented a substantial commitment. Over the nearly four years of the plan's existence, the aid provided to Europe annually amounted to 1.2 percent of the total U.S. gross national product (GNP).

Once the ERP had been formulated, the president, the cabinet, and many other officials threw their support behind it. The program provided that most food, raw materials, and machinery would be purchased in America and thus promised a substantial increase in American exports. For this reason, the program also found widespread support among business and agricultural leaders. Many political leaders viewed it as a means of containing communism through the use of American economic strength. Their reasoning became more compelling after heavy-handed Soviet intervention and repression in Czechoslovakia in the fall of 1947. Polls taken at the time, however, showed that a majority of the American people supported the ERP primarily on humanitarian grounds. Whatever the reason, Congress was swayed, and the European Recovery Act passed overwhelmingly on April 3, 1948.

SIGNIFICANCE

The Marshall Plan had a significant impact on European economic and cultural history, although scholars continue to disagree about the precise nature of that impact. For one thing, economic results varied considerably from nation to nation. During its first year, the ERP added more than 10 percent to the GNP of two nations, Austria and the Netherlands, and more than 5 percent to the GNP in five other nations, France, Iceland, Ireland, Italy, and Norway. In nations that suffered acute food shortages—West Germany, Austria, and the United Kingdom—more than one-third of Marshall Plan aid went for food supplies. In other nations, funding for raw materials, energy, and machinery surpassed that for food imports.

By bringing significant quantities of American capital and goods into Europe, the ERP contributed to a 32 percent rise in the GNP of the participating nations between 1948 and 1951. Food rationing disappeared, and the standard of living rose rapidly throughout the four years of the program. By 1950, most European nations had exceeded their prewar agricultural production levels. The ERP stimulated American investments and influence in Europe. American corporate investments increased more than twice as rapidly in Europe as in any other area. In addition to the large exports of machinery and supplies, the United States sent thousands of experts overseas. A major objective of the plan was to increase the productivity of the economies by increasing their efficiency. In the American view, it was necessary to increase efficiency, which lagged far behind that of the United States, in order to prevent a rapid rise in inflation while external aid was stimulating economic growth.

The Marshall Plan aided people indirectly, using a systems approach, and its objectives were for the long term. By providing raw materials from the United States for British factories, it enabled British workers to remain productively employed. Through promoting a fourfold increase in the number of tractors in France, it contributed to the elimination of hunger in France and in other countries as well. Through providing the machinery and transportation necessary for German coal production, it ensured that affordable energy was available during periods of inclement weather. By making labor more efficient, American experts helped retard inflation during a period of economic expansion, thus enabling European workers to retain their purchasing power.

From a broader policy perspective, the American consultants sought to decrease the power of industrial cartels, to increase the productive efficiency of European workers, and to promote free trade. These objectives were partially achieved, though the measure of success depended heavily on conditions in each nation. West Germany, for example, was still under American military government, so breaking the power of cartels in that country was relatively easy.

The ERP was by no means the sole cause of European postwar recovery, for economies as depressed as those of Europe were almost certain to improve, given existing conditions. Most scholars agree, however, that the ERP provided a powerful stimulus that hastened the recovery and alleviated human suffering. In addition, American influence furthered policies that American politicians believed were in the interest of the long-term economic health of the region. Politically, in nation after nation, economic resurgence had the effects that American planners had desired. As hopes for prosperity became reality, elections produced centrist and rightist governments at the expense of communists and their allies. Although these governments did not invariably assure all the freedoms found in the United States, they provided greater freedoms to their citizens than did the governments of Eastern Bloc nations. On the whole, they preserved freedoms of speech, religion, and the press.

In this respect, the ERP contributed to the American Cold War policy of containment and to the American view of a world order that assured fundamental political and economic freedoms. In another respect, the ERP benefited both the United States and Europe by establishing a mode of cooperation that made mutual defense more palatable. The cooperation and mutual planning mandated by the ERP contributed significantly to the formation of the North Atlantic Treaty Organization (NATO) in 1949. On the downside, the ERP leaders tacitly acknowledged the split in Europe between West and East that prompted the Soviet government to consolidate Eastern Europe into its own economic and defense plans and to refuse the extension of Marshall Plan benefits to areas under its control.

Stanley Archer

FURTHER READING

Bonds, John Bledsoe. *Bipartisan Strategy: Selling the Marshall Plan*. Westport, Conn.: Praeger, 2002. Study of the U.S. domestic campaign to convince Congress to pass the Economic Recovery Act. Bibliographic references and index.

Gaddis, John Lewis. *The Cold War: A New History*. New York: Penguin, 2005. A noted historian presents a concise overview of the Cold War, covering its origins, ideologies, and technologies.

Gimbel, John. *The Origins of the Marshall Plan*. Stanford, Calif.: Stanford University Press, 1976. This analytical book traces the origins of the ERP to American policy makers and to specific postwar events. Gimbel sees the East-West conflict as a minor influence on the development and implementation of the Marshall Plan. Includes notes on unpublished sources, extensive notes on published sources, and a good index.

Hogan, Michael J. *The Marshall Plan: America, Britain, and the Reconstruction of Western Europe, 1947-1952*. New York: Cambridge University Press, 1987. In his carefully researched and comprehensive analysis of the ERP, Hogan takes into account the arguments of its critics and concludes that it achieved its major economic and political purposes. Very extensive but unannotated bibliography. Good index.

Mee, Charles L., Jr. *The Marshall Plan: The Launching of the Pax Americana*. New York: Simon & Schuster, 1984. Mee provides a clearly written and balanced account of the formulation and adoption of the Marshall Plan, incorporating data and figures into the text. For the average reader, this book is perhaps the best introduction to the subject. Offers two useful appendixes including Truman's address and Marshall's Harvard speech as well as notes, bibliography, and index.

Milward, Alan S. *The Reconstruction of Western Europe, 1945-1951*. Berkeley: University of California Press, 1984. A detailed study of all aspects of the European economic recovery, the book provides numerous tables showing progress of the recovery in detail. Milward gives the background of the Marshall Plan and assesses its effects. Useful bibliography focuses on international sources. Brief index.

Pogue, Forrest C. *George C. Marshall: Statesman, 1945-1959.* New York: Viking Press, 1987. The fourth and final volume of the standard biography of Marshall, it gives an account of the formulation of the ERP. Pogue clarifies Marshall's contribution, differentiating it from the roles of other prominent diplomats and officials. Useful appendix, bibliography, notes, and index. Illustrated.

Price, Harry Bayard. *The Marshall Plan and Its Meaning.* Ithaca, N.Y.: Cornell University Press, 1955. A general and optimistic study of the ERP and its effects, the book places the Marshall Plan within the context of American aid throughout the world. Although many of Price's findings encountered later challenges, this early volume is still useful. Bibliographic references and index.

Schain, Martin, ed. *The Marshall Plan: Fifty Years Later.* New York: Palgrave, 2001. Compilation of essays devoted to revisiting the ERP, both to reevaluate its effects at the time and to examine its long-term impact on the Cold War and European economic history. Bibliographic references and index.

Thompson, Nicholas. *The Hawk and the Dove: Paul Nitze, George Kennan, and the History of the Cold War.* New York: Henry Holt, 2009. Profiles two highly influential figures in American foreign policy: Nitze helped drive the arms race, while his friend and rival Kennan advocated containment. Illustrated.

Wexler, Imanuel. *The Marshall Plan Revisited: The European Recovery Program in Economic Perspective.* Westport, Conn.: Greenwood Press, 1983. Wexler places the Marshall Plan in broad economic context and traces factors other than American aid that promoted or hindered economic recovery. His assessment finds that the ERP achieved a large measure of success. Good notes, usefully divided bibliography, and brief index.

SEE ALSO: Mar. 12, 1947: Truman Doctrine; Jan. 25, 1949: Soviet Bloc States Establish Council for Mutual Economic Assistance; Apr. 4, 1949: North Atlantic Treaty Organization Is Formed; July 1, 1950: European Payments Union Is Formed; Oct. 22, 1951: United States Inaugurates Mutual Security Program; Mar. 7, 1966: France Withdraws from NATO's Military Structure; Nov. 12, 1968-Dec., 1989: Brezhnev Doctrine Mandates Soviet Control of Satellite Nations.

JUNE 24, 1948-MAY 11, 1949

BERLIN BLOCKADE AND AIRLIFT

Faced with Soviet attempts to cut off West Berlin from the Western Allies' zones in Germany, the United States and Great Britain responded with an airlift, delivering more than 1.5 million tons of food and supplies to the city.

LOCALE: Berlin, Germany
CATEGORY: Diplomacy and international relations

KEY FIGURES

Joseph Stalin (Joseph Vissarionovich Dzhugashvili; 1878-1953), general
     secretary of the Central Committee of the Communist Party of the
     Soviet Union, 1922-1953, and premier, 1941-1953
Harry S. Truman (1884-1972), president of the United States, 1945-1953
Lucius DuBignon Clay (1897-1978), U.S. military governor in Germany and
     commander of U.S. forces in Europe
George C. Marshall (1880-1959), U.S. secretary of state, 1947-1949
Ernst Reuter (1889-1953), lord mayor of West Berlin

SUMMARY OF EVENT

The most important and dramatic confrontation between the United States and the Soviet Union in the formative period of the Cold War was the blockade of Berlin and the resulting airlift. The Soviet challenge to the West's rights of access to Berlin seems to have been designed not only to expel the Western powers from the former German capital but also to prevent the creation of a workable West German government. President Harry S. Truman, General George C. Marshall, and General Lucius DuBignon Clay, however, recognized that the continued Western presence in Berlin was a test of the determination of the Western powers regarding the German question. Therefore, they made it clear that the United States would not submit to Stalin's demands.

The problem in Berlin arose from the wartime agreements among the Allies for the postwar administration of Germany. Zones of occupation were agreed upon for Germany itself. Although Berlin was deep within the Soviet zone, each of the Allies controlled a sector in Berlin. U.S., British, and French authorities dutifully assumed their responsibilities in the ruined capital, seeking to cooperate with the Soviet authorities in the Allied Control Council (for all of Germany) and the Kommandatura (for Berlin). Soviet obstructionism, however, convinced U.S. leaders that the Soviet Union sought to dominate all of Berlin and eventually, the whole of Germany. The climax of this struggle was the municipal election of October 20, 1946, in greater Berlin. The result was an overwhelming victory for the Social Democrats and defeat for the Soviet-backed Socialist Unity Party. Soviet-inspired political and economic pressure on Berlin increased during 1947.

In early 1948, Great Britain and the United States developed plans to merge their two zones in western Germany economically, and the French were encouraged to cooperate. The Soviet Union protested these actions bitterly and responded by putting more economic pressure on the western sectors of Berlin. A communist coup in Czechoslovakia in February, 1948, incurred Western suspicions of Soviet intentions in Germany. In March, the London Conference (which included the United States, the United Kingdom, France, Holland, Belgium, and Luxembourg) recommended that West Germany be united to form a federal state and that it take part in the Marshall Plan of economic recovery. In response, the Soviet Union withdrew its representatives from the Allied Control Council in Berlin. On April 1, the Soviet Union began the "small Berlin blockade," by restricting land access and deliveries of food and fuel to Berlin.

U.S. leaders realized that should the Soviets cordon off Berlin entirely, the situation of the city's inhabitants and the token Western garrisons would be desperate. The Western sectors were entirely dependent upon provisions shipped in by rail, truck, and canal. There was no written agreement guaranteeing free access to Berlin by surface transportation, merely oral understandings. There was a specific agreement on air access between Berlin and West Germany, but few people believed that the needs of 2,250,000 people could be met by air transport alone.

Aware of the West's dilemma, the Soviets pushed forward with plans to isolate the city. Apparently, their goal was to discourage the economic and political unification of West Germany, and eventually to take control of Berlin, by demonstrating that the Western powers were unwilling or unable to protect their rights. The Western powers nevertheless went ahead with economic and currency reform in their zones of Germany, introducing the deutsche mark to replace the worthlessly inflated old currency, beginning on June 20, 1948. The full-scale Soviet blockade of West Berlin followed on June 24.

General Clay organized an immediate but modest airlift to keep the Western garrisons supplied, and he returned to Washington, D.C., to consult with President Truman in July. Clay favored forcing the issue with the Soviet Union by sending an armed transport convoy along the main highway from western Germany into the city. Secretary of State George Marshall favored an expanded airlift instead, coupled with a direct but informal approach to Stalin. Truman decided on the airlift rather than the armed convoy, and he told the U.S. ambassador in Moscow to contact Joseph Stalin, the Soviet dictator.

An airlift to ferry all necessary supplies for more than 2 million people was a most difficult undertaking. The logistic triumph would have proven fruitless if it had not been for the dogged determination of the people of West Berlin. Berliners knew Soviet troops could take over the city in a few hours. The Western allies had only sixty-five hundred combat troops in Berlin to face more than three hundred thousand troops in the Soviet zone. However, the Berliners refused to give in to fear, hunger, or discouragement. In December, Ernst Reuter, a Social Democrat and staunch opponent of communist rule, was elected lord mayor of West Berlin. During the blockade, many noncommunist professors abandoned Humboldt University in the Soviet sector and, with aid from the United States, established the Free University of Berlin in the U.S. sector. Reuter's leadership and the Free University became rallying points for the Berliners, strengthening their resolve.

The airlift proved more and more successful. Tons of fuel and food staples, and enough luxuries such as fish, coffee, and children's candies, arrived each day to buoy popular spirits. Politically, the blockade and airlift brought unintended and unwelcome results for the Soviet Union. Rather

Planes carrying supplies into Berlin unloading cargo at Tempelhof Airport. (Smithsonian Institution)

than forcing a humiliating retreat on the Western powers, the blockade showed the West to be a solid ally of the Berliners, willing to pay any price to save the people from either Soviet domination or war. West Germany continued on its way to becoming a unified state and eventually an ally of the North Atlantic Treaty Organization, rather than merely a conquered enemy. Truman, who was facing a difficult election campaign at home, emerged as a hero, willing to face up to communist threats without actually going to war. He not only ordered the full power of U.S. transport aircraft into the airlift but also moved B-29 bombers, capable of carrying atomic weapons, to British bases within range of Moscow. Soviet attempts to intimidate the U.S. and British fliers on airlift duty by holding "air maneuvers" along the approaches to the West Berlin airfields were brushed aside, and deliveries continued to increase, even in the bad winter weather.

At the same time, Truman made behind-the-scenes diplomatic efforts in an attempt to bring an end to the crisis. In August, 1948, the U.S. ambassador in Moscow spoke directly to Stalin about Berlin. At times, Stalin appeared reasonable, remarking that the United States and the Soviet Union were still allies. At other times, Stalin seemed elusive and belligerent, and Truman commented privately in September that he feared that the United States and the Soviet Union were slipping toward war.

By February, 1949, it had become clear that the Western powers could sustain the airlift indefinitely and that the blockade was driving the Germans into the arms of the West. Stalin hinted to a Western newsman that he was willing to give up his objections to the use of the West German deutsche mark in West Berlin and eventually drop the blockade. Soviet and U.S. diplomats soon began meeting secretly at the United Nations in New York.

In early May, the secret talks at the United Nations were nearing successful completion. Simultaneously, the West German parliamentary council was moving toward approval of the constitutional document that would establish the Federal Republic of Germany. On May 10, 1949, the Soviets published the orders for lifting their restrictions, and the next day, electrical power began flowing into West Berlin from East German power plants. The gates were lifted and the Berlin blockade was over. The airlift had lasted a total of 321 days, from June 24, 1948, until May 11, 1949, and brought into Berlin 1,592,787 tons of supplies.

SIGNIFICANCE

The achievements of the airlift were not without cost. It was a heavy burden for U.S. and British taxpayers—approximately $200 million—and the Berliners had to make do with very short rations. Moreover, accidental deaths did occur. Twenty-four planes crashed, and seventy-six persons lost their lives.

144

Although additional Berlin crises would occur, including the building of the Berlin Wall in 1961, the Berlin blockade and the airlift response had been a clear turning point in the history of post-World War II Europe. War had been avoided, the Soviet Union was forced to back down, and West Germany and West Berlin were clearly linked to the United States and Western Europe for the remainder of the Cold War. In addition, the United States had solidified its role as a world power willing to commit its resources to the advancement of democracy.

Theodore A. Wilson and Gordon R. Mork

FURTHER READING

Clay, Lucius D. *Decision in Germany.* Garden City, N.Y.: Doubleday, 1950. The U.S. commander in Germany recounts his personal experiences.

Ferrell, Robert H. *George C. Marshall.* Vol. 15 in *The American Secretaries of State and Their Diplomacy.* New York: Cooper Square, 1966. An exhaustive study of Marshall's tenure at the Department of State. The author relies on memoirs and other published information for most of his information.

Grathwol, Robert P., and Donita M. Moorhus. *American Forces in Berlin: Cold War Outpost, 1945-1994.* Washington, D.C.: Department of Defense, 1994. Partly a commemorative booklet, partly an illustrated documentary history, this well-illustrated book adds significant details to the U.S. achievements in Berlin.

McCullough, David. *Truman.* New York: Simon & Schuster, 1992. Portrays Truman's staunch response to the Berlin blockade crisis as one of the finest aspects of his presidency. Puts the whole matter into the context of U.S. political history.

Miller, Roger G. *To Save a City: The Berlin Airlift, 1948-1949.* College Station: Texas A&M University Press, 2000. Reveals both the airlift's local, operational details and its global, geopolitical ramifications, drawing on formerly classified documents. Bibliographic references and index.

Powaski, Ronald E. *The Cold War: The United States and the Soviet Union, 1917-1991.* New York: Oxford University Press, 1998. Traces the roots of the Cold War to czarist Russia and early America and contends that each nation's psychology led to the decades-long conflict.

Sewell, Mike. *The Cold War.* Cambridge, U.K.: Cambridge University Press, 2002. Concise introductory text that also covers the historiography of the Cold War. Contains illustrations and maps.

Shlaim, Avi. *The United States and the Berlin Blockade, 1948-1949: A Study in Crisis Decision-Making.* Berkeley: University of California Press, 1983. A scholarly analysis of United States decision making, step by step, during the crises of the blockade and airlift.

Tusa, Ann, and John Tusa. *The Berlin Airlift.* New York: Atheneum, 1988. A well-documented narrative account of the blockade and the airlift within the context of Cold War diplomacy.

SEE ALSO: July 17-Aug. 2, 1945: Potsdam Conference; Feb. 25, 1948: Communists Seize Power in Czechoslovakia; 1949-1961: East Germans Flee to West to Escape Communist Regime; Sept. 21-Oct. 7, 1949: Germany Splits into Two Republics; Aug. 13, 1961: Communists Raise the Berlin Wall; June 21, 1973: East and West Germany Establish Diplomatic Relations; Nov. 9, 1989: Fall of the Berlin Wall; July 16, 1990: Gorbachev Agrees to Membership of a United Germany in NATO.

■ OCTOBER 6, 1948

EARTHQUAKE DEVASTATES ASHGABAT AND KILLS UP TO 100,000 PEOPLE

A magnitude 7.3 earthquake leveled Ashgabat, the capital of the Turkmen Soviet Socialist Republic (later Turkmenistan) killing between 70,000 and 100,000 people. The scope of the disaster remained unknown outside Central Asia until 1973, when archival records were unsealed by local officials.

LOCALE: Ashgabat, Turkmen Soviet Socialist Republic, Soviet Union (now Ashkhabad, Turkmenistan)

CATEGORIES: Disasters; government and politics

KEY FIGURES

Joseph Stalin (Joseph Vissarionovich Dzhugashvili; 1878-1953), general secretary of the Central Committee of the Communist Party of the Soviet Union, 1922-1953, and premier, 1941-1953

S. Batirova (fl. mid-twentieth century), first secretary of the Communist Party of the Turkmen Soviet Socialist Republic, 1948

Saparmurat Niyazov (1940-2006), president of Turkmenistan, 1991-2006

SUMMARY OF EVENT

Ashgabat, capital of Turkmenistan, lies at the foot of the Kopet-Dag mountain range near the border with Iran, in a geologically unstable, earthquake-prone area. Ashgabat was founded as a czarist outpost in 1881 and grew without reference to local conditions. During World War II, evacuees from the war zone swelled the population to an estimated 150,000 people, most of whom lived in hastily built single-story houses of unreinforced brick and stone, with heavy roofs of packed clay. Schools, hospitals, and other public buildings also suffered from shoddy construction during wartime. Existing seismic standards, seldom met, greatly underestimated the earthquake danger. A 1929 quake had caused significant property damage, but the fault zone had been unusually inactive, a sign, perhaps, of an impending catastrophe.

Disaster struck at 1:17 A.M. on October 6, 1948. The few people awake at this time heard an ominous rumbling from the mountains, followed immediately by violent vertical shaking. Two strong shocks seconds apart reduced Ashgabat to rubble. No one had time to escape from collapsing buildings. Many of the survivors, conditioned by propaganda in the acute early phase of the Cold War, thought that the city had been hit by an American atomic bomb.

The quake severed all communications with the outside world. Hospitals, clinics, and pharmacies lay in ruins. In the first few hours, surviving uninjured members of the city's emergency services struggled heroically in darkness to render aid. Doctors, many of whom had served in war, retrieved equipment from the ruins and set up an emergency station in Karl Marx Square. By afternoon, reinforcements and supplies arrived from Tashkent and Baku. The sheer number of casualties, however, and the inherent difficulty of evacuating gravely wounded people, meant that aid came too late for many. Half of an estimated thirty thousand people with life-threatening injuries died from lack of prompt attention.

Immediately after the quake, city workers converged on the damaged central headquarters of the Communist Party, where after hastily consulting with the party's first secretary, S. Batirova, they commandeered an undamaged automobile and drove northward to a functioning telephone line. Soldiers stationed at the airport used an aircraft radio to contact Baku and Sverdlovsk. It was many hours before any details reached areas from which aid could be dispatched. Once aid was forthcoming, multiple impediments hindered delivery. The railway station was in ruins, tracks were blocked, the airport control tower was destroyed, and the airport and roads could not handle heavy traffic.

The precise death toll will never be known with certainty. Estimates range from a low of 400, postulated by *Nature* magazine in 1948, to a high of 110,000. The dead were buried in mass graves, and were not counted or identified. There were roughly 50,000 survivors, suggesting a death toll of 80,000 to 100,000, or about two-thirds of the population.

Like the enormous initial death toll, an inadequate emergency response was probably unavoidable in the poorest part of a country just emerging

147

from long years of war. As days progressed, however, the response from the rest of the Soviet Union became more and more problematic. On October 7, *Pravda* printed a brief article stating only that geologists at the Russian Academy of Sciences had detected a strong earthquake. Subsequently, there were reports of supply shipments and of the evacuation of the wounded, but no mention of the scope of devastation or the number of casualties. The international press used *Pravda*'s limited and incorrect reportage about the quake as the source for their own news reports.

A conspiracy of silence followed the destruction of Ashgabat. Most histories and almanacs of natural disasters omit the quake entirely. Soviet propaganda of the 1950's praised reconstruction efforts that used designs lacking seismological standards. A Soviet journalist who visited the city in 1953 later described being forbidden to photograph the omnipresent ruins or to report a march of weeping survivors to the mass graves on the outskirts of the city. Only in 1973, on the twenty-fifth anniversary of the event, did officials in Turkmenistan begin to open sealed archives and acknowledge the terrible calamity.

The silence accompanying the earthquake and its devastation is puzzling. The earthquake occurred during an acute phase of the Cold War, when both sides were eager not to expose their strategic vulnerabilities. However, the destruction of Ashgabat neither compromised the Soviet Union's defense system nor revealed grave internal weaknesses. Silence did nothing to improve domestic morale in Russia, and it created widespread resentment in Central Asia. Internationally the Soviet Union could have gained propaganda points by publicizing the disaster and then criticizing the lack of response from the West.

Soviet officials lived in fear of initiative-taking in 1948. Joseph Stalin's iron grip on the country, secured by sweeping purges, rewarded silence and timidity. The people responsible for aid to Ashgabat could not act on their own, and they risked incurring the deadly displeasure of a dictator if they approached him with a problem that could reflect badly on socialism and Stalin's leadership. The timidity surrounding the disaster snowballed; no one was willing to admit publicly that national response to an overwhelming natural disaster was so inadequate. Until Stalin's death in 1953, referencing the event was considered a dangerous move.

Soviet Central Asia—isolated, predominantly Muslim, with no history of emigration—had no advocates in the Western world. Consequently, even when the region became open to Westerners during perestroika, there were no efforts to raise awareness of the catastrophe nor to obtain the financial aid that undoubtedly is still needed decades after the disaster.

Silence translated into slow reconstruction. Having learned a bitter lesson, local planners insisted on seismologically sound building practices. Because they were in effect building a new city, planners could be innovative, if allowed to be. Reconstruction, however, would be expensive. The central Soviet government assigned low priority to erasing the scars of a disaster it never fully acknowledged. Substantial portions of the city remain in ruins, and a significant portion of the population still lives in temporary, or inadequate and unsafe, dwellings.

Turkmenistan's independence in 1992 brought a totalitarian government, which seems to be erasing or stalling what social and economic progress was made in the country under Soviet rule. Were an earthquake of comparable magnitude to strike the region, cities, structurally, would be far less vulnerable. The social infrastructure, however, especially emergency medical response, remains seriously weak after more than a decade of misadministration by the new government.

SIGNIFICANCE

The physical destruction and loss of life in the Ashgabat earthquake stunted development in the Turkmen Republic for decades. The psychological effects of not only the event but also the long period of silence and denial that followed shaped Turkmen national consciousness in ways that are difficult to quantify but undoubtedly significant.

A feeling of abandonment and lack of recognition fed the extreme, paranoid nationalism of Turkmenistan's dictator Saparmurat Niyazov. Niyazov lost his entire family in the 1948 earthquake; one can only speculate how years of living in denial of the central tragedy in one's life while being educated in Russia helped shape the leader.

Martha A. Sherwood

FURTHER READING

Abazov, Rafis. *Historical Dictionary of Turkmenistan.* Lanham, Md.: Scarecrow Press, 2005. The entry on Ashgabat devotes a half page to the quake and reconstruction, and lists the death toll at thirty thousand.

Bolt, Bruce A. *Earthquakes.* 5th ed. New York: W. H. Freeman, 2004. A standard textbook with descriptions of the geophysics of earthquakes and principles of antiseismological structural engineering. The Ashgabat earthquake is omitted from a table of worldwide historical disasters.

Nikonov, A. A. *Ashkhabadskoe Zemlietriasenie: Problemy I Reshenie Polvieka.* (Ashkhabad earthquake: problems and resolutions of half a century). Ashgabat, Turkmenistan, 1998. Discusses casualty estimates, faulty construction, reconstruction efforts, and means of avoiding future disasters. The author is a seismologist specializing in earthquake prediction.

_____. *Khronika Ashkhabadskoi Katastrophy.* (Chronicle of the Ashkhabad catastrophe). Ashgabat, Turkmenistan, 1998. Chronological account of the disaster, with quotes from eyewitnesses.

Skosirev, P. *Soviet Turkmenistan.* Moscow: Foreign Languages Publishing House, 1956. Propaganda notable for referring to reconstruction but omitting all other mention of the disaster. Useful historical background.

SEE ALSO: Jan. 25, 1949: Soviet Bloc States Establish Council for Mutual Economic Assistance; June 27, 1954: Soviet Union Completes Its First Nuclear Power Plant; Nov. 12, 1968-Dec., 1989: Brezhnev Doctrine Mandates Soviet Control of Satellite Nations; Nov. 11, 1970: Moscow Human Rights Committee Is Founded.

■ **DECEMBER 10, 1948**

UNITED NATIONS ADOPTS THE UNIVERSAL DECLARATION OF HUMAN RIGHTS

The United Nations' Universal Declaration of Human Rights was the first major document to provide a comprehensive and authoritative statement of international human rights norms.

ALSO KNOWN AS: International Bill of Human Rights
LOCALE: New York, New York
CATEGORIES: United Nations; human rights

KEY FIGURES
Eleanor Roosevelt (1884-1962), U.S. delegate to and chair of the U.N. Commission on Human Rights
John Humphrey (1905-1995), director of the Division of Human Rights and a principal author of the declaration
René Cassin (1887-1976), French delegate to the U.N. Commission on Human Rights and a principal author of the declaration
Charles Habib Malik (1906-1987), Lebanese representative to and rapporteur of the U.N. Commission on Human Rights
P. C. Chang (1892-1957), Chinese representative to and vice-chair of the U.N. Commission on Human Rights

SUMMARY OF EVENT

The United Nations Charter includes the promotion of human rights and fundamental freedoms among the principal purposes of the organization. It does not, however, specify their substance. One of the principal human rights contributions of the United Nations has been to forge an international normative consensus on a list of human rights. The central expression of that consensus is the Universal Declaration of Human Rights, adopted by the General Assembly on December 10, 1948.

The U.N. Commission on Human Rights, a permanent functional commission of the Economic and Social Council (ECOSOC), was given principal responsibility for drafting an international human rights covenant (treaty). The commission decided to prepare a nonbinding declaration as quickly as possible. This became the Universal Declaration. Meanwhile, work continued on the more difficult and more controversial task of producing a binding treaty, which was finally completed in 1966, in the form of two covenants, one dealing with civil and political rights, the other with economic, social, and cultural rights. They were opened for signature and ratification in that year. The Universal Declaration and the covenants together are frequently referred to as the International Bill of Human Rights.

At its first meeting, in January, 1947, the commission appointed a drafting committee made up of its three officers, Eleanor Roosevelt (United States), P. C. Chang (China), and Charles Habib Malik (Lebanon). In March, representatives from Australia, Chile, France, the United Kingdom, and the Soviet Union were added. During the summer, an outline (initially drafted by John Humphrey, the director of the Secretariat's Division of Human Rights and revised by the French delegate, René Cassin) was debated. By Christmas, a complete draft was circulated to governments for comment. On June 18, 1948, the full commission adopted a draft declaration.

In the fall of 1948, the Third (Social and Humanitarian) Committee of the General Assembly devoted eighty-one meetings to discussion of the draft declaration and nearly seventy proposed amendments. This arduous process was eased somewhat because the chair of the committee was Malik, the rapporteur of the Commission on Human Rights. On December 10, the committee completed its work. The full General Assembly adopted the Universal Declaration of Human Rights with none opposed and eight abstentions.

South Africa abstained because of the declaration's provisions on racial discrimination. Saudi Arabia abstained over its lack of rights for women and of rights to change one's religion. The other abstentions came from the Soviet Union and its allies, whose delegates believed that economic and social rights were not given enough emphasis. Thus, although the declaration was not adopted unanimously, no states voted against it and only two believed that it went too far (and even then only in a few areas).

The Universal Declaration of Human Rights begins with the claim that "recognition of the inherent dignity and of the equal and inalienable rights of all members of the human family is the foundation of freedom, justice and peace in the world." Article 1 echoes these sentiments of the preamble, holding that "all human beings are born free and equal in dignity and rights. They are endowed with reason and conscience and should act toward one another in a spirit of brotherhood." Articles two through twenty-eight then lay out a comprehensive set of human rights.

The Universal Declaration, however, contains no implementation or enforcement mechanisms. It is only a statement of principles and aspirations, without a mechanism or program for realizing them. In 1966, the International Human Rights Covenants gave binding international legal force to the rights of the Universal Declaration and established rudimentary international monitoring procedures. The covenants did not, however, fundamentally alter the substance of the declaration. There have also been important treaties dealing with particular human rights such as racial discrimination, women's rights, torture, and children's rights. These too are best seen as supplements to the Universal Declaration that give greater specificity to particular rights and establish international monitoring procedures. They do not significantly alter the norms laid out in the Universal Declaration.

The Universal Declaration remains the single most important statement of international human rights norms. It is widely commended by virtually all states, from all regions and all ideological perspectives—even those states that systematically violate its provisions. In recognition of its importance, most countries celebrate December 10 as Human Rights Day.

The Universal Declaration, however, has always been controversial. In particular, the relative weight of civil, political, economic, social, and cultural rights, which led to the abstention of the Soviet bloc states, remained a matter of intense controversy in the following decades. In fact, this issue often transformed international discussions of human rights in the 1950's and 1960's into exercises in Cold War ideological rivalry.

Nevertheless, the principle that all human rights are interdependent and indivisible, first established in the Universal Declaration, has largely prevailed. The Universal Declaration is not a list from which states may pick and choose as they see fit. Rather, it is a comprehensive set of minimum standards of domestic political behavior. The fundamental unity of all human rights, exemplified by the existence of a single Declaration containing both civil and political rights and economic, social, and cultural rights without any indication of categorical differences or priorities, has been central to the international definition of human rights since 1948.

Another complaint has concerned the alleged Western bias of the Universal Declaration. When it was drafted, most of Africa and much of Asia was under colonial rule. Only half of the commission's eighteen members, and only three of the eight members of the drafting committee, were from developing countries. One consequence was that the original declaration did not recognize the right of peoples to self-determination. That was remedied by the 1966 International Human Rights Covenants, also known as the International Covenant on Civil and Political Rights.

At the 1994 World Conference on Human Rights, China and certain Islamic countries challenged the idea of the universality of human rights, claiming that cultural differences had to be honored. Even taking such cultural differences into account, the vast majority of rights listed in the declaration flow from the inherent dignity of the human person, a principle that is hard to refute on cultural grounds. A number of critics in developing countries have argued that the Universal Declaration systematically disparages collective rights in favor of the individual rights emphasized in the West.

The most striking fact about the updated list of internationally recognized human rights is the persistence of the original list presented in the Universal Declaration. Virtually all the rights in the International Covenant on Political and Civil Rights, except for the right to self-determination, were enumerated in the Universal Declaration (although often in much less detail). Furthermore, only one right in the Universal Declaration (the right to own property) is not included in those covenants. The constitutions of some two dozen developing countries that achieved their independence after 1948 contain explicit references to the Universal Declaration, and many others have drawn their definition of rights from the Declaration, sometimes verbatim. Virtually all states treat the Declaration as an authoritative statement of international human rights norms.

SIGNIFICANCE

Before World War II, there were few explicit international human rights norms, although customary international law, and the natural law tradition on which it was largely based, contained the seeds of most modern human rights norms. Two centuries of the gradual ascendancy of positivist theories of international law, left individuals largely subject to the whims of their governments. Gradually, in the twentieth century, governments came to recognize again the need to take the treatment of human beings seriously at the international level.

The Treaty of Versailles, which ended World War I, established a (very weak and incomplete) system to protect minorities' rights through the League of Nations. The Treaty of Versailles also created the International Labor Organization, which began to deal with workers' rights issues in the 1920's. The 1926 International Slavery Convention dealt with slavery. Such international efforts to protect individual human rights were clearly exceptions.

Until 1945, the human rights practices of states were treated as internationally protected exercises of the sovereign prerogative of states. International human rights law basically did not exist. The human rights practices of other states simply were not considered legitimate matters for either bilateral or multilateral international action.

The Nuremberg Trials of 1945 introduced into international legal practice the idea of crimes against humanity. Nuremberg, however, dealt only with the particular case of the Holocaust and Nazi atrocities. It did not address human rights violations short of genocide or the practices of states other than Germany. Furthermore, the prosecution at Nuremberg was forced to deal with the uncomfortable fact that although the Nazis were obviously guilty of great moral crimes, such crimes against humanity had not been prohibited explicitly by prewar international law, there being few who would have thought that outlawing murder by millions was necessary, when murder itself was proscribed in the legal systems and moral codes of all nations.

The Universal Declaration was the United Nations' first major response to this distressing and embarrassing absence of an explicit international law of human rights, and the even more shocking claims made by governments about how they could abuse human beings in the name of racial purity or any other principle. The Universal Declaration, however, forthrightly refers to itself as "a common standard of achievement for all peoples and all nations." It does not claim to create binding international legal obligations. In fact, as a resolution of the U.N. General Assembly it is technically speaking only a recommendation to states.

Many lawyers, scholars, and activists have argued that over time, the declaration has become a part of customary international law. Whatever its technical legal status, the Declaration has become a political standard of reference in human rights diplomacy. Numerous U.N. General Assembly resolutions have reaffirmed the document's centrality. It is explicitly referred to as a standard in the European Convention for the Protection of Human Rights and Fundamental Freedoms and the Charter of the Organization of African Unity. Virtually all states use the Universal Declaration as a point of reference when defending or criticizing the human rights practices of other states or their own practices.

The Universal Declaration of Human Rights has become a normative standard of political legitimacy in the contemporary world. It is an authoritative international statement of the minimum standards of treatment that every state owes to all of its citizens.

Jack Donnelly

FURTHER READING

Berting, Jan, et al., eds. *Human Rights in a Pluralist World: Individuals and Collectivities.* Westport, Conn.: Meckler, 1990. Part one considers the Universal Declaration forty years after its formulation. The remaining parts focus principally on the relationship between individual and collective rights and varying cultural conceptions of human rights.

Donnelly, Jack. *Universal Human Rights in Theory and Practice.* 2d ed. Ithaca, N.Y.: Cornell University Press, 2003. This philosophical inquiry into the meaning of human rights and the policy contexts in which human rights operates is recommended for advanced students. References, index.

Humphrey, John P. *Human Rights and the United Nations: A Great Adventure.* Dobbs Ferry, N.Y.: Transnational, 1984. A sometimes engaging and always opinionated memoir of the United Nations' first director of the Division of Human Rights and author of the initial draft of the Universal Declaration.

Johnson, M. Glen. "The Contributions of Eleanor and Franklin Roosevelt to the Development of International Protection for Human Rights." *Human Rights Quarterly* 9 (February, 1987): 19-48. A look at the special contributions of Franklin Roosevelt in helping to inspire U.N. action on human rights and of Eleanor Roosevelt in bringing the Universal Declaration to fruition.

Morsing, Johannes. *The Universal Declaration of Human Rights: Origins, Drafting, and Intent.* Philadelphia: University of Pennsylvania Press, 1999. Historical study of the declaration meant to guide its interpretation in the present as well as to reveal the factors originally leading to its creation. Bibliographic references.

Ramcharan, B. G., ed. *Human Rights: Thirty Years After the Universal Declaration.* The Hague, the Netherlands: Martinus Nijhoff, 1979. Chapters 1, 2, and 7 deal with the Universal Declaration and later efforts at setting international human rights norms. The remaining chapters focus on strategies and institutions for implementing these norms.

Schwelb, Egon. *Human Rights and the International Community: The Roots and Growth of the Universal Declaration of Human Rights, 1948-1963.* Chicago: Quadrangle Books, 1964. An accessible general survey of the origins of the Universal Declaration and its place in the emergence of human rights as a significant issue in international relations in the postwar era.

Shelton, Dinah L., ed. *Encyclopedia of Genocide and Crimes Against Humanity.* 3 vols. Detroit, Mich.: Macmillan Reference, 2005. That there exists a three-volume encyclopedic work on genocide and crimes against humanity is most relevant here. Includes a glossary, maps, primary sources, and an index.

Tolley, Howard, Jr. *The U.N. Commission on Human Rights.* Boulder, Colo.: Westview Press, 1986. This is the authoritative work on the Commission on Human Rights. Chapter 2 briefly discusses the process of drafting in the general context of the political controversies in the commission during its early years.

United Nations Commission on Human Rights. "Universal Declaration of Human Rights." In *The Human Rights Reader,* edited by Walter Laqueur and Barry Rubin. Rev. ed. New York: New American Library, 1990. One of many sources for the text of the Universal Declaration, which deserves reading in its entirety.

Wagner, Teresa, and Leslie Carbone, eds. *Fifty Years After the Declaration: The United Nations' Record on Human Rights.* Lanham, Md.: University Press of America, 2001. Anthology detailing the impact the declaration had— and failed to have—on human rights and international law through the end of the twentieth century.

SEE ALSO: Apr. 25-June 26, 1945: United Nations Charter Convention; Nov. 3, 1950: United Nations General Assembly Passes the Uniting for Peace Resolution; Dec. 14, 1950: United Nations High Commissioner for Refugees Statute Is Approved; 1960's: Soviet Jews Demand Cultural and Religious Rights; Nov. 11, 1970: Moscow Human Rights Committee Is Founded; 1977-1981: Carter Makes Human Rights a Central Theme of Foreign Policy; Spring, 1978: China Promises to Correct Human Rights Abuses.

■ **DECEMBER 26, 1948**

HUNGARY'S COMMUNIST GOVERNMENT ARRESTS CARDINAL MINDSZENTY

Resistance by the Roman Catholic Church to communist repression in Hungary led to the arrest of the primate of Hungary, József Mindszenty, by the Communist Party government. Briefly freed during the 1956 Hungarian uprising, he then took refuge in the U.S. embassy in Budapest, where he remained for fifteen years before going into exile in Austria. His isolation and the fierce repression of the communist regime severely limited the strength and independence of the Catholic Church in Hungary.

LOCALE: Hungary
CATEGORIES: Religion, theology, and ethics; human rights; government and politics; organizations and institutions, crime and scandal

KEY FIGURES

József Mindszenty (József Pehm; 1892-1975), cardinal archbishop of
   Esztergom and primate of Hungary
Imre Nagy (1896-1958), prime minister of Hungary, 1953-1955, 1956
Mátyás Rákosi (Mátyás Rosenfeld; 1892-1971), general secretary of the
   Communist Party of Hungary
Joseph Stalin (Joseph Vissarionovich Dzhugashvili; 1879-1953), general
   secretary of the Communist Party of the Soviet Union, 1922-1953

SUMMARY OF EVENT

Following the World War II defeat of Nazi Germany in 1945, Hungary fell under the control of Joseph Stalin and the Soviet Union, which promptly installed a communist government there. Behind the scenes, real control over major governmental decisions remained in the hands of Soviet "advisers," who kept in constant contact with Moscow. The new government in Hungary was secured through intimidation, electoral fraud, and the infiltration and gradual elimination of legitimate opposition parties.

After 1947, under the leadership of Mátyás Rákosi, the pace of official repression increased dramatically: Between 1948 and 1953, more than 1.3 million Hungarians were brought to trial for a variety of political "crimes." Torture, execution, and long prison terms were the common fates of most real or imaginary enemies of the new Soviet regime.

In 1948, the Hungarian communists turned the apparatus of repression against religious bodies and the Roman Catholic Church in particular.

157

Scores of priests and other clergy were arrested, Church property was seized without compensation, and nearly all religious orders and voluntary institutions were closed. In the following year, 1950, the government then began to re-create religious bodies under government supervision and control. Critical to this project was the destruction of an independent Catholic hierarchy in Hungary, which, in the late 1940's, was led by the formidable primate József Mindszenty.

Mindszenty was a well-known figure in the Hungarian Catholic Church by World War I. During the brief communist revolution in 1919, he was imprisoned for opposition to communism. By the early 1940's, he was an active member of the conservative-traditionalist Smallholders' Party, which formed the bulwark of opposition to the fascist Arrow Cross Party. In 1944, he was made bishop of Veszprém. That year, the Arrow Cross Party, backed by Nazi Germany, overthrew the more moderate (though still German-allied) government of Miklós Horthy. Mindszenty opposed the fascists and their efforts to impose further anti-Semitic measures on the country and because of this was arrested and imprisoned for the remainder of the war. Following his release in 1945, he was named cardinal archbishop of Esztergom and primate of Hungary by Pope Pius XII.

Mindszenty strongly opposed communist efforts to control Catholic education and sought to maintain the independence of the Hungary Catholic Church in the face of increasing repression. On December 26, 1948, he was arrested by the communist security police and charged with treason, conspiracy against the government, and illegal use of foreign currency. During

Primate József Mindszenty.

his imprisonment, Mindszenty was beaten, drugged, and subject to sleep deprivation and other abuse and torture. When the prelate would not cooperate, the police created a forged confession of the cardinal's "crimes" as well as other incriminating but fake documents.

The trial that began on February 3, 1949, was a classic Stalinist show trial, featuring manufactured evidence, forgeries, and sensational charges, including charges that Mindszenty sought to incite the United States to attack Hungary. He was not allowed to present a defense and was convicted and sentenced to life in prison. The cardinal would remain in prison for the next seven years.

In 1953, following the death of Stalin and the revelation of some of his crimes against fellow communists, the power of his henchmen in Soviet-ruled countries of central and eastern Europe began to decline. In 1956, revolts broke out in East Germany and Poland but were quickly crushed, and more moderate communist leaders began to emerge throughout the region. In Budapest that October, a rally supporting a pro-reform Polish Communist Party quickly became a mass demonstration. The demonstrators were attacked by police, resulting in rioting and widespread unrest. The reform communist, Imre Nagy, was named leader of the Hungarian Communist Party and quickly released many political prisoners. The most important of those released was Mindszenty. The newly freed cardinal threw his full support behind the mass movement for independence from the Soviet Union. Within a few weeks, however, Soviet forces invaded Hungary and crushed the freedom movement, with great loss of life.

As the Soviets attacked Budapest, Mindszenty sought asylum in the U.S. embassy there, where he would spend the next fifteen years. This created a complicated diplomatic situation for the United States, which refused the demands of the pro-Soviet Hungarian government to release the cardinal to them. Beginning in the 1960's, it also created a difficult situation for the Vatican, which, under Pope Paul VI, sought to appease rather than confront communist regimes in Central and Eastern Europe. In 1964, without Mindszenty's approval, the Vatican struck an agreement with the Hungarian government, in which bishops would be approved by the government and clergy would swear an oath of loyalty to the regime. By then, the regime had achieved significant infiltration of Church structures and turned many clergy, including bishops, into informers.

In 1971, Mindszenty was allowed exile into Vienna, Austria. Nevertheless, he refused to give up his position as primate of Hungary, and his staunch opposition to communism and traditionalism complicated Paul VI's appeasement efforts. In 1973, he was stripped of his titles by the pope, though the office of primate remained unfilled until after his death.

SIGNIFICANCE

Cardinal Mindszenty, who died in the spring of 1975, remained an unbreakable foe of communist rule in Hungary, but the overwhelming power of the Soviet armed forces, the success of the Hungarian communist security apparatus in undermining the Church, and the willingness of the Vatican to compromise with communism during the early 1970's destroyed much of the Church's functional independence in Hungary and its ability to provide an effective moral voice. Mindszenty, however, became an important symbol of the desire of Hungarian Catholics for both political and religious freedom. Mindszenty became a hero to many opponents of communism and he inspired the formation of an American Catholic lay foundation whose goal remains the defense of Church independence and teachings.

John Radzilowski

FURTHER READING

Lendvai, Paul. *The Hungarians: A Thousand Years of Victory in Defeat.* Translated by Ann Major. Princeton, N.J.: Princeton University Press, 2003. A narrative history of the Hungarian people over the course of one thousand years.

Mindszenty, József Cardinal. *Memoirs.* New York: Macmillan, 1974. The English-language translation of Mindszenty's memoirs.

Molnár, Miklós. *A Concise History of Hungary.* New York: Cambridge University Press, 2001. A narrative account of the often-turbulent history of Hungary.

Shuster, George N. *In Silence I Speak: The Story of Cardinal Mindszenty Today and of Hungary's "New Order."* New York: Farrar, Straus and Cudahy, 1956. A contemporary account of Mindszenty's repression.

Toma, Peter A. *Socialist Authority: The Hungarian Experience.* New York: Praeger, 1988. Discussion of the legal and political apparatus of communist control in Hungary.

The Trial of József Mindszenty. Budapest: Hungarian State Publishing House, 1949. Official report by the communist government on the trial; for Western readers.

SEE ALSO: Sept. 25, 1953-Oct. 26, 1956: Polish Communist Government Arrests the Primate of Poland; Oct. 23-Nov. 10, 1956: Soviets Crush Hungarian Uprising; Nov. 12, 1968-Dec., 1989: Brezhnev Doctrine Mandates Soviet Control of Satellite Nations; 1989: Hungary Adopts a Multiparty System; July 1, 1991: Dissolution of the Warsaw Pact.

■ 1949-1961

EAST GERMANS FLEE TO WEST TO ESCAPE COMMUNIST REGIME

Hundreds of thousands of people migrated to the West after the partition of Germany into the German Democratic Republic (East Germany) and the Federal Republic of Germany (West Germany).

LOCALE: Germany

CATEGORIES: Immigration, emigration, and relocation; expansion and land acquisition

KEY FIGURES

Konrad Adenauer (1876-1967), chancellor of West Germany, 1949-1963

Walter Ulbricht (1893-1973), general secretary of the Central Committee of the Socialist Unity Party of East Germany

Harry S. Truman (1884-1972), president of the United States, 1945-1953

Joseph Stalin (Joseph Vissarionovich Dzhugashvili; 1878-1953), general secretary of the Central Committee of the Communist Party of the Soviet Union, 1922-1953, and premier, 1941-1953

Clement Attlee (1883-1967), prime minister of Great Britain, 1945-1951

Winston Churchill (1874-1965), prime minister of Great Britain, 1940-1945 and 1951-1955

SUMMARY OF EVENT

World War II may be seen as an amalgamation of many different conflicts. In Europe, in addition to being an ideological battle against fascism and a fight by a coalition of powers to stop Adolf Hitler's aggression, the war represented the continuation of a centuries-old struggle between Germany and Russia for mastery of central Europe. Thus, when the war ended in Germany's defeat, the Soviet Union not only desired expanded influence in that region but also found the way cleared to achieve such influence. Joseph Stalin, the Soviet ruler, wanted to ensure that the terms of the peace would keep Germany prostrate so that its resources could be used to rebuild the Soviet state.

Stalin's Western allies, the United States, Great Britain, and France, had less clear goals. Some Western leaders saw communism as constituting as great a danger as had fascism. They had joined Stalin only through military expediency, seeing Hitler as the more immediate threat. Others hoped that

161

the wartime alliance would result in continued Soviet cooperation with the Western powers' agendas after the peace.

Some in the West also agreed with Stalin that Germany should be reduced to impotency. They believed, perhaps unfairly, that the country had been responsible for both of the twentieth century's world wars and should therefore be severely punished. Henry Morgenthau, Jr., a presidential adviser and secretary of the treasury under President Franklin D. Roosevelt, suggested in 1943 that Germany be "pastoralized," so it could never make war again. France, which like the Soviet Union had suffered brutal occupation by the Nazis, particularly desired that potential future German aggression be curbed.

In the years following World War II, as Moscow imposed its own order on Eastern Europe through less than democratic means, Western skepticism grew concerning Stalin's commitment to European peace and independence. A civil war between communists and monarchists in Greece and the appearance of strong communist movements in France and Italy also contributed to the breakdown of the East-West coalition.

Geopolitical issues overrode even these ideological concerns. Neither Germany nor France remained strong enough to counterbalance the Soviet Union on the European continent. As early as October, 1944, British prime minister Winston Churchill and Stalin had agreed that there should be a formula for dividing Eastern Europe. In February, 1945, at Yalta in the Soviet Union, Churchill, Stalin, and Roosevelt developed further plans that placed Eastern Europe in the Soviet sphere and Western Europe in the Anglo-American sphere.

Roosevelt died in April, 1945, a month before the war in Europe ended. After the German surrender, Churchill and Stalin met with the new U.S. president, Harry S. Truman, at Potsdam, outside Berlin. There, they decided the fate of Germany. In the midst of the conference, British voters unseated Churchill's Conservative Party. Labour Party leader Clement Attlee became prime minister and replaced the venerable Churchill at Potsdam. The change did not greatly affect the negotiations in progress.

The Potsdam agreement called for the division of Germany into four zones—one American, one British, one French, and one Soviet. It treated Berlin separately but also divided it into four parts, even though it was situated geographically inside the Soviet zone. Furthermore, the treaty allowed the Soviets to take reparations, including machinery and produce, from their zone and from the others as compensation for the damage done to the Soviet Union under German occupation. France and other European countries occupied by the Nazis received similar, but lesser, compensations. The Soviets, in fact, removed industrial material from Germany as soon as they could, even before the agreements were in place.

The Soviet zone, the largest in area, encompassed about 40 percent of German territory, including most of eastern Prussia to the Weser River, Saxony, and Thuringia. In addition, the Germans surrendered their prewar territory east of the Oder and Neisse Rivers directly to the Soviet Union, Poland, and Czechoslovakia. Both of the latter were soon to fall under the complete domination of Moscow. Furthermore, all German conquests after 1938 were restored. The French zone, 10 percent of German territory, fell along the Rhine valley. The British zone, 20 percent, lay in the north. The United States' zone, 30 percent, was located in the southwest.

Stalin interpreted the meaning of democracy in a manner vastly different from that understood by the Western leaders. Moscow instituted systems of government in Eastern Europe that were controlled by communist parties through one-candidate elections. Opponents of the Moscow system were forced into silence or exile. The authorities even imprisoned or executed some. The West put pressure on native communists, sometimes extralegally, reducing their influence. The communist parties, however, were rarely completely outlawed. Moreover, Washington's Marshall Plan brought rapid economic recovery to Western Europe, further reducing the communists' appeal in both Eastern and Western Europe. The two camps rapidly went their separate ways. In 1946, Winston Churchill declared that an Iron Curtain had fallen across Europe. By 1948, the wartime alliance between the Soviet Union and the West had broken down completely. The Cold War had begun.

The split between the former Allies had repercussions for Germany. Each occupier created a temporary administration modeled on its own goals and precepts of government. In 1949, the Western allies—Great Britain, the United States, and France—relinquished their authority as occupying powers and united their sections into the new Federal Republic of Germany (West Germany), with a capital at Bonn. The first elections resulted in the anti-Nazi conservative Konrad Adenauer becoming chancellor. Berlin remained legally distinct, but its three Western sections were also united into a free city, West Berlin.

The Soviets followed suit. They declared East Germany the German Democratic Republic (GDR; German DDR), with East Berlin as its capital and Walter Ulbricht, a communist leader loyal to Moscow, as its prime minister. Already in 1948, Moscow had tried to restrict access to the city, even though access was guaranteed by treaty. An airlift, sponsored chiefly by the United States, had caused the plan of blocking the roads to backfire. The Kremlin had lifted the blockade.

The memory of the blockade in combination with the designation of East and West Germany as different nations struck terror into the Germans

East German leader Walter Ulbricht. (National Archives)

in the east. While others in the Soviet Bloc had little chance of leaving their homelands, Germans who lived in Berlin, or who could get there, could make their way to West Berlin simply by taking a subway ride. Once in West Berlin, they could join relatives or simply move themselves into the Federal Republic. By the end of 1951, the total number of Germans who had left the East for the West exceeded 1.5 million.

The lure of the West, especially the benefits provided by the airlift and the Marshall Plan, provided East Germans with more than enough incentive to give up all of their possessions and take the chance of relocating. The bleak future that the German Democratic Republic promised to its residents also provided such an impulse. In addition, the new governments of other Eastern European nations expelled almost eight million more Germans whose families had lived in those countries for generations. Most of these refugees came from the German territories that had been received as compensation by Poland, Czechoslovakia, and the Soviet Union. Their migrations further divided the two German states. Their division, perhaps more than any other condition, would come to symbolize the Cold War.

SIGNIFICANCE

The establishment of two Germanies was in many ways convenient for both the West and the Soviet Union. It allowed the World War II settlement to continue even after the alliance broke down. The Germans did not like this settlement, however, and West Germany never recognized the two-Germany policy. It even took measures against the policy, such as the Hallstein Doctrine, named after Walter Hallstein, a foreign office official. The Hallstein Doctrine stated that Bonn would not recognize any country that maintained diplomatic relations with the GDR. Exceptions were granted to the Soviet Union and some developing nations. Later, in the 1960's, Bonn modified the doctrine in order to establish relations with Eastern Europe, but unification remained a goal for West Germany.

In contrast, the Communist Party leaders of the GDR supported the two-Germany policy, since it served both Moscow's interests and their own. Only under this situation could they have an opportunity to govern, as it was clear that reunification would mean the end of communist power in Germany. The sovietization of East Germany, however, produced a great deal of hostility among the populace. In 1953, a mass uprising erupted.

Escape to the West through Berlin continued. Between 1949 and 1961, at least another 1.5 million East Germans migrated to the West. In the 1950's, Western aid rebuilt Western Europe, including West Germany and West Berlin. In the meantime, the states of Eastern Europe suffered under the burden of having to help build up the devastated Soviet Union as well as their own countries. As West Berlin became a beacon of prosperity, more and more East Germans decided to forsake their homes and migrate to the West.

Stalin died in 1953. His successor, Nikita S. Khrushchev, soon began a program of de-Stalinization, reversing some of Stalin's policies. Some liberalization took place in the East. The example of West Berlin and West Germany prospering in Europe spurred an economic revival in the east. Compared to other socialist countries, the GDR was a miracle in its own right, especially considering the facts that the Soviet Union continued to appropriate its goods and services as reparations and that it had not received the massive aid granted to West Germany. The exceptionally rapid development of the Federal Republic, however, increased the migrations to the West to a fever pitch.

While the Soviet Union and its allies could glory in technological accomplishments such as the first artificial satellite and piloted space flights, or in their huge military systems and intercontinental ballistic missiles (built and designed in large part by German engineers and scientists), the West continued to enjoy a consumer and societal miracle. West Germany joined the North Atlantic Treaty Organization (NATO) and the Common Market. The Federal Republic had become a world economic power. There were no lines or shortages, as there were in the East. The loss of East German citizens to the West became too much for both the Germans and the Soviets, especially since those who left were often among the most highly trained and skilled. On August 13, 1961, the authorities sealed the border, and in the next weeks the Soviets and East Germans erected a massive wall across Berlin that stood until 1989.

Frederick B. Chary

FURTHER READING

Backer, John H. *Winds of History: The German Years of Lucius DuBignon Clay.* New York: Van Nostrand Reinhold, 1983. A history of General Clay's administration of the American sector in Germany. Very well researched, with detailed documentation. Illustrations, index, and bibliography.

Botting, Douglas. *From the Ruins of the Reich: Germany, 1945-1949.* New York: New American Library, 1985. A history of Germany under Allied occupation, analyzing many different aspects. Very readable and well researched. Has some material on the refugee question. Illustrations, bibliography, and index.

Davidson, Eugene. *The Death and Life of Germany: An Account of the American Occupation.* New York: Alfred A. Knopf, 1961. Analysis of the period of German occupation from 1945 to 1953, especially in the American zone. It deals with the refugee question and the problems caused by the Cold War. Very well researched. Puts positive light on American rehabilitation efforts. Bibliography and index.

Keesing's Research Report. *Germany and Eastern Europe Since 1945: From Potsdam Agreement to Chancellor Brandt's "Östpolitik."* New York: Charles Scribner's Sons, 1973. The history of Germany from 1945 to 1970, based on contemporary news reports from the Keesing's archives linked together by a narrative. The first section deals with the occupation period. Contains material relating to East German refugees. Index, no bibliography.

McInnis, Edgar, Richard Hiscocks, and Robert Spencer. *The Shaping of Postwar Germany.* New York: Praeger, 1960. A survey of the German situation at the end of the 1950's. Considers the entire German question, including the refugees from the East. Gives a brief historical outline and focuses on the division by the superpowers, a comparison of the economics and politics in the two Germanies, the Berlin issue, and the dilemma of unification. Contains a chronology and maps as well as documentation and an index.

Offner, Arnold A. *Another Such Victory: President Truman and the Cold War, 1945-1953.* Stanford, Calif.: Stanford University Press, 2002. Analysis of Truman's role and how his policies affected political events in Germany, Greece, China, and Korea. Includes an index and a bibliography.

Pounds, Norman J. G. *Divided Germany and Berlin.* Princeton, N.J.: D. Van Nostrand, 1962. Part of a series of short geographical studies published for university students in the 1960's. The author, a leading geographer of Eastern Europe, surveys the German question at one of the peaks of the Cold War, shortly after the communists built the Berlin Wall. Examines the question of refugees. Bibliography and index.

Ruhm von Oppen, Beate, ed. *Documents on Germany Under Occupation: 1945-1954.* London: Oxford University Press, 1955. A selection of documents concerning the Allied occupation of Germany. Contains the texts of treaties, memoranda, protocols, and decrees from all occupying powers and concerning various issues, including the refugees and reparations. Contains a map and index.

Settel, Arthur, ed. *This Is Germany.* New York: William Sloane Associates, 1950. A collection of contemporary newspaper and magazine articles on occupied Germany, written by international correspondents. "March of Millions," by Denis Martin, concerns the refugees coming from Eastern Europe and East Germany into the Western zones. No index or bibliography.

Williams, Charles. *Adenauer: The Father of the New Germany.* New York: Wiley, 2001. A strong, well-researched biography of West Germany's first chancellor. Includes a bibliography and an index.

SEE ALSO: July 17-Aug. 2, 1945: Potsdam Conference; Feb. 25, 1948: Communists Seize Power in Czechoslovakia; June 24, 1948-May 11, 1949: Berlin Blockade and Airlift; Sept. 21-Oct. 7, 1949: Germany Splits into Two Republics; Aug. 13, 1961: Communists Raise the Berlin Wall; June 21, 1973: East and West Germany Establish Diplomatic Relations; Nov. 9, 1989: Fall of the Berlin Wall; July 16, 1990: Gorbachev Agrees to Membership of a United Germany in NATO.

■ JANUARY 25, 1949

SOVIET BLOC STATES ESTABLISH COUNCIL FOR MUTUAL ECONOMIC ASSISTANCE

The communist states replied to the U.S. Marshall Plan by establishing the Council for Mutual Economic Assistance, which Soviet leader Joseph Stalin saw as a means of enforcing Soviet-style economic development in Eastern Europe to counter Western influence. The agency became more active after Stalin's death but ceased to exist when the Soviet Union itself collapsed.

ALSO KNOWN AS: Comecon; CMEA; Moscow Joint Communiqué
LOCALE: Eastern Europe
CATEGORIES: Economics; trade and commerce; diplomacy and
international relations

KEY FIGURES

Joseph Stalin (Joseph Vissarionovich Dzhugashvili; 1878-1953), general
secretary of the Central Committee of the Communist Party of the
Soviet Union, 1922-1953, and premier, 1941-1953

Harry S. Truman (1884-1972), president of the United States, 1945-1953

George F. Kennan (1904-2005), American diplomat, 1926-1950

George C. Marshall (1880-1959), U.S. secretary of state, 1947-1949

Vyacheslav Mikhailovich Molotov (Vyacheslav Mikhailovich Skryabin; 1890-
1986), Soviet commissar of foreign affairs, 1939-1949 and 1953-1956

SUMMARY OF EVENT

On January 25, 1949, the Moscow Joint Communiqué was issued by Soviet
leader Joseph Stalin, as well as the heads of state of Bulgaria, Czechoslovakia, Hungary, Poland, and Romania. This document announced the founding of the Council for Mutual Economic Assistance (Comecon, or CMEA).
It represented the Soviet rejection of the United States' Marshall Plan
as the framework for postwar reconstruction, while simultaneously laying
the groundwork for a centralized system of diplomatic, economic, and military alliances in Eastern Europe designed to serve Soviet strategic interests.
The so-called Molotov Plan, meant as an alternative to the Marshall Plan,
marked the de facto division of Europe into two separate and mutually hostile blocs, a condition that was to last until the dissolution of the Soviet
Union in 1991.

From the very earliest stages of World War II, the Allied Powers were
forced to paper over numerous conflicts of interest among the coalition's
partners. The Atlantic Charter (1941) was originally intended to establish
an Anglo-American alliance against both Germany and the Soviet Union—
in spite of the fact that the United States had yet to enter the war, while the
Soviet Union had already entered on the side of the British and was fighting
for its very existence against Germany.

The Red Army faced the full fury of the Wehrmacht (German army), losing millions of soldiers while inflicting three-fourths of all the casualties suffered by Germany during the war. Meanwhile, despite numerous urgent requests from Stalin to open a second front in Europe, the United States and
Great Britain made no moves to comply until 1944. By this time, the Red
Army had already destroyed the Wehrmacht as a fighting force on the east-

ern front and was rapidly rolling back the remainder, occupying vast areas of eastern Europe in its drive to the German homeland.

Planning for the end of the war and the postwar recovery had begun in earnest by 1943. The planning process was dominated by the British and Americans, with no serious consideration of Soviet views or interests. The Soviets were resentful, and Stalin was increasingly determined to do whatever was required to guarantee the security of the Soviet Union in the postwar period. In the wake of Germany's invasion of his country, Stalin's vision of a stable and secure postwar order focused on the creation of a buffer zone of friendly states. Such a zone would close off the Polish corridor and eliminate Germany and any other potential invaders as military threats, albeit at the potential expense of the buffer states themselves. It would also establish an international peacetime sphere of influence within which Soviet hegemony would be unchallenged.

This approach was consistent with the outcomes of previous great power conflicts; furthermore, it comported handily with the plans of Great Britain and France for the reestablishment of their own colonial empires. However, the American plan was for a postwar order based on open markets in a system of intergovernmental organizations (IGOs) that would maintain the collective security of all nations. This plan was incompatible with the perceived needs of the Soviet Union. The United Nations (in which the Soviet Union had veto power) was the only international institution in which the Soviets regularly participated.

The United States saw the major challenges of the postwar period to be the reconstruction of Europe and Asia, the restoration of a stable world economy, the establishment of an effective system of collective security, and limiting the influence of the Soviet Union in world affairs. The "Truman Doctrine" refers to the speech (March 12, 1947) in which U.S. president Harry S. Truman declared it to be the duty of the United States to support any resistance to what might be considered an expansion of "communist influences" anywhere on the globe. This represented an embrace of the strategic doctrine of "containment," first articulated by George F. Kennan in 1946, and it was a foundational moment in the Cold War between capitalist and communist nations.

Kennan's work provided the theoretical rationale for the Truman Doctrine; he was also one of the chief authors of the Marshall Plan (named for then-secretary of state George C. Marshall). The plan was the economic counterpart to the Truman Doctrine. It was designed to support Western European nations in the task of material reconstruction and was based on the premise that prosperous nations were less vulnerable to communist influences. The Marshall Plan arose out of a series of negotiations among sixteen

Western European nations regarding an acceptable mechanism for distributing and managing American financial contributions to the rebuilding effort.

Under the plan, aid was conditional on the recipient's willingness to disclose all economic information to the United States, accept a fixed exchange rate for its currency, eliminate trade barriers, and adopt a number of other structural reforms. With those restrictions, Marshall Plan aid was available to all European nations, including the Soviet Union and its satellites. The Soviets sent Vyacheslav Mikhailovich Molotov, Stalin's minister of foreign affairs, to the Paris Meetings (June, 1946) to explore the terms for obtaining economic assistance, and he left after only a few days, declaring that the U.S. plan was an imposition on national sovereignty, because it required the disclosure of financial information that the Soviets deemed too sensitive to reveal to the world's capitalist powers. Moreover, the plan seemed to Molotov to be designed rapidly to rebuild Germany in order to aid in the U.S. containment strategy by reconstituting the German threat to the Soviet Union. Consequently, Moscow forbade all of its Eastern European satellite nations from receiving Marshall Plan aid.

Upon Molotov's return to Moscow in July of 1947, Stalin announced the Soviet response to the Marshall Plan: The Molotov Plan would be a program of in-kind aid and technical assistance, administered through a series of bilateral agreements between the Soviet Union and the nations under its influence. Stalin intended to use Soviet economic and military advantages to impose what he called the "socialist international division of labor" upon Eastern Europe. This division of labor essentially consisted of the provision of raw materials and energy resources to Eastern European countries by the Soviet Union, which would receive finished goods from the satellite nations in return. The agreements negotiated along these lines were designed to redirect trade flows, increase the degree of economic dependency of the subject states upon the Soviet Union, and create a mechanism for the extraction of reparations.

The Moscow Joint Communiqué of January, 1949, established Comecon as the institutional framework for the coordination of numerous national economic plans. The stated purpose of the organization was to coordinate economic planning and share technology among member nations. Members were all entitled to "sovereign equality," meaning "one-nation, one vote" in all decision-making processes. Each member was allowed to declare an "interest" in any matter under consideration; all participation was voluntary. The dominance of the Soviet economy in the region, however, gave the Soviets a disproportionate say in collective decisions. Nevertheless, they were unable to prevent countries from opting out of the organization, meaning that Comecon never obtained formal supranational authority.

Soviet commissar of foreign affairs Vyacheslav Mikhailovich Molotov. (Library of Congress)

The structure and proximate goals of Comecon evolved over the years to reflect the varying foci of Soviet security strategy. This approach to economic integration suffered from a variety of technical defects as regarded purely economic criteria for efficiency. It persisted, because Comecon served extremely well as an instrument for the advancement of the Soviet Union's fundamental strategic objectives: maintaining and extending the nation's political dominance within its sphere, using client states to finance Soviet reconstruction, maintaining the buffer zone of pliable regimes, and cultivating a group of dependent allied nations to bolster Soviet influence on the United Nations. Comecon was finally declared defunct with the dissolution of the Soviet Union on June 28, 1991.

SIGNIFICANCE

The formation of Comecon served to crystallize the existing and emerging Cold War lines of division between the United States and the Soviet Union, and it accelerated the growth of tension in the superpower rivalry. It also froze Germany's political structure, forcing the nation to remain partitioned for another four decades. Comecon served as an adjunct to the process of creating a system of communist military alliances known as the Warsaw Pact, and it did much to shape the relatively favorable image the Soviets enjoyed among the less developed nations within its sphere. It probably carried within it the seeds of its own destruction, however, since the satellite nations received relatively favorable terms on the resources they received from the Soviets for most of the period. This implicit subsidy to the Soviets' client states turned out to be a measure that the Soviet economy could ill afford in the long run.

Ivan Weinel

FURTHER READING

Berger, Helge, and Albrecht Ritschl. "Germany and the Political Economy of the Marshall Plan, 1947-1952: A Re-Revisionist View." In *Europe's Postwar Recovery*, edited by Barry Eichengreen. New York: Cambridge University Press, 1995. Argues that the linkage of several issue areas through the conditionality of Marshall Plan aid served a wider purpose than simply assisting in postwar rebuilding: It was also intended to foster a much tighter degree of European economic integration than was actually achieved.

Gaddis, John Lewis. *We Now Know: Rethinking Cold War History.* New York: Oxford University Press, 1997. Addresses the question as to whether the Cold War was inevitable; his answer is in the affirmative.

Judt, Tony. *Postwar: A History of Europe Since 1945.* New York: Penguin Press, 2005. Provides a very thorough look at the economic histories of Eastern European countries.

LaFeber, Walter. *America, Russia, and the Cold War: 1945-2006.* New York: McGraw-Hill. 2008. Focuses on relations between the United States and the Soviet Union and examines causes and effects of the conflict. Contains illustrations and maps.

McMahon, Robert J. *The Cold War: A Very Short Introduction.* New York: Oxford University Press, 2003. Broad, accessible overview of the Cold War that covers key events and themes. Contains illustrations, maps, and index.

Powaski, Ronald E. *The Cold War: The United States and the Soviet Union, 1917-1991.* New York: Oxford University Press, 1998. Argues that the roots of the Cold War extend to czarist Russia and early America and examines the national psychology led to the decades-long conflict.

Riasanovsky, Nicholas V., and Mark Steinberg. *A History of Russia.* 7th ed. New York: Oxford University Press, 2005. Excellent overview of the roots of the Cold War conflict; includes chapters on the transition into capitalism at the end of the twentieth century.

Walker, Martin. *The Cold War: A History.* New York: Henry Holt, 1995. Argues that the Cold War helped maintain global stability and promoted economic growth.

SEE ALSO: Apr. 3, 1948: Marshall Plan Provides Aid to Europe; Sept. 21-Oct. 7, 1949: Germany Splits into Two Republics; Oct. 23, 1954: Western European Union Is Established; May 14, 1955: Warsaw Pact Is Signed; Oct. 23-Nov. 10, 1956: Soviets Crush Hungarian Uprising; 1968-Dec., 1989: Brezhnev Doctrine Mandates Soviet Control of Satellite Nations; Aug. 20-21, 1968: Soviet Union Invades Czechoslovakia; Nov. 12, 1968-Dec., 1989: Brezhnev Doctrine Mandates Soviet Control of Satellite Nations; Dec., 1991: Dissolution of the Soviet Union.

■ APRIL 4, 1949

NORTH ATLANTIC TREATY ORGANIZATION IS FORMED

Twelve democracies established the North Atlantic Treaty Organization, or NATO, as an association for mutual defense against the Soviet Union.

ALSO KNOWN AS: NATO
LOCALE: Western Europe; Washington, D.C.
CATEGORIES: Diplomacy and international relations; organizations and institutions

KEY FIGURES
Dean Acheson (1893-1971), U.S. secretary of state, 1949-1953
George C. Marshall (1880-1959), U.S. secretary of state, 1947-1949
Joseph Stalin (Joseph Vissarionovich Dzhugashvili; 1878-1953), general secretary of the Central Committee of the Communist Party of the Soviet Union
Harry S. Truman (1884-1972), president of the United States, 1945-1953
Arthur Hendrick Vandenberg (1884-1951), senator from Michigan and leader of the movement for a bipartisan foreign policy

SUMMARY OF EVENT
On April 4, 1949, the United States and eleven other nations (Belgium, Canada, Denmark, France, the United Kingdom, Iceland, Italy, Luxembourg, the Netherlands, Norway, and Portugal) signed a treaty of alliance establishing the North Atlantic Treaty Organization (NATO), committing the signatories to the principle of common security on a regional basis. By joining,

the United States took a precedent-shattering step; it had never before concluded a military alliance in peacetime with any European state. Participation in NATO meant that the United States had modified one of its oldest principles, which stemmed from the advice of George Washington and Thomas Jefferson: to avoid entangling alliances.

The genesis for such an alliance emerged from the Truman administration's containment policy, with the fundamental objective of opposing Soviet expansionist efforts in Europe after World War II. The United States had committed itself in the 1947 Truman Doctrine to assisting European nations facing civil war or external threats from the Soviet Union, led by Joseph Stalin.

Also in 1947, Secretary of State George C. Marshall proposed the more ambitious European Recovery Program. Economic aid through this costly effort, better known as the Marshall Plan, greatly assisted the European economy after the program began in 1948. There was widespread belief in the United States, however, that Europe's full economic and psychological recovery would not be possible until Europeans believed themselves safe from the threat of the Soviet Red Army. Thus, military security was essential for continued economic recovery.

Several major events in 1948 revealed the widening Cold War in Europe. A communist coup d'état in Czechoslovakia, the Soviet blockade of Berlin (lasting into 1949), and other Soviet actions convinced the Truman administration of the need for more extensive, long-term U.S. involvement in Europe. Despite appeals from European leaders for the creation of a common front, however, Truman was not sufficiently confident of public and congressional support to move directly toward an alliance. In June, the Senate approved the Vandenberg Resolution, named for Senator Arthur Hendrick Vandenberg, the major proponent of the movement for a bipartisan foreign policy. The Senate vote of 64-4 declared support for U.S. participation in regional arrangements for "continuous and effective self-help and mutual aid." This pronouncement was interpreted by some as an attempt to limit presidential power in foreign affairs rather than as a sincere expression of support for collective security. Only after the presidential election of 1948 and cautious discussions with the principal European nations did the Truman administration act to move the United States away from its traditional isolationism.

In March, five European nations—Great Britain, France, Belgium, the Netherlands, and Luxembourg—signed the Brussels Pact, a fifty-year defensive alliance. Its terms obligated the signatories to come to the aid of any member attacked by an aggressor. The Brussels Pact nations invited the United States to participate, but there were numerous obstacles to concerted action at that time, even though the Vandenberg Resolution showed

U.S. interest in a mutual security system. In January, 1949, more positive support was expressed in Truman's inaugural address, which promised that the United States would contribute to the defense of friendly nations.

The United States began negotiations with a number of European states, with the aim of creating a cooperative system of military security against the presumed Soviet threat to Western Europe. These discussions were criticized by some people in the United States and especially by communist authorities in Moscow. They accused the United States of undercutting the United Nations and jeopardizing world peace by forming a bloc of states for aggressive purposes. The United States answered this accusation by pointing out that article 51 of the U.N. Charter allowed for regional defense pacts, and that the proposed alliance clearly was defensive in character.

Dean Acheson, who succeeded Marshall as secretary of state in early 1949, believed that the United States should look to military and diplomatic arrangements to meet the communist challenge rather than rely upon the institutional procedures of the United Nations, which could be blocked by a Soviet veto. Negotiations achieved the desired objective of an expanded association of democratic states. In ceremonies in Washington, D.C., on April 4, the North Atlantic Treaty was signed by representatives of twelve nations—Belgium, Canada, Denmark, France, Iceland, Italy, Luxembourg, the Netherlands, Norway, Portugal, the United States, and the United Kingdom. They reaffirmed their support of the United Nations, vowed to cooperate in the maintenance of the stability and well-being of the North Atlantic region, and promised to work together for collective defense and the preservation of peace and general security.

Although the pact bound its members to settle international disputes by peaceful means, article 5 stated that "the Parties agree that an armed attack against one or more of them in Europe or North America shall be considered an attack against them all." Any attack would be met by armed force, if necessary. Each member state was permitted to adopt its own response to aggression after consultation with its allies. The treaty provided for the establishment of the NATO council, on which each of the signatory states was to be represented. The council created a defense committee and other departments to develop measures for the nations' common defense. No signatory was committed absolutely to go to war, but the treaty was a powerful moral commitment to aid members threatened by aggression. The treaty was to be in effect for at least twenty years and could be renewed.

Senate hearings on the North Atlantic Treaty, while not endangering its chances of ratification by the United States, resulted in sometimes bitter debate concerning the wisdom of U.S. involvement. Prominent national political figures, such as Senator Robert A. Taft, warned against the United States assuming major long-term responsibilities. These discussions revealed that the Truman administration could not anticipate all the military implications of the new alliance. Nevertheless, on July 21 the Senate approved the North Atlantic Treaty by a vote of 82-13. Eleven of the thirteen who voted "no" were Republicans, but both Republicans and Democrats supported the treaty. By late August, following ratification by member governments, NATO officially formed.

SIGNIFICANCE

The adoption of the pact demonstrated the signatories' willingness to make military commitments for their common security. Although NATO was never used in actual combat with the Soviet Union, its formation illustrated

NATO's EUROPEAN MEMBER STATES, 1955

the unity of spirit and dedication of its Western democracies. Members who entered NATO later included Greece and Turkey (1952), West Germany (1955), and Spain (1981). NATO succeeded in fulfilling its primary purpose of creating a viable military counterweight to Soviet power.

With the collapse of communist systems in the states of Eastern Europe in 1989, followed by the disintegration of the Soviet Union in 1991, the relevance and functions of NATO had to be reconsidered. Despite the apparent end of the Cold War, all member governments agreed that the organization still served the primary objective of promoting stability within Europe, even as new problems (such as the Yugoslav civil war) appeared on the horizon. That conflict blossomed in the mid-1990's, eventually provoking a NATO response, primarily in the form of air strikes against Serbian forces, and NATO participation in the Dayton Peace Accord follow-up implementation.

When civil war broke out in Kosovo, NATO members circumvented the United Nations, making the decision to bomb Serbia for its refusal to sign an ultimatum to allow NATO peacekeepers to deploy in Kosovo and to permit Kosovo's autonomy. NATO forces were prominent in the post-bombing period of Kosovo reconstruction. This event was unprecedented in NATO history, and required the organization to rethink its mission as a defense alliance. No NATO country was under attack; rather, NATO intervened in the domestic affairs of a nonmember state on humanitarian grounds.

NATO subsequently took yet another unprecedented step by undertaking military operations outside Europe, when in August, 2003, it assumed responsibility for military and security operations in Afghanistan after the United States toppled the Taliban regime for its assumed complicity in the September 11, 2001, terrorist attacks in the United States. Clearly, NATO has broken the mold and redefined itself.

Several East European states formerly associated with the Soviet Union applied during the 1990's for NATO membership, fearful of the possibility of a resurgence of Russian expansionism. Eventually, nine former communist countries of Eastern Europe or former Soviet Socialist Republics were admitted to NATO, after the organization decided to move forward with enlargements. These countries included Bulgaria, the Czech Republic, Hungary, Poland, Romania, and Slovakia, as well as the former Soviet Socialist Republics of Estonia, Latvia, and Lithuania. Slovenia, once a part of the former Yugoslavia, was also admitted, bringing NATO's membership to twenty-six nations in the first decade of the twenty-first century. Three other countries from the Balkans region are under consideration for membership, including Albania, Croatia, and Macedonia. Moscow has viewed NATO enlargement with suspicion, but has been in no position to prevent it.

Theodore A. Wilson and Taylor Stults

FURTHER READING

Acheson, Dean. *Present at the Creation: My Years in the State Department.* New York: Norton, 1969. Memoirs of the U.S. secretary of state at the time of NATO's formation.

Feis, Herbert. *From Trust to Terror: The Onset of the Cold War, 1945-1950.* New York: Norton, 1970. Provides a detailed account of the issues and crises during the Cold War in the later 1940's.

Judge, Edward H., and John Langdon. *The Cold War: A History through Documents.* Upper Saddle River, N.J.: Prentice-Hall, 1999. Collection of more than 130 primary sources including speeches, agreements, and declarations, arranged chronologically.

Kaplan, Lawrence S. *NATO and the United States: The Enduring Alliance.* New York: Twayne, 1988. A solid survey of the United States's relationship with its NATO partners.

Osmanczyk, Edmund Jan. *The Encyclopedia of the United Nations and International Agreements.* Edited by Anthony Mango. 4 vols. 3d ed. Philadelphia: Taylor & Francis, 2003. Provides brief but detailed entries on a variety of international organizations and agreements at the global level.

Rose, Clive. *Campaigns Against Western Defense: NATO's Adversaries and Critics.* New York: St. Martin's Press, 1985. An unusual perspective on NATO that assesses its opponents.

Schmidt, Gustav, ed. *A History of NATO: The First Fifty Years.* New York: Palgrave, 2001. A comprehensive three-volume history of NATO, from its formation in 1949 through the end of the twentieth century. Highly recommended.

Sherwen, Nicholas, ed. *NATO's Anxious Birth: The Prophetic Vision of the 1940's.* New York: St. Martin's Press, 1985. Diverse topical essays discuss the formative period of the alliance.

Truman, Harry S. *Memoirs: Years of Trial and Hope, 1946-1952.* Garden City, N.Y.: Doubleday, 1956. The president's account of the events and negotiations leading to the Western alliance in the late 1940's.

Urwin, Derek W. *The Community of Europe: A History of European Integration Since 1945.* New York: Longman, 1995. A compact, yet detailed history of the various organizations carrying out European integration after World War II.

Vandenberg, Arthur H. *The Private Papers of Senator Vandenberg.* Edited by Arthur H. Vandenberg, Jr. Boston: Houghton Mifflin, 1952. Observations of a prominent supporter of Western defense.

SEE ALSO: Mar. 5, 1946: Churchill Delivers His Iron Curtain Speech; Mar. 12, 1947: Truman Doctrine; Apr. 3, 1948: Marshall Plan Provides Aid to

Europe; Jan. 25, 1949: Soviet Bloc States Establish Council for Mutual Economic Assistance; Nov. 3, 1950: United Nations General Assembly Passes the Uniting for Peace Resolution; Oct. 22, 1951: United States Inaugurates Mutual Security Program; May 14, 1955: Warsaw Pact Is Signed; Sept. 1-5, 1961: Nonaligned Movement Meets; Mar. 7, 1966: France Withdraws from NATO's Military Structure; July 1, 1991: Dissolution of the Warsaw Pact.

■ JUNE, 1949

NINETEEN EIGHTY-FOUR PORTRAYS TOTALITARIANISM AND MIND CONTROL

George Orwell's most powerful warning against totalitarianism fulfilled his stated desire to make political writing into an art; it represents the single most famous example of the science-fiction subgenre known as dystopian literature.

LOCALE: London, England
CATEGORY: Literature

KEY FIGURES
George Orwell (Eric Arthur Blair; 1903-1950), British writer
Fredric Warburg (1898-1981), British publisher and Orwell's friend

SUMMARY OF EVENT
When *Nineteen Eighty-Four* was published in June, 1949, George Orwell had entered the last phase of his chronic illness. Despite his persistent stubborn hopes of a full recovery from the respiratory problems and tuberculosis that plagued his adult life, he must also have felt a strong sense of urgency. The speed of the planning and writing of the book, completed in two years, exceeded even his usual astoundingly short periods of composition, especially considering that his work on the book was interrupted constantly by periods of hospitalization.

As Michael Shelden recounts in his 1991 biography of Orwell, the book was to be Orwell's self-described most important work. It was impelled by his cumulative disappointment in socialism as an effective deterrent to fascism and perhaps by a subconscious realization of his own precarious mortality. Orwell wanted *Nineteen Eighty-Four* to be his best creative work, a distillation of language, style, and ideas that would convey most compellingly his desire to make political writing into an art. It was also to be the strongest expression of the moral vision that shaped both Orwell's life and his writing.

Orwell's commitment to the idea of the constant struggle for freedom from tyranny of any kind—physical, political, or spiritual—began early in his adult life. Having failed to win entrance to the University of Oxford following his largely mediocre and unhappy school career, he more or less stumbled into joining the Indian Imperial Police in Burma (present-day Myanmar). His maternal grandmother still lived there, and his father, a lifelong minor functionary in the Indian Civil Service, believed that Orwell could follow a similarly secure, respectable, and patriotic career.

Although he did his conscientious duty in his lonely five-year tenure (1922-1927), Orwell hated the Imperial Police. He came to loathe the values that had fueled British empire building, especially the paternalistic concept of "the white man's burden," and to understand with a mixture of sympathy and fear the extent of the hatred that the Burmese felt toward their British rulers. "Shooting an Elephant" (1936), one of the many penetrating, luminously written autobiographical essays that Orwell was to produce, powerfully portrayed the dilemma of authority in which a British civil servant with a lively conscience could find himself anywhere in the sprawling British Empire.

The forging of Orwell's social consciousness begun in Burma continued through his sojourns in London and Paris between 1927 and 1929. Periodically, and by choice, he lived as a tramp and menial laborer on the fringes of these two great cities, endangering his already precarious health and threatening his personal autonomy.

Orwell's first, strongly autobiographical, book, *Down and Out in Paris and London* (1933), chronicled these experiences. Its generally good reviews marked the permanent adoption of his pen name George Orwell and gave him the opportunity to complete *Burmese Days* (1934), a very personal and vivid novel based on his Imperial Police experience. Its mixed success gave Orwell the means to abandon a wretched job to write full-time, marry, and move to the Hertfordshire countryside, where he and his wife, Eileen, ran a small country store.

A Clergyman's Daughter (1935) and *Keep the Aspidistra Flying* (1936) were the resulting two novels. In them, he explored both the writing of pure fiction (largely a failure) and more memorably the lives of two alienated, emotionally starved individuals stifled by the rigid morality of middle-class England. In these novels' central protagonists lay the seeds of Winston Smith's character and his lonely struggle for personal fulfillment.

The rise of fascism in Europe during the 1930's stirred Orwell's interest

George Orwell. (Library of Congress)

in socialism, which, he declared in his next nonfiction work, *The Road to Wigan Pier* (1937), was the only ideological and political movement that could stand in opposition to fascism. In 1936, Orwell went to Spain, eventually joining the International Brigade to fight the Fascists led by Francisco Franco. He recounted his difficult sojourn in Spain in *Homage to Catalonia* (1938), in which his disillusionment with internal party politics and his political idealism are expressed in some of his best writing to that time. In typical fashion, he understated his own dedication and heroism in that struggle.

Recovering slowly from a bullet wound to the throat, an exhausted Orwell conceived and wrote his next novel, *Coming Up for Air* (1939), during a "rest cure" in Morocco. Its lyrical depiction of the South English countryside (later echoed in *Nineteen Eighty-Four*'s Edenic Golden Country) was undercut by a strong sense of doom, soon given credibility by the Luftwaffe's devastation of England's major cities and much of its southern landscape during World War II.

Orwell devoted himself courageously to the civil defense of England throughout the war. His writing during this period was confined to a series of more and more confident and incisive essays and reviews, in which he polished both his prose and his insightful political commentary into brilliance. In 1945, he published *Animal Farm*, the political fable that was finally to bring him enormous popular fame. This satirical indictment of the Russian

Revolution's worst aspects appealed to the public imagination in Great Britain and North America just as the Cold War was beginning. *Animal Farm* paved the way for *Nineteen Eighty-Four* and elucidated Orwell's opinion that socialism itself was not the danger: the Soviet model and its power-hungry leaders were.

Animal Farm was arguably a masterpiece, but *Nineteen Eighty-Four* was the work toward which Orwell's vision, through almost all of his other fiction and nonfiction, had been developing. At its center lies Orwell's perception that power and its abuse are the essential evils against which humanity must always pit itself. In the novel, under the all-seeing, paternalistic eye of Big Brother, Winston Smith (embodying in his given name the fierce spirit of Winston Churchill and in his surname, common man) struggles to preserve his memory, emotions, identity, and above all his hope against the forceful repressiveness of the sterile totalitarian society in which he exists.

The principles of INGSOC (English Socialism), summarized in a trio of paradoxical slogans, provide the regime's overtly simple public ideology. The welfare of the state is not the real raison d'étre of INGSOC, which is instead dedicated to the complete subjugation of its people to the power of a tiny elite. Control of daily life is pervasive and absolute. Although Smith recognizes this truth intellectually, he clings stubbornly to the hope that one day the mass of the "proles" (proletarians, or working-class people) will rise up and overthrow the tyrants. Expressing Orwell's socialism, Smith recognizes that "if there is hope, it lies in the proles." Even his recognition of the proles' current apathy and debasement does not quench either his optimism or a will to survive that he perceives as endemic to humans. "DOWN WITH BIG BROTHER," writes Smith repeatedly in his illicit diary.

Smith eventually is subjugated to the Party's power through torture inflicted physically, mentally, and emotionally. The torture is carried out meticulously and with leisurely certainty by O'Brien, Big Brother's Mephistophelian spokesman and a man in whom Smith had mistakenly sensed an ally. Despite the explication of the Party's overwhelming control that O'Brien unfolds, Smith clings as long as possible to his own belief: "I *know* that you will fail. There is something in the universe—I don't know, some spirit, some principle—that you will never overcome." The novel's closing sentence—"He loved Big Brother"—seems to signify Smith's defeat, however, as Smith is a lone individual and he struggles as an individual. The only hope to change the system and eliminate Big Brother, the book implies, is a mass uprising: If there is hope, it lies in the proles.

The novel's projected title was *The Last Man in Europe*. On January 25, 1949, Orwell and his publisher, Fredric Warburg, agreed on *Nineteen Eighty-Four* as a more suitable title, arrived at simply by reversing the last two digits of the novel's year of completion. The original title does embody much of the novel's central vision. Smith indeed can be seen as Europe's "last man," the articulator of humankind's desire to be free, the representative of what Orwell called elsewhere in a poem "the crystal spirit." As well, the word "Europe" in the novel's first title conjures the specter of thousands of years of history (however bloody at times), civility, and culture crushed under tyranny's heel. Whatever its title, the novel made vividly clear Orwell's main intention: to warn against authoritarianism in general, whether right or left in the political spectrum. That he made his political point so well in a book that also succeeded as a work of fiction is a tribute to Orwell's formidable powers as a writer.

SIGNIFICANCE

Orwell died in January, 1950, so he certainly was aware of the huge popular success of *Nineteen Eighty-Four* and its critical acclaim, but he could not have envisioned its lasting domination in the literary firmament. "Orwellian" is an adjective now popularly used to describe fictional and nonfictional governments and societies characterized by repression or diabolical ideologies; the widespread recognition of at least Orwell's last two fictional works is testimony to their impact.

Critical acclaim for *Nineteen Eighty-Four* in both Great Britain and the United States was even more positive and widespread than it had been for *Animal Farm*, with respected writers such as V. S. Pritchett, Lionel Trilling, and Aldous Huxley weighing in with praise. Any criticism from socialists that the novel was an attack on socialism in particular Orwell denied swiftly and firmly in letters and articles he wrote in response. He reaffirmed his support of socialism as an ideology, though he continued to criticize its abuses.

A general fear of Joseph Stalin's continued power, underscored by acceleration of the Cold War and the rise of McCarthyism in the United States, made Orwell's reading public especially vulnerable to fears of the future and the loss of personal freedom. Interestingly, 1949 also saw the production of Arthur Miller's *Death of a Salesman*, which portrayed poignantly the tragedy of that inveterate dreamer, lover of the pastoral, and "little" man, salesman Willie Loman, obsessed with his stifling urban life and his total failure to "measure up."

Right up to his premature death, Orwell displayed his own "crystal spirit," hopeful to the end that he would get well, burning as usual to get on with other writing projects. His legacy to humanity has been his clear-eyed vision and sharp, luminous prose, urging readers over and over again to embrace the socialist ideal as a means to and fight for freedom against tyranny.

Jill Rollins

Further Reading

Bloom, Harold, ed. *George Orwell's "Nineteen Eighty-Four."* Philadelphia: Chelsea House, 2004. Compilation of essays by leading scholars, examining Orwell's work from a variety of angles. Bibliographic references and index.

Calder, Jenni. *"Animal Farm" and "Nineteen Eighty-Four."* Philadelphia: Open University Press, 1987. Part of a series of short introductory books about major writers, texts, and literary concepts. Seven chapters link common thematic, stylistic, and political aspects of the two novels. "Suggestions for Further Reading" is geared to student work on Orwell's principal novels. Helpful and straightforward.

George Orwell and "Nineteen Eighty-Four." Trivandrum: Institute of English, University of Kerala, 1985. The papers of conference speakers who represent the cream of Orwell scholars. The novel is examined under four topics: "The Test," "The Man," "The Book," and "Its Meaning Today." A comprehensive, annotated bibliography follows. Invaluable for in-depth study of the novel.

Gleason, Abbott, Jack Goldsmith, and Martha C. Nussbaum, eds. *On "Nineteen Eighty-Four": Orwell and Our Future.* Princeton, N.J.: Princeton University Press, 2005. Compilation of revised papers presented at a 1999 conference on the lessons of *Nineteen Eighty-Four* for the present and the future. Bibliographic references and index.

Howe, Irving, ed. *Orwell's "Nineteen Eighty-Four": Text, Sources, Criticism.* 2d ed. New York: Harcourt Brace Jovanovich, 1982. This essential compendium consists of the text of the novel and eight more parts comprising short, succinct selections by and about Orwell and his works; criticism by such luminaries as Aldous Huxley, Bertrand Russell, and Lionel Trilling; reviews of the novel; analyses of totalitarianism; and recent views.

Meyers, Jeffrey. *A Reader's Guide to George Orwell.* London: Thames & Hudson, 1975. In clear, straightforward chapters, Meyers guides readers through the Orwell canon. Chapter 8 is a particularly interesting theory of the novel's sources of inspiration. Bibliography and index included.

_____, ed. *George Orwell: The Critical Heritage.* London: Routledge & Kegan Paul, 1975. An enormously rich collection of critical writing, mainly book reviews in whole or in part, on all of Orwell's fiction and nonfiction, including posthumous. Essential study compiled by the preeminent Orwell expert.

Reilly, Patrick. *"Nineteen Eighty-Four": Past, Present, and Future.* Twayne's Masterwork Studies 30. Boston: Twayne, 1989. A scholarly work in two sections. The first discusses historical context, the novel's importance, and its critical reception; the second is a series of four interpretations, quite idiosyncratic, of the novel's several themes. Very thorough bibliography and index.

Shelden, Michael. *Orwell: The Authorized Biography.* New York: Harper-Collins, 1991. An exhaustively researched chronicle of Orwell's life, inspiration, and works, written in lucid prose. Includes photos, bibliographies of primary and secondary sources, comprehensive source notes, and an excellent, thorough, useful index. The viewpoint is somewhat biased in places, but fact and commentary are generally well balanced. Absorbing and essential.

Whiffield, Stephen. *The Culture of the Cold War.* 2d ed. Baltimore: Johns Hopkins University Press, 1996. Describes and analyzes the anticommunist rhetoric that flourished in the popular culture of the 1940's and 1950's, including films, television, and literature. Includes bibliography and index.

Woodcock, George. *Orwell's Message: 1984 and the Present.* Madeira Park, B.C.: Harbour, 1984. Woodcock was Orwell's friend and a respected critic who perhaps knew Orwell and his writings most intimately. He presents a reassessment of the novel in four thorough, informative chapters. Index.

SEE ALSO: Mar. 5, 1946: Churchill Delivers His Iron Curtain Speech; Jan. 22, 1953: *The Crucible* Allegorizes the Red Scare Era; Oct., 1957: Pasternak's *Doctor Zhivago* Is Published; Dec. 3, 1963: Havel's *The Garden Party* Satirizes Life Under Communism; Feb. 13, 1974: Soviet Union Expels Solzhenitsyn.

■ **SEPTEMBER 21-OCTOBER 7, 1949**

GERMANY SPLITS INTO TWO REPUBLICS

The formation of two German republics—the German Democratic Republic and the Federal Republic of Germany—powerfully symbolized the division of Cold War-era Europe into two hostile blocs: Eastern socialist and Western democratic.

ALSO KNOWN AS: German partition
LOCALE: Bonn and Berlin, Germany
CATEGORIES: Expansion and land acquisition; government and politics

KEY FIGURES

Konrad Adenauer (1876-1967), chancellor of the Federal Republic of
  Germany and chairman of the Christian Democratic Union, 1949-1963
James Francis Byrnes (1879-1972), U.S. secretary of state, 1945-1947
Lucius DuBignon Clay (1897-1978), U.S. Army general and military
  governor of the U.S. occupation zone, 1947-1949
Theodor Heuss (1884-1963), president of the Federal Republic of Germany
  and chairman of the Free Democratic Party, 1949-1959
Walter Ulbricht (1893-1973), head of the ruling Socialist Unity Party of East
  Germany

SUMMARY OF EVENT

Set in motion by passage of the Basic Law on May 23, 1949, the formal establishment of the Federal Republic of Germany (FRG) and the German Democratic Republic (GDR) occurred on September 21 and October 7, 1949,
respectively. The creation of these two separate German states was the ultimate consequence of the Cold War between the United States and the Soviet Union that evolved soon after the defeat of Nazi Germany. The division
of Germany came to symbolize the division of the world into Eastern and
Western blocs and represented one of the most serious threats to world
peace.

At the close of World War II, the Allied Powers had concerned themselves only in a limited way with the future of Germany. In effect, they had
decided to divide the prewar territory of the German Reich into eight separate parts. The most important were the four zones of occupation. The capital city of Berlin was given separate special status, placed under four-power
control and divided into four occupation sectors. East Prussia was divided,
the northern half given to the Soviet Union and the southern half placed
under Polish administration, along with all the territory east of a line
formed by the Oder and the western Neisse rivers. In addition, the Saar region was given special status and placed under French control.

Regarding the control machinery for the occupation zones, it was stipulated that each Allied commander in chief would function as military governor in his respective occupation zone. Matters of common concern to all of
occupied Germany were to be dealt with by an Allied Control Council.
These arrangements were intended to be temporary, pending more detailed and permanent agreements for the uniform political and economic
administration of Germany. Such agreements, however, would not materi-
alize for thirty-five years.

At the Potsdam Conference in the summer of 1945, the victorious Allies
reiterated their intentions for defeated Germany. These included complete

disarmament and demilitarization; the eradication of all vestiges of Nazism and the restructuring of German political life along democratic lines; the destruction of the industrial cartels and monopolies; and the extraction of reparations. At this time, major differences regarding the future of Germany between the United States and the United Kingdom on one side and the Soviet Union on the other were already apparent. Disagreement over the issue of reparations was the major reason for the failure to reach a permanent agreement on all of occupied Germany.

The United States and the United Kingdom were becoming apprehen-

PARTITION OF GERMANY, 1949

West German chancellor Konrad Adenauer. (Library of Congress)

sive about Soviet power extending deep into central Europe, and they envisioned a revived Germany serving as a barrier to the expansion of communism. Conversely, the Soviet Union was unwilling to relinquish its claim to participate in the determination of p3olicies regarding the western zones and to face the prospect of having the resources of that area turned against it. In the end, it was agreed that each occupying power could draw reparations from its own zone and the Soviet Union, in view of the greater industrial wealth in the western zones, would receive from these zones an additional 25 percent of the industrial equipment considered unessential for the German peace economy.

The provisions were highly ambiguous and the subject of considerable polemics between the occupying powers. A major item of contention was whether the Soviet Union's share of reparations should be derived from the removal of plants existing at the end of the war or from current production. The United States refused to allow payments from current production.

The functioning of the Allied Control Council came to an end when the Soviet commandant walked out of the Control Council on March 20 and the Soviet military administration began to impose a blockade on Berlin shortly thereafter. As the hostilities and suspicions between the powers mounted, the Soviets used their control over the military and civilian traffic between the western sectors and Berlin to retaliate for what they considered hostile acts. In this case, it was the introduction into West Berlin of the German mark, the new currency of the western zones. On July 24, the Soviets halted all rail and road traffic with the West. The Berlin blockade was the most serious crisis of the evolving Cold War. The United States responded by supplying the daily needs of the western sectors through the most massive airlift in history, for a period of eleven months. The consequence was the definite split of Berlin.

The sobering crisis also had the effect of ending the stubborn French opposition to the creation of a West German government. Moreover, the path was clear for twelve nations to respond to the United States' initiatives and to negotiate the North Atlantic Treaty, signed on April 4, 1949.

The United States and the United Kingdom had already agreed to an economic fusion of their zones as early as December, 1946. The area, known as Bizonia, was to become self-sustaining in three years and thus reduce occupation costs. With the assistance of selected German leaders, an administrative machinery was established in Frankfurt. By 1947, an economic council was in existence, the members of which were selected by the popular branches of the newly established provincial legislatures within Bizonia. This body could adopt and promulgate ordinances, with the approval of the Anglo-American Bipartite Board. Soon an executive committee and a German high court were added to the Economic Council. Thus, the organs of a central German government were gradually emerging for the American and British zones. The growing split between the Soviet Union and the three western Allies ultimately induced France to join in the establishment of a central German government for all three western zones.

The United States had been on public record since September, 1946, when Secretary of State James Francis Byrnes declared that the United States would grant the German people the right to manage their own affairs, as soon as they were able to do so in a democratic manner. This matter was more deliberately taken up at the meeting of the Council of Ministers in London, in February, 1948. In addition to the three western Allies, Belgium, the Netherlands, and Luxembourg were participating in the deliberations. At this time, basic agreement on the fusion of the three western zones was achieved.

As the four-power control apparatus had come to a complete standstill in mid-1948, the western Allies proceeded with specific trizonal arrangements. The heads of the various German provincial governments were empowered by the military governors to convene a constituent assembly for the purpose of drafting a democratic, federal constitution. The German assembly, apprehensive about finalizing the division of Germany and desirous to give the formal arrangements a kind of provisional status, called itself "Parliamentary Council" and the new constitution came to be referred to as "Basic Law." The composition of the Parliamentary Council reflected the proportionate strength of the political parties. Konrad Adenauer, the chairman of the Christian Democratic Union (CDU), was elected the presiding officer.

SIGNIFICANCE

On May 23, 1949, the Basic Law was formally adopted. The Allies approved it with some reservations and negotiated for the arrangements paving the way for civilian control. Residual occupation powers were exercised by a new Allied High Commission. Following the first postwar elections, the new Parliament convened in Bonn for its inaugural session on September 7. A federal convention elected Theodor Heuss, the chairman of the Free Democratic Party (FDP), as federal president. Heuss then nominated Adenauer for federal chancellor. Adenauer was elected by the Parliament with a one-vote margin and formed a coalition government. Thus, all the basic arrangements being attended to, the Federal Republic of Germany was officially launched in a formal ceremony on September 21.

The Soviet Union strongly and bitterly protested the establishment of the West German state. In its zone, however, fundamental societal changes had been made, with the objective of eliminating all aspects of capitalism and creating a socialist society. The Soviet military administration had for some time permitted the formation of German central organs. These were controlled by the communist-dominated Socialist Unity Party (SED), under the effective leadership of Walter Ulbricht. The Soviet Union was, therefore, able to follow suit quickly in the formal division of Germany. It authorized the drafting of a constitution for an East German state. On October 7, the so-called German People's Council convened in Berlin and voted unanimously to transform itself into the provisional People's Chamber of the German Democratic Republic and adopted the new constitution, thereby formally launching the GDR. Germany would remain divided until the dramatic events of 1989 with the fall of the Berlin wall and the formal treaty of reunification on October 3, 1990.

Manfred Grote and Steve D. Boilard

FURTHER READING

Adenauer, Konrad. *Memoirs, 1945-1953.* Translated by Beate Ruhm von Oppen. Chicago: Henry Regnery, 1966. West Germany's first chancellor describes the first years after the defeat of Hitler. Also examines the establishment of the Federal Republic of Germany.

Clay, Lucius D. *Decision in Germany.* Garden City, N.Y.: Doubleday, 1950. A detailed, firsthand account of the occupation of defeated Germany by the Allies, and the subsequent partition and division of the country. Clay was the military governor of the U.S. occupation zone.

LaFeber, Walter. *America, Russia, and the Cold War: 1945-2006.* New York: McGraw-Hill. 2008. Focuses on the fraught relations between the United States and the Soviet Union and how their conflict manifested worldwide. Contains illustrations and maps.

Fulbrook, Mary. *A Concise History of Germany.* 2d ed. New York: Cambridge University Press, 2004. A recommended historical study that includes the chapters "The Two Germanies, 1945-1990," "The Federal Republic of Germany Since 1990," and "Patterns and Problems of German History." Includes maps.

Kitchen, Martin. *A History of Modern Germany, 1800-2000.* Malden, Mass.: Blackwell, 2006. A comprehensive historical study of Germany to the end of the twentieth century. Includes maps.

Sewell, Mike. *The Cold War.* Cambridge, U.K.: Cambridge University Press, 2002. Concise introductory text that also covers the historiography of the Cold War. Contains illustrations and maps.

Sowden, J. K. "Division 1949-1955." In *The German Question, 1945-1973: Continuity in Change.* New York: St. Martin's Press, 1975. Chapter 4 presents an account of the procedural details surrounding the creation of West and East Germany.

Turner, Henry Ashby, Jr. "The Birth of Two New Governments." In *Germany from Partition to Reunification.* New Haven, Conn.: Yale University Press, 1992. Chapter 2 gives a brief account of the formal creation of the two German states.

United States Senate. Committee on Foreign Relations. *Documents on Germany, 1944-1970.* Washington, D.C.: Government Printing Office, 1971. Includes text of numerous official documents relating to the division of Germany.

SEE ALSO: Feb. 4-11, 1945: Yalta Conference; July 17-Aug. 2, 1945: Potsdam Conference; Mar. 5, 1946: Churchill Delivers His Iron Curtain Speech; June 24, 1948-May 11, 1949: Berlin Blockade and Airlift; 1949-1961: East Germans Flee to West to Escape Communist Regime; Aug. 13, 1961: Communists Raise the Berlin Wall; June 21, 1973: East and West Germany Establish Diplomatic Relations; Nov. 9, 1989: Fall of the Berlin Wall; July 16, 1990: Gorbachev Agrees to Membership of a United Germany in NATO.

■ FEBRUARY 14, 1950

STALIN AND MAO PEN A DEFENSE PACT

The Defense Pact signed in Moscow formalized the political alliance between the two leading powers of the international communist movement. The alliance governed their relations in the 1950's and contributed to the bipolar character of the Cold War.

ALSO KNOWN AS: Sino-Soviet alliance
LOCALE: Moscow, Soviet Union
CATEGORY: Diplomacy and international relations

KEY FIGURES
Mao Zedong (Mao Tse-tung; 1893-1976), chairman of the Chinese
    Communist Party, 1935-1976, and top Chinese leader, 1949-1976
Joseph Stalin (Joseph Vissarionovich Dzhugashvili; 1878-1953), general
    secretary of the Central Committee of the Communist Party of the
    Soviet Union, 1922-1953, and premier, 1941-1953
Nikita S. Khrushchev (1894-1971), first secretary of the Communist Party of
    the Soviet Union, 1953-1964, and premier, 1958-1964

SUMMARY OF EVENT
On October 1, 1949, Mao Zedong, the chairman of the Chinese Communist Party, having defeated the nationalist forces of Chiang Kai-Shek, proclaimed the creation of the People's Republic of China (PRC). Immediately, the PRC was recognized by the Soviet Union. The United States was among the states that chose not to recognize the PRC. At that time, the Soviet Union and the West had been engaged in a Cold War for some four years. There was little doubt which side the PRC would choose to align with. In mid-1949, Mao had declared his policy of "leaning to one side" as a commitment to the global forces of socialism. Mao and Stalin shared a belief in the doctrine of Marxism-Leninism (though they interpreted that doctrine differently), but more important, they had a common enemy in the United States. There were also serious differences between them. Mao wanted the restoration to China of concessions made to the Soviet Union by the 1945 Sino-Soviet treaty; he wanted more economic assistance than Moscow was prepared to give; and he wanted recognition from the Soviet leadership as an equal in the struggle against Western imperialism. Thus, even as they considered themselves partners, Stalin and Mao were also rivals.

To resolve their differences and formulate a common strategy, Mao went to Moscow in mid-December, 1949. The fact that he found it necessary to remain in Moscow for eight weeks was an indication that the negotiations were intensive and contentious. The result was the signing on February 14, 1950, of a thirty-year treaty of friendship, alliance, and mutual assistance. It provided for common action against aggression by Japan or any country acting in collaboration with Japan. The real target was the United States. Each power agreed to render military and other assistance should the other become involved in a war with Japan or any state allied with Japan.

On the contentious issue of Soviet concessions in China, Mao scored several major victories. Stalin agreed to surrender Soviet rights to ownership by 1952 of the Changchun Railroad without compensation. By the end of that year, Stalin also agreed to withdraw Soviet troops from Port Arthur. The fate of Dalian was left undetermined. A separate communique specified that both parties would recognize the independence of the Mongolian People's Republic, a territory (Outer Mongolia) that the Chinese would have preferred to be a part of China. Stalin's financial assistance was minimal, even niggardly. He agreed to loan China $300,000,000 (with interest) over the period 1950-1954. Overall, the terms of the 1950 alliance contained benefits and costs to both parties. However, Mao departed Moscow dissatisfied with the dominating role played by Stalin, who left no doubt which of the partners was senior and which junior.

Fundamentally, the Sino-Soviet alliance transformed the balance of power in East Asia. That transformation made possible the Korean War, which broke out some four months later. The impetus for the North Korean attack on South Korea came from Kim Il Sung, North Korea's leader. Stalin, assuming the success of the operation, gave his consent subject to Mao's willingness to go along. Mao had some reservations about the timing of the attack but agreed to have China serve as a supply zone for the operation. Mao could not have known when the war began on June 25 that Chinese involvement would go well beyond supply operations. The success of the American campaign in the fall of 1950 brought American troops close to the Yalu River, the border between China and North Korea, threatening to destroy Kim Il Sung's regime. Stalin pressured Mao to intervene, which he did on October 19, 1950. Chinese intervention turned back the American advance. By the spring of 1951, the battle lines had hardened roughly along the original North Korean-South Korean demarcation zones, where they remained until the truce agreement in July, 1953, ended the fighting. China had won a dramatic victory but at a terrible price: some 900,000 killed or wounded. Though there were disagreements between the communist allies on the strategy and financing of the Korean War, the net impact of the war was to cement the Sino-Soviet alliance. Their successful assault on American troops gave the Chinese prestige in their efforts to prove themselves worthy of a leadership role in the world communist movement.

The Sino-Soviet alliance remained strong until the end of the 1950's. Nikita S. Khrushchev, Stalin's successor, even expanded upon the benefits given to the Chinese by his predecessor. His first foreign trip, in September-October, 1954, was to Beijing. He was the first party leader to visit Mao, a fact of enormous symbolic significance to the Chinese. Khrushchev agreed to turn over to China the Lushan naval base and Soviet shares in joint companies in Manchuria and Xin Jiang. Economic cooperation between the two countries reached new levels. Reversing its policy under Stalin, the Kremlin provided state-of-the-art technology to the Chinese. There was also a dramatic increase in the number of Soviet experts and advisors sent to China. With some reluctance, the Soviet Union in October, 1957, promised to supply China with a prototype nuclear weapon. That commitment was later withdrawn.

Problems in the relationship developed in the late 1950's. Moscow became apprehensive about the radical character of Mao's domestic program and his aggressiveness in foreign policy. Khrushchev's policy of "peaceful coexistence" conflicted with China's willingness to confront the United States over Taiwan. As evidence mounted that China's nuclear program was designed to build an atomic bomb rather than for energy, the Kremlin in 1959 terminated nuclear assistance. From 1957 through 1959, distinct but muted criticisms of the other side were made in Moscow and Beijing. By 1959, Khrushchev and Mao each came to view the other as a threat to his own ambitions. Up to that time, the existence of a rupture in communist relations was unknown in the West. That changed on April 16, 1960, with the publication in China of an article "Long Live Leninism." The split in the alliance was openly acknowledged. A new stage in the Cold War had developed, and with it Chinese and Soviet relations with the West changed as well.

SIGNIFICANCE

The Sino-Soviet pact of February, 1950, profoundly shaped relations between the two communist states and the character of the Cold War during the 1950's. It established what many in the West believed to be a monolithic bloc of communist states. Prior to this alliance, the Cold War had been fought largely in Europe. With the alignment of China with the Soviet bloc, the struggle became global. The most immediate consequence of the pact was its impact on the Korean War. Though the text of the Sino-Soviet alliance made no mention of Korea, the pact created the political framework that made the war in Korea inevitable. It guaranteed that both states would cooperate in the effort to extend communist rule to South Korea, though no one could know at the time exactly what contributions each would make. As the Korean War worked itself out from 1950 through 1953, the costs turned out to be much higher for the Chinese than for the Soviets, a fact that in the longer term contributed to the Sino-Soviet split in the 1960's. Another consequence of the alliance and the Korean War was an increase in the antagonism between the PRC and the United States. Following the intervention by communist Chinese forces in Korea in the fall of 1950, Sino-American relations sharply deteriorated. President Harry S. Truman sent the Seventh Fleet to neutralize the Taiwan Strait. The United States imposed an economic embargo on the PRC and vigorously opposed the representation of Beijing in the United Nations. Not until serious differences later developed between Moscow and Beijing was it possible for a rapprochement between the two adversaries. With that rapprochement, the structure of international politics moved from bipolarity to tripolarity.

Joseph L. Nogee

FURTHER READING

Borisov, O. B., and B. T. Koloskov. *Soviet-Chinese Relations, 1945-1970.* Bloomington: Indiana University Press, 1975. Reflects official Soviet line toward China. Emphasis is on conflict with China during the 1960's, but chapter 2 covers the Sino-Soviet pact. Highly polemical.

Hunt, Michael H. *The Genesis of Chinese Communist Foreign Policy.* New York: Columbia University Press, 1996. Scholarly study of modern Chinese history relying heavily on Chinese-language sources including party documents and the memoirs and writings of Mao Zedong.

Jian, Chen. *Mao's China and the Cold War.* Charlotte: University of North Carolina Press, 2001. Examines Mao Zedong's political motives and argues that China's break with the Soviet Union and subsequent reconciliation with the United States turned the tide of the Cold War. Contains illustrations and maps.

Schwartz, Harry. *Tsars, Mandarins, and Commissars: A History of Chinese-Russian Relations.* Rev. ed. Garden City, N.Y.: Anchor Books, 1973. Short popular survey of Sino-Soviet relations written from an American perspective.

Westad, Odd Arne, ed. *Brothers In Arms: The Rise and Fall of the Sino-Soviet Alliance, 1945-1963.* Stanford, Calif.: Stanford University Press, 2000. Scholars from China, Russia, the United States, and Western Europe use documentation available in the post-Soviet period to reassess the Sino-Soviet Alliance. A lengthy introduction gives a comprehensive yet concise overview of the 1950 alliance.

Zubok, Vladislav, and Constantine Pleshakov. *Inside the Kremlin's Cold War: From Stalin to Khrushchev.* Cambridge, Mass.: Harvard University Press, 1996. Influential book using documents made available after Soviet collapse. Fine coverage of Stalin's foreign policy beliefs.

SEE ALSO: May 14, 1955: Warsaw Pact Is Signed; Spring, 1957: Mao's Hundred Flowers Campaign Begins; Beginning 1958: Mao's Great Leap Forward Brings Chaos to China; Feb. 11, 1966: Cuba Signs a Commercial Agreement with the Soviet Union; Mar. 2-Oct. 20, 1969: Sino-Soviet Tensions Mount Along the Ussuri River Border; Oct. 25, 1971: People's Republic of China Is Seated at the United Nations; Jan. 1, 1979: United States and China Establish Full Diplomatic Relations.

■ **JUNE 25, 1950-JULY 27, 1953**

KOREAN WAR

The first test of the U.S. policy of containment articulated in the Truman Doctrine, the Korean conflict escalated from a U.N.-led "police action" to a confrontation between the United States and the People's Republic of China.

ALSO KNOWN AS: Korean conflict
LOCALE: Korean Peninsula
CATEGORIES: Wars, uprisings, and civil unrest

KEY FIGURES
Harry S. Truman (1884-1972), president of the United States, 1945-1953
Douglas MacArthur (1880-1964), military governor of Japan, 1945-1951, and supreme commander of U.N. forces in Korea, 1950-1951
Kim Il Sung (1912-1994), premier of the Democratic People's Republic of Korea, 1948-1972, and general secretary of the Korean Workers' Party, 1946-1994
Syngman Rhee (1875-1965), president of the Republic of Korea, 1948-1960
Dwight D. Eisenhower (1890-1969), president of the United States, 1953-1961
Joseph Stalin (Joseph Vissarionovich Dzhugashvili; 1878-1953), general secretary of the Central Committee of the Communist Party of the Soviet Union, 1922-1953, and premier, 1941-1953

Summary of Event

At the end of World War II, Korea was a nation divided to allow for occupation by several members of the victorious Allied coalition. The so-called Hermit Kingdom, which had been under Japanese control for many years, was occupied by Soviet and U.S. forces, and the thirty-eighth parallel was set as a temporary line of demarcation. In their zone north of the parallel, the Soviets organized a communist regime, which was named the Democratic People's Republic of Korea (North Korea) in 1948. An old-time communist, Kim Il Sung, was its first premier. In the south, various elements struggled for power until the party of the "father of Korean nationalism," Syngman Rhee, won a United Nations-sponsored election. On August 15, 1948, Rhee became president of the Republic of Korea (South Korea).

Both Korean governments were determined to achieve unification on their own terms. Large-scale guerrilla incursions into the south were supported by the North Koreans, and retaliatory raids by South Korean forces kept the divided country in a state of crisis. Despite this situation, U.S. troops were withdrawn in June, 1949, leaving behind only a small group of technical advisers. South Korea, whose army was small, ill-trained, and poorly equipped, faced an adversary that possessed an army of 135,000 men equipped with modern Russian weapons. North Korea also had between 150 and 200 combat airplanes.

Although South Korean leaders and some in the United States feared that North Korea might attack across the thirty-eighth parallel at any time, Secretary of State Dean Acheson gave further evidence of the United States' disinterest by stating on January 12, 1950, that South Korea was not within the "defense perimeter" of the United States in the Pacific. Some authorities have suggested that Acheson's remarks sent misleading signals to North Korea about the United States' commitment to the security of South Korea. As yet, there is no documentary evidence to determine if these remarks had any effect on either North Korea or the Soviet Union. However, after the fall of the Soviet Union, historians found evidence to suggest that Joseph Stalin was deeply involved in planning the initial invasion and secretly supplied North Korea with Soviet pilots to counter U.S. airpower.

The attack came on June 25, 1950. North Korean armed forces—armored units and mechanized divisions supported by massed artillery—struck without warning across the demarcation line. Meeting only uncoordinated resistance, North Korean tanks were moving into the outer suburb of Seoul, the capital of South Korea, within thirty-six hours. Contrary to communist expectations, the United States reacted swiftly and with great determination. With U.S. encouragement, the United Nations Security Council met in special session on the day of the attack. The Soviet Union was boycotting the council at the time, and a resolution calling for an immediate end to hostilities and withdrawal of North Korean forces to their former positions on the thirty-eighth parallel was passed unanimously.

When the United Nations resolution was ignored by North Korea, the Security Council convened on June 27, and adopted a resolution that recommended that members "of the United Nations furnish such assistance to the Republic of Korea as may be necessary to repel the armed attack." President Harry S. Truman ignored recommendations of caution and acted to enforce the U.N. resolutions. On June 27, he committed U.S. air and naval forces to the conflict, as well as ground forces previously stationed in Japan.

These commitments were inadequate to stem North Korean advances. By the end of June, more than half of South Korea's army had been destroyed, and U.S. units were forced to fight countless rearguard actions in a retreat southward. In early August, a defense perimeter was created around the important port of Pusan, and after intense fighting, a stable defense line was assured. As U.S. forces and contingents from fifteen other nations arrived, General Douglas MacArthur, commander in chief of the Far East and supreme commander of U.N. forces, decided to employ his troops not in a frontal offensive from Pusan but in a daring amphibious landing at Inchon, a west coast port just miles from Seoul. This brilliantly conceived but risky operation, launched on September 15, 1950, was a great success. The North Korean army, threatened with encirclement, was forced to retreat back across the thirty-eighth parallel.

With the North Korean forces in retreat, the U.N. command was forced to make the single most important decision of the war: Should the retreating North Koreans be chased across the demarcation line? Pressed by public demands for total victory, the Truman administration cited the Security Council's resolution and gave MacArthur authorization to pursue the North Korean troops across the thirty-eighth parallel. MacArthur already had decided to take this step. He was confident that the North Korean army was effectively destroyed and that the Soviet Union and China would not risk a confrontation with U.N. forces led by the United States. The first crossing took place on October 1. United Nations and South Korean forces sped north, and by late November they were nearing the Yalu River boundary between North Korea and the People's Republic of China.

The seesaw struggle was reversed once again by the entry of Chinese "volunteers" into the war. Chinese leaders had warned that they would not allow North Korea to be invaded and would come to the aid of their communist allies. U.S. intelligence services and MacArthur had dismissed these threats as rhetoric, but it soon became clear that Beijing was not bluffing. By late October, thousands of Chinese soldiers had crossed the Yalu River. A month later,

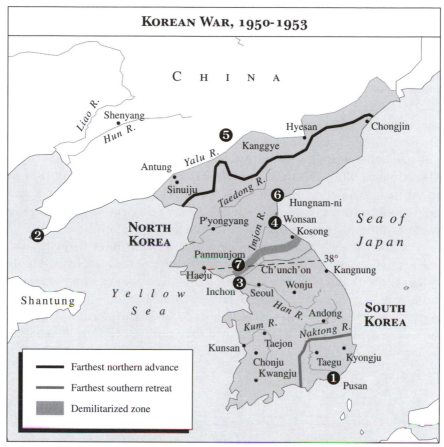

KOREAN WAR, 1950-1953

(1) Main U.N. base. (2) Russian-Chinese naval installation. (3) Sept. 15, 1950, U.N. forces land. (4) Oct. 8, 1950, U.N. forces land. (5) Nov. 26, 1950, Chinese attack. (6) Dec. 9, 1950, U.N. forces evacuate. (7) July 27, 1953, armistice signed.

they struck at the exposed flank and rear of MacArthur's overextended armies. By early December, U.N. troops were again in headlong retreat.

In the United States, there was widespread fear of an expanded war in Korea. A Gallup poll estimated that 55 percent of the people in the United States believed that World War III had begun soon after the Chinese entry into the war. A new line was organized south of the thirty-eighth parallel, and through the remaining winter and early spring months, the lines fluctuated from south of Seoul to north of the thirty-eighth parallel. On April 11, Truman relieved MacArthur of his U.N. and U.S. commands, after MacArthur publicly questioned Truman's prohibition on U.S. bombing of North Korean supply depots inside China. MacArthur's support of a wider war against the People's Republic of China had long been opposed by Truman, who feared an even greater conflict with the Soviet Union.

Military stalemate was finally reached in July, 1951. The conflict deteriorated into trench warfare, which was marked by indecisive but bloody fighting, at which the Chinese were particularly adept. The situation lasted for two cruel years. During this time, more than one million U.S. troops served in Korea. For much of this period, talks went on, seeking a cease-fire and armistice. On June 10, 1951, communist and U.N. delegations began negotiations, talks initiated by the North Koreans and welcomed by the majority of people in the United States. Most of the talks took place in the city of Panmunjom, located in the no-man's-land between the two armies. The talks broke down repeatedly because of antagonism generated by North Korean accusations of germ warfare, disputes over prisoner-of-war exchanges, and other issues.

The stalemate was a source of mounting frustration in the United States, where it influenced both the rise of McCarthyism and the election of Republican Dwight D. Eisenhower to the presidency. Eisenhower won support by promising to go to Korea if elected. He kept his pledge, but the visit had no noticeable effect on the success of the peace talks. The North Korean and Chinese negotiators ultimately modified their position on forcible repatria-

General Douglas MacArthur (right) visiting the front lines, accompanied by Major General Courtney Whitney (second from left) and Lieutenant General Matthew B. Ridgway (center, with three stars on cap), who was later to replace him as commander of United Nations ground forces in Korea. (National Archives)

tion of prisoners, and an armistice agreement was signed at Panmunjom on July 27, 1953. It provided for a cease-fire and for withdrawal of both armies two kilometers from the existing battle line, which ran from coast to coast from just below the thirty-eighth parallel in the west to thirty miles north of it in the east. The agreement also provided for the creation of the Neutral Nations Supervisory Commission to carry out the armistice terms. It further called for a political conference to settle all remaining questions, including the fate of prisoners who refused to return to their homelands. The political conference was never held, and relations between North and South Korea deteriorated because of each Korea's claims on "unification" with the other.

SIGNIFICANCE

The Korean war lasted three years and one month and took more than four million lives. There was little celebration in the United States at its conclusion. Upon signing the armistice in Panmunjom, U.S. commander Mark W. Clark declared, "I cannot find it in me to exalt at this hour." General Omar N. Bradley later observed that the conflict was "the wrong war, in the wrong place, at the wrong time, with the wrong enemy." Some commentators did commend the United States' resolve in containing communism and defending South Korea, but after the deaths of 54,000 troops, 100,000 wounded, 8,000 missing in action, and a cost of 22 billion dollars, most people in the United States were simply relieved that the fighting had ceased.

A symbol of the war's unique status in history was the fact that the United States never formally declared war on China. President Truman simply referred to the military hostilities in Korea as a United Nations "police action." Because it was quickly followed by the United States' protracted war in Vietnam, the Korean War soon became known as "the forgotten war."

After the 1953 armistice, both the United States and the Soviet Union moved to fortify their positions on the Korean peninsula. Apart from isolated incidents at the border between the two Koreas, the two sides avoided open military conflict. Lacking an agreement to end hostilities, North and South Korea remained in a state of war, and more than a million troops were stationed guarding the 150-mile demilitarized zone. The United States continued to provide South Korea with military aid and stationed thousands of U.S. troops in the country.

Theodore A. Wilson and Lawrence I. Clark

FURTHER READING

Blair, Clay. *The Forgotten War: America in Korea, 1950-1953.* New York: Times Books, 1987. A well-researched, comprehensive examination of the origins and conduct of the Korean War. Index.

Edwards, Paul M. *The Korean War.* Westport, Conn.: Greenwood Press, 2006. Part of the Daily Life Through History series, this book by a Korean War veteran and prolific scholar details the experiences of the individual troops fighting in Korea. Bibliographic references and index.

Hastings, Max. *The Korean War.* New York: Simon & Schuster, 1987. An in-depth examination of military operations of the nations involved in the Korean War, from a British military historian. Chronology of the war, bibliography, index.

Hoyt, Edwin P. *The Day the Chinese Attacked: Korea, 1950.* New York: McGraw-Hill, 1990. An investigation of the misperceptions and policy failures in the United States and China that led to the Chinese entry into the Korean War in October, 1950. Bibliography, index.

Hughes, Matthew, and Matthew S. Seligmann. *Does Peace Lead to War? Peace Settlements and Conflict in the Modern Age.* Stroud, Gloucestershire, England: Sutton, 2002. Traces the roots of major international conflicts of the twentieth century to failed peace accords. Bibliographic references and index.

James, D. Clayton, and Anne S. Wells. *Refighting the Last War: Command and Crisis in Korea, 1950-1953.* New York: Free Press, 1993. Provides a detailed examination of the conduct of the leadership, personalities, and viewpoints of President Truman, Douglas MacArthur, Matthew B. Ridgeway, Mark Clark, and Turner Joy. Index.

Levering, Ralph B. *The Cold War: A Post-Cold War History.* 2d ed. Arlington Heights, Ill.: Harlan Davidson, 2005. Reassesses the Cold War in light of archival materials that were released after the collapse of the Soviet Union. Includes detailed analysis of the wars in Korea and Vietnam and the Cuban Missile Crisis.

Levine, Alan J. *Stalin's Last War: Korea and the Approach to World War III.* Jefferson, N.C.: McFarland, 2005. In addition to detailed information on the military campaign in Korea itself, this text provides a global history of the Korean War, emphasizing its crucial place in Cold War history and the events relating to the war, in Europe, Asia, and North America. Bibliographic references and index.

Stokesbury, James L. *A Short History of the Korean War.* New York: William Morrow, 1988. A brief introduction to the sources, conduct, and outcome of the Korean War. Suggested readings, index.

Whelan, Richard. *Drawing the Line: The Korean War, 1950-1953.* Boston: Little, Brown, 1990. Using declassified documents, this detailed examination of the war focuses mainly on the war's roots and the effects of U.S. politics on the Korean War.

SEE ALSO: Mar. 12, 1947: Truman Doctrine; Nov. 4, 1952: Eisenhower Is Elected President; Jan. 5, 1957: Eisenhower Doctrine; Nov. 14, 1961: Kennedy Expands U.S. Involvement in Vietnam; Aug. 7, 1964-Jan. 27, 1973: United States Enters the Vietnam War; Jan. 23, 1968: North Korea Seizes the USS *Pueblo*; Sept. 1, 1983: Soviet Jets Shoot Down Korean Air Lines Flight 007.

■ JULY 1, 1950

EUROPEAN PAYMENTS UNION IS FORMED

Sixteen European nations formed the European Payments Union, an organization designed to coordinate Marshall Plan expenditures and aid the rebuilding of European infrastructure damaged or destroyed in World War II. Formally created on July 1, 1950, the union was intended to be temporary, and it dissolved in 1958. It was succeeded by the European Monetary Agreement.

ALSO KNOWN AS: EPU

LOCALE: Paris, France

CATEGORIES: Banking and finance; diplomacy and international relations; trade and commerce

KEY FIGURES

Konrad Adenauer (1876-1967), chancellor of the Federal Republic of Germany, 1949-1963

Ernest Bevin (1881-1951), foreign secretary of the United Kingdom, 1945-1951

Clement Attlee (1883-1967), prime minister of the United Kingdom, 1945-1951

Winston Churchill (1874-1965), British prime minister, 1940-1945 and 1951-1955

Harry S. Truman (1884-1972), president of the United States, 1945-1952

George C. Marshall (1880-1959), U.S. secretary of state, 1947-1949

SUMMARY OF EVENT

With victory over Nazi Germany assured but still distant in early 1945, the United States and the United Kingdom began to envision the postwar era. Critical to their designs of winning the peace were programs such as the Bretton Woods system, which locked the value of the U.S. dollar to an ounce of gold, and the International Monetary Fund, which aimed to assist countries with balance-of-payment difficulties. Both plans sought to encourage and facilitate trade liberalization on an international scale. This was deemed all the more necessary after 1947, when relations soured with former wartime ally the Soviet Union. The United States then looked to shore up "democratic," "free-market economies" in Western Europe to win a budding Cold War. An instrumental part of this new U.S. strategic endeavor was the European Recovery Program (ERP), known more commonly as the Marshall Plan.

The ERP had been inaugurated in 1948 but proposed as early as 1947 by U.S. secretary of state George C. Marshall, working for the administration of President Harry S. Truman. The ERP established two entities of great importance: the European Cooperation Administration (ECA) in Washington, and its subsidiary, Organization for European Economic Cooperation (OEEC), located in Paris. Though Western economies were already well on their way to recovery, with many having already reached and in some cases surpassed their pre-1938 production levels, the $12.4 billion that the ERP pumped into Europe certainly did not hurt. Though not as well known as either the Marshall Plan or the North Atlantic Treaty Organization (NATO)—which constituted the military arm of the larger Cold War project while the ERP addressed the economic—the European Payments Union (EPU) was designed to tip the balance in favor of capitalism. It also sought to regulate Germany and to prevent the spread of Soviet influence.

Before turning to consider the demands and interests of each of the more significant countries participating in this economic entity, itself a masterstroke of diplomatic bargaining, it is necessary to examine how the EPU functioned. The basic principle behind the EPU was the facilitation of European trade. A member-state created a line of credit with the group (multilaterally) rather than with another individual country (bilaterally). A credit limit or "quota" was established, based on a nation's annual economic output. That nation was then allowed to use that credit to "purchase" a given commodity or service from another state. Though a country might be a "debtor" to a particular trading partner, that debt would be cancelled by a "credit" held with still another party or parties. Credits and debts were thus mutually offsetting among member-states. Incentives were built into the system such that debtors were not overly penalized, and creditors not unduly rewarded.

Nonetheless, once a country exhausted its credit, a sliding scale of interest rates encouraged the correction of the imbalance. Trade liberalization smoothed the process of general exchange, but it also was an equally important goal of the EPU. Trade liberalization encouraged and, in some cases, required the reduction of import and export restrictions, doing for Europe

British prime minister Clement Attlee. (Library of Congress)

what the International Monetary Fund sought globally. The purpose here was to promote competition, which would in turn boost productivity and efficiency and eliminate overlap, thereby ensuring European integration through economic interdependency and planning.

Each participating country brought its own agendas to the bargaining table over the formation of the EPU. Some nations were more important than others in sheer economic terms. Their participation or exclusion thus threatened to change the dynamic of the entire group. Perhaps most important was Great Britain, which, just before the collapse of Nazi Germany, had witnessed the ouster of its Conservative leader Winston Churchill. Into the breach had stepped Prime Minister Clement Attlee. His new Labour Party government promptly set about instituting a welfare state derived from the principles and successes of war planning if not socialism.

In addition to protecting national sovereignty, British foreign secretary Ernest Bevin, in 1950, also sought to protect five years of Labour restructuring and nationalizations. In this case, the perceived threat was the challenge an EPU might represent for a Great Britain exposed to the financial volatility of other European powers. Equally important was the protection of the British Commonwealth, an economic bloc forged with former crown colonies. There, the pound sterling reigned supreme. Bevin hardly wished to see

English prerogatives eroded here, any further than they already had been by the power of the U.S. dollar in the post-1945 world. Such forthrightness was referred to as "British exceptionalism." This exceptionalism was tacitly but grudgingly accepted by the United States, which had the interests of other continental powers to attend to.

France wanted Great Britain to join the EPU, but not because of any innate trans-Channel fondness. In the eyes of the Fourth Republic, the English necessarily counterbalanced the might of the Federal Republic of Germany (West Germany). Germany—though reduced to rubble and divided into two countries (West and East) independently overseen by the "super-powers" of the United States and the Soviet Union, respectively—was still more than capable of dominating the continent economically. West German chancellor Konrad Adenauer, a Christian Democrat, felt that only through cooperation and integration with the rest of Western Europe could his country atone internationally for Nazi atrocities. This especially motivated his desires to smooth Franco-German relations throughout his tenure of office, which lasted until 1963. The United States sought nothing less. Postwar programs such as the Marshall Plan and the EPU aimed to root the Federal Republic to a continent looking west across the Atlantic, and not east to the orbit of Moscow.

Diplomatic wrangling—begun in late 1949 and not truly finished until the de facto establishment of the EPU in July, 1950—somehow managed to please or at least appease all parties. It even protected Great Britain's Commonwealth interests, reaffirming the status of the British pound as an international currency and even, perhaps, foreshadowing Britain's abstinence from participation in using the euro.

SIGNIFICANCE

The EPU was a true diplomatic success. Just one year before its formation, a number of setbacks had seemed to indicate that power might be shifting eastward. In 1949, the Soviet Union, for instance, broke the nuclear monopoly of the United States. Also, communists led by Mao Zedong seized power in China. Southeast Asia was astir with "Red" partisans, leading, ultimately, to the Korean War (1950-1953). The United States itself was aflame with McCarthyism, intent on rooting out communist sympathizers on its own soil.

As was the case with the establishment of NATO in 1949, the EPU was formed to recapture the forward momentum Western Europe had possessed but then feared it had lost. Neither the EPU nor the Marshall Plan were solely responsible for what would be known as the European "economic miracle," running, roughly, from the war's 1945 conclusion to the oil crisis of 1973. Nevertheless, both programs contributed at the outset to the staggeringly successful economic booms the Western powers would register across the period. Ultimately, the European Coal and Steel Community, also established in 1950 under the Schuman Plan, would best represent the Europe of the future. Until its abandonment with the Rome Treaties of 1958, however, the EPU was instrumental in promoting liberalization and integration, laying a basis for a cooperation that would endure. This was perhaps necessary in the transition from war-torn continent to economic and political union.

R. O'Brian Carter

FURTHER READING

Dinan, Desmond. *Europe Recast: A History of European Union.* Boulder, Colo.: Lynne Rienner, 2004. A rigorous yet rewarding examination of the long road to the Maastricht Treaty of the early 1990's and beyond.

Eichengreen, Barry. *Globalizing Capital: A History of the International Monetary System.* Princeton, N.J.: Princeton University Press, 1996. A detailed appraisal of the links between international economics and global politics from 1870 to the close of the twentieth century.

Gillingham, John. *European Integration, 1950-2003: Superstate or New Market Economy?* New York: Cambridge University Press, 2003. Assesses the EPU within the broader context of growing European economic and political union.

Hogan, Michael J. *The Marshall Plan: America, Britain, and the Reconstruction of Western Europe, 1947-1952.* New York: Cambridge University Press, 1987. A sophisticated analysis of the larger European Recovery Program of which the EPU was a part.

Kaplan, Jacob J., and Günther Schleiminger. *The European Payments Union: Financial Diplomacy in the 1950's.* Oxford, England: Clarendon Press, 1989. An essential monograph exploring the EPU in all of its nuances.

Maier, Charles S. "The Two Postwar Eras and the Conditions for Stability in Twentieth-Century Western Europe." *American Historical Review* 86 (April, 1981). An interpretive essay that argues that the Marshall Plan did not "save" Europe but merely contributed to furthering its economic recovery.

Schain, Martin, ed. *The Marshall Plan: Fifty Years Later.* New York: Palgrave, 2001. Essays evaluate the European Recovery Plan's contemporary and long-term impact on the Cold War and European economies. Bibliographic references and index.

SEE ALSO: Apr. 3, 1948: Marshall Plan Provides Aid to Europe; Jan. 25, 1949: Soviet Bloc States Establish Council for Mutual Economic Assistance; Oct. 23, 1954: Western European Union Is Established; July 19-20, 1956: Foreign Aid Is Withdrawn from Egypt's Aswan High Dam Project; May-June, 1968: French Students and Workers Rebel Against the Political Order; Aug. 1, 1975: Helsinki Accords Offer Terms for International Cooperation.

■ OCTOBER 7, 1950

CHINA INVADES AND BEGINS RULE OF TIBET

The Chinese invasion of Tibet and the subsequent Chinese rule and modernization of the country led to savage repression and widespread environmental destruction.

LOCALE: Tibet

CATEGORIES: Wars, uprisings, and civil unrest; expansion and land acquisition; environmental issues; human rights

KEY FIGURES

Mao Zedong (Mao Tse-tung; 1893-1976), founder and chairman of the Chinese Communist Party who ordered the invasion of Tibet

Dalai Lama (Tenzin Gyatso; b. 1935), fourteenth Dalai Lama and Tibetan religious leader, who resisted Chinese ravishment of Tibet and its traditional theocratic culture

Panchen Lama (1938-1989), Buddhist religious leader, whom the Chinese used to replace the Dalai Lama

Jawaharlal Nehru (1889-1964), Indian prime minister, who gave sanctuary to the Dalai Lama

Ngabo Ngawang Jigme (1910-2009), Tibetan cabinet member, who collaborated with the Chinese

Dan Guansan (Tan Kuan-san; fl. mid-twentieth century), Chinese military commander at the time of the 1959 Tibetan revolt

SUMMARY OF EVENT

In September, 1949, the Chinese Communist Party, led by its founder Mao Zedong, completed its seizure of power in mainland China. Chinese Nationalist forces under Chiang Kai-shek fled to Taiwan. In July, 1949, the Chinese Nationalist Mission and its puppet, the Panchen Lama, had been expelled from Tibet as a signal that Tibetans were reasserting the independence of their theocratic country. On October 7, 1950, however, claiming officially that "Tibet is part of China," Chinese communist troops invaded Eastern Tibet and the Tibetan Question emerged as a long-standing matter of Cold War contention.

Although China's People's Liberation Army (PLA) easily defeated the small and antiquated Tibetan forces, the Chinese refrained initially from driving the PLA to the Tibetan capital in Lhasa. Instead, their approach toward Tibetans appeared conciliatory. To that end, they respected Tibetan monasteries, seats and symbols of Tibet's theocratic government. They further agreed that Tibetan religion would be respected and that Tibet's supreme religious leader, the fourteenth Dalai Lama, then in exile, would be welcome to return to Lhasa. As a goodwill gesture, captured Tibetan soldiers were released.

By May, 1951, the Chinese "liberation" of Tibet appeared to be based upon mutual cooperation and conciliation. This seemed to be confirmed by the signing in Beijing, also in May, of the first Sino-Tibetan treaty in one thousand years. The treaty defined Tibet as part of China, something the Chinese had asserted for centuries, and something Tibetan officials were constrained to acknowledge.

During the next three years, however, the Chinese tightened their control over Tibet. PLA troops appeared in Lhasa, and new military highways were constructed through formidable terrain to afford the PLA reliable linkages to home. At the same time, Sino-Tibetan relations deteriorated. Few Tibetans showed any inclination to embrace communist ideology, despite Chinese attempts to subvert the religious authority represented by Tibet's thousands of monasteries. Chinese demands for the replacement of certain Tibetan officials likewise met with resistance.

Discontent had become endemic in Tibet by 1954, when the Dalai Lama was invited to Beijing; while there, he discussed the creation of a "Unified Preparatory Committee for the Autonomous Region of Tibet." During his absence (even though food and fuel were scarce in Tibet) Tibetans kept their resistance in check, fearing the Dalai Lama was Mao's hostage. Upon the Dalai Lama's return, however, Eastern Tibet erupted in guerrilla warfare, and Tibetan armed assaults on the Chinese swiftly exploded elsewhere. After a Chinese garrison near Lhasa was annihilated, Chinese reaction turned savage. Lamas and monks were humiliated, beaten, tortured, and slain. Monasteries were shelled. Ordinary people were terrorized, women were raped, and children were forcibly taken from their homes and sent to China for "reeducation." Sacred Tibetan books, relics, and other religious objects were seized or destroyed, as the Chinese, their patience gone, sought to eradicate what they perceived as a backward people and a theocratic regime mired in medieval practices.

In January, 1959, when the Dalai Lama was summoned again to Beijing, he demurred on grounds that he was undergoing lengthy and strenuous religious examinations—a response infuriating to antireligious communists. Shortly thereafter, in March, when the Dalai Lama accepted an invitation to attend festivities at a Chinese military post in Lhasa, a Chinese official was killed by Tibetans who were fearful that the Dalai Lama had entered a Chinese trap. The Chinese Military Area Command under General Dan Guansan thereupon sought to crush the rebellion with maximum force. The Dalai Lama and thousands of refugees escaped to India, where Indian prime minister Jawaharlal Nehru gave them sanctuary, while the Tibetan cabinet denounced the treaty with China and reclaimed Tibetan independence. Other cabinet officers, such as Ngabo Ngawang Jigme and enemies of the Dalai Lama, collaborated with the Chinese.

China's subsequent efforts to eradicate all opposition in Tibet set the

stage for disaster in both the human environment and in the ecology of the region. The human environment was savaged in the name of modernization. International monitors estimated that, over the course of the next decade, about 1.2 million Tibetans were killed or were forcibly resettled in China. Hundreds of thousands were pressed into forced labor, while more than 100,000 Tibetans fled into exile. Nearly all of Tibet's four thousand lamaseries and monasteries were looted or destroyed. Millions of Han Chinese were brought in to colonize Tibet, and by 1980 Han Chinese outnumbered native Tibetans.

Traditional Tibetan agriculture and other industries previously serving the Dalai Lama and a regime of monks were wiped out. Tibet's economic resources were exploited for the benefit of Chinese settlers and the Chinese army; Tibetans received only the surpluses. Chinese-style communes appeared everywhere, and massive attempts to reeducate the remaining Tibetans were initiated. Nearly complete destruction of any remaining Tibetan culture occurred between 1966 and 1968 during the Chinese Cultural Revolution.

SIGNIFICANCE

The Chinese communists modernized Tibet. They transformed its agriculture; established a modern transport and communication network; opened a number of coal, graphite, and boron mines; founded many light industries; doubled the number of hydroelectric plants by 1970; electrified the country; drastically improved sanitation facilities and urban infrastructures; and altered traditional Tibetan trade routes. For exiled Tibetans and the Dalai Lama's close followers, however, the price for such modernization was excessive.

Living standards for native Tibetans—in contrast to Chinese settlers—remained low. Worse, according to evidence weighed by the International Commission of Jurists, an independent legal association, the Chinese in Tibet were guilty of "the gravest crime of which any . . . nation can be accused . . . the intent to destroy, in whole or in part, a national, ethnic, racial, or religious group as such." A conference of Buddhists in Indonesia castigated the Chinese for their assaults on the Dalai Lama and the Tibetan Buddhists, while in September, 1973, the Soviet Union charged the Chinese with genocide in Tibet. The U.S. State Department consistently decried Chinese repressions and violations of human rights in Tibet from the 1950's into the 1990's. After Mao's death in 1976, many Chinese unofficially acknowledged such depredations but attributed them to the infamous and by-then discredited Gang of Four, a group that dominated the Cultural Revolution in China during the mid-1960's. Officially, the Chinese government

211

The Dalai Lama (left) in India shortly after fleeing Tibet in 1959. (National Archives)

continued to emphasize the undeniable progress of modernization in Tibet.

The impetus for China's seizure and forced modernization of Tibet sprang from Tibet's strategic geographical position. Tibet flanked China's Xinjiang Province, which the Chinese believed was vulnerable to Soviet ambitions. Such concerns were exacerbated after the rift in Sino-Soviet cooperation in 1960. Furthermore, the Chinese had long-standing disputes along their borders with India. They believed that this geopolitical situation placed them in a vise between Soviet and Indian territorial interests. Not least, after the Korean War, in which the Chinese intervened against the United States and its United Nations allies from 1950 to 1953, the Chinese worked swiftly to develop an arsenal of nuclear weapons and long-range missiles.

Of these strategic considerations, none was more important to the Chinese than the military integrity of Sinkiang Province. Sites in sparsely populated and inhospitable Sinkiang were the centers of China's first atomic installations. The province was a major source of uranium ores; with Soviet assistance, the Chinese produced weapons-grade uranium there. Rising Sino-Soviet tensions along Sinkiang's border with Soviet Kazakstan during the next few years prompted the Chinese to seek a safer haven in Tibet for some Lop Nor atomic facilities.

Although the precise location of the Tibetan nuclear sites was not disclosed, *The New York Times* reported in 1969 that the sites were located in high valleys among the mountains north of the Himalayas, where they were unlikely to be struck by Soviet bombs or missiles. In Western Tibet, too, by 1974, the Chinese had deployed between fifty and one hundred ballistic missiles with 1,500-mile ranges, all with nuclear warheads. In addition, the Chinese constructed at least twenty-five new airbases across southern Tibet north of the Himalayas, principally on the Chang Thang plateau.

The environmental impacts of these nuclear installations, test sites, missile ranges, and airbases were reported by international observers to have been severe. Nomadic herdsmen, for example, who traditionally had tended their flocks in Western Tibet near Rudok, were forced from their ranges by Chinese officials. The building of steel mills, roads, mines, and military installations destroyed the alpine grasses upon which Tibetan yak herds depended. The herdsmen themselves were obliged to enter agricultural communes and adapt to sedentary ways, or they were assigned to forced labor. In many subtle ways the region's ecology was altered. Although Chinese settlers introduced modern agricultural machinery and new crops and soon claimed significant increments to the crops' yields, food supplies for native Tibetans remained scarce into the 1980's.

Environmental changes that accompanied the development of Chinese atomic weaponry in Tibet and adjacent Sinkiang were more dramatic. On October 1, 1964, the Chinese detonated their first atomic bomb at Lop Nor, and additional bombs were tested, several in atmospheric bursts, during the next two decades.

Meanwhile, Tibetan resistance to Chinese authority continued. Khamba tribesmen in Eastern Tibet persisted in using guerrilla warfare that they had begun in the early 1950's against the Chinese. Likewise, the revolt that erupted in Lhasa in 1959 spread throughout the country, and resistance never entirely disappeared. In 1989, the still-exiled Dalai Lama was awarded the Nobel Peace Prize for his pacific resistance to Chinese violations of human rights in Tibet and for the international attention that he had drawn to the environmental damage that accompanied Chinese development in Tibet.

Clifton K. Yearley

FURTHER READING

Barber, Noel. *From the Land of Lost Content: The Dalai Lama's Fight for Tibet.* Boston: Houghton Mifflin, 1970. Barber, an experienced international observer, recounts the Dalai Lama's early struggles against the Chinese in Tibet. Chapters represent a month-by-month account of the 1959 revolt. Map of Lhasan plain and a historical appendix.

Gilbert, Rodney Yonkers. *Genocide in Tibet: A Study in Communist Aggression.* New York: American-Asian Educational Exchange, 1959. Presents evidence that the Chinese sought to eliminate the native Tibetan population through a combination of killings, wholesale removal of Tibetans to China, forced labor, Chinese colonization of Tibet, and the eradication of Tibetan Buddhism and the Tibetan language. Maps, bibliography.

Karan, Pradyumna P. *The Changing Face of Tibet.* Lexington: University of Kentucky Press, 1976. An excellent survey of the impact of Chinese ideology upon the physical, economic, political, and cultural landscapes of Tibet. Gives a balanced account of the Chinese invasion and the beginnings of Chinese modernization in Tibet. Maps, photographs, extensive bibliography, index.

Kolås, Åshild, and Monika P. Thowsen. *On the Margins of Tibet: Cultural Survival on the Sino-Tibetan Frontier.* Seattle: University of Washington Press, 2005. A study of the state, preservation, and survival of Tibetan culture—including language, literature, visual arts, museums, performing arts, festivals, and religion—in the context of Chinese influence in the region.

Lamb, Alastair. *Asian Frontiers: Studies in a Continuing Problem.* New York: Praeger, 1964. A scholarly analysis of the problems presented to China (and other Asian powers) by vulnerable and contested frontiers. Provides insights into Chinese and Soviet concerns over Xinjiang and Tibet, as well as China's and India's quarrels over the China-India, Nepalese, Bhutan, and Tibetan borders. Notes, bibliography, index.

Normanton, Simon. *Tibet: The Lost Civilization.* New York: Viking Press, 1988. A lavishly illustrated survey of Tibet and of the colonial rivalries that exposed its people to Western powers during the first half of the twentieth century. Chapters dealing with the last days of old Tibet and events behind the so-called Bamboo Curtain are especially relevant. Many splendid photographs.

Sperling, Elliot. *The Tibet-China Conflict: History and Polemics.* Policy Studies 7. Washington, D.C.: East-West Center Washington, 2004. A recommended resource that examines the ongoing history of conflict between Tibet and China.

Suyin, Han. *Lhasa: The Open City.* New York: Putnam, 1977. Permitted to visit Tibet in 1975, Suyin recounts her firsthand observations of Tibet fifteen years after the Chinese invasion. Emphasis is upon China's modernization of once-feudal Tibet. Despite a distinctive pro-Chinese bias, there is much useful information in this well-written work. Map, illustrations, notes, bibliography, valuable index.

Westad, Odd Arne. *The Global Cold War: Third World Interventions and the Makings of Our Times.* Cambridge, U.K.: Cambridge University Press, 2007. Examines the aftermath of the Cold War in terms of globalization and American interventionism in developing nations. Illustrated.

SEE ALSO: Jan. 29, 1955: Formosa Resolution Is Signed into Law; Jan., 1953: China Begins Its First Five-Year Plan; Spring, 1957: Mao's Hundred Flowers Campaign Begins; Beginning 1958: Mao's Great Leap Forward Brings Chaos to China; May, 1966: Cultural Revolution Begins in China; Oct. 25, 1971: People's Republic of China Is Seated at the United Nations; Feb. 21, 1972: Nixon Opens Trade with China; Sept. 9, 1976: Death of Mao Zedong Leads to Reforms in China; Feb. 17-Mar. 16, 1979: China Invades Vietnam.

■ November 3, 1950

United Nations General Assembly Passes the Uniting for Peace Resolution

Uniting for Peace, a resolution passed during the Korean War by the General Assembly, was designed to circumvent a Soviet veto that likely would have blocked the efforts of the Security Council to defend South Korea from North Korean aggression. The resolution's long-term purpose was to ensure that the United Nations could act similarly in any future crisis involving the need to keep the peace.

LOCALE: Lake Success, New York
CATEGORIES: United Nations; organizations and institutions

KEY FIGURES
Dean Acheson (1893-1971), U.S. secretary of state, 1949-1953
John Foster Dulles (1888-1959), member of the U.S. delegation to the United Nations, 1946-1949, and later U.S. secretary of state, 1953-1959
Jacob Malik (1906-1980), Soviet permanent representative to the United Nations, 1948-1952
Warren Austin (1877-1962), American permanent representative to the United Nations, 1946-1953

SUMMARY OF EVENT

In June and July, 1950, the United Nations Security Council passed three resolutions calling on U.N. members to help defend the Republic of Korea (South Korea) after North Korean forces invaded the independent nation. The Soviet Union could have used its veto to block these measures, but six months earlier it had begun a boycott against the United Nations to protest the denial of U.N. membership to the People's Republic of China. A U.N. commission that had been in Korea when the Korean War began reported that North Korea had attacked first, providing critical justification for U.N. military intervention.

U.S. state department officials quickly recognized the potential benefits in having similar commissions monitoring events in other trouble spots around the world. Responding to this proposal, Warren Austin, the American permanent representative at the United Nations, recommended instead that the Security Council establish one observation commission with authority to visit any area with a threat to peace. U.S. secretary of state Dean Acheson agreed. On July 28, he cabled a draft resolution calling for the creation of the Security Council Fact-Finding and Observation Commission to the United Kingdom and to France, requesting comments on Austin's proposal. Both London and Paris raised objections, arguing that the proposal left too much initiative to the commission, appeared to bypass the authority of the Security Council, and conflicted with an exact reading of the U.N. charter.

Acheson decided not to introduce the resolution, but he informed Britain and France that the United States would continue to study methods for strengthening the peacekeeping abilities of the United Nations, to include relying on the U.N. General Assembly. On August 1, Soviet delegate Jacob Malik returned to the Security Council and began his term as president. By August 9, Malik's use of procedural steps to delay action on Korea convinced Acheson that a resolution was necessary to circumvent such obstructionism. Paving the way for passage, Washington began turning to the General Assembly for support of the U.N. Command in Korea and worked to promote its role in the maintenance of peace and security. Acheson cabled London that the next session of the General Assembly offered a unique opportunity to utilize the lessons and psychological impact of the Korean crisis to strengthen the U.N. system for defending peace.

On September 19, Acheson addressed the opening session of the fifth General Assembly, reminding participants that articles 10, 11, and 14 of the charter vested in the assembly "responsibility for matters affecting international peace." Acheson called for steps to organize the General Assembly to discharge its responsibility promptly and decisively in cases where a single

216

member prevented action at the Security Council. The British immediately voiced concerns, claiming the proposal conflicted with a strict reading of the charter. The French worried about empowering the assembly because of its size and occasional irresponsible behavior. Washington countered that its resolution provided only for amending assembly procedures, not the charter, and that the resolution would not lead to a transfer of power from the council to the assembly. Under duress, Britain and France gave unenthusiastic support to what came to be called the Acheson Plan. On September 25, Washington sent a slightly redrafted text of the resolution to other friendly U.N. delegations. Six nations—Britain, Canada, France, the Philippines, Turkey, and Uruguay—joined the United States as cosponsors of the measure.

The Uniting for Peace resolution, submitted on October 3, had four provisions. First, it authorized seven members of the Security Council in a procedural vote or a majority of the assembly to call an emergency session of the General Assembly within twenty-four hours. Second, it established the Peace Observation Commission to provide independent information about areas with threats to peace. The commission would function only when the council, the assembly, or an interim committee directed it to do so. Third—in the

U.S. secretary of state Dean Acheson. (Library of Congress)

217

case of a "threat to the peace, breach of the peace or act of aggression"—if the Security Council, "because of lack of unanimity of its permanent members" does not "exercise its primary responsibility," then the General Assembly shall consider the matter and make "appropriate recommendations to members for collective measures." These recommendations include, "in the case of a breach of the peace or act of aggression[,] the use of armed force when necessary to maintain and restore international peace and security."

Each member nation was encouraged to create and maintain an armed force for deployment as a U.N. unit to enforce the peace. Finally, the resolution established the Collective Measures Committee, which had to study before September 1, 1951, the methods that can be used to coordinate actions by individual states in strengthening peace and security. The resolution invited members to inform the committee of the measures taken to carry out this recommendation.

U.S. delegate John Foster Dulles carried the Uniting for Peace resolution through its review before the first committee and in plenary debates. The Soviet Union insisted that the resolution was illegal because under the charter, only the Security Council could take action to maintain peace and security. India warned that the measure would make the assembly an extension of the North Atlantic Treaty Organization (NATO). On November 3, however, the General Assembly voted 52-5 for approval, with India and Argentina abstaining. Forming that same day was the Collective Measures Committee (CMC), which consisted of Australia, Belgium, Brazil, Britain, Canada, Egypt, France, Mexico, the Philippines, Turkey, the United States, and Venezuela.

In late November, Chinese forces staged a massive offensive in the Korean War that prompted units from the United Nations into rapid retreat. In January, 1952, the United States pressed for a resolution condemning China for aggression in Korea and requesting the CMC to recommend further punitive action. On February 1, the General Assembly, using the Uniting for Peace mechanism for the first time, approved a resolution that branded China an aggressor and established the Additional Measures Committee with the same members as the CMC. In 1954, after submitting three reports to the assembly, the CMC assumed standby status, but then it played no role in a series of subsequent Cold War crises.

SIGNIFICANCE

Because only the Soviet Union and its allies voted against passage of the important Uniting for Peace resolution, it soon became clear that it was the United States that dominated the United Nations early in the Cold War. In 1956, however, Moscow joined with Washington in advocating action in the

General Assembly to end the Suez Canal crisis when Britain and France used their vetoes to immobilize the Security Council.

During the Six-Day War in 1967, the Soviets acted under the Uniting for Peace resolution to secure an emergency special session of the assembly. The assembly did not comply with the Soviet request, however; only in Korea in 1950 did the United Nations use force to restore peace. Unlike the Security Council, the General Assembly is not permitted to pass binding resolutions obligating members to act; the assembly can only recommend a course of action.

Also, the assembly became increasingly more diverse after 1960, adding developing nations as members. It also began embracing neutrality and also defied American dominance of proceedings. As a result, the Uniting for Peace resolution failed to create the system of collective security that Acheson had desired. During the Kosovo crisis in 1998, both Russia and China threatened to veto any Security Council resolution authorizing military operations. NATO could have asked the General Assembly to approve its armed intervention, but it acted without using the moribund Uniting for Peace mechanism.

James I. Matray

FURTHER READING

Acheson, Dean. *Present at the Creation: My Years in the State Department.* New York: W. W. Norton, 1969. Provides a firsthand account of why the United States proposed the Uniting for Peace resolution.

Bourantonis, Dimitris, and Konstantinos Magliveras. "Anglo-American Differences over the United Nations During the Cold War: The Uniting for Peace Resolution." *Contemporary British History* 16 (Summer, 2002): 59-76. Argues that the Uniting for Peace resolution created friction in Anglo-American relations because of differing beliefs about the proper role of the United Nations.

Buergenthal, Thomas, Dinah Shelton, and David P. Stewart. *International Human Rights in a Nutshell.* 3d ed. St. Paul, Minn.: West Group, 2002. Describes the essential contents of regional and international human rights agreements, ranging from the U.N. Charter to European, inter-American, and African documents on human rights.

Finger, Seymour Maxwell. *Your Man at the U.N.: People, Politics, and Bureaucracy in Making Foreign Policy.* New York: New York University Press, 1980. Presents a concise description of the Uniting for Peace resolution, arguing that it reinforced legal and moral justification for U.S. action in Korea.

Mazuzan, George T. *Warren R. Austin at the U.N., 1946-1953.* Kent, Ohio: Kent State University Press, 1977. Considers the resolution shortsighted, noting that Austin played only a small role in its passage because he maintained unwarranted faith in the effectiveness of the Security Council.

Osmanczyk, Edmund Jan. *The Encyclopedia of the United Nations and International Agreements*. Edited by Anthony Mango. 4 vols. 3d ed. Philadelphia: Taylor & Francis, 2003. Provides brief but detailed entries on a variety of international organizations and agreements applicable on a global level.

Ryan, Stephen. *The United Nations and International Politics*. New York: St. Martin's Press, 2000. Explains that the Uniting for Peace resolution was the most important of a series of mechanisms that the United States first used during the Greek civil war to circumvent the Soviet veto.

SEE ALSO: Dec. 10, 1948: United Nations Adopts the Universal Declaration of Human Rights; June 25, 1950-July 27, 1953: Korean War; Dec. 14, 1950: United Nations High Commissioner for Refugees Statute Is Approved; Apr. 10, 1953: Hammarskjöld Is Elected U.N. Secretary-General; Dec. 14, 1955: United Nations Admits Sixteen New Members; July, 1960: United Nations Intervenes in the Congolese Civil War; 1963-1965: Crisis in U.N. Financing Emerges Over Peacekeeping Expenses; Oct. 25, 1971: People's Republic of China Is Seated at the United Nations; 1990-1994: United Nations Admits Many New Members.

■ DECEMBER 14, 1950

UNITED NATIONS HIGH COMMISSIONER FOR REFUGEES STATUTE IS APPROVED

By adopting this statute, the United Nations and international community reaffirmed their commitment to protect and assist persons with a well-founded fear of persecution if they returned to their homelands.

LOCALE: New York, New York
CATEGORIES: United Nations; laws, acts, and legal history; immigration, emigration, and relocation; human rights

KEY FIGURES
Gerrit Jan van Heuven Goedhart (1901-1956), first United Nations high commissioner for refugees

J. Donald Kingsley (1908-1972), director-general of the International
  Refugee Organization, 1949-1952, who presided over its transfer of
  authority to the U.N. high commissioners office
Trygve Lie (1896-1968), secretary-general of the United Nations, 1946-1952

SUMMARY OF EVENT

The Office of the United Nations High Commissioner for Refugees (UNHCR),
under U.N. secretary-general Trygve Lie, was created on December 14,
1950. This event, however, did not mark the first effort by the international
community to address the problem of large-scale refugee migrations. In
1921, the League of Nations appointed Fridtjof Nansen to the post of high
commissioner for refugees for the purpose of grappling with refugee problems associated with the Bolshevik revolution in Russia. Later, Nansen extended protection and assistance to Armenians, Assyro-Chaldeans, and
Turks fleeing from turmoil attending the collapse of the Ottoman Empire.
Efforts by the League of Nations on behalf of refugees continued officially
until the organization's dissolution in 1946.

During World War II and its immediate aftermath, several organizations
were established to deal with the nearly thirty million displaced persons and
refugees in Europe. Many of these people were homeless, destitute, and
highly vulnerable, especially during Europe's cold winters. The United Nations Relief and Rehabilitation Administration (UNRRA), established in
1943, cared for and assisted millions of displaced persons and repatriated
some six million persons before it was replaced by the Preparatory Commission for the International Refugee Organization (PCIRO) in 1947. The Intergovernmental Committee on Refugees (IGCR), first established in 1938
to deal with the Jewish refugee problem spawned by Nazi anti-Semitic policy
in Germany, also briefly took responsibility in 1946 for Nansen refugees who
had been under the care of the League of Nations.

In 1947, work on behalf of refugees and displaced persons in Europe was
consolidated under the authority of the PCIRO and in 1948 under the fully
constituted but temporary mandate of the International Refugee Organization (IRO). By this time, Cold War politics were chilling international relations, and the IRO contended not only with a large number of war-displaced
persons but also with new arrivals from behind the Iron Curtain. In 1946,
the U.N. General Assembly reaffirmed the principle that no persons fearing
persecution could be compelled to return to their country of origin against
their will, even if their governments insisted upon their return, as many East
European governments did. Thus, although the IRO was charged with exploring repatriation of refugees and displaced persons as the solution of
first preference, thousands of East Europeans refused to go home, so the

IRO explored possibilities of settlement in their countries of first asylum or resettlement to third countries.

Under the leadership of its directors-general, including J. Donald Kingsley, more than one million persons were resettled in third countries during the IRO's operations, mainly in the United States, Australia, Israel, and Canada. Nevertheless, by the time the IRO was liquidated and its protection function shifted to the UNHCR in 1951, there were still about 400,000 refugees under the IRO mandate who had not been resettled.

With the IRO's mandate fast approaching its conclusion, the General Assembly on December 3, 1949, established another temporary successor agency. Wrangling over the exact nature and extent of this new agency's mandate centered on whether it should be responsible for material assistance and the very expensive resettlement operations conducted by the IRO or merely for protection of refugees until resettlement was effected by another agency. The United States, which had financed up to 70 percent of the IRO's work, wished to see expenditures for refugee operations reduced, while West European countries worried about the political and economic implications of a large and lingering refugee population in their territories. The Soviet Union and East European countries resented the creation of any agency that would protect and assist exiles from their territories and refused to become members of the UNHCR, which they viewed as a tool of Western capitalism.

The upshot of these variable pressures was the creation of an agency whose responsibilities included, first and foremost, protection of refugees. The UNHCR also was given responsibility for material assistance to refugees, but its initial budget, provided out of the regular U.N. budget, included only administrative expenses, not operational ones, and any efforts by the UNHCR to raise revenue from governments or private sources directly was subject to General Assembly approval.

Under its statute, the UNHCR had no direct responsibility for resettlement of refugees; this function was later placed in the hands of the Intergovernmental Committee for European Migration. The UNHCR was given responsibility for seeking permanent solutions for refugees, which included not only repatriation and local integration but also third-country resettlement. More important, the statute's definition of the term "refugee" was sufficiently elastic to include all persons previously classified as refugees by the IRO and other persons who could show a well-founded fear of persecution if returned to their country of nationality. The definition was universal in nature, and—unlike the definition incorporated in the 1951 Convention Relating to the Status of Refugees, which contained time restrictions—was potentially applicable whenever refugee problems might arise. Moreover, the statute stipulated that the UNHCR's work was entirely nonpolitical in nature, focusing rather on the social and humanitarian aspects of refugee situations.

Answering to the General Assembly through the U.N.'s Economic and Social Council, and working under the supervision of an advisory committee composed of governments and other interested parties, Gerrit Jan van Heuven Goedhart was named to a three-year term as the UNHCR's first high commissioner and assumed his position on January 1, 1951. Operating under the statute's initially restricted and temporary, but potentially elastic, mandate, van Heuven Goedhart aggressively carved out a permanent and effective UNHCR role not only for protecting but also for assisting refugees. He won permission from the General Assembly to seek funds for emergency assistance in 1952. In 1953, the General Assembly extended the UNHCR's mandate from three to five years, and in 1954 the high commissioner was allowed to seek funds for a Program of Permanent Solutions. In the same year, the UNHCR won the first of two Nobel Peace Prizes.

Measured in human terms, the early success of the UNHCR not only meant that refugees would be spared from forcible repatriation to countries that might persecute them but also that they would be provided with care and assistance until they could find new and permanent homes. In addition to protection and assistance, the UNHCR provided hope for a better future to destitute and homeless people who otherwise might have died or languished in poverty. In time, and contrary to the initial hopes and expectations of its founders, global events dictated that the UNHCR could not remain a temporary and fragile holding operation. Hundreds of thousands of European refugees benefited from its work in the early 1950's, and as time passed millions more would benefit in every corner of the globe.

SIGNIFICANCE

The true impact of the General Assembly's decision to create the UNHCR cannot be measured solely by its immediate effects. With a budget in 1952 of little more than $700,000 and only about 400,000 European refugees under its care, the UNHCR's birth was not an especially auspicious one. Nevertheless, and despite periodic budgetary crises throughout its history, the UNHCR matured into an agency responsible for the protection and welfare of some sixteen million refugees throughout the world. Its annual budgets regularly approached or exceeded $500 million by the early 1990's. After that time, the numbers of refugees declined, in part due to successful repatriation programs and the resolution of refugee-producing disputes. UNHCR budgets in the early twenty-first century ranged between $350-400 million, as the refugee population dropped below ten million. Nevertheless, counting internally displaced persons and others of concern to the UNHCR, more than nineteen million persons fell under its mandate in 2005, and it maintained a physical presence in 116 countries.

As refugee situations developed in Africa and Asia during the 1960's and 1970's, the U.N. General Assembly encouraged the UNHCR to extend its protection and assistance functions to non-European contexts, despite the 1951 Convention Relating to the Status of Refugees' restriction that considered only those persons fleeing from persecution as a result of events prior to January 1, 1951, as refugees. This extension of UNHCR good offices was made easier when, in 1967, a protocol to the 1951 convention formally removed the time limitations. Thus, over the years—informally and through ad hoc procedures before 1967 and more formally and routinely since then—the UNHCR has extended its protection and assistance to refugees in developing countries where civil war, domestic upheaval, and political persecution, often exacerbated by drought and famine, have produced refugee flows of monumental proportions.

The hallmark of the UNHCR has been its ability to adapt to changing circumstances and to cope with the often very difficult political circumstances that surround refugee situations. Having started on tenuous footing with a fragile consensus among governments, the UNHCR, under the leadership of several high commissioners, has proven its worth as an indispensable element of the international refugee protection and assistance network.

Robert F. Gorman

FURTHER READING

Chandler, Edgar H. S. *The High Tower of Refuge.* New York: Praeger, 1959. This book, written by a former director of the Service to Refugees of the World Council of Churches, offers an inspiring and compassionate from-the-trenches perspective about refugees and relief workers, the very constituencies for which UNHCR was created and upon which it relies to carry out its mandate. Photographs, index, short bibliography.

Fullerton, Maryellen. "The International and National Protection of Refugees." In *Guide to International Human Rights Practice,* edited by Hurst Hannum. 4th ed. Ardsley, N.Y.: Transnational, 2004. Examines the international community's role in protecting political and other refugees. Recommended for study of the legal implications of refugee status and human rights.

Gordenker, Leon. *Refugees in International Relations.* New York: Columbia University Press, 1987. A thoughtful and balanced analysis of the global refugee problem and the role of the UNHCR. Using the notion of forced migrations as the test for defining refugees, the author discusses realistic ways in which the international community can respond to contemporary refugee emergencies and resolve long-term refugee situations. Bibliography, index.

Gorman, Robert F. *Coping with Africa's Refugee Burden: A Time for Solutions.* Boston: Kluwer, 1987. This book describes the difficulties encountered by the UNHCR and other bodies in meeting the assistance needs of asylum (developing) countries and their local populations, whose well-being is often adversely affected by large numbers of refugees. Figures, tables, bibliography, index.

Gowlland-Debbas, Vera, ed. *The Problem of Refugees in the Light of Contemporary International Law Issues.* Boston: Martinus. Nijhoff, 1996. A good resource exploring refugee concerns in the context of late-twentieth-century international law and policy.

Holborn, Louise W. *Refugees, a Problem of Our Times: The Work of the United Nations High Commissioner for Refugees, 1951-1972.* 2 vols. Metuchen, N.J.: Scarecrow Press, 1975. The definitive work on the formation of the UNHCR and its first two decades of work. Highly detailed and voluminously documented, this book serves as a sequel to Holborn's work on the UNHCR's predecessor, the IRO. Charts, tables, index, bibliography.

Marrus, Michael R. *The Unwanted: European Refugees in the Twentieth Century.* New York: Oxford University Press, 1985. This painstakingly researched, comprehensive, and readable history of Europe's refugee problem traces in detail Jewish and European refugee flows and the international politics that spawned them from the late nineteenth century to the creation of the UNHCR. An excellent treatment of League of Nations and pre-UNHCR international policy responses. Bibliography, index.

Shawcross, William. *The Quality of Mercy: Cambodia, Holocaust, and Modern Conscience.* New York: Simon & Schuster, 1984. This journalistic account of the conflicting interagency mandates and governmental policies that plagued the Cambodian relief effort provides insight into the difficulties that the UNHCR and other international and private relief agencies encounter in highly politicized situations. Lacks consultation with academic sources but is strong on interviews. Source section, index.

The State of the World's Refugees, 2006: Human Displacement in the New Millennium. New York: Oxford University Press, 2006. A 237-page report by the UNHCR. Focuses on the ongoing task of the agency for the new century and beyond.

Vernant, Jacques. *The Refugee in the Post-War World.* New Haven, Conn.: Yale University Press, 1953. This lengthy encyclopedic work meticulously catalogs the global refugee situation as it existed at the inception of the UNHCR. Early chapters summarize the refugee problem and international agency responses to it. Subsequent chapters catalog the legal, economic, and social status of refugees by country of reception. Charts, bibliography, index.

Zarjevski, Yefime. *A Future Preserved: International Assistance to Refugees.* Oxford, England: Pergamon Press, 1988. Chronicles the formation and growth of the UNHCR to the mid-1980's. Surveys refugee situations in various regions while documenting how the UNHCR gradually strengthened its capacity to provide protection and assistance to refugees. Bibliography, index.

Zolberg, Aristide R., Astri Suhrke, and Sergio Aguayo. *Escape from Violence: Conflict and the Refugee Crisis in the Developing World.* New York: Oxford University Press, 1989. Three refugee specialists provide a comprehensive assessment of the factors that motivate and exacerbate refugee flows in the developing world. The role of the UNHCR is ably and extensively analyzed. Exhaustively documented and footnoted. Index, no bibliography.

SEE ALSO: Nov. 29, 1947-July, 1949: Arab-Israeli War Creates Refugee Crisis; Dec. 10, 1948: United Nations Adopts the Universal Declaration of Human Rights; 1949-1961: East Germans Flee to West to Escape Communist Regime; Aug., 1954-May, 1955: Operation Passage to Freedom Evacuates Refugees from North Vietnam; 1960's: Cubans Flee to Florida and Receive Assistance; Oct. 25, 1971: People's Republic of China Is Seated at the United Nations; May, 1975: Indo-Chinese Boat People Begin Fleeing Vietnam; Apr. 1-Sept. 25, 1980: Mariel Boatlift.

■ 1951-1952

TELLER AND ULAM DEVELOP THE FIRST HYDROGEN BOMB

Inspired by the work of Ulam and others, Teller proposed a workable concept that led to the construction of a thermonuclear device called the hydrogen bomb, the most powerful bomb ever exploded.

ALSO KNOWN AS: H-bomb; superbomb
LOCALE: Los Alamos, New Mexico; Marshall Islands, Micronesia
CATEGORIES: Science and technology; engineering

KEY FIGURES

Edward Teller (1908-2003), Hungarian-born American theoretical physicist
Stanislaw Ulam (1909-1984), Polish-born American mathematician

SUMMARY OF EVENT

A few months before the 1942 creation of the Manhattan Project, the United States-led effort to build an atomic (fission) bomb, Enrico Fermi suggested to Edward Teller that such a bomb could release more of the energy that binds atomic nuclei together by heating a mass of the hydrogen isotope deuterium and igniting the fusion of hydrogen into helium. These were also the thermonuclear reactions in stars, making them shine and radiate heat, that Hans Bethe, George Gamow, and Teller had been studying in the United States since 1934. Initially, Teller dismissed Fermi's idea, but later in 1942, in collaboration with Emil Konopinski, he concluded that a hydrogen bomb, or superbomb, could be made.

German scientists were working on an atomic bomb, and with Teller's advocacy, the superbomb received serious consideration within the Manhattan Project. To increase the probability of success for the concept then championed by Teller, Konopinski suggested that the rare heavy isotope of hydrogen—tritium—should be added also as fusion fuel. An atomic bomb had not yet been produced, and in 1944 the Los Alamos Laboratory governing board concluded that Teller's proposed superbomb would require more tritium than could be available for some time. J. Robert Oppenheimer, then director at Los Alamos, stated that after World War II, the United States should make every effort to determine the practical feasibility of a hydrogen bomb. In the meantime, Teller worked less on the atomic bomb, devoting his time to investigating the superbomb.

With the war over and the atomic bomb a proven reality, Teller returned to Los Alamos in 1946 to chair a secret conference on the superbomb attended by, among other Manhattan Project veterans, Stanislaw Ulam and Klaus Emil Julius Fuchs. Supporting the investigation of Teller's concept, the conferees requested a more complete mathematical analysis of his own admittedly crude calculations on the hydrodynamics of the fusion reactions. In 1947, Teller believed that these calculations might take years. Two years later, however, for Teller, with his parents in a Hungary that was now within the folds of the Iron Curtain, and for his supporters, the Soviet Union's explosion of an atomic bomb meant that America's Cold War adversary was hard at work on its own superbomb. Even when new calculations cast further doubt on his designs, Teller began a vigorous campaign for a crash development of the superbomb, or H-bomb.

For several reasons, Oppenheimer and the General Advisory Committee

(GAC) of the Atomic Energy Commission (AEC) in 1949 did not endorse Teller's urgent demands. The GAC did not find evidence to support a high probability of success in Teller's design to warrant massive expenditures at that time. Also, the GAC was certain that with modest funding and existing facilities, the addition of fusion components to an atomic bomb would boost efficiency by several orders of magnitude, producing yields of about 200,000 tons of TNT (trinitrotoluene). Any weapon with a greater explosive yield than that, the GAC observed, could only be used to commit genocide. Teller, however, was gaining important political and military support. For him, it was a moral imperative of the United States to be the first nation to develop such a weapon.

In 1950, the same year that Fuchs admitted passing information to the Soviet Union about U.S. nuclear weapons programs, the Korean War broke out, and President Harry S. Truman decided to approve an all-out effort to build the H-bomb. The basic design under consideration remained Teller's classic superbomb, one that consisted of liquid deuterium and tritium configured within an atomic device. During that year and into the spring of 1951, however, Ulam, Cornelius J. Everett, Fermi, Frederick de Hoffman, and the ENIAC computer had disproved the workability of Teller's design. That some other design might work, however, remained a possibility.

Scientists did not doubt that fusion reactions could be induced by the explosion of an atomic bomb. The basic problem was simple and formidable; how could fusion fuel be heated and compressed long enough to achieve significant thermonuclear burning before the expansion of the fireball from the atomic explosion blew the assembly apart? During these difficult months, the collaboration of these individuals and others, and verification provided by ENIAC, moved them closer to a practical solution of building a workable H-bomb. As a group, however, their recollections and contemporary documentation revealed that they were hoping to discover that an H-bomb could not be built by any nation. Early in 1951, however, a major part of the ultimate solution came from Ulam, who proposed using the energy from an exploding atomic bomb to induce significant thermonuclear reactions in adjacent fusion fuel components.

This arrangement of materials became known as the Teller-Ulam configuration, that is, the physical separation of the A-bomb primary from the secondary's fusion fuel; all H-bombs are cylindrical, with an atomic device at one end and the other components filling the remaining space. In Teller's unexpected approach, energy from the exploding primary could be transported by X rays at near-light speed, thus affecting the secondary before the arrival of the explosion. De Hoffman's work verified and enriched the new concept.

MAKING THE H-BOMB

In this excerpt from "The Work of Many People," an article in the February 25, 1955, issue of the journal Science, *Edward Teller reflected on the journey that made the first hydrogen bomb explosion a reality:*

No one expected to approach the conditions of the solar interior [the Sun] in any of our experiments. No container would have withstood the temperatures; no familiar source could deliver the energy in the necessary concentrated form. Then, in December 1938, Otto Hahn and Lise Meitner discovered fission. . . .

I do not know how many scientific experiments have been made under conditions as exotic or in a place [Elugelab Island] as beautiful as was the setting for the first thermonuclear experiment. There must have been other events as strange, exciting, and unforgettable. What remains most clear in my mind is the contrast between the spectacular explosion, which in itself meant nothing, and the small piece of paper handed to me by my good friend, Louis Rosen, which showed that the experiment was a success.

Now, moderated X rays from the primary would in the secondary irradiate a reactive plastic medium surrounding concentric and generally cylindrical layers of fusion and fission fuel. Instantly, the plastic becomes a hot plasma that compresses and heats an inner layer of fusion fuel, which in turn compresses a central core of fissile plutonium to supercriticality. Thus compressed and bombarded by fusion-produced, high-energy neutrons, the fission element expands rapidly in chain reaction from the inside out, further compressing and heating the surrounding fusion fuel, resulting in the liberation of more energy and fast neutrons that induce fission in a fuel casing-tamper made of normally stable uranium 238.

The device to test Teller's new concept weighed more than 60 tons with its equipment to refrigerate the hydrogen isotopes. Like all the H-bomb prototypes, concepts were given workable forms by the Los Alamos Laboratory, with which Teller was no longer affiliated. During Operation Ivy, the bomb was tested at Elugelab Island in Eniwetok Atoll on November 1, 1952. Exceeding the expectations of all concerned and vaporizing the island, the explosion equaled 10.4 million tons of TNT, or about seven hundred times greater than the atomic bomb used on Hiroshima in 1945. An emergency capability version of this device weighing about 20 tons was prepared for delivery by specially modified Air Force B-36 bombers.

In development at Los Alamos before the 1952 test was a device weighing only about 4 tons, a "dry bomb" that did not require cryogenic equipment or liquid fusion fuel; when sufficiently compressed and heated in its molded-powder form, the new fusion fuel component, lithium-6 deutride, instantly produces tritium. This concept was tested during Operation Castle at Bikini Atoll in 1954 and produced a yield of 15 million tons of TNT, the largest-ever nuclear explosion by the United States. Not until 1956, in Operation Cherokee-Redwing, did the United States explode an H-bomb dropped from an aircraft, an Air Force B-52 bomber.

SIGNIFICANCE

The successful explosion of a Teller-inspired thermonuclear device in 1952 gave impetus to an ongoing global nuclear arms race. Teller was not alone in believing that the world could produce many nuclear and thermonuclear-capable nation-states and that some would threaten the United States.

During these early years of military and ideological confrontation with the Soviet Union, Teller advocated and received in 1952 a second nuclear weapons facility, the Lawrence-Livermore National Laboratory in California. For many years within the scientific community there existed disagreement over weapons development and the role that such weapons should play in national defense policy making. Prior to the identification of Teller's

The first hydrogen bomb explosion vaporizing Elugelab Island on November 1, 1952. (Courtesy, National Nuclear Security Administration/Nevada Site Office)

name with the H-bomb, it had been Oppenheimer, Los Alamos, and the A-bomb receiving attention. Oppenheimer and others on technical and moral grounds had initially opposed building the H-bomb, seeking instead an international moratorium on its development. For many years in the future, the expression of such concerns within the weapons community would not be tolerated.

With anticommunist activity and legislation reaching a peak, Oppenheimer's loyalty was questioned. During Oppenheimer's security clearance hearing held by the AEC in 1954, Teller's testimony against his former superior at Los Alamos and consistent critic of his early H-bomb designs proved decisive. President Dwight D. Eisenhower endorsed the AEC findings, and Oppenheimer's security clearance for work in classified nuclear areas was withdrawn. Teller became the scientific adviser in the nuclear affairs of the nation to presidents, from Eisenhower to Ronald Reagan. The widespread blast and fallout effects of H-bombs assured the mutual destruction of combatants. Teller knew that the availability of H-bombs encouraged but did not guarantee the deterrence of use.

A long-standing schism developed within the U.S. scientific community between the supporters of Teller or Oppenheimer and the combatants over the issue of nuclear test ban treaties. Teller consistently advised against U.S. participation with the Soviet Union in a moratorium on nuclear weapons testing. Largely based on Teller's advocacy of retaining the prerogative to test underground, the United States rejected a total moratorium in favor of the 1963 Limited Test Ban Treaty.

During the 1980's, Teller, among others, convinced President Reagan to embrace the Strategic Defense Initiative (SDI). Teller argued that SDI components, such as the space-based Excalibur, a nuclear bomb-powered X-ray laser antiwarhead weapon proposed by the Lawrence-Livermore National Laboratory, would make thermonuclear war not so much unimaginable as theoretically impossible.

Teller's hawkish views provoked dislike from the Left, but he also earned numerous awards, including the Albert Einstein Award, the National Medal of Science, and the Presidential Medal of Freedom, the latter presented by President George W. Bush less than two months before Teller's death on September 9, 2003.

Eric Howard Christianson

FURTHER READING

Bethe, Hans. "Comments on the History of the H-Bomb, 1954." In *The American Atom: A Documentary History of Nuclear Policies from the Discovery of Fission to the Present, 1939-1984*, edited by Robert C. Williams and Philip L. Cantelon. Philadelphia: University of Pennsylvania Press, 1984. Nobel laureate Bethe provides a critical eyewitness assessment of Teller's role in the H-bomb program, describes Teller's early designs and why they would not work, and declares Ulam's work essential. Argues that Teller's direction of the program was itself an inhibiting factor and defends the technical skepticism of Oppenheimer and the GAC in 1949.

Goodchild, Peter. *Edward Teller: The Real Dr. Strangelove.* Cambridge, Mass.: Harvard University Press, 2004. A good work of history that examines the scientific legacy of the "father of the H-bomb." Much of the work is based on interviews with Teller and on archival material.

Hoffman, David. *The Dead Hand: The Untold Story of the Cold War Arms Race and Its Dangerous Legacy.* New York: Doubleday, 2009. Describes American and Soviet strategies and decision making related to the superpowers' nuclear arsenals. Includes discussion of the continued threat posed by these weapons after the breakup of the Soviet Union. The title refers to a Soviet plan to create a system to automatically retaliate after a nuclear attack. Contains illustrations and maps.

Kelly, Cynthia C., ed. *Oppenheimer and the Manhattan Project: Insights into J. Robert Oppenheimer, "Father of the Atomic Bomb."* Hackensack, N.J.: World Scientific, 2006. A concise but comprehensive history of Oppenheimer's scientific legacy. Bibliography, index.

————. *Remembering the Manhattan Project: Perspectives on the Making of the Atomic Bomb and Its Legacy.* Hackensack, N.J.: World Scientific, 2004. A report on the proceedings of the 2002 Atomic Heritage Foundation's Symposium on the Manhattan Project, held in Washington, D.C. Bibliography, index.

Kevles, Daniel J. *The Physicists: The History of a Scientific Community in Modern America.* New York: Alfred A. Knopf, 1977. A valuable study for understanding the changing twentieth century relationships between academic and industrial science, and the military. Extensive bibliography.

Morland, Howard. *The Secret That Exploded.* New York: Random House, 1981. Based on information in the public domain, Morland conjectured the secret of the Teller-Ulam configuration. In 1979, the federal government sued his employer, *The Progressive* magazine, to prevent publication of his diagrams. To avoid further revelations, the government conceded the case; in 1979, the article and more accurate diagrams were published. Includes diagrams of H-bomb schemata, photographs of facilities, processes of fabrication, and H-bombs.

Rhodes, Richard. *Dark Sun: The Making of the Hydrogen Bomb.* New York: Simon & Schuster, 1995. Still the best of the many books released to coincide with the fiftieth anniversary of the first atomic explosion. Authoritative, extensively documented, and highly readable.

_____. *The Making of the Atomic Bomb.* New York: Simon & Schuster, 1986. The discussion of the H-bomb in this Pulitzer Prize-winning book draws on and confirms the claims and observations of Bethe, Ulam, York, Morland, and others. Exhaustive bibliography and diagrams and photographs of nuclear bombs and the original emergency-capability thermonuclear bomb.

Teller, Edward. "The Hydrogen Bomb: The Work of Many People." In *Better a Shield than a Sword: Perspectives on Defense and Technology.* 1955. Reprint. New York: Free Press, 1987. Teller's recollection of H-bomb development. He acknowledges his indebtedness to many others but does not grant Ulam major status in the solution of the H-bomb problem.

Ulam, Stanislaw. "Thermonuclear Devices." In *Perspectives in Modern Physics: Essays in Honor of Hans A. Bethe,* edited by R. E. Marshak. New York: Interscience, 1966. Adds credibility to the belief that while an H-bomb was theoretically possible, Teller had no practicable idea of how to realize it until the spring of 1951. As other sources confirm, Ulam's contributions were more than architectural.

York, Herbert F. *The Advisors: Oppenheimer, Teller, and the Superbomb.* 1976. Stanford, Calif.: Stanford University Press, 1989. York, the first director of the Lawrence-Livermore National Laboratory, corroborates the accounts of others. York believed Ulam's contributions were critical and discusses the emergence of Teller as the authority on nuclear matters. Extensive bibliography.

SEE ALSO: Aug. 6 and 9, 1945: Atomic Bombs Destroy Hiroshima and Nagasaki; Mar. 1, 1954: Nuclear Bombing of Bikini Atoll; July 9, 1955-early 1960's: Scientists Campaign Against Nuclear Testing; Aug. 5, 1963: Nuclear Powers Sign the Limited Test Ban Treaty; Oct. 16, 1964: China Explodes Its First Nuclear Bomb; Mar. 5, 1970: Nuclear Non-Proliferation Treaty Goes into Effect; May 26, 1972: SALT I Is Signed; June 18, 1979: SALT II Is Signed; Aug. 10, 1981: United States Announces Production of Neutron Bombs; Oct., 1983: Europeans Demonstrate Against Nuclear Weapons.

■ SEPTEMBER 1, 1951

SECURITY PACT IS SIGNED BY THREE PACIFIC NATIONS AGAINST COMMUNIST ENCROACHMENT

Australia, New Zealand, and the United States signed a security treaty called the ANZUS pact to ally against possible Chinese or Soviet aggression in the Pacific region. The pact demonstrated a commitment to contain communism by coordinating the military forces of the three countries. Although the United States considered New Zealand to have gone on leave from the arrangement in 1984, the framework continued. With the end of the Cold War in 1989, new forms of cooperation have emerged among the three nations.

ALSO KNOWN AS: ANZUS pact; Security Treaty Between Australia, New Zealand, and the United States of America

LOCALE: San Francisco, California

CATEGORIES: Diplomacy and international relations; organizations and institutions; military history

KEY FIGURES

Dean Acheson (1893-1971), U.S. secretary of state, 1949-1953

John Foster Dulles (1888-1959), U.S. foreign policy adviser to the secretary of state, 1950-1953

Percy Spender (1897-1985), Australian minister for external affairs, 1949-1951

Frederick Widdowson Doidge (1884-1954), New Zealand minister for foreign affairs, 1949-1951

SUMMARY OF EVENT

Immediately after World War II, Australia pressed for a regional security arrangement, but the United States was hesitant. Soon, however, several events gave greater urgency to the idea. In 1949, communists won the civil war in China. February, 1950, saw the signing of the Sino-Soviet Treaty of Friendship and Mutual Assistance, and in June, North Korea's army entered South Korea. Australia and New Zealand were the first countries to join the United States in sending troops to defend South Korea within the U.N. Command in Korea.

In 1949, U.S. secretary of state Dean Acheson appointed John Foster Dulles as U.S. foreign policy adviser to handle several specific tasks. Dulles felt that a power vacuum existed because demilitarized Japan was still under Allied occupation, so communist countries were moving to fill the void. Accordingly, Dulles considered a peace treaty with Japan to be a top priority. Australia and New Zealand, opposed to the possibility of Japanese rearmament, said that they would be interested in signing a Japanese peace treaty only if they were included in a formal defensive arrangement involving the United States. Dulles then went to Canberra, Australia, in February, 1951, to meet Australian minister for external affairs Percy Spender and New Zealand minister for foreign affairs Frederick Widdowson Doidge to discuss proposals for a defensive arrangement among the three countries. Promising military aid to both countries, Dulles then prepared a draft trilateral treaty, which was signed during the first day of the Japanese peace conference in San Francisco, California, on September 1, 1951.

The treaty came into force on April 29, 1952, one day after the Treaty of Peace with Japan went into effect. The aim was to send a signal to Beijing and Moscow that all three Western-oriented countries were determined to stop any new aggressive moves in the Pacific. To avoid the impression that the treaty dealt with the entire Pacific area, the acronym ANZUS—Australia, New Zealand, United States—was accepted in August at the inaugural meeting of the council, the principal organ set up by the treaty.

Articles 4 and 5 state that armed attacks "on the metropolitan territory of any of the Parties, or on the island territories under its jurisdiction in the Pacific" should be reported immediately to the United Nations Security Council. Until the Security Council acts, ANZUS countries are authorized to coordinate their own actions to meet aggression, but there is no guarantee that the countries will come to each other's aid in response to such attacks.

ANZUS was not negotiated in a vacuum, as all three countries were involved in other military arrangements in the late 1940's and the 1950's. The UKUSA Agreement, which also involved Canada and the United Kingdom and later New Zealand, was formed for the purposes of military intelligence cooperation. The armies of the United States, the United Kingdom, Canada, and Australia also formed an agreement known as ABCA; New Zealand joined later. Australia, New Zealand, and the United Kingdom formed the ANZAM Defense Committee, which evolved into the Anglo-Malayan Defense Agreement with the addition of Malaya in 1963. All three ANZUS countries also became members of the Southeast Asia Treaty Organization (SEATO), which had similar goals from 1955 to 1976. Possible overlapping arenas provided some flexibility to all member countries to operate on some tasks in one organization that might have difficulties in another.

In 1962, the ANZUS treaty area was clarified to include the three original countries as well as the many Pacific island territories then under the jurisdiction of the ANZUS powers. In the early twenty-first century only the Tokelau Islands, still a part of New Zealand, would appear to be covered as an island territory.

SIGNIFICANCE

ANZUS had little effect in accomplishing its original aim, which presumably became a nonissue with the end of the Cold War. However, practically, ANZUS provided a framework for regular civilian and military consultation among nations. The treaty council was designed for civilian consultation among foreign ministers, resulting in annual declarations of unified foreign policy goals. Military cooperation, which began in 1952 with a meeting at Pearl Harbor in Hawaii, consisted primarily of intelligence briefings and consultations through the office of the U.S. commander in chief of Pacific forces. The United States has provided military training to officers from Australia and New Zealand. The countries also have engaged in joint naval exercises, standardized equipment, and harmonized their operational doctrines. Allies of the United States also can purchase the latest military technology and often rely on U.S. military logistics.

Australia later agreed to establish facilities for signals intelligence and to test long-range missiles. Signals intelligence, derived from communications satellites, provides an important source of information about military as well as terrorist activities. Australia and the United States have continued to cooperate within the framework of the treaty, holding meetings, since 1985, known as Australia-United States Ministerial Talks (AUSMINS); the relationship was further confirmed by the talks of 1986, which issued the so-called Sydney Statement. Australia and New Zealand, however, continued to maintain their ANZUS relationship despite Washington's reclassification of New Zealand as "a friend, but not an ally."

Michael Haas

FURTHER READING

Bercovitch, Jacob, ed. *ANZUS in Crisis: Alliance Management in International Affairs.* New York: St. Martin's Press, 1988. Explains how New Zealand's refusal to allow nuclear-powered or nuclear-armed naval ships from the United States to dock in its country fractured ANZUS relations between the two nations.

Buckley, Roger. *The United States in the Asia-Pacific Since 1945.* New York: Cambridge University Press, 2002. An overview of American relations with East Asia since the end of World War II that puts the creation of SEATO into context and examines such themes as Asian concerns about colonialism and the American fear of communism.

Holdich, Roger, et al., eds. *The ANZUS Treaty, 1951.* Canberra, A.C.T.: Department of Foreign Affairs and Trade, 2001. A thorough analysis of the treaty's provisions and how they have applied to military contingencies in the Cold War and beyond.

McIntire, W. David. *Background to the ANZUS Pact: Policy-Making, Strategy, and Diplomacy, 1945-1955.* New York: Palgrave Macmillan, 1995. An analysis of the early years of ANZUS.

Tow, William, and Henry Albinski. "ANZUS: Alive and Well After Fifty Years." *Australian Journal of Politics and History* 48 (June, 2002): 153-173. Argues for the continued import of ANZUS, basing its vitality on its mutual cultural and political complementarity.

SEE ALSO: Feb. 14, 1950: Stalin and Mao Pen a Defense Pact; Sept. 8, 1951: Treaty of Peace with Japan Is Signed in San Francisco; Oct. 22, 1951: United States Inaugurates Mutual Security Program; Sept. 8, 1954: SEATO Is Founded; Nov. 22-Dec. 8, 1956: Cold War Politics Mar the Melbourne Summer Olympics; Aug. 8, 1967: Association of Southeast Asian Nations Is Formed.

■ SEPTEMBER 8, 1951

TREATY OF PEACE WITH JAPAN IS SIGNED IN SAN FRANCISCO

The Allied Powers signed the official peace treaty with Japan, ending World War II in Asia and the Pacific. The treaty reintegrated Japan into the community of nations.

ALSO KNOWN AS: Treaty of San Francisco; Japanese Peace Treaty; San Francisco Peace Treaty

LOCALE: San Francisco, California

CATEGORIES: World War II; diplomacy and international relations; wars, uprisings, and civil unrest

KEY FIGURES

John Foster Dulles (1888-1959), U.S. senator from New York, 1949; special consultant to the secretary of state, 1950-1951; and U.S. secretary of state, 1953-1959

Douglas MacArthur (1880-1964), military governor of Japan, 1945-1951;
   and supreme commander of U.N. forces in Korea, 1950-1951
Shigeru Yoshida (1878-1967), prime minister of Japan, 1946-1947 and 1948-
   1954

SUMMARY OF EVENT

On September 8, 1951, delegates from the United States, Japan, and forty-six other nations met in San Francisco and signed the Treaty of Peace with Japan. World War II had ended in August, 1945, after the United Statesdropped two atomic bombs on the Japanese cities of Hiroshima and Nagasaki. However, Cold War concerns and fears of renewed Japanese aggression against developing nations delayed the writing of the official peace treaty.

In August, 1945, the United States began a military occupation of Japan; General of the Army Douglas MacArthur oversaw the occupation force as the governor of Japan. During the occupation, MacArthur's staff wrote a new Japanese constitution that permanently disarmed Japan, so it would never again become a military power, and MacArthur instituted liberal reforms designed to democratize the country. Had the peace treaty with Japan been written during this period, its terms would most likely have been rather harsh, but the Japanese treaty initially progressed slowly. Despite being allied in World War II, the United States and the Soviet Union had divergent views on how to treat postwar Japan. Furthermore, the postwar division of Germany between various occupying powers demonstrated the possible problems with a Japanese peace treaty written to satisfy the conflicting requirements of both the Americans and the Soviets.

Writing a peace treaty could not be delayed perpetually, and when Mao Zedong won the Chinese Civil War and declared the establishment of the People's Republic of China on October 1, 1949, Asia rapidly turned into a focal point for U.S. foreign policy. With China's adoption of communism, the Harry S. Truman administration came to view Japan as a potential stabilizing force in Asia and made plans to keep Japan's industrial potential free from Soviet influence. A continued occupation of Japan seemed counterproductive to that goal, and the Truman administration began placing more importance on drafting a peace treaty.

The United States primarily sought to use the peace treaty as a means of ensuring an anticommunist orientation in Japan, an orientation that it hoped would deny Japanese trade to the Soviet Union. In order to ensure success, American leaders believed, the peace treaty could not be punitive and had to allow Japan the ability to reestablish its industrial base. American planners also believed that Japan needed to rearm after the treaty was

U.S. State Department official and later U.S. secretary of state John Foster Dulles. (Library of Congress)

signed, so its military strength could help offset communist power in the region. With these goals in mind, Truman appointed John Foster Dulles as special consultant to the secretary of state in charge of helping create a Japanese peace treaty on April 6, 1950.

Dulles arrived in Japan in late June, 1950. The week of his arrival, North Korea invaded South Korea, thereby starting the Korean War. The outbreak of the war caused Dulles to believe that rearming Japan was one of the most important aspects of the peace treaty negotiations. He believed that the Japanese would readily accept rearmament, but when Dulles began meeting with Japanese prime minister Shigeru Yoshida, he quickly learned this was not the case.

The United States envisioned a massive rearmament that would give Japan a significant defensive and offensive capability. This force would include a large army, a substantial navy, and a modern air force. Yoshida, on the other hand, merely wanted a strong security force. He saw the need for a few small ships to patrol Japan's coastal waters and a small air force to provide for a modicum of self-defense, but he could not envision the Japanese people rebuilding a large modern military. Dulles attempted to persuade Yoshida that Japan had a right to a substantial defensive force, but the prime minister argued that the Japanese people had had their fill of war and militarism. Dulles never managed to reverse Yoshida's position, and the peace treaty did not rearm Japan.

Trade was another aspect of the treaty discussions. The Americans feared that an open economic relationship between communist China and Japan would lead to the communist subversion of Japan, and the Truman administration threatened to deny the United States' good will if Japan instituted trade with Red China. Dulles could not force rearmament, but he did compel Japan to restrict its Chinese trade. Yoshida grudgingly complied with the trade restrictions, because Dulles told him the Senate would veto the peace treaty without such protections in place.

After working out most of the principal details with Japan, Dulles traveled to many other nations in the region to receive their input on the treaty. Dulles found leaders in these nations reluctant to support the lenient treaty the United States favored, so the United States agreed to enter into mutual security treaties with Australia, New Zealand, and the Philippines to ensure their support of the American version of the peace treaty. Additionally, Dulles negotiated a security treaty with Japan, since he could not convince Yoshida of the necessity of rearmament.

With drafts of the peace and security treaties in place, the United States hosted the San Francisco Peace Conference in September, 1951. Forty-eight nations attended the conference for the treaty signing, but the Soviet Union, the People's Republic of China, and the Republic of China (Taiwan) did not attend. The Soviet Union refused to accept the treaty, and the United States had not invited the governments of China or Taiwan. Communist China was not invited because the United States refused to accept its government as legitimate, and participation by the Nationalist Chinese government on Taiwan would have been too controversial at the time.

In the treaty, Japan renounced its sovereignty over most of the territories it had acquired before and during World War II. These included Sakhalin, Korea, Taiwan, Manchuria, Hong Kong, the Kuril Islands, P'eng-hu (the Pescadores), and the Spratly Islands. While the treaty stipulated that Japan no longer controlled these areas, it did not specify who did. Japan also agreed to accept all judgments of the International Military Tribunal of the Far East, which tried war criminals. Finally, Japan agreed to negotiate separate treaties with those former enemies who desired reparations payments not specified in the peace treaty.

SIGNIFICANCE

Due to the trade restrictions enacted in the Treaty of San Francisco, Japan had significantly less trade with the People's Republic of China than with Western Europe. However, the restrictions were lifted when the United

States began to normalize relations with China during the Richard M. Nixon administration. Despite this lost trade, however, the leniency of the treaty, coupled with its savings on defense expenditures, allowed Japan to reindustrialize rapidly and to rebuild its infrastructure so that it became one of the leading world economic powers by the 1960's. Taiwan concluded separate peace arrangements and signed the Treaty of Taipei with Japan in 1952. However, the lack of a treaty with the Soviet Union or the People's Republic of China, coupled with ambiguity in the Treaty of San Francisco concerning disposition of Japanese territories, led to disputes with Russia over the sovereignty of the Kuril Islands and disputes with China over the ownership of the Senkaku Islands. Japan concluded its treaty obligations when it made its last reparations payment to the Philippines in 1976.

John K. Franklin

FURTHER READING

Buckley, Roger. *The United States in the Asia-Pacific Since 1945.* New York: Cambridge University Press, 2002. An overview of American relations with East Asia since the end of World War II that puts the Japanese Peace Treaty into context. The work examines such themes as Asian concerns about colonialism and the American fear of communism.

Dower, John W. *Embracing Defeat: Japan in the Wake of World War II.* New York: W. W. Norton, 2000. Pulitzer Prize-winning account of postwar Japan and the American occupation. Particularly helpful in portraying the differences between Japanese and American cultures during this period.

Hughes, Matthew, and Matthew S. Seligmann. *Does Peace Lead to War? Peace Settlements and Conflict in the Modern Age.* Stroud, Gloucestershire, England: Sutton, 2002. Traces the roots of major international conflicts of the twentieth century to failed peace accords. Bibliographic references and index.

Immerman, Richard. *John Foster Dulles: Piety, Pragmatism, and Power in U.S. Foreign Policy.* Wilmington, Del.: SR Books, 1999. Brief biography of Dulles that touches on the role he played in negotiating the Japanese Peace Treaty and compares his work on the peace treaty to his foreign policy positions as secretary of state.

Yoshitsu, Michael. *Japan and the San Francisco Peace Settlement.* New York: Columbia University Press, 1983. Based on Japanese-language sources, this work gives a good glimpse at Yoshida's goals for Japan's future when negotiating the peace treaty.

SEE ALSO: Aug. 6 and 9, 1945: Atomic Bombs Destroy Hiroshima and Nagasaki; June 25, 1950-July 27, 1953: Korean War; Sept. 8, 1954: SEATO Is Founded; Jan. 29, 1955: Formosa Resolution Is Signed into Law; Nov. 14, 1961: Kennedy Expands U.S. Involvement in Vietnam; Aug. 7, 1964-Jan. 27, 1973: United States Enters the Vietnam War; Nov. 7, 1973: U.S. Congress Overrides Presidential Veto to Pass the War Powers Act.

■ **OCTOBER 22, 1951**

UNITED STATES INAUGURATES MUTUAL SECURITY PROGRAM

Mutual security, a hybrid strategy of military and economic aid, became the framework for economic development assistance to developing nations.

ALSO KNOWN AS: Mutual Security Act of 1951
LOCALE: Washington, D.C.
CATEGORIES: Economics; diplomacy and international relations

KEY FIGURES
Harry S. Truman (1884-1972), president of the United States, 1945-1953
Dwight D. Eisenhower (1890-1969), president of the United States, 1953-1961

SUMMARY OF EVENT
The concept of mutual security emerged in 1951 as a strategy for the containment of communism. The concept dominated U.S. foreign aid policy for a decade, much longer than its originators had anticipated. By the mid-1950's, however, the military thrust of the mutual security program yielded to the idea of "competitive coexistence." The Cold War rivalry shifted to economics, trade, and technology, but with deference to military imperatives. The tactical shift from militarism to mercantilism began with the establishment of the International Cooperation Administration in 1955, which replaced the Foreign Operations Administration, set up in 1953 at the height of military motives for the disbursement of aid.

The shift to competitive coexistence led a conceptual expansion in foreign assistance, multilateral as well as bilateral, including the guaranteeing of private investments against foreign confiscation in 1954, the establishment of the International Finance Corporation (IFC) in 1955, the creation of the Development Loan Fund (DLF) in 1957, and the founding of the International Development Association (IDA) in 1960. In the 1960's, long-term development assistance emerged as the focus of U.S. foreign aid.

The idea of collective security emerged as a response to post-World War II challenges. The end of the war engendered the prospects and problems of peaceful coexistence. America's response included the extension of assistance to its wartime allies, legislative approval for U.S. commitment to the World Bank and the International Monetary Fund (IMF), the capital expansion of the Export-Import Bank (EXIMBANK), and financial support for the relief efforts of the United Nations. By 1947, problems seemed to outweigh prospects of mutual coexistence, particularly in the light of communist militarism and ideological ventures in the Middle East, Central and Eastern Europe, and the Far East.

The postwar posture of subversive communism prompted a turn in U.S. foreign policy. In an address to Congress on March 12, 1947, President Harry S. Truman postulated a global policy of democracy and self-determination. The Truman Doctrine, responding to events in Greece and Turkey, called for U.S. aid to peoples of the free world in their struggles against the pressures of armed dictatorship or external forces. The president requested and received congressional authorization for $400 million in military, economic, and technical assistance to Greece and Turkey.

On the heels of Truman's prescription for global democracy came the proposal by Secretary of State George C. Marshall, on June 5, 1947, for the European Recovery Program, or Marshall Plan. The urgency of the proposal was soon underscored by ideological developments and Soviet incursions into Czechoslovakia and Italy. Congress then passed the Economic Cooperation Act of 1948, which established the Economic Cooperation Administration (ECA), the first autonomous agency for the conduct of U.S. foreign aid. Although the ECA's framework enhanced private-public sector cooperation in foreign policy, some sections of the U.S. business community were concerned by the strain placed on the domestic economy by the efforts to give aid to Europe.

The formation of the North Atlantic Treaty Organization (NATO) and the passage of the U.S. Mutual Defense Assistance Act, both in 1949, signified a shift in concern from economic recovery to rearmament. The need for collective defense against Chinese and Soviet communism overshadowed Truman's initiative for a program of bilateral and multilateral support for economic and industrial self-reliance in developing nations. Congressional response to the proposal was clear. The Foreign Economic Assistance Act of 1950 authorized an initial $35 million for technical assistance, with $1 billion for NATO under the Mutual Defense Assistance Program.

The need for development aid as part of U.S. foreign assistance was recognized in the Foreign Economic Assistance Act of 1950, which established the Technical Cooperation Administration as a semiautonomous unit of the Department of State. A bill to empower EXIMBANK to guarantee U.S. private investments against foreign expropriations did not survive the legislative process. EXIMBANK had been created in 1934 as a government agency to assist domestic exporters via short-term loans.

The European Recovery Program and Truman's initiatives came under increased fire. Some critics wanted a military focus in the packaging of foreign assistance and were unfavorably disposed to economic rationalizations for aid. The outbreak of armed conflict between the communist North Koreans and the Republic of Korea, as well as the reversals suffered by U.S. forces there at the close of 1950, appeared to support the critical disposition of some legislators to Truman's economic bent in foreign policy.

Truman, in an effort to assuage Congress and secure the necessary authorizations, agreed to a package deal under the omnibus rubric of mutual security. The Mutual Security Act of 1951 eliminated the Economic Cooperation Administration and established the Mutual Security Agency. The act, originally slated to expire after three years, was reconstituted in 1954 without further reference to its life span. A one-year limit placed by the act on economic assistance was eventually repealed.

The mutual security program thus began as a hybridized package of military and economic tools for the containment of communism. Under H.R. 5113 of 1951 (October 22), Congress authorized the appropriation of $7.49 billion for the program, including $5 billion for NATO and nearly $1 billion in additional authorizations for global military assistance. The authorizations for economic and technical aid were less generous, with the lion's share for NATO nations. Congress, however, directed that no less than 10 percent of reauthorized funds be disbursed as development loans. The structuring of the mutual security program would come to reflect altered perceptions of its aims.

SIGNIFICANCE

The heightened perception of the need for collective security in the early 1950's dictated, to a large extent, the denomination, packaging, and destination of foreign aid. The 1950's was a decade of mutual security, giving way to a decade of development in the 1960's. Unlike programs under the Foreign Assistance Act of 1961, those in the mutual security program lacked a developmental focus. Until the mid-1950's, the concept and content of foreign assistance were conditioned by America's concerns with communist efforts in Indochina, Formosa (Taiwan), Korea, and parts of Europe. Within that conceptual frame, the decade of mutual security involved little concern for the economic and social development of poor nations.

The program did not concentrate on mobilizing or utilizing private resources for the achievement of its economic objectives. Unlike the Marshall Plan, the program failed to create an elaborate framework of government-business partnerships for the transfer of private resources for business development abroad. The mutual security program also limited its guarantees against confiscation. It offered private U.S. investors small incentives for business participation in the economic aspects of the mutual security program, instead relying increasingly on multilateral approaches to foreign investment and development. Unlike the Foreign Assistance Act of 1961, which established mechanisms for the mobilization of entrepreneurial skills and private resources for development assistance, the Mutual Security Act lacked affirmative provisions against foreign nationalizations, expropriations, and other "takings" of private direct investments.

President Dwight D. Eisenhower toughened the ideological and functional tendons of the mutual security program. By Executive Order 10458 of June 1, 1953, he abolished the Technical Cooperation Administration and moved its functions to the Mutual Security Agency, which itself was eliminated as the primary vehicle of foreign aid two months later. The functions of the Mutual Security Agency, including those of the Institute of Inter-American Affairs, passed to the Foreign Operations Administration.

The shifting fronts of the Cold War defined the packaging and, therefore, the impact of the mutual security program. The categories of benefits under the program expanded in response to the exigencies of the rivalry. Under H.R. 10051 of 1954, Congress appropriated $184 million for development assistance and $116 million for technical cooperation. Further, Congress set aside 30 percent of development funds for disbursement as direct loans. Under H.R. 9678, Congress authorized the president to provide a maximum of $200 million in guarantees against foreign confiscation of U.S. private investments. Development loans and guarantees soon became staples of assistance.

Title I of the Agricultural Trade Development and Assistance Act of 1954 enhanced the value of otherwise inconvertible currencies by accepting them as payments for U.S. surplus commodities. The currencies then were returned to the local economies as loans and grants from the United States. At a multilateral level, the United States proposed the formation of the International Finance Corporation to boost the flow of investment capital to the poor nations. In 1955, that corporation, capitalized at $100 million, was formed as an affiliate of the World Bank. Congress approved U.S. participation with an initial contribution of $35,168,000.

An obvious shift was under way in the mutual security program. By Executive Order 10610 of June 30, 1955, the Foreign Operations Administration was eliminated and replaced with the International Cooperation Administration (ICA). The ICA, a quasi-independent body within the State Department, came into being as the challenges of competitive coexistence were beginning to be realized. The content of foreign assistance gradually shifted to economic packages. The Eisenhower Doctrine proposed military as well as economic aid to the nations of the Middle East and was followed by the president's recommendation to Congress for the creation of a Development Loan Fund for the benefit of needy friendly nations.

The Mutual Security Act of 1957 (PL 85-477) established the Development Loan Fund as a lending division of the International Cooperation Administration to provide subsidized low-interest loans in developing areas. The DLF became a government corporation in 1958. In 1959, the Mutual Security Act raised to $1 billion, from $500 million, the investment guarantee coverage for foreign confiscations and restricted new guarantees to investments in developing areas.

By 1960, Congress was moving toward significant reductions in U.S. bilateral assistance as part of an ongoing review of the mutual security program. Congress at the same time increased appropriations to multilateral agencies. The legislature approved measures for the establishment of the International Development Association (IDA), as an affiliate of the World Bank, to provide long-term low-interest loans to developing nations. In 1960, Congress authorized U.S. participation in the IDA and a contribution of $320 million toward the IDA's initial capitalization of $1 billion. By 1964, the IDA had advanced $778 million in credit to twenty-two nations.

In 1961, President John F. Kennedy proposed far-reaching reforms including the elimination of the mutual security program and the separation of military aid from economic programs. The president proposed changes for long-term development assistance and administrative effectiveness that were reflected in the Foreign Assistance Act of 1961. The act eliminated the International Cooperation Administration and transferred its remaining functions, together with the Development Loan Fund, to the Agency for International Development (USAID). Despite its limitations, the mutual security program provided the conceptual plank for the institutionalization of development assistance in subsequent decades.

FURTHER READING

Akinsanya, Adeoye A. *The Expropriation of Multinational Property in the Third World.* New York: Praeger, 1980. Examines the causes and rationales of expropriation in the less industrialized countries as well as the policy reactions of capital-exporting nations. Offers thoughtful insights into the sensitivities of economic nationalism in Africa, Asia, Latin America, and the Middle East.

Hogan, Michael J. *The Marshall Plan: America, Britain, and the Reconstruction of Western Europe, 1947-1952.* New York: Cambridge University Press, 1987. The element of corporatism in government-business exchanges is discussed. It appears to account for the success of the European Recovery Program. The mutual security program, on the other hand, did not have the full benefit of similar corporatist exchanges between business and government.

Horowitz, David, Peter Carroll, and David Lee. *On the Edge: A New History of Twentieth Century America.* St. Paul, Minn.: West, 1990. A well-written discussion, in chapters 9 and 10, of U.S. foreign policy postures under Truman and Eisenhower. Includes factual reviews of Cold War politics and the anticommunist crusade at home and abroad.

Kaufman, Burton I. *Trade and Aid: Eisenhower's Foreign Economic Policy, 1953-1961.* Baltimore: Johns Hopkins University Press, 1982. A standard work on the interface of trade and aid during the Eisenhower administration. The practical implications of Eisenhower's policy of competitive coexistence are thoroughly examined in lucid prose.

Leigh-Phippard, Helen. *Congress and U.S. Military Aid to Britain: Interdependence and Dependence, 1949-1956.* New York: St. Martin's Press, 1995. Extensive study of U.S.-British relations during the early Cold War; includes several chapters on mutual security and mutual defense programs. Bibliographic references and index.

Lillich, Richard B. *The Protection of Foreign Investment: Six Procedural Studies.* Syracuse, N.Y.: Syracuse University Press, 1965. The protection of foreign direct investments has been a thorny matter in international law and relations. The enduring quality of this monograph lies in its detached and seemingly objective commentary. It examines the safeguards against foreign "takings."

McMahon, Robert J. *The Cold War: A Very Short Introduction.* New York: Oxford University Press, 2003. Broad, accessible overview of the Cold War that covers key events and themes. Contains illustrations, maps, and index.

Nwogugu, E. I. *The Legal Problems of Foreign Investment in Developing Countries.* Manchester, England: Manchester University Press, 1965. An authoritative assessment of the legal and juridical regimen affecting property rights across national borders, including the attitudes of developing nations toward international law and regulation.

Pastor, Robert A. *Congress and the Politics of U.S. Foreign Economic Policy, 1929-1976.* Berkeley: University of California Press, 1980. The study brings historical perspectives to the politics and partisanship of foreign affairs and economic policy. In many ways, domestic politics and business interests defined policy and policy implementation in foreign relations.

Penrose, Edith. *The Large International Firm in Developing Countries.* London: Allen & Unwin, 1968. The role of the multinational corporation as a remote actor in the conduct and outcome of foreign policy has been an interesting area of study. Penrose brings to light the daunting position of multinational firms in the peripheral, but crucial, economies of developing nations.

Schwarzenberger, Georg. *Foreign Investments and International Law.* London: Stevens, 1969. The principles of public international law are considered as they affect or relate to alien property rights. The discussion on the treatment of alien property rights and safeguards is instructive.

Walker, Martin. *The Cold War: A History.* New York: Henry Holt, 1995. Argues that the Cold War helped maintain global stability and promoted economic growth.

Wennergren, E. Boyd, et al. *The United States and World Poverty.* Cabin John, Md.: Seven Locks Press, 1989. Examines the relationship between foreign assistance and the war on global poverty. The authors present useful statistical evidence on income, productivity, and growth patterns.

SEE ALSO: Mar. 12, 1947: Truman Doctrine; Apr. 3, 1948: Marshall Plan Provides Aid to Europe; Apr. 4, 1949: North Atlantic Treaty Organization Is Formed; 1954: Eisenhower Begins the Food for Peace Program; May 14, 1955: Warsaw Pact Is Signed.

■ **NOVEMBER 4, 1952**

EISENHOWER IS ELECTED PRESIDENT

The election of a Republican war hero to the U.S. presidency ended two decades of Democratic domination of the White House. During his two terms in office, Dwight D. Eisenhower would see the nation recover from World War II, as it entered the Cold War.

ALSO KNOWN AS: U.S. presidential election of 1952
LOCALE: United States
CATEGORY: Government and politics

KEY FIGURES

Dwight D. Eisenhower (1890-1969), supreme commander of NATO forces in Europe, 1951-1952, and president of the United States, 1953-1961

Joseph McCarthy (1908-1957), U.S. senator from Wisconsin, 1947-1957

Richard M. Nixon (1913-1994), U.S. senator from California, 1950-1953, vice president, 1953-1961, and later president, 1969-1974

Adlai E. Stevenson (1900-1965), governor of Illinois, 1949-1953, and presidential candidate, 1952 and 1956

Robert A. Taft (1889-1953), U.S. senator from Ohio, 1939-1953

Harry S. Truman (1884-1972), president of the United States, 1945-1953

SUMMARY OF EVENT

As the United States moved into a new decade in 1950, the Democrats had been in power in Washington for eighteen years, Cold War tensions seemed to be melting into a hot war in Korea, and apprehensive citizens suspected that communists and corruption were lurking behind the scenes in the administration of Harry S. Truman. With the approach of the 1952 election, the Democratic Party found itself facing several serious liabilities. The public tended to blame the incumbent party for many of the problems that had beset the postwar United States, a tendency that was exacerbated by the long tenure of the Democrats and by the sweeping changes instituted by President Franklin D. Roosevelt and by Truman, his vice president and successor.

Adding to the Democratic Party's problems was the disclosure, prior to the election, of several instances of Democratic corruption. Democrats were charged not only with plundering at home but also with blundering abroad. China had fallen to communists, allegedly because of the administration's mishandling of foreign affairs in Asia. The situation in the Korean War was tense and uncertain. The peace talks had bogged down, and Truman's dismissal of General of the Army Douglas MacArthur indicated to many that the Democrats had no will to win the war. The Republican Party seized on this issue, claiming that something decisive needed to be done in Korea.

To escalate the United States' concern about communists, Senator Joseph McCarthy had been painting vivid pictures of communist infiltration of the U.S. government, especially in the State Department. Despite his excesses and outright falsifications, McCarthy's charges hurt the Democrats, who had held power when these networks reached their apex: Because the Democrats had been in office for almost twenty years, many people held them responsible for this supposed communist subversion of the government.

Other problems plagued the Democrats, including the high cost of living. The Korean War had produced a need for heavy spending, adding inflationary pressure to the postwar financial boom and the record expenditures of World War II. Fear of inflation was widespread. Many people in the United States, especially Republicans, believed that it was time to balance the budget and reduce government spending.

The Republicans had problems too, however. As the Republican National Convention drew near, a split within the party seemed imminent. Senator Robert A. Taft and his followers advocated an isolationist, anti-New Deal platform. The senator's foreign policy appealed to many Republicans and gained widespread support in the traditionally isolationist Midwest. However, many powerful Republican leaders feared that Taft had made too many enemies within the party to gain unanimous support. Because he had attached his name to the Taft-Hartley labor law and was bitterly despised by the labor establishment and millions of rank-and-file union members, the Ohio senator had lost much support from significant segments of the voter population.

Many Republicans thus favored a less controversial figure for the nomination. General of the Army Dwight D. Eisenhower—supreme commander of Allied forces in Europe during World War II, president of Columbia University, and temporary head of North Atlantic Treaty Organization (NATO) forces in Europe—seemed perfect for the job. After the general at last

Dwight D. Eisenhower at his first inauguration on January 20, 1953. (Library of Congress)

declared that he was a Republican, Senator Henry Cabot Lodge, Jr., of Massachusetts encouraged his nomination.

Following primary victories in New Hampshire and Minnesota, Eisenhower defeated Taft on the first ballot, 595 to 500. To appease the Taft wing of the party and to give the ticket youth and Western representation, Senator Richard M. Nixon of California was chosen as the vice presidential candidate. Eisenhower, however, did not back Nixon fully until after a dramatic television appearance by the Californian, when, challenged to explain aspects of his financial background, Nixon made the famous televised Checkers speech, in which he listed his earnings and debts and noted that the only gift he ever had accepted was a cocker spaniel named Checkers. Eisenhower astutely observed that the response to the speech—more than 300,000 letters and telegrams to the Republican National Committee positive to Nixon, as well as thousands of pro-Nixon phone calls—made Nixon a political asset.

The leading candidates for the Democratic nomination included Vice President Alben W. Barkley and Senator Estes Kefauver of Tennessee. Governor Adlai E. Stevenson of Illinois declared that he would not run but would accept a party draft. After a struggle on the convention floor, Stevenson was nominated on the first ballot. Senator John Jackson Sparkman of Alabama was given the vice presidential slot to appease the South. Although the Democratic platform was soft on civil rights and included support of state control of tidelands oil, two prominent Democratic governors, James Francis Byrnes of South Carolina and Allen Shivers of Texas, declared their support for Eisenhower. It thus became respectable to be a Southern Republican, and the Democratic hold on the South was cracked at last.

During the campaign, several Republican policies became evident. The Tennessee Valley Authority, Social Security, and certain other New Deal institutions would be retained by a Republican administration. Eisenhower announced that his party had no basic quarrel with established Democratic economic dogma. He did promise to balance the budget, reduce federal outlays, lower taxes, safeguard free enterprise, lessen government interference in business, and place fewer curbs on industry.

However, the issues of the Korean War and communists in the federal government overshadowed domestic economic policy. On the subject of the war, Eisenhower declared that he would go to Korea, although he did not specify what he expected to accomplish by going. Americans, tired of the Korean quagmire, found hope in the Republican candidate's pledge; the hero of World War II could certainly solve the sideshow events of Korea. On the communist issue, Eisenhower did not make the McCarthy smear tactics a part of his personal campaign. Nevertheless, he did not disavow McCarthy's aims and in symbolic ways accommodated the emotional thrust of the Red hunt.

"Ike," as the public called Eisenhower, also had a strong historical trend in his favor: In the nineteenth century, whenever a party needed to break the opposing party's momentum, it had nominated a general, usually with success in November. William Henry Harrison, Zachary Taylor, and Ulysses S. Grant were not career politicians, but they had parlayed their military successes and images as strong leaders into peacetime political victories. Unlike those politician-generals, Eisenhower held a rank—general of the army, or five-star general—that required him by law to remain on active duty for life. Therefore, because a president cannot also be an active member of the armed forces, he had to resign his commission in the U.S. Army before he could take office as president.

Stevenson, with his urbane and lofty rhetoric, proved no match for the genial and likable general as a vote-getter. The commonly held assumption that Stevenson had elevated U.S. political thinking and therefore appealed to educated and intellectual voters, whereas Eisenhower, often portrayed as dull and lacking in sophistication, appealed only to less-educated voters, has been disputed: Analysis of polling behavior has suggested that the less educated the voter, the more likely he or she was to vote for Stevenson, and the more educated the voter, the more likely he or she was to vote for Eisenhower. College-educated voters preferred Eisenhower by a margin of two to one.

Even Democratic suggestions that a new depression would follow Republican victory were not enough to stem the tide. Eisenhower won thirty-nine states, including four in the so-called Solid South, and 442 electoral votes to Stevenson's nine states and 89 electoral votes. The Republican Party narrowly gained control of Congress but retained it for only the first two years of Eisenhower's tenure. In the Senate, the Republicans had a four-seat majority in 1954, losing two seats since 1952. The Democrats retained their hold on the governorships and of state and local government in the Southern states that went for Eisenhower.

SIGNIFICANCE

President Eisenhower, reelected in 1956, presided over most of the 1950's in the United States. He is therefore associated, whether rightly or wrongly, with most of the developments of that decade. In addition to helping define the Cold War, the 1950's and the Republican presidential administration that presided over them are linked with an era of great economic expansion. During the decade, Americans went beyond simply recovering from the Depression and World War II to flourish, as capitalism functioned in its least controversial and apparently most benign form. The mass media was pervasive enough to present a general image of American prosperity and happiness. It was also limited and monovocal enough to efface the racial and cultural tensions that would explode a decade later. Eisenhower thus benefited both from actual peace and prosperity and from perceived peace and prosperity, as he seemed to be the president of a decade-long golden age.

Fredrick J. Dobney and Larry Schweikart

FURTHER READING

Ambrose, Stephen E. *Eisenhower: Soldier, General of the Army, President-Elect, 1890-1952*. New York: Simon & Schuster, 1983. A classic biography of Eisenhower by an illustrious biographer who is sympathetic to the general.

Boyle, Peter G. *Eisenhower.* New York: Pearson/Longman, 2005. Part of the Profiles in Power series, this book looks at both Eisenhower's strengths as a leader of a nation and his weaknesses as a leader of a political party. Bibliographic references and index.

Childs, Marquis. *Eisenhower: Captive Hero.* New York: Harcourt, Brace & World, 1958. An unfavorable treatment of Eisenhower and his administration.

Eisenhower, Dwight D. *The White House Years: Mandate for Change, 1953-1956.* Garden City, N.Y.: Doubleday, 1963. The first volume of Eisenhower's memoirs, which covers his first term and the campaign of 1952.

Johnson, Walter. *How We Drafted Adlai Stevenson.* New York: Alfred A. Knopf, 1955. One of the leaders of the draft movement describes in detail the preconvention and convention activities of his committee and argues that the draft was genuine.

Klehr, Harvey, et al. *The Secret World of American Communism.* Translated by Timothy Sergay. New Haven, Conn.: Yale University Press, 1995. This translation of Russian documents provides a revealing look at Communist Party operations in the United States from the Soviet perspective.

LaFeber, Walter. *America, Russia, and the Cold War: 1945-2006.* New York: McGraw-Hill. 2008. Focuses on relations between the United States and the Soviet Union and examines causes and effects of the conflict. Contains illustrations and maps.

McKeever, Porter. *Adlai Stevenson: His Life and Legacy.* New York: Morrow, 1989. The best biography to date of Stevenson.

Parmet, Herbert S. *Eisenhower and the American Crusades.* New York: Macmillan, 1972. A renowned presidential scholar examines the campaign and the reasons Eisenhower chose to run. A large portion of the book is devoted to the 1952 election.

Schweikart, Larry, and Dennis Lynch. "Government and Politics." In *American Decades, 1950-1959*, edited by Richard Layman. Detroit, Mich.: Gale, 1994. A detailed look at the 1952 and 1954 elections, including analyses of voting data.

Williamson, Daniel C. *Separate Agendas: Churchill, Eisenhower, and Anglo-American Relations, 1953-1955.* Lanham, Md.: Lexington Books, 2006. Detailed account of American foreign policy under Eisenhower during the first three years of his administration, focused on his cooperation and contention with British prime minister Winston Churchill and the extent to which they helped define the Cold War and the post-World War II world.

SEE ALSO: Apr. 4, 1949: North Atlantic Treaty Organization Is Formed; July 10, 1954: Eisenhower Begins the Food for Peace Program; Jan. 5, 1957: Eisenhower Doctrine; July 29, 1958: Congress Creates the National Aeronautics and Space Administration; Jan. 17, 1961: Eisenhower Warns of the Military-Industrial Complex; Apr. 17-19, 1961: Bay of Pigs Invasion.

■ JANUARY, 1953

CHINA BEGINS ITS FIRST FIVE-YEAR PLAN

By implementing the First Five-Year Plan, the new People's Republic of China moved decisively toward centrally planned, large-scale national economic development.

ALSO KNOWN AS: First Five-Year Plan of the People's Republic of China for Developing the National Economy
LOCALE: People's Republic of China
CATEGORIES: Government and politics; economics

KEY FIGURES

Mao Zedong (Mao Tse-tung; 1893-1976), chairman of the Chinese Communist Party, 1935-1976, and top Chinese leader, 1949-1976
Zhou Enlai (Chou En-lai; 1898-1976), chief foreign minister of the Chinese Communist Party, 1935-1976, and premier of China, 1949-1976
Liu Shaoqi (Liu Shao-ch'i; 1898-1969), president of the People's Republic of China, 1959-1968
Deng Xiaoping (Teng Hsiao-p'ing; 1904-1997), general secretary of the Chinese Communist Party, 1956-1967, and later de facto leader of China
Chen Yun (1905-1995), Chinese economic planner
Peng Dehuai (P'eng Te-huai; 1898-1974), Chinese military leader

SUMMARY OF EVENT

One aspect of Cold War rivalry concerned the growth and prosperity of domestic economies in the rival Eastern and Western blocs. The implementation of China's First Five-Year Plan was the beginning of the country's centrally planned economic development and industrialization. From 1953 to 1957, production more than doubled; numerous factories, roads, and dams were built. By 1957, 97 percent of land was collectivized, or put under state control. The Great Leap Forward in 1958 attempted to decentralize the economic management system. The Great Leap Forward ended in January, 1961, after poor harvests in 1959 and 1960 and termination of Soviet technical aid in 1960.

The People's Republic of China was established in October, 1949. Its first three years were a period of rehabilitation. By 1952, the gross value of industrial output had grown to two and a half times that of 1949 and exceeded prewar levels by almost 25 percent. Agricultural output also exceeded prewar levels.

In late 1952, Chinese leaders decided to undertake long-term economic development. Because of lack of experience in both economic planning and advanced technology, Chinese leaders had to rely heavily on foreign aid for their economic development. At that time, the Soviet Union was the only country willing and able to provide China with economic and technical assistance. With little alternative, Chinese leaders adopted the Soviet model for China's economic development.

The First Five-Year Plan started in January, 1953, although final details were not agreed upon, and the plan was not published until July, 1955. The most important proposal in the plan was to raise to about 20 percent the share of the nation's resources to be invested, and to use these resources for the development of heavy industry. The acquisition of investment resources was to be achieved by imposing compulsory purchases and taxes on agriculture and private industry and by earning high profits in state-owned industries. The controlled allocation of resources was to be accomplished through a Soviet-style apparatus for the central planning of state industry and wholesale, retail, and foreign trade. Control of foreign trade was particularly crucial, since the strategy adopted required that China sell agricultural products to pay for industrial goods and materials supplied by the Soviet Union. It is important to note that the plan did not call for immediate nationalization of private industry and commerce.

Planning was adopted gradually in China. The State Statistical Bureau was set up on October, 1952. The chief organ of planning, the State Planning Commission, was established in 1952 and was placed under the State Council when the latter was made the supreme executive body by the 1954 constitution. At the same time, a State Construction Commission was organized to oversee capital investment under the First Five-Year Plan, which covered the 1953-1957 period. The complete title of the plan is the First Five-Year Plan of the People's Republic of China for Developing the National Economy.

The method of central planning adopted, based on Soviet experience, was that of "material balances," sometimes referred to as input-output analysis. In this system, tables are prepared to indicate, based on experience and expectations, how the output of each industry or sector of the economy is distributed among all producing industries or sectors, plus final demand. With such a table of interconnecting balances, it is then possible to project the pattern of demand for each sector's output that will be generated by a given planned rate and pattern of growth and to compare it with the supplies likely to be made available by existing capacities and their planned expansions. If balance between anticipated supply and demand is lacking, the plan is adjusted and the possibility of using foreign trade to fill the gaps is explored.

The fundamental task of the chinese plan was to implement 156 development construction projects that were designed with Soviet assistance. During this period, 145 construction projects were to be started or completed. Eleven others were scheduled to start during the period of the Second Five-Year Plan (1958-1962).

Until November, 1957, China's planning system was highly centralized, in the sense that a fairly large number of targets of different kinds were drawn up and their fulfillment directly supervised by the central government. These targets applied to an originally small but rapidly growing number of goods. As both the number of commodities and the number of enterprises for which the center assumed responsibility grew rapidly in the course of the 1950's, the maintenance of such a high degree of centralization of both planning and management became increasingly cumbersome. In 1957 and 1958, the government adopted a series of decentralization measures in order to delegate some of its responsibilities to the localities, increase the scope for local initiative, and strengthen central control of the most important plan targets and enterprises.

Total planned investment by the state for the five-year period came to 76.640 billion yuan ($32.154 billion at the official exchange rate of 2.46 yuan to the U.S. dollar). Some three-fifths of state investment was to be devoted to capital construction. About three-fifths of that was earmarked for industry, most of it for heavy industry, fuel production, and machine building. Agricultural investment was to be limited to a little more than 1 billion yuan, or 2.4 percent of planned capital construction. The Chinese leadership was always acutely aware of the need for agricultural surpluses as a condition for rapid industrialization.

Impatient with the gradual pace of collectivization set by the First Five-Year Plan, Mao Zedong called for an immediate acceleration of agricultural collectivization. Mao's impact on agricultural collectivization was dramatic. By March, 1956, more than 90 percent of Chinese peasants were in cooperatives, and by 1957 virtually all were in the higher-stage cooperatives. Thus an agricultural collectivization anticipated to take fifteen years according to the First Five-Year Plan was completed in little more than one year. The results, however, were unsatisfactory. Mao's expectation that changes in ownership and organization would produce immediate economic effects was belied by events. By the fall of 1957, it was apparent that the growth of agriculture was still too slow, that urban unemployment was a serious problem, and that relations with the Soviet Union, on which industrial assistance depended, were worsening. This crisis led Mao to launch the most extraordinary economic adventure that the world has ever seen, the Great Leap Forward of 1958.

SIGNIFICANCE

The First Five-Year Plan scored major successes in laying the foundations for industrialization strategy in China. The First Five-Year Plan achieved a dramatic increase in industrial production across a broad sector of goods. Most of the plan targets had already been fulfilled by the end of 1956. Political and economic difficulties arising out of the First Five-Year Plan, however, had serious consequences. First, there was inadequate growth of agricultural production and procurement. Grain output stagnated. Second, planning and administration, in their highly centralized form, had become increasingly ineffective as the economy grew in size and complexity, and especially after most industry and commerce came under direct state control in 1956. Third, the industrialization strategy of the First Five-Year Plan had proved incapable of solving the unemployment problem.

From 1953 to 1957, China's population grew from 582.6 million to 646.5 million. According to official statistics, industrial production grew during those five years at an annual rate of 18 percent, while agricultural production rose 4.5 percent a year and the output of food grains by 3.7 percent, barely surpassing the population's growth rate. Bottlenecks in the production of raw materials forced planners to reconsider the development plan.

In general, economic performance was quite good during the period of the First Five-Year Plan, even though the growth was unbalanced between industry and agriculture. The average annual growth rate of national income reached 8.9 percent. The high level of investment spending in industry resulted in a high rate of industrial growth. Within the industrial sector, the annual growth rate of steel output in terms of quantity was 31.8 percent. Chemical fertilizer production increased by 29.3 percent annually, and electric power by 20.4 percent. The annual increase rate of grain production, in contrast, was only 4 percent, and production of cotton increased by 4.7 percent annually.

The First Five-Year Plan had a number of drawbacks. First, the plan required large forced savings from the agricultural sector. Second, the plan placed undue concentration of investment in such heavy industries as steel at the expense not only of agriculture but also of light and consumer goods industries. Third, the plan required a high degree of centralization and the development of an elaborate bureaucratic structure to implement, control, and check the plan according to fixed targets and quotas.

In establishing urban industries, setting up management systems, embarking on long-term planning, and providing for scientific and technical education, the Chinese in the early 1950's had only the Soviet Union to turn to for models, assistance, and advice. The Soviet Union was willing to provide assistance in the form of plants, machinery, and systems of organization and management, which inevitably resembled their counterparts at home.

In the latter stages of the First Five-Year Plan, hundreds of thousands of peasants were mobilized to build roads and dredge canals. The Great Leap Forward began in March, 1958, when some sixty million peasants were assigned to build and operate millions of factories and backyard furnaces.

The first people's commune was organized in April, 1958. In August, the Chinese Communist Party adopted a resolution on the establishment of people's communes in rural areas. Following its provisions, cooperatives everywhere were merged immediately into communes. By the end of September, 1958, there were 26,425 communes in the rural areas, representing 98.2 percent of the total number of peasant households. The commune was a much larger and more advanced form of collectivization than the cooperative. The people's commune was the basic social structure combining industry, agriculture, trade, education, and the military.

As the Great Leap Forward went on into 1959, administrative confusion deepened, and the consequences of strain, of the misuse of resources, and of sheer human exhaustion became increasingly serious. When the end came, it coincided with the withdrawal of Soviet assistance and a succession of natural disasters. The results were appalling.

Soviet aid to China was in the form of interest-bearing loans, not grants. Some Chinese leaders were not satisfied with the prices the Soviets set for their equipment and plants or with the interest rate charged for loans.

Chinese government posters extolling communist programs during the 1950's. (National Archives)

China had to repay these loans with its products, gold, and foreign currencies. Investments thus had to pay off quickly, and at rates above the rate of interest charged by the Soviets, if investment was not to be a drain on the Chinese economy.

Mao spelled out his strategies for achieving the objective of the Great Leap Forward in two simple slogans: "walking on two legs" and the "five dualities." Walking on two legs meant that growth should be balanced between industry and agriculture. The five dualities were to develop industry and agriculture simultaneously, to develop light industry and heavy industry simultaneously, to develop large enterprises simultaneously with medium-sized and small enterprises, to develop state industry and local industry simultaneously, and to use traditional production technology and modern production technology simultaneously.

In 1958, 700,000 small blast furnaces were built to produce steel, and 100,000 small coal pits were set up. These blast furnaces and coal pits were staffed by inexperienced workers who used old production processes. Mao knew that building modern steel mills would take several years and huge amounts of capital investment. He attempted to substitute labor for capital by using outdated technology.

During the Great Leap Forward, some statistics on increased production were based on exaggeration and fabrication. Millions of tons of pig iron, much substandard and all a long way from being steel, were produced in backyard furnaces. The pig iron accumulated along railways that could not possibly handle its movement, causing serious bottlenecks in the transport system. In 1958, when the Great Leap Forward and commune programs were launched, there was a good harvest. In 1959, heavy floods and drought laid waste to almost half of the cultivable land. Then, in 1960, floods, drought, and pests ravaged millions of acres. To make matters worse, the Soviets withdrew all of their technicians and advisers from China in June, 1960, because of disagreements concerning development strategy. The drastic reduction in agricultural production stalled the drive for rapid development of industry.

The Great Leap Forward ended in failure because the program merely promoted "excessive targets," with cadres issuing arbitrary decisions. The Great Leap Forward was not carefully planned and was rashly implemented, causing a huge waste of both material and human resources. The estimated loss during the years of the Great Leap Forward, 1958-1960, amounted to $66 billion. But worse still was the massive human toll in the starvation of upwards of 30 million people.

The chaotic situation in China's economy was exacerbated by the unexpected withdrawal in August, 1960, of all Soviet economists and technicians working in China. China learned a bitter lesson from the surprise Soviet withdrawal. Facing growing criticism from both domestic and foreign sources, Mao resigned from the presidency of the People's Republic of China and gave the position to Liu Shaoqi. In the early 1960's, China's economy entered a period of recovery and consolidation. The relatively peaceful development of China's economy was once again disrupted by the Cultural Revolution of 1966.

Guoli Liu

FURTHER READING

Chan, Alfred L. *Mao's Crusade: Politics and Policy Implementation in China's Great Leap Forward.* New York: Oxford University Press, 2001. Argues that the Great Leap Forward was the result of Mao's personal policies and plans for China, rather than being the result of Chinese bureaucratic politics or other collective, cultural and economic phenomena. Bibliographic references and index.

Cheng, Chu-yuan. *China's Economic Development: Growth and Structural Change.* Boulder, Colo.: Westview Press, 1982. Discusses China's economic development and the operation of its economic system, with a focus on institutional change as a major determinant of economic growth.

Fairbank, John K. *The United States and China.* 4th ed. Cambridge, Mass.: Harvard University Press, 1983. The best single thematic introduction to China's history, civilization, and contemporary evolution. Includes an extensive annotated bibliography.

Howe, Christopher. *China's Economy: A Basic Guide.* New York: Basic Books, 1978. An introduction to China's economy, including the following subjects: population and human resources, organization and planning, agriculture and industry, foreign trade, and the standard of living.

Li, Hua-Yu. *Mao and the Economic Stalinization of China, 1948-1953.* Lanham, Md.: Rowman & Littlefield, 2006. Crucial background to the First Five-Year Plan, focused on Chinese economic strategies and development during the five years preceding the plan. Bibliographic references and index.

Prybyla, Jan S. *The Political Economy of Communist China.* Scranton, Pa.: International Textbook, 1970. Chapters 3, 4, and 5 directly address issues related to the First Five-Year Plan.

Riskin, Carl. *China's Political Economy: The Quest for Development Since 1949.* New York: Oxford University Press, 1991. Examines the economy of China between 1949 and 1985. This textbook discusses both the Maoist approach to economic development and the post-Mao economic reforms.

Rozman, Gilbert, ed. *The Modernization of China.* New York: Free Press, 1981. A collective work by nine scholars, integrating modernization theory with Chinese socioeconomic and political development, from historical and comparative perspectives.

Tsao, James T. H. *China's Development Strategies and Foreign Trade.* Lexington, Mass.: Lexington Books, 1987. A concise account of China's economic development and foreign trade. Supported by extensive statistical data.

Westad, Odd Arne, ed. *Brothers In Arms: The Rise and Fall of the Sino-Soviet Alliance, 1945-1963.* Stanford, Calif.: Stanford University Press, 2000. Scholars from China, Russia, the United States, and Western Europe use documentation available in the post-Soviet period to reassess the Sino-Soviet Alliance. A lengthy introduction gives a comprehensive yet concise overview of the 1950 alliance.

SEE ALSO: Oct. 7, 1950: China Invades and Begins Rule of Tibet; Spring, 1957: Mao's Hundred Flowers Campaign Begins; Beginning 1958: Mao's Great Leap Forward Brings Chaos to China; 1959-1961: Famine Devastates China; Oct. 16, 1964: China Explodes Its First Nuclear Bomb; May, 1966: Cultural Revolution Begins in China; Oct. 25, 1971: People's Republic of China Is Seated at the United Nations; Feb. 21, 1972: Nixon Opens Trade with China; Sept. 9, 1976: Death of Mao Zedong Leads to Reforms in China.

■ **January 15, 1953-December 2, 1954**

McCarthy Hearings

U.S. senator Joseph McCarthy launched investigative hearings into the possible communist infiltration of the U.S. government. In combination with the House of Representatives' similar hearings, McCarthy's rhetoric and his investigations came to symbolize the dangers posed to democracy and civil rights of the anticommunist paranoia that characterized the Cold War.

Also known as: Executive Sessions of the Senate Permanent Subcommittee on Investigations of the Committee on Government Operations
Locale: Washington, D.C.
Categories: civil rights and liberties; social issues and reform

Key Figures
Joseph McCarthy (1908-1957), U.S. senator from Wisconsin, 1947-1957, and chair of the Committee on Government Operations and its Permanent Subcommittee on Investigations, 1953-1954
Roy M. Cohn (1927-1986), chief counsel to the U.S. Senate Permanent Subcommittee on Investigations
Alger Hiss (1904-1996), former U.S. State Department official accused of espionage
Owen Lattimore (1900-1989), American professor of Far Eastern affairs
Margaret Chase Smith (1897-1995), U.S. senator from Maine, 1949-1973
Harold R. Velde (1910-1985), U.S. representative from Illinois, 1949-1957, and chair of HUAC, 1953-1954
Arthur V. Watkins (1886-1973), U.S. senator from Utah, 1947-1959

Summary of Event
On February 9, 1950, Senator Joseph R. McCarthy of Wisconsin addressed the Ohio County Women's Republican Club of Wheeling, West Virginia. He said, "While I cannot take the time to name all of the men in the State Department who have been named as members of the Communist Party and members of a spy ring, I have here in my hand a list of two hundred and five that were known to the secretary of state as being members of the Communist Party and who nevertheless are still working and shaping the policy of the State Department." Later, McCarthy revised his figures downward to fifty-seven, but the shocking allegations were that the secretary of state knew of these persons, and that they continued nonetheless to shape U.S. government policies.

McCarthy was exploiting a sensitive and emotional issue, for it was a known fact that there had been communists in the government, the labor movement, certain intellectual circles, and "popular front" organizations shortly before, during, and after World War II. Communist cells had functioned in Washington, D.C., during the 1930's, numbering among their members government officials such as Alger Hiss, whom an admitted communist agent, Whittaker Chambers, had named on August 3, 1948, as a prewar member of the Communist Party. Hiss brought a libel suit but was eventually indicted on charges of perjury and sentenced to five years in prison. Hiss had been highly regarded, and his conviction fueled growing Cold War fear that if he could be a communist, almost anyone might be guilty of such subversion.

Fear of communism, to be sure, had existed well before World War II. In the early 1920's, in the wake of the Bolshevik Revolution of 1917, Attorney General A. Mitchell Palmer and a young J. Edgar Hoover had led the charge against "foreign" elements in public life, resulting in such phenomena as the Red Scare of 1919-1920. Boom and depression also encouraged people to look for enemies outside the mainstream "American" ideals of motherhood, apple pie, and patriotism. America-first movements manifested themselves in a variety of ways, from Huey P. Long to Father Coughlin to the Ku

Senator Joseph McCarthy (left) with his legal counsel Roy M. Cohn during Senate subcommittee hearings in 1954. (Library of Congress)

Klux Klan. Anticommunist fervor seemed justified by events such as the Russian purge trials and executions of 1936-1938 and, more important, the signing of the Russo-Nazi Pact in August, 1939.

After World War II, the Soviet determination to build a world power led President Harry S. Truman to form his policy of containment and, on March 22, 1947, to institute a "loyalty order" to ensure detection and removal of subversive elements within the government. Bolstered by the Smith Act of 1940—which required that aliens in the United States register with the government and which made it unlawful for anyone to preach the overthrow of the U.S. government—such policies led to the conviction and sentencing of communist spies but also threatened innocent people with unfashionable political affiliations.

Lives were being ruined, such as those of the Hollywood Ten, a group of film writers and directors who in 1947 appeared before the House Committee on Un-American Activities (HUAC), chaired by Harold R. Velde, and refused to "name names"; they were supported by a cadre of famous actors who flew to Washington for the event. The Ten were subsequently blacklisted by Hollywood executives and did not work in their chosen profession for years afterward. Some in the entertainment community did inform, but many more—actor Zero Mostel and folksinger Pete Seeger among them—appeared at the hearings and denounced HUAC's investigations, refusing to inform. Although many Americans recognized the dangers of a growing paranoia, others wanted action to eradicate what seemed a communist conspiracy in their midst.

Thus, when the specter of a home-grown communist conspiracy was raised, a fearful nativist element existed to give it legitimacy, and Joseph McCarthy, the Republican senator from Wisconsin, appeared as the incarnation of that nativism and the nemesis of communism. After his appearance before the women's club in Wheeling, McCarthy—unable to name two hundred five, eighty-five, or even fifty-seven communists in the State Department—shifted his attack to Professor Owen Lattimore, whom he called "the top espionage agent" in the United States, and to certain diplomats.

Some Republicans thought that McCarthy had struck a rich vein that might yield political treasures (perhaps the presidency in 1952), but other Republicans, including Senator Margaret Chase Smith, disagreed. She did not want the Senate being used for "selfish political gain at the sacrifice of individual reputations and national unity." A committee headed by Millard Tydings, Democratic senator from Maryland, investigated McCarthy's accusations and concluded that McCarthy had perpetuated "a fraud and a hoax" on the Senate and the American people, and that his statements represented "perhaps the most nefarious campaign of half-truths and untruth in

---

SENATE CENSURE OF MCCARTHY

The U.S. Senate "condemned" and hence censured Senator Joseph McCarthy on December 2, 1954, effectively ending not only the hearings, which began in March, 1951, but also McCarthy's political career.

Resolved,

That the Senator from Wisconsin, Mr. McCarthy, failed to cooperate with the Subcommittee on Privileges and Elections of the Senate Committee on Rules and Administration in clearing up matters referred to that subcommittee which concerned his conduct as a Senator and affected the honor of the Senate and, instead, repeatedly abused the subcommittee and its members who were trying to carry out assigned duties, thereby obstructing the constitutional processes of the Senate, and that this conduct of the Senator from Wisconsin, Mr. McCarthy, is contrary to senatorial traditions and is hereby condemned.

---

the history of the Republic." McCarthy's defenders rushed to his support, and he was able to continue his crusade for another four years.

In 1953, McCarthy became the chairman of the Senate Committee on Government Operations, giving him control of its Permanent Subcommittee on Investigations. He used this position to hold hearings of his own, becoming more sensational, strident, and unbelievable and even associating the Democratic Party with communist tendencies. The first hearing held by the subcommittee under McCarthy's leadership was on January 15, when Russell W. Duke was questioned. McCarthy also used his position to denounce Charles E. Bohlen's appointment as ambassador based on his close alignment with the foreign policy of Franklin D. Roosevelt and Harry S. Truman (Bohlen was confirmed anyway), and he then claimed that the Democratic Party was a perpetrator of twenty years of treason.

SIGNIFICANCE

Senator McCarthy caused his own downfall in the late spring of 1954, when he displayed ruthlessness during the nationally televised Army-McCarthy hearings before an audience of more than eighty million people. McCarthy had charged Secretary of the Army Robert T. Stevens, along with Brigadier General Ralph W. Zwicker, of covering up espionage activities at Ft. Monmouth's Signal Corps Engineering Laboratories. The Army countercharged that McCarthy and Roy M. Cohn, counsel to McCarthy's Senate subcommittee, were attempting to exert pressure on the Army and the War Department. Cohn resigned on July 20, although McCarthy was cleared. Finally, on September 27, a Senate committee headed by the venerable Arthur V. Watkins of Utah recommended that McCarthy be censured.

McCarthy's reign of terror was effectively ended on December 2, 1954, when the Senate condemned him for bringing the Senate "into dishonor and disrepute" and thus impairing that institution's "dignity." It was later proven that many communist cells had as many double agents working for the United States as there were die-hard converts. Perhaps the ultimate lesson of the McCarthy hearings is that, when a people allows the freedoms they cherish to be compromised by innuendo, fear, and finger-pointing, those freedoms may be in greater danger from their supposed defenders than from any other threats, no matter how real they may be.

William M. Tuttle and Paul Barton-Kriese

FURTHER READING

Cohn, Roy. *McCarthy.* New York: New American Library, 1968. Written by one of McCarthy's main associates, this book proffers a flattering account of McCarthy's rise and fall.

Cook, Fred J. *The Nightmare Decade: The Life and Times of Senator Joe McCarthy.* New York: Random House, 1971. Cook, a former FBI agent, sees McCarthy as a person who was able to twist fact and fiction together to create the type of reality he wanted, and needed, to see.

Fried, Richard. *Nightmare in Red: The McCarthy Era in Perspective.* New York: Oxford University Press, 1990. A study of the anticommunist movement in the United States after World War II up to the beginning of Dwight D. Eisenhower's presidency in 1952.

Navasky, Victor S. *Naming Names.* New York: Viking Press, 1980. The editor of the liberal periodical *The Nation* provides a meticulously researched history of the HUAC hearings in this "moral detective story" that seeks answers to the question, "What happens when a state puts pressure on its citizens to betray their fellows?"

Newman, Robert. *Owen Lattimore and the "Loss" of China.* Berkeley: University of California Press, 1992. One of the major suspected "spies" accused by McCarthy and the political and ideological storms waged around him. An excellent picture of life in the United States during the McCarthy years.

Oshinsky, David M. *A Conspiracy So Immense: The World of Joe McCarthy.* New York: Oxford University Press, 2005. Exploration of the Cold War mentality in the West, Joseph McCarthy's exploitation of it, and the effects of McCarthyism on American society. Bibliographic references and index.

Schrecker, Ellen. *The Age of McCarthyism: A Brief History with Documents.* Boston: St. Martin's Press, 1994. An excellent overview of the McCarthy years, collecting many important primary documents.

Winkler, Allan. *The Cold War: A History in Documents.* New York: Oxford University Press, 2000. Includes excerpts from Arthur Miller's *The Crucible* among speeches by Winston Churchill, Harry S. Truman, Joseph Stalin, and other major Cold War figures. Also contains a collection of photos and cartoons related to nuclear weapons.

SEE ALSO: 1947-1951: Blacklisting Depletes Hollywood's Talent Pool; Oct. 20, 1947: HUAC Investigates Hollywood; Jan. 22, 1953: *The Crucible* Allegorizes the Red Scare Era; June 19, 1953: Rosenbergs Are Executed for Peacetime Espionage.

■ **JANUARY 22, 1953**

THE CRUCIBLE ALLEGORIZES THE RED SCARE ERA

Arthur Miller's play examining the infamous Salem, Massachusetts, witchcraft hysteria and trials of the seventeenth century was an allegory of the persecution of American communists by the House Committee on Un-American Activities during the Red Scare era of the late 1940's and early 1950's.

LOCALE: New York, New York
CATEGORY: Theater;

KEY FIGURES
Arthur Miller (1915-2005), American playwright
Joseph McCarthy (1908-1957), U.S. senator from Wisconsin, 1947-1957, and chair of the Committee on Government Operations, 1953-1954
Martin Dies, Jr. (1900-1972), U.S. representative from Texas, 1931-1945 and 1953-1959, and chair of the Special Committee to Investigate Un-American Activities, 1938-1944
Elia Kazan (1909-2003), Turkish-born stage and film director

SUMMARY OF EVENT

Renowned American playwright Arthur Miller was born in New York in 1915. He began his writing career after graduating from the University of Michigan with an English degree in 1938. He was married several times, most famously to actor Marilyn Monroe from 1956 to 1961, and he fathered several children. His first Broadway play, *The Man Who Had All the Luck*, appeared in 1944. He is best remembered for his Pulitzer Prize-winning 1949 play *Death of a Salesman*, which is considered a modern American classic. His 1955 work *A View from the Bridge* also won a Pulitzer Prize. Miller was politically active throughout most of his career, and many of his works dealt with their characters' personal conflicts with social or political events.

The Crucible, which first appeared on Broadway on January 22, 1953, was Miller's fictionalized account of the historical 1692 witchcraft trials in Salem, Massachusetts. The mass hysteria surrounding the hunt for witches in Salem served as an allegory for the mass hysteria of the Red Scare, begun during the Cold War that developed between the United States and the So-

Early 1953 editorial cartoon by Reg Manning lampooning Senator Joseph McCarthy's claim that communists were infiltrating every branch of the U.S. government by showing McCarthy himself popping out of a drawer in Secretary of State John Foster Dulles's desk. (Library of Congress)

viet Union in the post-World War II period. The U.S. government, mainly the House Committee on Un-American Activities (HUAC) led by Democratic congressman Martin Dies, Jr., had launched an investigation designed to target suspected Communist Party members in all areas of life, including government, educational institutions, labor unions, and the entertainment industry. The repression engendered a climate of fear throughout the country, as people were afraid to speak out as the accused found their names on blacklists, which hindered their employability and ruined many lives.

Republican senator Joseph McCarthy also investigated communist infiltration of the U.S. government, using his position as the chair of the Senate Committee on Government Operations and of its Permanent Subcommittee on Investigations to focus the subcommittee's activities in that direction. McCarthy was extremely public in his activities and charges, intentionally cultivating and amplifying the anticommunist hysteria of the early 1950's. His leading role in creating this climate led to its being known as McCarthyism. The popularity of McCarthyism was peaking at the time *The Crucible* appeared on Broadway.

The characters accused of witchcraft in the play's seventeenth century Salem resembled those Americans accused of communist sympathies during the Red Scare of the twentieth century United States: They both faced the personal conflict of self-preservation versus conscience. Salem's Puritan inhabitants believed in the existence of witches and of the ability of people to enter into compacts with the Devil, exchanging their souls for worldly benefits.

When the play begins, a group of young girls, including the Reverend Samuel Parris's daughter Betty and niece Abigail Williams, have been discovered dancing in the woods. The townspeople are quick to suspect witchcraft. The girls and the Parrises' slave Tituba then begin accusing various townspeople of bewitching them in order to save themselves from suspicion and punishment. At the behest of the strong-willed Abigail, the girls act as if possessed, creating mass hysteria throughout the town.

A series of witchcraft trials begins, presided over by Massachusetts deputy governor Danforth and Judge John Hathorne. Danforth is more concerned with preserving the court's reputation than with finding the truth. The leaders of those opposed to the trials are the Reverend John Hale and John Proctor, whose earlier affair with Abigail ultimately leads to her accusations against him and his wife Elizabeth. At first, Proctor wants no involvement with the trials, but he ultimately decides to admit his adultery in court, risking his reputation to discredit Abigail's accusations and reveal the truth. Elizabeth is then brought forth to confirm his testimony, but she unknowingly seals John's fate by lying that he has remained faithful to her. Proctor is taken to jail and ultimately must decide whether to falsely sign a confession to save his life or to stand by his principles and maintain his innocence, which will surely lead to his execution. He ultimately refuses to confess and implicate his friends and goes to face a hero's death.

During the Red Scare, many Americans faced similar (although usually not life and death) decisions. A number of Miller's friends and acquaintances, including noted director Elia Kazan, were accused of belonging to the Communist Party. Miller himself faced investigation as a suspected communist, which gave him a personal connection to the themes of *The Crucible*. Miller was interested in exploring times when fear and self-preservation seemed to be opposed to truth and rational thought. The Salem witchcraft trials served as an apt allegory to the Red Scare, as both events dealt with periods of mass hysteria when people were ruled by their emotions. The paranoid searches for the Devil in Massachusetts and for communist subversion in the United States were out of proportion to any actual danger that may have existed. Although the play met mixed reviews and a short original run on Broadway, it played well internationally, and its reputation has grown.

SIGNIFICANCE

McCarthyism began to die out after McCarthy destroyed his own popularity by appearing to be belligerent and insulting during the nationally televised 1954 Army-McCarthy hearings in the Senate. For many, the nail in McCarthy's coffin was his confrontation with journalist Edward R. Murrow. Murrow, a heroic war correspondent during World War II, attacked McCarthy on national television. McCarthy responded by labeling as communistic a public figure whose patriotism was beyond reproach in the public mind.

McCarthy was censured by the Senate for acting "contrary to senatorial traditions" and spent the remainder of his days disgraced and ignored, dying shortly thereafter in 1957. The hunt for communist subversives within the United States, however, continued on a smaller scale through organizations such as the John Birch Society, formed in 1958. HUAC, moreover, was still powerful into the 1960's, and anticommunism continued to guide U.S. foreign policy toward communist nations such as the Soviet Union, China, Vietnam, and Cuba.

Miller was called to testify before HUAC in 1956 and was found guilty of holding communist beliefs, a verdict that was later reversed in an appeals court. In his testimony, Miller faced the same conflict as that of his characters in *The Crucible*: whether or not to succumb to the social pressure to implicate others. Miller admitted to attending meetings but denied being a communist, and he refused to name any of those who had attended meetings with him, leading to a citation for contempt. Miller was blacklisted from television, film, and radio and denied a passport by the U.S. government. He entered into a public dispute with noted director Elia Kazan, who had earlier provided the names of eight others who had been members of the Communist Party. *The Crucible* would become one of Miller's most well-known and widely produced plays and was made into feature films on several occasions.

Marcella Bush Trevino

FURTHER READING

Abbotson, Susan C. W. *Student Companion to Arthur Miller.* Westport, Conn.: Greenwood Press, 2000. Includes a biographical section, including a look at Miller's confrontation with HUAC and a discussion of eight of his major plays. Includes a bibliography and list of critical studies and reviews of his work.

Bigsby, Christopher W. E., ed. *The Cambridge Companion to Arthur Miller.* New York: Cambridge University Press, 1997. Provides introductions to and analysis of Miller's plays, as well as of his other literary contributions, and places them in historical context. Includes a chronology.

Fariello, Griffin. *Red Scare: Memories of the American Inquisition.* New York: Avon Books, 1995. Contains numerous firsthand accounts of those who were affected by the U.S. government's persecution of communists during the Red Scare era, including Arthur Miller himself.

Fitzgerald, Brian. *McCarthyism: The Red Scare.* Mankato, Minn.: Capstone Press, 2006. Presents a variety of primary documents from the period from the late 1940's through the mid 1960's, with commentary.

Gottfried, Martin. *Arthur Miller: His Life and Work.* Cambridge, Mass.: Da Capo Press, 2003. Recounts Miller's life and artistic career, including a chapter on *The Crucible* and information on his conflict with HUAC during the Red Scare era.

Miller, Arthur. *Timebends: A Life.* New York: Penguin Books, 1995. An autobiographical account of Miller's life and works in his own words.

Schrecker, Ellen. *The Age of McCarthyism: A Brief History with Documents.* New York: Palgrave Macmillan, 1994. Two sections provide a comprehensive history of the era and a number of primary documents, including new archival evidence. Includes headnotes, a chronology, and a bibliographical essay.

Whiffield, Stephen. *The Culture of the Cold War.* 2d ed. Baltimore: Johns Hopkins University Press, 1996. Describes and analyzes the anticommunist rhetoric that flourished in the popular culture of the 1940's and 1950's, including films, television, and literature.

Winkler, Allan. *The Cold War: A History in Documents.* New York: Oxford University Press, 2000. Includes excerpts from Arthur Miller's *The Crucible* among speeches by Winston Churchill, Harry S. Truman, Joseph Stalin, and other major Cold War figures. Also contains a collection of photos and cartoons related to nuclear weapons.

SEE ALSO: 1947-1951: Blacklisting Depletes Hollywood's Talent Pool; Oct. 20, 1947: HUAC Investigates Hollywood; Jan. 15, 1953-Dec. 2, 1954: McCarthy Hearings.

■ **MARCH 5, 1953**

DEATH OF STALIN

The death of Joseph Stalin ended several decades of dictatorial rule and terminated the initial stages of a new wave of purges in the Soviet Union.

LOCALE: Moscow, Soviet Union (now in Russia)
CATEGORY: Government and politics;

KEY FIGURES

Lavrenty P. Beria (1899-1953), chief of the secret police under Stalin, 1938-1953

Nikita S. Khrushchev (1894-1971), first secretary of the Communist Party of the Soviet Union, 1953-1964, and premier, 1958-1964

Georgi M. Malenkov (1902-1988), deputy premier of the Soviet Union, 1946-1953, premier, 1953-1955

Joseph Stalin (Joseph Vissarionovich Dzhugashvili; 1878-1953), general secretary of the Central Committee of the Communist Party of the Soviet Union, 1922-1953, and premier, 1941-1953

SUMMARY OF EVENT

On March 4, 1953, Radio Moscow announced that on March 1, Joseph Stalin had suffered a stroke, which had led to partial paralysis with heart and breathing difficulties. On the morning of March 6, it reported that Stalin had died on the evening of March 5. He was seventy-four years old at the time of his death.

The news aroused consternation throughout the country that Stalin had ruled for more than a quarter of a century. In the wider world marked by Cold War tension, Stalin's death was also greeted with mixed concern and apprehension. Following Lenin's death in January, 1924, Stalin had become the most powerful figure in the party and governed the nation until his own death nearly three decades later.

Stalin had led his people victoriously through World War II, which brought death and destruction to the Soviet Union on an unprecedented scale as a result of the Nazi invasion, and he seemed to be the indispensable center about which all Soviet life revolved. Despite the terror, bloodshed, and suffering associated with his policies, Stalin provided the security of the familiar in Soviet citizens from the poorest collective farmers to the top leaders of the Communist Party. It was logical that his associates feared the possible disruptive consequences in the aftermath of his death and the removal of his dominating and guiding hand.

In the last years of his life, Stalin had been preparing to plunge his people once again into the suffering and killing that had characterized his rule. Suspicious of everyone and growing more paranoid in his final years, the old dictator appeared to be setting the stage for a repeat performance. The death penalty, abolished in 1947, was restored to deal with "spies and traitors." The so-called Leningrad Affair of 1949 led to further demotions and even execution of significant party leaders. The Soviet press, by the early 1950's, published numerous criticisms and even denunciations of individuals and groups.

Events surrounding the Nineteenth Party Congress of October, 1952, provided ominous signs of the purge spreading throughout the highest echelons of the party and extending to other areas of society to produce another destructive wave of terror. Technically, the actions of the Congress did not on the surface look unduly serious. A new leadership committee, the Presidium, replaced the ruling Politburo, substantially increasing its membership as compared to its predecessor. Significant changes modified the Secretariat as the Communist Party's central bureaucratic and organizational structure. Rumors began to spread that even the most important of Stalin's associates during the previous fifteen years were among those likely to be demoted, ousted from power in the government or the Communist Party, or possibly arrested.

Moreover, a major part of Stalin's scheme was the conscious use of political anti-Semitism, a clear threat to the Jewish population of the Soviet Union. The dossier which Stalin prepared against his intended victims included numerous indictments of prominent Jews in the party and the government bureaucracy. Anti-Semitic language and the prevalence of Jews among the alleged "criminals" seemed to indicate that Stalin planned to capitalize upon existing anti-Semitism in Russia to get public support for at least the beginning of his purge. Allegations of Jews recruited by the Ameri-

Funeral procession for Joseph Stalin moving through Moscow's Red Square. (National Archives)

can Central Intelligence Agency (CIA) to work for "American-Zionist imperialism" inside the Soviet Union became more frequent. The executions of several Jews in 1952, after allegations of collaboration with Russia's enemies, further added to the atmosphere of suspicion and fear.

Most frightening of all was the announcement in January, 1953, of the discovery of the Doctors' Plot, which charged that nine prominent doctors, six of whom were Jews, had been guilty of trying to kill, by improper medical treatment, leaders of the Communist Party and the armed forces. The list of allegedly murdered victims included Andrei Zhdanov, the party leader of Leningrad and widely believed to have been Stalin's choice as his eventual heir, who died in 1948. The secret police and investigative agencies came under special attack for their apparent laxity in discovering these opponents. It became clear that Stalin was piecing together allegations involving assassination plots, economic crimes, sabotage, and collaboration with foreign enemies in which prominent party figures and many lesser officials would be swept up and punished.

Only his death saved Russia from the bloodshed that would have followed the implementation of his plans. On March 4, Soviet authorities announced that Stalin suffered a major stroke on the night of March 1-2. A brain hemorrhage caused major paralysis of his right side, plus loss of speech and consciousness. The medical team provided what care they could, even using leeches to reduce the blood pressure of their patient. He died at 9:50 P.M. on March 5.

In announcing Stalin's death and in their speeches in succeeding weeks, Communist Party leaders, fearing civil disorder upon the death of the much feared leader, appealed to the people in the name of "collective leadership" to remain calm. They took steps to tighten control over the party and other political and economic organs by placing themselves in key positions. The powerful party leaders carefully avoided any suggestion that any individual would rule the party as Stalin had done. Georgi M. Malenkov became Soviet premier, while Nikita S. Khrushchev assumed the responsibility as head of the party.

SIGNIFICANCE

Stalin's successors began almost immediately to reduce the most hated features of the Stalinist system, including the secret police apparatus and the terror by which it had infected Russian life. The Doctors' Plot was admitted to have been fabricated, and those physicians still in prison were released. By the end of the year, it was announced that Lavrenty Beria had been ousted as head of the secret police, expelled from the party, and executed. Articles in the party newspaper *Pravda* assured the people that their rights under the Soviet constitution would be respected and that more consumer goods would be made available. Thus, the Communist Party, under the concept of "collective leadership," rode out of the days of uncertainty, fear, and turmoil surrounding Stalin's death, and a new era in Russian history began, even as a new and less confrontational phase of the Cold War began with Khrushchev's explorations of avenues of peaceful coexistence..

George F. Putnam and Taylor Stults

FURTHER READING

Bortoli, Georges. *The Death of Stalin*. New York: Frederick A. Praeger, 1975. The title is misleading, as this account traces events from 1952 through Stalin's death and effectively juxtaposes general social conditions with the activities of the Communist Party leadership.

Brent, Jonathan, and Vladimir Namurov. *Stalin's Last Crime*. New York: HarperCollins, 2003. A study of the events leading up to Stalin's death, particularly the "Doctors' Plot" and the apparent preparations for a major pogrom against the Soviet Jewish population.

Conquest, Robert. *Stalin: Breaker of Nations*. New York: Penguin Books, 1991. This psychological study emphasizes Stalin's paranoia and his desire to achieve massive power.

Fürst, Juliane, ed. *Late Stalinist Russia: Society Between Reconstruction and Reinvention.* New York: Routledge, 2006. Focused account of the last eight years of Stalin's regime conveys the state of the Soviet Union at the time of his death. Bibliographic references and index.

Hyde, H. Montgomery. *Stalin: The History of a Dictator.* New York: Farrar, Straus & Giroux, 1972. A critical assessment of Stalin, but a solid biography.

Leffler, Melvyn. *For the Soul of Mankind: The United States, the Soviet Union and the Cold War.* New York: Hill & Wang, 2007. Examines Stalin's death and three other critical missed opportunities for peace between the Soviet Union and the U.S. Contains illustrations and maps.

Radzinsky, Edvard. *Stalin: The First In-Depth Biography Based on Explosive Documents from Russia's Secret Archives.* New York: Doubleday, 1996. A Russian historian provides more information based on previously inaccessible files.

Salisbury, Harrison E. *Moscow Journal: The End of Stalin.* Chicago: University of Chicago Press, 1961. Engaging and detailed account of conditions in the Soviet Union in the late Stalin era, including Stalin's demise, by a *New York Times* correspondent living in Moscow.

Ulam, Adam B. *Stalin: The Man and His Era.* Boston: Beacon Press, 1989. Expanded edition of an earlier biography of Stalin by a highly regarded Soviet scholar at Harvard University.

Volkogonov, Dmitri. *Stalin: Triumph and Tragedy.* New York: Grove Weidenfeld, 1991. Substantial biography by a noted Russian historian provides a postcommunist perspective of Stalin.

SEE ALSO: Feb. 4-11, 1945: Yalta Conference; July 17-Aug. 2, 1945: Potsdam Conference; Mar. 5, 1946: Churchill Delivers His Iron Curtain Speech; 1948: Soviets Escalate Persecution of Jews; 1955-1964: Brezhnev Rises in Communist Ranks; Feb. 25, 1956: Khrushchev Denounces Stalinist Regime; Oct. 13-14, 1964: Khrushchev Falls from Power; Nov. 12, 1968-Dec., 1989: Brezhnev Doctrine Mandates Soviet Control of Satellite Nations.

■ **APRIL 10, 1953**

HAMMARSKJÖLD IS ELECTED U.N. SECRETARY-GENERAL

Following his nomination by the U.N. Security Council, Swedish civil servant and diplomat Dag Hammarskjöld was elected by the U.N. General Assembly to the position of secretary-general. No one could have foretold then that he would become the organization's most activist secretary-general, a person of great courage.

LOCALE: New York, New York
CATEGORIES: United Nations; diplomacy and international relations; organizations and institutions

KEY FIGURES
Dag Hammarskjöld (1905-1961), Swedish U.N. secretary-general, 1953-1961
Trygve Lie (1896-1968), Norwegian U.N. secretary-general, 1946-1952
Lester B. Pearson (1897-1972), Canadian delegate to the U.N. General Assembly, 1946-1957, and later prime minister, 1963-1968

SUMMARY OF EVENT
Two trends formed a backdrop to the emergence of the practically unknown Dag Hammarskjöld on the world scene in April, 1953: first, the Cold War between the Soviet-led communist bloc and the Washington-led Western capitalist democracies and second, the decolonization of the dependencies of the former European empires and the birth pains inherent in that process. The intertwining of these two developments made the 1950's a particularly challenging time for the United Nations' chief executive and head administrator—the secretary-general—and for the institution itself.

Trygve Lie, the first incumbent, had been marginalized by the Soviet bloc for his allegedly pro-Western position in the U.N.-sponsored action in the Korean War of 1950-1953. In April, 1953, Lie still had a chance that his mandate would be renewed, since the Soviets once again barred the candidacy of Canada's Lester B. Pearson, as they had done in 1946 for a different reason. There seemed to be a momentary impasse.

Then a "dark horse" emerged from the shadows, one about whom so little was known that few could hold anything against him. This compromise candidate was Dag Hammarskjöld, who had worked first for the Swedish government and then in its delegation to the United Nations in 1951 and 1952. His name was submitted to the Security Council by the French ambassador to the United Nations, Henri Hoppenot. On April 7, 1953, Hammarskjöld received ten of the council's eleven votes. The only abstention in the council's recommendation to the General Assembly was that of Nationalist China, the island of Taiwan (formerly Formosa) ruled by the government of General Chiang Kai-shek. The reason for Taiwan's abstention was that Sweden had recognized the regime of its adversary, the People's Republic of China, as the legitimate representative of the Chinese people. On April 10, 1953, by secret ballot, the General Assembly confirmed Hammarskjöld's appointment by a vote of fifty-seven for, one against, and one abstention. He was immediately installed as U.N. secretary-general.

Hammarskjöld's eight-and-one-half-year tenure was marked by his insistence on being an activist secretary-general: "an instrument, a catalyst, an inspirer," as he phrased it. Under repeated assaults by the Soviet representatives, he would constantly stress his necessarily neutral position as an international civil servant. Indeed, were it not for Hammarskjöld's nearly religious devotion to his job and his stated commitment to fill even the slightest vacuum created by the indecision and stalemate that characterized the major policy-making organs of the United Nations—especially its Cold War-locked Security Council—he would probably not have become the world's most celebrated peacemaker. Given the stalemate of the Cold War, however, there was considerable decision-making space to fill on the international stage, and Hammarskjöld took full advantage of this political void by practicing his quiet, behind-the-scenes, and often personal diplomacy.

Hammarskjöld certainly did not make much headway as head of the U.N. Secretariat or as chief coordinator of the broader U.N. family, including its specialized agencies. The vested interests in both bodies resisted his attempts at coordination and reform. In addition, when Hammarskjöld assumed his responsibilities in April of 1953, a trend was developing toward recruiting professional staff in senior U.N. positions based on the geographic distribution of their countries of origin. An unwritten quota system (which eventually was to reach the level of the general secretariat itself) was being instituted, rather than one based on an applicant's meritorious qualifications for a given job.

Despite these difficulties, Hammarskjöld did not tarry in promoting his view that, where a political organ did not speak out clearly, the secretary-general could implement policy. Indeed, he believed that using the power of the U.N. Secretariat to fill the international power vacuum was an obligation. He relied on the U.N. Charter, U.N. Security Council decisions, General Assembly resolutions, common-law precedent, principle, or any other basis that he could find or even invent to justify his actions.

Hammarskjöld's quiet, behind-the-scenes style of diplomacy became evident as early as 1954, when he interceded with the leaders of "Red China," as the People's Republic of China was widely known, to free eleven American airmen whose plane had been shot down near the North Korean-Chinese border during the Korean War. The General Assembly had asked Hammarskjöld to obtain their release in accordance with the Armistice Agreement of July 27, 1953, which had concluded the fighting between the U.N.-sponsored coalition led by the United States and its North Korean-Chinese adversaries. On his trip to Beijing, Hammarskjöld convinced the Chinese leaders that his intercession was strictly of a personal nature, since the United Nations had not, at that point, recognized the People's Republic of China but rather had seated the Nationalist (Taiwanese) Chinese delegates. Even though the United Nations had failed on five earlier occasions, Hammarskjöld now succeeded, and the American fliers were eventually freed.

Another move that greatly enhanced Hammarskjöld's prestige and that of the United Nations was the creation of the initial peacekeeping force—the United Nations Emergency Force (UNEF)—used after the British-

Dag Hammarskjöld. (Library of Congress)

French-Israeli invasion of Egypt's Suez Canal Zone in November of 1956. UNEF interposed itself between the forces of the tripartite invaders and the defending Egyptians and supervised the evacuation of the threesome by early 1957. The idea of establishing blue-helmeted peacekeepers had been in fact that of Canada's Lester B. Pearson, but Hammarskjöld's name became most closely identified with it as one of his longest-lasting legacies.

Hammarskjöld also managed to fill space in Lebanon in 1958 through the expanded United Nations Observation Group in Lebanon (UNOGIL), which replaced the ten thousand U.S. Marines ordered to that Middle Eastern country to stabilize a volatile situation. The secretary-general then arranged to provide Jordan with his personal representative's good offices to prevent a threatened forcible regime-change there. In 1959, Hammarskjöld used similar techniques to settle a territorial dispute between Cambodia and Thailand.

Hammarskjöld was not always so successful—or lucky. At one point, he attempted to play a role in the matter of the United States toppling Jacobo Arbenz Guzmán, a democratically elected Guatemalan leftist president who had nationalized the American-owned United Fruit Company. Hammarskjöld was told in no uncertain terms by the U.S. delegate to the Security Council, Henry Cabot Lodge, Jr., that the United Nations lacked jurisdiction to address the matter. If anything, the coup fell under the jurisdiction of the Organization of American States (where the United States was dominant), not the world organization, despite Hammarskjöld's opposite interpretation of the U.N. Charter's provisions.

Similarly, when Soviet forces invaded Hungary to help quash its uprising against communist rule, the veto-bound Security Council (and equally impotent General Assembly) placed the matter in Hammarskjöld's hands. With the exception of some humanitarian relief, the secretary-general was unable to persuade the Soviets to change their policy. The Hungarian communist authorities even refused to grant an entry visa to Hammarskjöld, who had wished to obtain firsthand information in Budapest.

Great-Power politics also triumphed over Hammarskjöld's efforts to intercede in France's quashing of the Algerian war of liberation and in the French army's refusal to evacuate the Tunisian port of Bizerte, which had ostensibly become independent in 1956. Indeed, French president Charles de Gaulle gave Hammarskjöld to understand that de Gaulle was not prepared to share his country's foreign policy with the secretary-general. These setbacks, however, paled in comparison with Hammarskjöld's most intense but ineffective efforts in the newly independent Congo in 1960-1961, efforts that ultimately cost him his life.

SIGNIFICANCE

Hammarskjöld demonstrated the extent to which the secretary-general's initiatives could be pushed by an individual dedicated to the cause of peace. There is no question that his efforts saved lives (in Egypt in 1956 and very possibly elsewhere). Hammarskjöld set a benchmark, as his 1961 posthumous Nobel Peace Prize evidences, by which his successors have been measured.

Peter B. Heller

FURTHER READING

Ask, Sten, and Anna Mark-Jungkvist, eds. *The Adventure of Peace: Dag Hammarskjold and the Future of the United Nations.* New York: Palgrave Macmillan, 2005. Includes essays on Hammarskjöld's statesmanship and artistic qualities.

Gordenker, Leon. *The U.N. Secretary-General and Secretariat.* New York: Routledge, 2005. Outlines the roles and responsibilities of secretary-general and secretariat of the United Nations. Part of the Global Institutions series.

Heller, Peter B. *The United Nations Under Dag Hammarskjöld, 1953-1961.* Lanham, Md.: Scarecrow Press, 2001. Assays the U.N. secretary-general both as an individual and as a professional.

Johnson, Edward. "'The Umpire on Whom the Sun Never Sets:' Dag Hammarskjöld's Political Role and the British at Suez." *Diplomacy and Statecraft* 8, no. 1 (1997): 249-278. Explains how Hammarskjöld's activism, while extricating the tripartite forces from Egypt in 1956 and 1957, gave the British doubts about the secretary-general's value to their foreign policy.

Urquhart, Brian. *Hammarskjold.* New York: Harper & Row, 1987. An authoritative and laudatory reevaluation of the secretary-general's significance by a contemporary associate.

Vargo, Marc E. *Noble Lives: Biographical Portraits of Three Remarkable Gay Men—Glenway Wescott, Aaron Copland, and Dag Hammarskjöld.* New York: Harrington Park Press, 2005. Speculates on the possible origins of Hammarskjöld's alleged sexual preference, which he supposedly hid from the world and from himself.

SEE ALSO: Apr. 25-June 26, 1945: United Nations Charter Convention; Feb. 1, 1946: First U.N. Secretary-General Is Selected; June 18-27, 1954: United Fruit Company Instigates a Coup in Guatemala; July, 1960: United Nations Intervenes in the Congolese Civil War.

■ June 19, 1953

Rosenbergs Are Executed for Peacetime Espionage

With the Cold War deepening, a recent war in Korea against communist forces, and an escalating nuclear arms race, the electrocution of Julius and Ethel Rosenberg for treason and conspiracy to pass nuclear secrets to the Soviet Union was a first for the United States: the execution for espionage during peacetime. Their deaths opened a long period of continuing controversy about the guilt or innocence of the accused.

Also known as: Crime of the Century
Locale: Ossining, New York
Categories: Crime and scandal; government and politics

Key Figures

Julius Rosenberg (1918-1953), convicted of espionage and treason and
 sentenced to die by electrocution
Ethel Rosenberg (1915-1953), convicted of passing atomic secrets to the
 Soviets and sentenced to die by electrocution
Morton Sobell (b. 1918), codefendant, who repeatedly invoked his Fifth
 Amendment rights during the trial
Klaus Fuchs (1911-1988), German-born physicist, who worked on the
 creation of the atomic bomb and passed information to the Soviets
Harry Gold (1910-1974), courier of atomic secrets
David Greenglass (b. 1922), brother of Ethel Rosenberg and primary
 witness for the prosecution
Alexander Feklisov (b. 1914), former KGB officer

Summary of Event

The arrest and confession in 1950 of Klaus Fuchs, a German-born physicist who had been educated at the University of Edinburgh and who had subsequently worked on the Manhattan Project in Los Alamos, New Mexico, led the Federal Bureau of Investigation (FBI) to his spy courier, known to Fuchs only as "Raymond." Raymond was, in fact, Harry Gold, who, in 1950, confessed to his part in a spy ring that involved a technician at Los Alamos named David Greenglass. Once Greenglass was arrested, he implicated his wife, Ruth; his sister, Ethel Rosenberg; and his brother-in-law, Julius Rosenberg. Ruth was never arrested, but Julius was arrested in May and Ethel was arrested in August.

David Greenglass confessed his involvement in a spy ring, stating that he had been persuaded by Julius to pass information through a courier named "Raymond" to the Soviet Union. Greenglass had drawn an illustration of the explosive device used to detonate the atomic bomb while he was working at Los Alamos. He also testified that Ethel typed his handwritten notes about the atomic bomb, providing the crucial evidence that was to convict her.

Morton Sobell, who allegedly tried to recruit Max Elitcher into the Rosenberg spy ring, stood trial with the Rosenbergs. He refused to testify by repeatedly invoking the Fifth Amendment. Greenglass received a fifteen-year prison sentence but was released after only ten years. Sobell received a thirty-year sentence and served eighteen years. Julius and Ethel Rosenberg, however, received the death penalty. In his sentencing statement, Judge Irving Kaufman stated that while Julius was the prime mover in the conspiracy, Ethel was also guilty, "a full-fledged partner" in crime. He also blamed the Rosenbergs for "the Communist aggression in Korea," adding that they were responsible not only for the more than fifty thousand casualties in that arena but also for the "millions more innocent people [who] may pay the price of your treason."

Despite numerous attempts to win a stay of execution, even to delay the Rosenbergs' execution beyond its scheduled Sabbath date, the Rosenbergs' execution took place on June 19, 1953. To avoid executing the two on the Sabbath, the execution time was moved forward to 8 P.M. When the Rosenbergs were informed that not only would they not receive a stay but that their execution had been moved forward, they refused a last meal and chose to spend their remaining hours talking together. Three newspaper reporters were stationed in the death house and were to be the only "outside" witnesses to their execution. FBI agents had been posted in the death house for an extended stay in case either of the Rosenbergs "broke" and confessed.

A few minutes before 8:00 P.M., Julius, facing electrocution first, entered the execution chamber. Shaved patches covered his legs and head, areas where electrodes would attach more effectively to his body. Although he squinted at the bright lights and his knees may have buckled as he approached the electric chair, he was quite calm and said nothing. A leather helmet was placed over his head so that witnesses would not see the severe facial contortions and ruptured eyes that would accompany his electrocution. He received the standard amount of electric shock and was pronounced dead at 8:06 P.M.

After the smell of Julius's urine and burned flesh was masked by a strong solution of ammonia, Ethel was led to the chamber. She was also very calm, and stopped to kiss one of her female guards on the cheek and then shake hands with another. She walked to the chair without aid and then looked di-

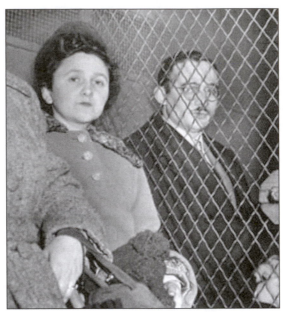

Julius and Ethel Rosenberg. (Library of Congress)

rectly at the three outside witnesses. Once her straps and helmet were secured, she received the same amount of electric shock given her husband, one short and two long shocks. The attending doctor checked for a heartbeat and was surprised when her heart was still beating: She was still alive. She was administered more shocks and died after being electrocuted for four minutes and fifty seconds.

The execution of the Rosenbergs produced different reactions at home and abroad. There were mass demonstrations against their deaths in France and Italy and other places, but demonstrations in the United States were mixed, as many Americans celebrated the executions. As many as eight thousand people attended the funeral of the Rosenbergs the following Sunday, June 21. Their two sons were placed with a foster family, and despite attempts to move them, they remained in the home of Abel and Anne Meeropol until they reached adulthood.

Over the next five decades a sometimes fierce debate raged over the Rosenbergs' guilt or innocence. Their two sons, Robert and Michael Meeropol, maintain that their parents were framed by the government and that they were innocent. While J. Edgar Hoover called their actions "the crime of the century," many historians and scientists doubt that the information provided by David Greenglass could have enabled Soviet scientists to build an atomic bomb. Much of the information in his confession was incorrect. The information provided by Fuchs during World War II was much more sophisticated and may have been the basis for Soviet nuclear development.

SIGNIFICANCE

To some extent, the execution of the Rosenbergs still haunts the American psyche. In 1995, the CIA released the first of its double-encrypted Soviet files, the Venona files, revealing new evidence in the case. Not even these files have laid the case to rest, however. Historian Robert Radosh believes that the government pushed the limits of U.S. law in seeking the death penalty for the Rosenbergs, leading to a "grave miscarriage of justice." The FBI hoped that one or both of them would break and provide the names of a U.S. spy ring. Also, many argue that the government also may have used the Rosenbergs as an example of the fate of spies.

One of the most shocking of the documents provided by the FBI included an interrogation plan with the following question to be addressed to Julius: "Was your wife cognizant of your activities?" Alexander Feklisov, the Russian behind Julius Rosenberg, has stated that while Julius was involved in passing electronic secrets to the Soviets, he was a minor figure in the atomic espionage, and that Ethel knew little or nothing of the spy ring. Finally, in 2002, Greenglass, in a *60 Minutes* episode, stated that he had lied about Ethel's involvement to save his own family and to lessen his own sentence.

Yvonne Johnson

FURTHER READING

Feklisov, Alexander. *The Man Behind the Rosenbergs.* New York: Enigma Books, 2001. Feklisov was Julius Rosenberg's Russian contact and friend. He describes Rosenberg as a volunteer spy who did not want money but worked toward a Soviet future.

Meeropol, Robert. *An Execution in the Family.* St. Martin's Press, 2003. A moving memoir by the son of Julius and Ethel Rosenberg, recounting his search for truth and his conclusion that his parents did not receive a fair trial.

Radosh, Ronald, and Joyce Milton. *The Rosenberg File: A Search for the Truth.* 2d ed. New Haven, Conn.: Yale University Press, 1997. Julius Rosenberg reportedly spied for the Soviet Union, but Radosh argues that neither he nor Ethel deserved to die. He also demonstrates that the evidence against Ethel was weak at best.

Roberts, Sam. *The Brother: The Untold Story of the Rosenberg Case.* New York: Random House, 2003. In an interview with the author, David Greenglass confesses that he does not remember if Ethel Rosenberg actually typed the atomic bomb notes. The author agrees with others that the evidence against Ethel was too weak to secure a conviction.

SEE ALSO: Aug. 6 and 9, 1945: Atomic Bombs Destroy Hiroshima and Nagasaki; 1951-1952: Teller and Ulam Develop the First Hydrogen Bomb; Jan. 15, 1953-Dec. 2, 1954: McCarthy Hearings; Jan. 22, 1953: *The Crucible* Allegorizes the Red Scare Era; June 27, 1954: Soviet Union Completes Its First Nuclear Power Plant; July 9, 1955-early 1960's: Scientists Campaign Against Nuclear Testing.

■ **SEPTEMBER 25, 1953-OCTOBER 26, 1956**

POLISH COMMUNIST GOVERNMENT ARRESTS THE PRIMATE OF POLAND

Resistance by the Roman Catholic Church to communist repression in Poland led to the arrest of Stefan Wyszyński, the primate of Poland. Wyszyński became a symbol of defiance and was eventually released when the Church and the government reached an agreement that allowed the Church to remain independent. Events surrounding Wyszyński's arrest would help to spark the nonviolent Solidarity movement in 1980.

LOCALE: Poland
CATEGORIES: Religion, theology, and ethics; human rights; organizations and institutions; crime and scandal

KEY FIGURES
Stefan Wyszyński (1901-1981), cardinal archbishop of Gniezno, 1948-1981, and primate of Poland, 1948-1981
Bolesław Bierut (1892-1956), president of Poland, 1947-1952, prime minister of Poland, 1952-1956, and general secretary of the Polish United Workers Party
Joseph Stalin (Joseph Vissarionovich Dzhugashvili; 1878-1953), general secretary of the Central Committee of the Communist Party of the Soviet Union, 1922-1953, and premier, 1941-1953

SUMMARY OF EVENT
Following the defeat of Nazi Germany, the Soviet Union under Joseph Stalin attempted to establish total control over Poland using a small native Communist Party, led by Bolesław Bierut and backed by Soviet security and military forces. Poland's new leaders, however, lacked popular legitimacy. Most

Poles remained loyal to the noncommunist government in exile in London and tacitly supported the noncommunist underground resistance forces, both of which sought to reestablish Poland's independence.

As early as 1943, Soviet forces began to wage a campaign of covert killing against resistance forces. After 1945, this became a campaign of mass terror, with arrests, imprisonment, and executions of many of the leaders and rank and file of the anti-Nazi resistance movement. A virtual civil war raged in many parts of the country from 1944 to 1956, and communist forces killed approximately thirty thousand people, mostly civilians, in an effort to stamp out proindependence forces. In 1947, communist authorities rigged the national elections, effectively making even peaceful opposition illegal.

The one major institution in Poland that remained outside communist control was the Roman Catholic Church. The Church had long been a symbol of Polish independence, especially during the nineteenth century when Poland had been partitioned by its more powerful neighbors. During World War II, the Church had again emerged as a symbol of resistance to Nazi and Soviet occupations. Thousands of priests and other religious had been

Cardinal Stefan Wyszyński (in robe) posing with the family of U.S. attorney general Robert F. Kennedy in Poland in 1964. (AP/Wide World Photos)

imprisoned and murdered by Poland's occupiers, including a number of bishops.

Among the most important figures in the Church in Poland in the years following the war was Stefan Wyszyński. During the war, he had served as a chaplain to a partisan unit. In 1946, he was named bishop of Lublin and in 1948 his fellow bishops elected him primate of Poland and archbishop of Gniezno—the leading bishop in the country. Wyszyński had an unbending will and a determination to preserve the freedom of the Church and to protect the rights of those facing government persecution. He soon became a major enemy of the new regime.

The communist authorities made destruction of the Church a major goal, to be accomplished both through direct repression—arrests and murders of priests and religious and terrorizing the faithful—as well as through subversion, spying, and efforts to create dissension and division among Poland's Catholics. A special section of the ministry of the interior was set up to conduct anti-Church activities. Despite these efforts, the communists made few inroads with the populace in turning them against the Church's authority.

In 1950, Wyszyński agreed to a treaty with the authorities that would have regulated church-state relations and mitigated repression. This agreement was considered highly controversial since it pledged that the Church would not support the underground movement and would remain loyal to the state. However, the government had little intention of honoring the agreement and continued its campaign against the Church.

Wyszyński tried to avoid direct conflict with the communist authorities, preferring to emphasize the Church's role as defender of moral values, but the continuing repression led him to speak out against the government's effort to restrict religious freedom. The Bierut regime considered his speaking a direct challenge as well as an opportunity to break the power of the Church. On September 25, 1953, Wyszyński was arrested, placed in a prison in Grudziadz, and later transferred to house arrest in two monasteries in southern Poland. During the three-year period of his imprisonment, repression continued against the Church. More than one thousand priests were arrested, and there were frequent raids on parishes, schools, convents, and monasteries. Far from squelching Wyszyński or the Church, the arrest of Wyszyński added to his stature and the position of the Church. Wyszyński's quiet dignity and his refusal to compromise his morals made him a hero in the eyes of ordinary Poles and an international symbol of peaceful resistance to communism.

The strength of communist repression began to falter after the death of Stalin in 1953 and the revelation of his crimes against other communists. In

1956, the Polish communist leader Bierut died amid growing unrest among Polish workers. In June, 1956, communist police killed scores of workers in Poznań who had been protesting food shortages and poor working conditions. The new communist leadership moved away from overt repression and backed away from confrontation with the Church. On October 26, the government released Wyszyński. The Polish primate and government also reached a tacit agreement in which the government would not interfere with the Church, and priests and bishops would refrain from direct criticism of the authorities.

Although the communist authorities maintained efforts to subvert the Church and spying continued unabated, the period of relative calm after Wyszyński's release allowed the Church to rebuild its educational, media, and pastoral activities. Priests and bishops did not directly attack the government, but they continued to draw clear distinctions between the message of the Christian Gospels and the corruption and brutality of the authorities.

SIGNIFICANCE

Wyszyński's arrest and subsequent release proved to be critical for the subsequent history of the Cold War in East-Central Europe. His arrest and release marked the first time communist repression had been successfully confronted through peaceful means. Because of the primate's strong stand in forcing the government to back down from its effort to destroy the Church, the Catholic Church in Poland emerged as the only bastion of independent thought in the entire communist bloc. It operated the only legal periodicals and the only university outside government control. Because of this, the Church remained an institution of freedom and a beacon for those who hoped for the spread of freedom and human rights.

Wyszyński was made a cardinal in 1957 and was Poland's greatest moral leader. He also became the mentor for the young archbishop of Kraków, Karol Josef Wojtyła. Following Wyszyński's example, Wojtyła soon emerged as a powerful voice in his own right, both inside Poland and within the Catholic Church internationally. In 1978, Wojtyła was elected Pope John Paul II, the first non-Italian pope since the sixteenth century.

John Radzilowski

FURTHER READING

Berglund, Sten, and Frank Aarebrot. *The Political History of Eastern Europe in the Twentieth Century: The Struggle Between Democracy and Dictatorship*. Lyme, N.H.: E. Elgar, 1997. Detailed examination of the oscillation between freedom and totalitarian regimes in pre- and postwar Eastern Europe.

Chodakiewicz, Marek Jan. "The Pope's Secret File." *American Spectator*, March, 2006. Details anti-Church efforts by the communist regime in Poland.

Davies, Norman. *God's Playground: A History of Poland.* Vol. 2, *1795 to the Present.* New York: Columbia University Press, 1982. The standard history of Poland. Recommended.

Kloczowski, Jerzy. *A History of Polish Christianity.* New York: Cambridge University Press, 2000. A concise overview of the history of the Church in Poland, with a chapter on the communists and Wyszyński.

Radzilowski, John. *A Traveller's History of Poland.* Boston: Interlink, 2006. The most recent narrative history of Poland.

Wyszyński, Stefan. *A Freedom Within: The Prison Notes of Stefan Cardinal Wyszyński.* Translated by Barbara Krzywicki-Herburt and Walter J. Ziemba. San Diego, Calif.: Harcourt Brace Jovanovich, 1984. Wyszyński's own diary and notes provide essential insight into the conditions of his imprisonment as well as his moral and philosophical beliefs.

SEE ALSO: Dec. 26, 1948: Hungary's Communist Government Arrests Cardinal Mindszenty; May 14, 1955: Warsaw Pact Is Signed; Feb. 25, 1956: Khrushchev Denounces Stalinist Regime; Aug. 20-21, 1968: Soviet Union Invades Czechoslovakia; Nov. 12, 1968-Dec., 1989: Brezhnev Doctrine Mandates Soviet Control of Satellite Nations; June-Sept., 1989: Poland Forms a Noncommunist Government.

■ NOVEMBER 9, 1953

CAMBODIA GAINS INDEPENDENCE FROM FRANCE

Cambodian king Norodom Sihanouk helped to wrest Cambodian independence from France, making him a national hero and raising the hopes of Cambodians that they could remain free of communist domination threatening the region.

LOCALE: Cambodia
CATEGORIES: Independence movements; colonialism and occupation; government and politics

290

KEY FIGURES

Norodom Sihanouk (b. 1922), king of Cambodia, r. 1941-1955, 1993-2004
Son Ngoc Thanh (1908-1977), prime minister of Cambodia, 1945, 1972,
    1945-1972, and anti-Sihanouk rebel leader, 1952-1970
Samdech Penn Nouth (1906-1985), Cambodian ally of Sihanouk
Vincent Auriol (1884-1966), president of the French Republic, 1947-1954

SUMMARY OF EVENT

The ancient kingdom of Cambodia lost its independence to Siam (now Thailand) in 1369 and later became a vassal state, dependent on Siam and Vietnam, in the early nineteenth century. In 1863, in face of Vietnamese aggression, the French established the protectorate of Cambodia, which they incorporated into their colonial Union of Indochina in 1887. In 1897, France reduced the Cambodian king to a mere figurehead. Initially, during World War II (1939-1945), Japan allowed the French colonial administration to remain in place in Cambodia, and the French installed Norodom Sihanouk as Cambodian king in September, 1941.

On March 9, 1945, the Japanese ended French rule over Cambodia, and nine days later, King Norodom Sihanouk created the independent Kingdom of Cambodia, naming himself prime minister. He was succeeded by Cambodian nationalist Son Ngoc Thanh on August 14. However, even after Japan's World War II surrender to the Allies on August 15, the Allies still considered Cambodia's government as a Japanese puppet and allowed the French to reestablish their colonial rule. On October 17, the returning French arrested Son Ngoc Thanh, convicted him of treason, and exiled him to France, ending Cambodian independence again.

Sihanouk began negotiating with the French over degrees of Cambodia's independence. Soon there arose, in late 1945, a multifarious anti-French nationalist rebel movement called the Khmer Issarak—supported by Thailand—which was opposed to the king and included communist elements. Cautiously, the French chose to grant Cambodia limited independence. On May 6, 1947, Sihanouk proclaimed a new constitution for Cambodia, giving himself vaguely regulated powers as head of state.

Negotiating further with the French, Sihanouk worked out a treaty that granted Cambodia limited independence within the French Union, a status he called "fifty percent independence," which went into effect on November 8, 1949, even though Cambodia's antimonarchist national assembly never ratified the treaty. On February 7, 1950, the United States recognized Cambodian independence, and was joined by most Western countries in that recognition. France, however, maintained a great degree of control in Cambodia, which led Sihanouk to strive for a better solution.

Cambodian king Norodom Sihanouk. (National Archives)

With antimonarchists winning the elections of 1951, Sihanouk requested that the French release Son Ngoc Thanh, whom he considered an ally. Son Ngoc Thanh made a triumphant return to Phnom Penh on October 29. Soon, Son Ngoc Thanh clashed with the French and on March 9, 1952, left to join forces with the Khmer Issarak, forming his own rebel group, the Khmer Serei (free Cambodians). Jolted to win back popularity, Sihanouk, on June 15, 1952, took direct power as prime minister and declared he would achieve real independence within three years.

On January 24, 1953, Sihanouk declared martial law in Cambodia and made his ally Samdech Penn Nouth prime minister. On February 9, Sihanouk left for France to try to win full independence. In France, on March 5 and 18 and on April 3, Sihanouk wrote three letters to the French president, Vincent Auriol, declaring that the communist-infiltrated Khmer Issarak would succeed in Cambodia unless the French Republic achieved full independence for Cambodia. The French officials who were meeting with Sihanouk dismissed this claim. Frustrated with the French, Sihanouk left France on April 11. He traveled to the United States and Canada, lobbying for a completely independent Cambodia.

Publishing a pro-independence royal declaration in *The New York Times* on April 19 created momentum for Sihanouk, as he began to positively influence Western public opinion. The French opened negotiations with Prime Minister Penn Nouth, who returned to Cambodia without desired results on May 12, two days before Sihanouk's return from Japan.

On June 13, continuing his high-stakes gamble with the French, Sihanouk went to Bangkok, proclaiming he would return only to a free Cambodia. Rejected by Thailand, Sihanouk went to his royal residence near the ancient monument of Angkor Wat in an autonomous zone of Cambodia under control of his ally, Lieutenant Colonel Lon Nol.

France, troubled by its deteriorating military situation in neighboring Vietnam, where the communist Viet Minh fought a large-scale anticolonial war, sought to limit its losses in Cambodia by being conciliatory. On July 3, 1953, rather than overthrow Sihanouk as king, the French government declared it was prepared to bestow full independence to the three Indo-Chinese countries of Cambodia, Laos, and Vietnam. In the ensuing negotiations, Sihanouk insisted on full sovereignty and won on his terms. On August 29, Cambodia gained control of its police and judiciary from the French, and on October 17, it gained full command of its army.

On November 9, Sihanouk arrived to triumphal Cambodian welcome at his Royal Palace in Phnom Penh, after traveling some 180 miles from Angkor Wat, cheered along by the Cambodian people. At the Royal Palace, Sihanouk declared Cambodian independence and formally accepted the withdrawal of French power, which was symbolized by the resignation of the last French high commissioner of Cambodia, Jean Risterucci.

In spite of this emotional and symbolic day, full independence for Cambodia remained unsettled. France still held authority over economic and fiscal decisions. Because most Cambodians regarded Sihanouk as a national hero after November 9, the Khmer Issarak movement that had controlled perhaps half of rural Cambodia by 1952 quickly faded. Rebellious Son Ngoc Thanh went into exile in Vietnam.

But on the horizon ominous clouds of Cold War contention gathered. Communist Viet Minh forces fighting the French in Vietnam, however, moved into Cambodia as sanctuary in April, 1954, and the Cambodian army could not dislodge them. The communists also sought to carve out a part of Cambodia to be ruled by the Vietnamese-dependent Khmer People's Revolutionary Party (KPRP), similar to the situation emerging in a soon-to-be-divided Vietnam. Sihanouk's general, Saukam Khoy, defeated the KPRP in battle in the spring of 1954, ensuring Cambodian territorial integrity. The defeated KPRP fled to North Vietnam.

At the conclusion of the Geneva Conference on July 21, 1954, it was agreed that all foreign troops such as French and Viet Minh forces would leave Cambodia by October and that Cambodia, while a neutral country, was free to enter into alliances under the principles of the charter of the United Nations. At a conference in Paris in December, 1954, France agreed to the final transfer of economic and financial authority to Cambodia. On December 20 the former colonial power of France finally recognized Cambodian independence.

SIGNIFICANCE

King Norodom Sihanouk succeeded not only in his high-stakes political gamble to win Cambodia's modern independence but also thwarted French hopes to keep its colonial power in a Southeast Asian nation where opposition to French rule was not resisted with military force. The ensuing prestige of Sihanouk among Cambodians, coupled with Khoy's success on the battlefield in 1954, seemed to ensure the emergence of an independent and neutral Cambodia that would not fall victim to communism, which threatened to advance throughout Asia.

However, despite its independence, Sihanouk's Cambodia saw itself inextricably drawn into the war that engulfed North Vietnam and South Vietnam. Although Sihanouk pursued a policy of neutrality, North Vietnamese troops violated Cambodian neutrality and territorial integrity once Hanoi decided on armed struggle against the Republic of Vietnam (South Vietnam) in late 1959. By the early 1960's, North Vietnamese troops and South Vietnamese communist insurgents entered Cambodia either by force or forced agreements.

Ultimately, Cambodian independence under Sihanouk proved too fragile to withstand the cataclysmic forces of the Vietnam War , and its Cold War implications. Annoyed with Sihanouk's acceptance of North Vietnam's use of his independent country as sanctuary, even though it was born out of necessity forced by Cambodia's military inability to oppose it, the United States accepted the March 18, 1970, coup of Prime Minister Lon Nol against Sihanouk. By strongly aligning Cambodia to the United States and formally abolishing the monarchy on October 9, Lon Nol immediately faced Khmer Rouge aggression that was immeasurably aided by exiled Sihanouk's alliance with these ultracommunist Cambodian rebels. The Khmer Rouge captured Phnom Penh on April 17, 1975. Their genocidal regime caused Cambodia's invasion by Vietnam in December, 1979, leading yet again to its loss of independence. Full national sovereignty was reestablished in 1993, with the country bearing the wounds of the Khmer Rouge murdering more than 1.6 million of its own people.

R. C. Lutz

FURTHER READING

Chandler, David. *A History of Cambodia.* 3d ed. Boulder, Colo.: Westview Press, 2000. Chapter 10 of this critically acclaimed standard historical work covers the independence struggles and more.

Osborne, Milton. *Sihanouk: Prince of Light, Prince of Darkness.* Honolulu: University of Hawaii Press, 1994. Competent biography illuminating Sihanouk's mercurial character, his strengths, and his weaknesses. Covers the independence movement in detail.

Sihanouk, Norodom, with Wilfred Burchett. *My War with the CIA: Cambodia's Fight for Survival.* London: Penguin Books, 1974. Written while Sihanouk was in exile in Beijing and allied with the murderous Khmer Rouge, which was fighting a civil war in Cambodia. Sihanouk blames the United States for interfering with Cambodian independence.

_____. *War and Hope: The Case for Cambodia.* New York: Pantheon Books, 1980. Written while Sihanouk was in exile after the Vietnamese expelled the Khmer Rouge from the city of Phnom Penh.

Westad, Odd Arne. *The Global Cold War: Third World Interventions and the Makings of Our Times.* Cambridge, U.K.: Cambridge University Press, 2007. Examines the aftermath of the Cold War in terms of globalization and American interventionism in developing nations. Illustrated.

SEE ALSO: Nov., 1946-July, 1954: Nationalist Vietnamese Fight French Control of Indochina; Aug., 1954-May, 1955: Operation Passage to Freedom Evacuates Refugees from North Vietnam; Sept. 8, 1954: SEATO Is Founded; Dec. 14, 1955: United Nations Admits Sixteen New Members; Aug. 7, 1964-Jan. 27, 1973: United States Enters the Vietnam War; Mar., 1973: U.S. Troops Leave Vietnam; May, 1975: Indo-Chinese Boat People Begin Fleeing Vietnam; Feb. 17-Mar. 16, 1979: China Invades Vietnam; Sept., 1989: Vietnamese Troops Withdraw from Cambodia.

■ **FEBRUARY 15, 1954**

CANADA AND THE UNITED STATES ESTABLISH THE DEW LINE

To counter the threat of a Soviet air attack across the North Pole on populations and military establishments on the North American continent, the United States and Canada agreed to establish the Distant Early Warning (DEW) system, consisting of a series of radar stations designed to detect approaching aircraft.

ALSO KNOWN AS: Distant Early Warning system
LOCALE: Artic Circle, Canada, and Greenland
CATEGORIES: Diplomacy and international relations; military history; engineering

KEY FIGURES

Harry S. Truman (1884-1972), president of the United States, 1945-1953
Dwight D. Eisenhower (1890-1969), president of the United States, 1953-1961
Louis St. Laurent (1882-1973), prime minister of Canada, 1948-1957
Harold R. Bull (1893-1976), lieutenant general in the U.S. Army
Brooke Claxton (1898-1960), minister of defense in Canada, 1948-1954

SUMMARY OF EVENT

Even before World War II ended, the Western nations fighting against Adolf Hitler's Nazi Germany knew that they would soon be facing another enemy—their ally against the Nazis, the Soviet Union. The United States felt especially threatened by the Soviets' aggressive behavior in Europe and Asia, but Canada was also concerned, because if the Soviets were to launch an air assault on the United States, their route would cross Canadian soil. As a result, shortly after the war ended, both countries began constructing radar sites to provide warnings of Soviet air attacks. Unfortunately, these sites were often close to major population centers and hence afforded barely an hour's warning—far too little time to conduct wholesale evacuations. A number of military and political strategists in both countries believed that a system integrating the efforts of the two North American countries could prove beneficial to both nations.

Before any system could be developed, however, technical problems regarding the capability and reliability of advanced radar systems had to be solved. In the late 1940's and early 1950's, a number of scientists were commissioned by both governments to explore the technical feasibility of such systems. In 1952 the Lincoln Summer Study Group, a conference of scientists meeting in Boston, reviewed the issue once more and assured themselves that technology developed by scientists at McGill University in Canada could be used as the basis for a radar system that would be capable of long-range detection. If placed far enough north, this system could provide as much as six hours' notice of an impending Soviet attack. The Lincoln Summer Study Group recommended strongly that the U.S. government invest in such a project.

Surprisingly, not everyone in the United States was in favor of creating a strong system of defense. After the war, strategies that were being developed

THE DEW LINE

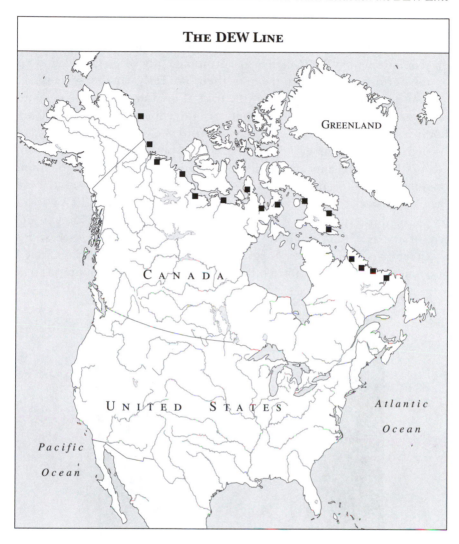

by the newly created U.S. Air Force to counter the Soviet air threat stressed offensive operations. For years, the Air Force fought plans to strengthen air defense systems, fearing that funds for these programs would be taken from money allocated to increase the number of aircraft in the U.S. fleet. Nevertheless, other members of the government, concerned that American cities might be vulnerable to Soviet attack, pressed President Harry S. Truman to commit to some form of national air defense system. Although he deliberated with both military and political advisers for quite some time, shortly before leaving office Truman signed a National Security Council (NSC) order authorizing the development of a comprehensive early warning system to give between three and six hours' notice of an impending attack. This formal commitment by the United States prompted officials in Canada to step up their efforts to develop and deploy their own early warning systems.

There was some willingness on the part of the Canadians to enter into agreements for joint operations, but the government of Prime Minister Louis St. Laurent was skeptical of American offers. The Canadians were concerned that large numbers of American service personnel stationed in Canada would give the appearance that their nation was somehow little more than a satellite of its neighbor to the south. Canadian minister of defense Brooke Claxton, who had been working independently to build his country's armed forces, saw the U.S. government's move toward a joint air defense force as a thinly disguised takeover of Canadian military operations and a rebuke of Canadian sovereignty. Nevertheless, while politicians fumed and feuded, Canadian air force officers began working with counterparts in

Canadian prime minister Louis St. Laurent. (National Archives)

the United States to build systems for sharing information, thus laying the groundwork for more formal efforts at joint operations that followed in the administration of U.S. president Dwight D. Eisenhower.

When the Soviet Union successfully detonated a hydrogen bomb in 1953, military officials in the United States gave up opposition to deployment of a defensive system. There was now general agreement that early warning was necessary so that the Strategic Air Command could launch its bombers before they were destroyed on the ground, which would make it impossible for the United States to launch a counterattack. Another special commission, established in 1953 and headed by one of Eisenhower's military associates, Lieutenant General Harold R. Bull, again recommended that the United States invest in an early warning network. In February, 1954, Eisenhower approved an NSC recommendation to deploy the system and signed a bill authorizing construction of the Distant Early Warning (DEW) Line. Under the terms of the bill, the United States agreed to pay the full costs of constructing radar sites above the Arctic Circle. As a second line of defense, Canadians built the Mid-Canada Line, a series of stations about midway between the Arctic Circle and the U.S.-Canadian border. Even before these were fully operational, a third line of stations running on both sides of the border, the Pinetree Line, was installed near major population centers.

Construction of the stations north of the Arctic Circle was a major engineering feat. All work had to be done during the short summers in the region, and materials had to be transported by air or sled to most locations. More than twenty-five thousand people were employed in construction. Sixty-three stations were erected between Alaska in the west and Baffin Island in the east. The stations varied in size. Some were small and intended to be unstaffed. A number were designed to be operated by a crew of three. The major stations were small cities that included housing, dining, and recreation accommodations for larger crews. A complex system of electronic transmissions linked all the stations and various military headquarters in Canada and the United States. Work began on stations above the Arctic Circle in 1955. Despite brutal weather conditions, the entire line of stations was built in two years. The system was declared fully operational July 31, 1957, and integrated into the air defense networks of both countries.

SIGNIFICANCE

The highly publicized efforts to create an early warning system against Soviet attack raised public awareness in both the United States and Canada about the menace posed by the communist juggernaut. Americans already accustomed to carrying out a number of defensive measures against impending nuclear attack took some comfort in knowing that the two countries were working together to thwart Soviet aggression. Unfortunately, because the radars were designed primarily to detect aircraft, the DEW Line's effectiveness was severely limited after the Soviets developed intercontinental ballistic missiles (ICBMs) that were similar to those deployed by the United States. Nevertheless, the system of joint command and control developed to coordinate this air defense system evolved into one of the most notable military organizations of the Cold War era, the North American Air Defense Command (NORAD), which was announced on August 1, 1957. Located deep inside a mountainside command post in Colorado, NORAD served for more than three decades as the principal command and control center for air defense operations on the North American continent.

Laurence W. Mazzeno

FURTHER READING

Eglin, James M. *Air Defense in the Nuclear Age: The Post-War Development of American and Soviet Strategic Defense Systems.* New York: Garland, 1988. Describes the evolution of air defense strategies in the United States and the Soviet Union; two chapters focus on the emergence in both countries of systems aimed at detecting enemy incursions.

Jockel, Joseph T. *No Boundaries Upstairs: Canada, the United States, and the Origins of North American Air Defence, 1945-1958.* Vancouver: University of British Columbia Press, 1987. Analysis of U.S.-Canadian relationships during the years when the two countries collaborated to develop air defenses against Soviet attacks.

Hoffman, David. *The Dead Hand: The Untold Story of the Cold War Arms Race and Its Dangerous Legacy.* New York: Doubleday, 2009. Describes American and Soviet strategies and decision making related to the superpowers' nuclear arsenals. Includes discussion of the continued threat posed by these weapons after the breakup of the Soviet Union. The title refers to a Soviet plan to create a system to automatically retaliate after a nuclear attack. Contains illustrations and maps.

Lackenbauer, P. W., et al. *The Distant Early Warning (DEW) Line: A Bibliography and Documentary Resource List.* Calgary, Alta.: Arctic Institute of North America, 2005. Contains a brief history of the creation and operation of the DEW Line; reproduces several key documents regarding the establishment and maintenance of the system.

Ranson, Rick. *Working North: DEW Line to Drill Ship.* Edmonton, Alta.: NeWest Press, 2003. Anecdotes about construction of the DEW Line radar stations provide a vivid sense of the environmental conditions under which the stations were built and operated.

SEE ALSO: Apr. 4, 1949: North Atlantic Treaty Organization Is Formed; May 12, 1958: Canada and the United States Create NORAD; Jan. 17, 1961: Eisenhower Warns of the Military-Industrial Complex; Oct. 6, 1986: Soviet Nuclear Submarine Sinks in the Atlantic.

■ MARCH 1, 1954

NUCLEAR BOMBING OF BIKINI ATOLL

The U.S. government tested a multimegaton bomb on Bikini Atoll, contaminating Bikini and several other of the Marshall Islands. The atoll was virtually obliterated by the explosion.

ALSO KNOWN AS: Bravo
LOCALE: Bikini Atoll, Marshall Islands, Micronesia
CATEGORIES: Environmental issues; atrocities and war crimes; science and technology; health and medicine

KEY FIGURES
Ben Wyatt (fl. mid-twentieth century), American military governor of the Marshall Islands in 1946
Juda Kessibuki (fl. mid-twentieth century), king of the Bikini Islanders in 1946
Tomaki Juda (b. c. 1944), youngest son of King Juda; Bikinian mayor, 1972-2000, and senator, 2000-
Lekoj Anjain (1953-1972), youngest child on Rongelap when the bomb exploded, who died of leukemia at the age of nineteen

SUMMARY OF EVENT
On March 1, 1954, the United States exploded a seventeen-megaton bomb on Bikini Island, one of the Marshall Islands in the South Pacific. The residents of Bikini had been relocated several years earlier, but the inhabitants of two other atolls downwind of the blast were neither removed nor warned. They suffered a variety of illnesses, many severe, from the effect of fallout. Related health problems would continue to occur.

The Marshall Archipelago consists of twenty-nine coral atolls and five coral islands in eastern Micronesia. The land area, scattered over 375,000 square miles of ocean, adds up to less than seventy square miles, mostly in atolls. Atolls are formed by coral growing upward from submerged volcanic

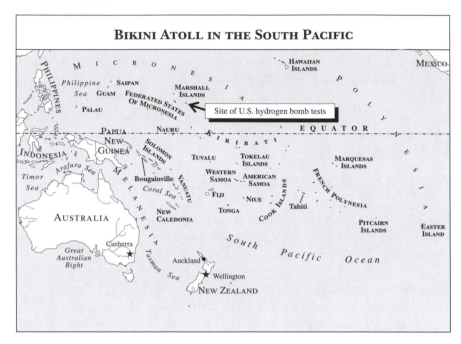

BIKINI ATOLL IN THE SOUTH PACIFIC

peaks, creating circles or semicircles of islands and reefs enclosing protected lagoons. Bikini, one of the northernmost atolls, was composed of twenty-six islands on a reef around a lagoon. The islanders relied on the atoll's abundant marine life for food, but they also grew coconuts and arrowroot, occasionally supplemented by pigs, chickens, and land crabs.

The Marshall Islands were controlled for forty years by the Japanese until the end of World War II, when the archipelago became a trusteeship of the U.S. government. Five weeks after the end of the war, the U.S. joint chiefs of staff began to look for a site for a series of atomic tests. Bikini was chosen because it had a deep-water harbor where target vessels could anchor, it was isolated, and it had a small and easily relocated population of 166 people.

In February, 1946, Commodore Ben Wyatt, American military governor of the Marshalls, flew to Bikini to ask the islanders to leave their land, and Chief Juda Kessibuki assented. The Bikinians were moved to the uninhabited atoll of Rongerik, one-quarter the size of their former home, and left with a two-week supply of food and water. The carrying capacity of Rongerik was insufficient for the new population, and the people soon suffered from hunger and malnutrition.

In June of that year, the bombing of Bikini began, and by December, Eniwetok, another atoll in the Marshall Islands, was also requisitioned. Its inhabitants were moved to a much smaller atoll, with the same results. After two years of near starvation and many requests for help, the Bikinians were moved again. Kili, their new home, was an island, not an atoll with a protected lagoon for fishing. Once again, malnutrition set in.

On March 1, 1954, the United States exploded a hydrogen bomb over Bikini Atoll. This bomb, named Bravo, had more than one thousand times the force of the bomb that had been dropped on Hiroshima, and it was designed to maximize radioactive fallout. Despite a weather report indicating winds headed toward the islands of Rongelap, one hundred miles east of Bikini, and Utirik, three hundred miles east, the inhabitants of the islands were neither removed nor warned.

After the blast, lime from the Bikini reef that had been melted in the blast fell on Rongelap in a white powder, accumulating to a depth of one and one-half inches. Unaware of its nature, children played with it as if it were snow, and the entire population continued to drink water from catch basins and to gather and eat food on which the substance had fallen. By nightfall, the inhabitants found their hair falling out and their skin itching and burning. Many experienced vomiting, achiness, and weakness.

The U.S. Navy vessels nearby were instructed not to rescue the residents for two days. The people of Utirik were rescued three days later. All the 239 irradiated Marshallese were transported to Kwajalein Atoll, where a team of U.S. radiation experts was flown in to study and examine them. In the weeks that followed, the islanders' blood platelet levels fell by 50 percent, and stillbirths and miscarriages were reported.

The International Commission on Radiological Protection recommends a maximum dose of 0.5 units of radiation (rems) per year; 200 to 300 rems is expected to cause a 50 percent death rate in a nuclear war. It was estimated that the people on Rongelap received a dose of 175 rems, and the people on Utirik 14 rems. These numbers refer only to whole-body exposure; exposure to specific body parts was higher because of the properties of ionizing radiation and the ingestion of contaminated food and water.

The Navy never explained the two- and three-day delays in evacuating the Marshall Islanders but did admit in early 1994 that its personnel had been aware of the wind forecast. Critics have charged that the delay may have been a deliberate attempt to create a population that could be studied to understand the effects of radiation. In the 1940's, standards for medical experimentation on human subjects were lower than they have become since.

SIGNIFICANCE

Prior to the bombing of Bikini Atoll, the only data on the effects of radiation exposure came from the explosions in Hiroshima and Nagasaki, where the direct effects of the blasts had to be taken into account as well. At that time, medical opinion held that the only effects of radiation exposure were immediate. After the initial examination of the radiation victims on Kwajalein Atoll, the Atomic Energy Commission (AEC) assigned a medical team from Brookhaven National Laboratory in New York to examine and record the health of the Marshallese over time.

Three months after the blast, the people from Utirik were allowed to return home. The people from Rongelap were returned after three years, although the AEC acknowledged that some radioactivity lingered on their island. Returning along with the Rongalapese were some residents who had not been on the island at the time of the blast and who subsequently became affected through the food they ate there.

On their return, the islanders found the ecology of the atoll altered. Animals they had left behind were dead or sick, as were plants and trees. The residents were instructed not to eat arrowroot or coconut crabs, but when food supplies from outside ran low, as they often did, anything edible was consumed. Brookhaven reported that when the people returned to Rongelap, their body levels of radioactivity soared, but the inhabitants were not told, nor were they urged to leave.

The next few years brought more miscarriages and stillbirths. The Brookhaven team, however, was expecting their subjects' health to return to normal. It was not until 1964, ten years after the bombing, that thyroid abnormalities began to appear in the Brookhaven data, proving for the first time that radioactive fallout has long-term effects. By the 1980's, approximately forty thyroid tumors had been found in the Rongelap population, four of which were malignant. Furthermore, 90 percent of the people who were under age twelve at the time of the explosion contracted thyroid disease. On Utirik, there were sixteen cases of tumors, three of which were malignant. The high rate of thyroid problems was thought to stem from the similarity of radioactive iodine 131 to normal, stable iodine, which the thyroid gland readily absorbs.

Growth retardation was found in some children who had been under age ten at the time of the blast, particularly boys who had been under five. In 1972, Lekoj Anjain, who had been the youngest child on Rongelap in 1954, died of leukemia.

One important implication of these data was that the younger the persons exposed, the more susceptible they were to radiation-induced disease. Cataracts became frequent among the population. The Marshall Islanders developed the highest rate of diabetes in the world, which may have been caused by the bomb, the subsequent rapid change of diet, or both. A higher-than-normal rate of an assortment of health problems, from anemia to cervical erosion, has been shown, but the incidences have been too few for clear conclusions to be drawn.

The Marshallese were critical of the quality of the health care provided them by the Brookhaven team, and they have been joined in their criticism by other medical personnel who questioned aspects of the research methodology. One departing Brookhaven doctor criticized the program for looking exclusively for evidence of what experts had previously predicted. Throughout the 1960's and early 1970's, Brookhaven focused on the effects of acute radiation, in effect dismissing blame from low- and middle-level radiation. This clean bill of health was used by the U.S. nuclear industry, which was at that time promoting nuclear energy as so healthy that radiation units were referred to as "units of sunshine." Not until 1976 did Brookhaven formally acknowledge that it had been wrong in disregarding the information available from Utirik, where radiation exposure was less but where the proportion of thyroid cancers and malignancies was actually higher.

Bombing continued in the Marshalls until 1958. In 1967, the AEC told the Bikinians that they could return. From four to five million dollars was spent cleaning up the atoll; fifty thousand new trees were planted, and homes were built. In 1971, 150 islanders returned. Within one year, new studies of the islands' radiation levels were requested, but not until 1978 was one done. That test confirmed that the Bikinians had been exposed to unacceptably high levels of contamination. The Bikinians left again, and the United States declared the island uninhabitable for at least another fifty years.

The Bikinians returned to the island of Kili, remaining dependent upon canned and packaged food from the United States and still wishing to return to their homeland. They own a trust fund of more than a million dollars in resettlement and compensation money, but that is nowhere near enough to restore their islands. Under the leadership of Mayor Tomaki Juda, son of the chief who ceded the Bikini Islands to the United States in 1946, they considered allowing one of the islands to be used as a nuclear waste repository, since it is already the most contaminated spot on Earth. Meanwhile, the Marshall Islanders experienced the symptoms of years of displacement as alcoholism, juvenile delinquency, and suicide, previously unknown in the culture, abounded.

Bravo provided the first opportunity for scientists to study the effects of radioactive fallout on a human population not affected by the actual explosion of a bomb. The initial data were skewed by the biases of the scientists involved, but by the late 1970's, the data that emerged showed the seriousness of even middle and low doses of radiation. These data were used by antinuclear activists in the United States concerned about power plant

305

safety and nuclear waste disposal sites. Bravo left behind a legacy of displaced islanders, of communities riddled with disease, and of islands contaminated for years to come. Although political and security factors dominated international efforts to achieve a ban on nuclear testing, gradually the environmental and health factors also gained wider notice. A partial nuclear test ban treaty was promulgated in 1963.

Maya Muir

FURTHER READING

Alcalay, Glenn H. "The Aftermath of Bikini." *Ecologist* 10 (December, 1980): 346-351. A good short summary of the social and environmental situation of the atolls by an anthropologist who worked to gain compensation for the Bikini Islanders.

Bertell, Rosalie. "The Marshallese." In *No Immediate Danger: Prognosis for a Radioactive Earth.* Toronto, Ont.: Women's Educational Press, 1985. An analysis of the nuclear industry by one who opposes it. The author, a senior cancer research scientist, acted as a consultant for the Citizens' Advisory Committee on the Accident at Three Mile Island. A well-documented case, with footnotes and index.

Davis, Jeffrey. "Bikini's Silver Lining." *The New York Times Magazine,* May 1, 1994, 47-73. An update on the Bikinians, focusing on the human story. Detailed but journalistic.

Dibblin, Jane. *Day of Two Suns: U.S. Nuclear Testing and the Pacific Islanders.* New York: New Amsterdam Books, 1988. A journalistic account focusing on the experiences of the islanders effected. Very readable. Footnotes.

Kiste, Robert C. *The Bikinians: A Study in Forced Migration.* Menlo Park, Calif.: Cummings, 1974. An anthropological examination of the effects of displacement on the Bikinians. Scholarly and detailed, with footnotes and bibliography.

Thompson, Nicholas. *The Hawk and the Dove: Paul Nitze, George Kennan, and the History of the Cold War.* New York: Henry Holt, 2009. Profiles two highly influential figures in American foreign policy: Nitze helped drive the arms race, while his friend and rival Kennan advocated containment. Illustrated.

U.S. Congress. House Committee on Resources. *The United States Nuclear Legacy in the Marshall Islands.* Washington, D.C.: Government Printing Office, 2005. Official twenty-first century assessment of the U.S. government's liability and obligations to the people of the Marshall Islands resulting from the Bikini Atoll nuclear tests. Bibliographic references.

SEE ALSO: Aug. 6 and 9, 1945: Atomic Bombs Destroy Hiroshima and Nagasaki; July 9, 1955-early 1960's: Scientists Campaign Against Nuclear Testing; Aug. 5, 1963: Nuclear Powers Sign the Limited Test Ban Treaty; Oct. 16, 1964: China Explodes Its First Nuclear Bomb; Mar. 5, 1970: Nuclear Non-Proliferation Treaty Goes into Effect; May 26, 1972: SALT I Is Signed; June 18, 1979: SALT II Is Signed; Oct. 16, 1980: China Conducts Atmospheric Nuclear Test; Oct., 1983: Europeans Demonstrate Against Nuclear Weapons.

■ JUNE 18-27, 1954

UNITED FRUIT COMPANY INSTIGATES A COUP IN GUATEMALA

Owners of the United Fruit Company forestalled agrarian reform in Guatemala by using the Central Intelligence Agency to overthrow the legitimate government of Jacobo Arbenz Guzmán.

ALSO KNOWN AS: Operation PBSUCCESS
LOCALE: Guatemala City, Guatemala
CATEGORIES: Government and politics; colonialism and occupation; wars, uprisings, and civil unrest

KEY FIGURES

Jacobo Arbenz Guzmán (1913-1971), president of Guatemala, 1951-1954
Henry Cabot Lodge, Jr. (1902-1985), U.S. senator from Massachusetts, 1937-1944 and 1947-1953, and delegate to the United Nations, 1953-1960
Allen Dulles (1893-1969), U.S. director of central intelligence, 1953-1961
John Foster Dulles (1888-1959), U.S. secretary of state, 1953-1959
Jorge Ubico Casteñeda (1878-1946), president of Guatemala, 1931-1944
Juan José Arévalo Bermejo (1904-1990), president of Guatemala, 1945-1951
Carlos Castillo Armas (1914-1957), president of Guatemala, 1954-1957

SUMMARY OF EVENT

Ownership of land in Guatemala is among the least equitably distributed in the Western world. The vast proportion of foreign-owned holdings not in cultivation has always tempted reformers. As a principal landholder in Central America, the United Fruit Company (UFCO) was particularly vulnerable to pressures for land reform.

The regime of President Jorge Ubico Casteñeda was supported by the landed aristocracy and foreign-owned agribusinesses, which Ubico allowed to operate with almost complete autonomy and without taxation. When it was expedient, Ubico reduced the daily minimum wage to be paid to field hands and had leaders of reform movements executed. To maintain stability, under these social pressures, in the region surrounding the Panama Canal, the United States government contributed generously to Guatemala's military establishment.

Following this repressive, almost feudal reign that ended with Ubico's forced resignation in 1944, the governments of Juan José Arévalo Bermejo and Jacobo Arbenz Guzmán seemed socially visionary. Arévalo introduced a social security program, expanded rural education, and instituted open elections. He encouraged cooperatives to aid the peasants whose ownership of tiny parcels of land maintained them in poverty and dependence on foreign employers in a country that showed, by its exports, that it could be self-sustaining.

Pressure for social reform led inevitably to rising feeling against foreign-owned corporations such as UFCO and its subsidiary, the International Railway of Central America. The railway became particularly vulnerable when Arbenz proposed a highway to compete with it. Loss of the transport monopoly for its crops would directly affect United Fruit as well as other agricultural firms.

On June 27, 1952, Arbenz introduced Decree 900, an agricultural land reform act that expropriated farms that had more than 223 acres not in cultivation. Expropriated land was to be distributed to land-poor peasants in plots of 42.5 acres. This was to enable them to sustain their families without being required to work for UFCO or other large landowners for low wages. All expropriated land was to be paid for with government bonds. During the eighteen-month program, 100,000 families received plots. About 1.5 million acres were distributed, for which the owners were paid more than $8 million.

The United Fruit Company had been allowed to claim a very low taxable value for its land to reduce its tax liability, and it was this taxable worth that was used to set the payments for expropriated land. The company thought this to be inequitable and asked the U.S. State Department to intervene. The State Department demanded millions of dollars more, asking for $75 an acre. The government of Guatemala had set the price at $2.99 an acre. Because the land in dispute had been acquired by UFCO only twenty years earlier for $1.48 an acre, Guillermo Toriello, the foreign minister of Guatemala, coldly refused the State Department request.

While the governments of the two nations argued this question, the

United States saw other disturbing developments in Guatemala. Many exiled communists, particularly from Peru and Chile, lived in Central and South America at the time. When Arbenz formed agencies to manage his agrarian reforms, he selected some of the educated and willing workers he needed from among these communist émigrés. He resisted pressure from the United States to purge them from his government, saying that Guatemala was a country where all views were welcome.

In May, 1954, a shipment of weapons from Czechoslovakia arrived in Puerto Barrios, Guatemala, ostensibly to replenish the armories of the Guatemalan military, which had been barred from buying arms from the United States since 1948 as a result of a treaty disagreement. This shipment alarmed many in the United States, who saw it as part of a communist plot to infiltrate Central America.

In the United States, the Cold War climate and the fear of encroaching communism was having a profound effect on internal policy. Senator Joseph McCarthy had elevated himself to prominence by alerting Americans

Guatemalan Liberation Army leader Carlos Castillo Armas (front, third from left) entering Guatemala City to join forces with the regular Guatemala army on September 28, 1954. (AP/ Wide World Photos)

to real and imagined communist plots in every profession, most notably Hollywood film production. He also suggested communist influence in the Central Intelligence Agency (CIA). Whether there was any communist threat in the CIA is unimportant. The agency thought that a demonstration of its loyalty was desirable to disarm suspicions.

Owners of UFCO included several who occupied positions of prominence in the United States government and the United Nations. The Lodge family was heavily invested, as were the Dulles brothers—Allen, director of the CIA, and John Foster, the secretary of state. When further expropriations of idle land owned by UFCO were made, the CIA was directed to plan and execute a clandestine operation to effect a coup in Guatemala. This action, called "Operation PBSUCCESS," was intended to protect the holdings of United States corporations and discourage further growth of communist influence in Central America.

On June 18, 1954, Guatemala was invaded by rebels from across the border in Honduras following aerial harassment of the capital and the port of San Jose by aircraft owned by the United States and by the United Fruit Company. The capital was defended in desultory fashion by six obsolete warplanes of American manufacture.

When the assault began, Ambassador Henry Cabot Lodge, Jr., the United States' delegate to the United Nations Security Council, was president of the council. He introduced a motion to transfer consideration of the Guatemalan "affair" from that international arena to the Organization of American States, which was dominated politically by the United States. He argued that the Guatemalan situation constituted a civil war. The Soviet Union vetoed the motion, representing the affair as an American effort to stifle a commercially uncooperative government.

France introduced a resolution ordering a truce and restraining Security Council members from further participation in the conflict. That action soothed the fears of the nations surrounding Guatemala but had no effect on the actual conflict. On June 27, 1954, Arbenz went on Guatemalan radio and surrendered. Many of his countrymen missed the broadcast, which was jammed by the CIA.

Carlos Castillo Armas replaced Arbenz as president of Guatemala. In a short while, the expropriated lands were returned to the foreign corporations, and labor unions were disbanded. There was widespread bloodshed as workers sought in vain to retain the real and potential reforms gained during the Arévalos and Arbenz regimes. A military response, supported by assistance from the United States, was necessary to restore order. The military continued for decades to sustain the conservative government of Guatemala and offer protection to foreign investments there.

SIGNIFICANCE

Operation PBSUCCESS had three primary effects on the economy of the Western Hemisphere. First, the two desired outcomes of the coup—restoration of UFCO property and rejection of communist influence in Guatemala—were secured. The pre-Arbenz system of agricultural management was restored to the United Fruit Company and its sister corporations. In an agreement negotiated with President Armas himself, UFCO recovered all of its expropriated lands, and a new, modest income tax plan was negotiated to the company's benefit.

A second effect on the Guatemalan economy was caused by President Armas's action to cancel the registration of 533 union locals advocating the rights of banana workers as well as other unions not associated with UFCO directly but having an economic relationship, such as the railway workers. Active union organizers on UFCO farms were assassinated. Organized reaction against the new economic policies was thus effectively prevented until the rise of outlaw guerrilla groups.

The third important effect of the coup on the Guatemalan economy was the growth of a strong and lasting enmity to the new regime and to the United States' involvement in its emergence. The new government became synonymous in people's minds with the *frutera*, as UFCO was called in Latin America. Modern movements advocating human rights and social reform largely bypassed Guatemala, lest they also be painted by the United States as "communist" and similarly attacked.

As a consequence of these changes, the social and economic situation in Guatemala returned to what it had been in the first half of the twentieth century. Land ownership, skewed heavily in favor of a few large landowners before Arbenz's Decree 900, was again so skewed. Most small landowners were unable to support their families on the parcels available to them, many on infertile mountainsides.

To earn the sustenance their families required, these small landholders worked on the plantations. Lacking other lodging in the lowlands, many moved their families temporarily directly onto the fields they worked. There they were vulnerable to the health effects of chemicals that, in the absence of modern ecological controls, were generously applied.

Guerrillas intent on maintaining instability engaged in ongoing efforts to cripple the activity of the large foreign companies and to discourage new investment. Domestic and foreign firms increasingly sheltered their capital by moving it out of Guatemala. The necessities of life, such as fuel and food, increasingly had to be imported, driving Guatemala's economy downward and its debts to others upward.

One lasting effect of the reversal of the reform movement by Operation

PBSUCCESS was a greater availability of labor in the cities, as rural people fled the oppressive conditions and starvation wages of the plantations. Unfortunately, the instability of the country's government discouraged investment to utilize this resource.

The political climate of Guatemala following Operation PBSUCCESS made it impossible to establish a large tax base in the regions actually producing the profits for the foreign owners. Without tax revenues consistent with the value of the land and its products, governmental investment in social, educational, and developmental programs was severely limited.

These severe conditions on the farms resulted in the same migration to the cities found elsewhere in Latin America. Unfortunately, the unsettling factors caused by the militantly conservative government prevented evolution of social programs and infrastructure necessary to keep pace with this influx. Poverty and substandard living conditions plagued cities as well as farms.

Growth of the economy, which was near 5 percent in the years immediately after the coup, ceased. External debt, which was $51 million in 1960, rose into the billions of dollars. Foreign aid declined sharply as the nations of Europe and North America experienced tightening in their own economies. Improvement in the social or economic lot of the people of Guatemala seemed unlikely until something akin to the reforms of 1944-1954 recurred.

Loring Emery

FURTHER READING

Adams, Richard. *Crucifixion by Power.* Austin: University of Texas Press, 1970. Covers the period 1944-1966. A comprehensive study of demographics, economics, politics, social development, and government of Guatemala. Includes many tables of economic and demographic interest and thorough investigations of the development of power and wealth.

Barry, Tom. *Central America Inside Out.* New York: Grove Weidenfeld, 1991. Barry presents discussions on the government, politics, foreign policy, human rights, military, police, economy, social development, foreign influence, and U.S. military aid for the seven Central American states. Included are discussions of the contributions of the church, guerrillas, civilian police, and communications media to social and economic growth.

Barry, Tom, Beth Wood, and Deb Preusch. *Dollars and Dictators.* New York: Grove Press, 1983. A popularized study of the effects that U.S. corporations and the U.S. government have on social programs, agriculture, politics, and economics in the Central American countries. Included are tables and lists of investments by corporations in Central American nations.

Cullather, Nick. *Secret History: The CIA's Classified Account of Its Operations in Guatemala, 1952-1954.* Stanford, Calif.: Stanford University Press, 1999. History of the CIA coup in Guatemala, originally commissioned by the CIA itself as a classified document for internal use only and later released to the public. Mandatory reading for students of the coup. Bibliographic references and index.

Galeano, Eduardo. *Open Veins of Latin America.* New York: Monthly Review Press, 1973. A historical account of the exploitation of Central and South America by outsiders. Presented are studies of the opening, exploitation, and modern development of the regions as various mineral and agricultural products were discovered and brought to market. Written from an advocacy viewpoint showing strong antipathy to exploitation.

Horowitz, Irving. *Latin American Radicalism.* New York: Random House, 1969. A series of reports on leftist and nationalist impulses in Latin America. It begins with a study of the politics and government of Latin America in the period immediately after World War II. Treatises on social conditions and economic conditions follow.

Schlesinger, Stephen, and Stephen Kinzer. *Bitter Fruit.* 2d ed. Cambridge, Mass.: Harvard University Press, 2005. The authors present a minutely detailed account of the events leading to the CIA's coup against Jacobo Arbenz. Written as an exposé of the "dirty tricks" in the action, the book still serves as an important reference for the minutiae of the period surrounding the coup.

Sewell, Mike. *The Cold War.* Cambridge, U.K.: Cambridge University Press, 2002. Presents a concise overview of the Cold War that also covers the politics of historiography. Contains illustrations and maps.

SEE ALSO: Jan. 15, 1953-Dec. 2, 1954: McCarthy Hearings; July 26, 1956-Jan. 8, 1959: Cuban Revolution; Apr. 27-May 15, 1958: Nixon Faces Riots on Tour of Latin America; Apr. 17-19, 1961: Bay of Pigs Invasion; Apr., 1962: Brazil Nationalizes U.S. Businesses; Oct. 22-28, 1962: Cuban Missile Crisis; July 17, 1979: Somoza Is Forced Out of Power in Nicaragua.

■ **JUNE 27, 1954**

SOVIET UNION COMPLETES ITS FIRST NUCLEAR POWER PLANT

In 1954, the Soviet Union became the first country to construct a nuclear facility to produce electrical power.

ALSO KNOWN AS: Obninsk power plant
LOCALE: Obninsk, Soviet Union
CATEGORIES: Science and technology; energy; engineering

KEY FIGURES

Nikita S. Khrushchev (1894-1971), first secretary of the Communist Party of the Soviet Union, 1953-1964, and premier, 1958-1964
Joseph Stalin (Joseph Vissarionovich Dzhugashvili; 1878-1953), general secretary of the Central Committee of the Communist Party of the Soviet Union, 1922-1953, and premier, 1941-1953

SUMMARY OF EVENT

On June 27, 1954, the world's first atomic power station began operation in the Soviet Union, in Obninsk. Cold War competition in the nuclear sphere also advanced significantly. Using enriched uranium, the plant generated five thousand kilowatts (kw) and initiated peacetime nuclear power generation in the Soviet Union. Four years later, in 1958, the Siberian atomic power station in Novosibirsk opened with a capacity more than one hundred times that of the Obninsk station; the Leningrad atomic power facility, with a capacity of 2 million kilowatts, opened at approximately the same time.

Soviet research in nuclear energy originated in studies of atomic nuclei done by D. D. Ivanenko in 1932 and was worked out in greater detail by I. Tamm two years later. Based on that work, supplemented by work later in the 1930's by Y. I. Frenkel and others, a group of Soviet scientists developed several experimental nuclear reactors for scientific research and laid the groundwork for Soviet applied physics. Serious work started on the Obninsk reactor in 1949, shortly after the Soviets exploded their first atomic bomb. A poem, "Atoms for Peace," written to commemorate the event, reflected a major purpose of the station, namely, to deflect attention from the Soviet Union's military nuclear program.

On the basis of data gathered after the Obninsk plant went into operation, Soviet scientists were able to develop large quantities of artificial radioactive isotopes in nuclear reactors. Those experiments led to atomic research in such fields as metallurgy, biology, medicine, and agriculture. The city of Obninsk emerged as an important research center, with institutes of medical radiology, physics and energetics, and meteorology.

After successfully generating power from the Obninsk station, the Soviet Union focused more seriously on nuclear engineering for civilian needs. Before that, virtually all nuclear engineering in the country had been done for military purposes. After Obninsk, a new trend began in power engineering, a trend that gained international approval at the First International Scientific and Technical Conference on the Peaceful Uses of Atomic Energy in Geneva in August, 1955.

The Siberian atomic power plant (completed in 1958) was constructed next, but ambitious attempts to add other facilities waned in the late 1950's as the economic realities of plant construction became clearer. In June, 1959, Deputy Premier Frol Kozlov visited the United States and said that his country had decided to cut back its nuclear power program because of the costs. Not until 1964 did the Soviets resume construction of nuclear plants, with the Beloyarsk industrial atomic power plant. That system used direct superheating of steam in the nuclear reactor, which made it possible to use ordinary modern turbines with few alterations. This was followed by a series of different types of power plants, including a boiling-water type that was noted for its smooth layout.

The costs of operating the plants fell steadily. Subsequent plants, such as the Novovornezhskaia atomic plant that used cooled-water systems, were designed and constructed not only for the immediate power they generated but also as demonstration models for industrial use and the advantages of atomic power engineering. In 1969, the first fast-breeder reactor opened at Ulyanovsk, followed by the Shevchenko reactor in 1973. Despite the slowdown in construction on new reactors after the 1986 Chernobyl disaster, atomic power plant construction was not halted altogether. The Zaporozhye plant went into operation as early as December, 1986. By 1991, the Soviet Union had 114 nuclear power stations in operation with a total capacity of 37.4 million kilowatts. Work had stopped at sixty sites by 1991, however, because of safety concerns.

Generating cheap electrical energy through nuclear power was a long-held dream of the Soviet Communist Party and its leaders. Joseph Stalin, Communist Party leader and premier of the Soviet Union for more than thirty years, had been captivated by electrical power, and he had pushed the country into a massive electrical construction program in the 1930's. The Soviet Union became the most electrified nation on earth (to the point that electric shock treatments were the preferred method of torture for the secret police, the KGB). When the Soviet Union exploded its first atomic bomb in 1949, at least three years before Western observers thought it possible, a new source of energy for electrical power generation emerged, although for the first five years the entire Soviet atomic energy effort went toward military requirements.

Even so, the Soviets preceded both Great Britain and the United States in applying nuclear power to the generation of electricity; Great Britain opened its first industrial atomic station in 1956, and the United States opened the Shippingport, Pennsylvania, atomic plant in 1957 (the Brookhaven, New York, plant, commissioned in 1947, was the first U.S. peacetime plant, but it was devoted to research). Although the incident at Chernobyl slowed the expansion of nonmilitary nuclear plants, the Soviet Union nevertheless joined Japan and several European countries in extensive construction of atomic energy stations. In some ways, that was unusual, given the vast resources in natural gas and oil within the country's borders.

The United States did not, however, lag far behind the Soviet Union. This was in large part attributable to the efforts of Admiral Hyman G. Rickover, who had learned of the potential of nuclear fission as a method of ship propulsion while visiting Oak Ridge, Tennessee, in 1946, and who pushed the U.S. Navy to adopt nuclear power for its submarine program in the early

The Shippingport, Pennsylvania, nuclear reactor vessel during construction in 1956. (Library of Congress)

1950's. Rickover held a position unmatched in the Soviet Union because he maintained concurrent membership in the Navy (ultimately as assistant chief of nuclear propulsion) and the Atomic Energy Commission, and he intended the Navy to prove the feasibility and reliability of nuclear reactors for power generation in the civilian sector as well as for military uses. He oversaw production of the USS *Nautilus*, which was launched in 1954, and subsequent nuclear submarine programs (as well as nuclear surface ships) well into the 1970's.

The Soviet Union, meanwhile, came to rely even more heavily on nuclear energy. Of the three major energy sources in the country—oil, coal, and gas—the first did not offer much cause for optimism at the time the first Soviet nuclear reactor was constructed. The second, coal resources, was once considered to hold out great hope for the Ukraine and, ultimately, the rest of the country. The output gradually fell, however, and safety problems increased. Over time, the Siberian production facilities started to replace the European coalfields, but overall production did not rise as predicted. Oil, on the other hand, promised tremendous rewards, especially as an export product in the 1970's when prices rose. Labor problems, poor equipment, and the hostile Siberian environment resulted in less oil actually being pumped than predicted by the politicians. Only Soviet gas production came up to expectations, but that did not occur until the 1980's and was insufficient to offset the shortfalls in oil and coal.

Although it was not explored as a major supplier of energy in the Soviet Union when first established in 1954, nuclear energy began to be seen as a way to plug the energy gap and at the same time furnish energy to Warsaw Pact nations without depleting the oil revenues from exports to Western countries. The chief engineer of the Beloyarsk plant told U.S. vice president Richard M. Nixon in 1959 that the Soviet Union did not see nuclear power as the most important way of obtaining electrical energy. Others were not convinced; academician A. A. Blagonravov, for example, in 1957 proposed a system of small atomic power plants on mobile caterpillar tracks for the far northern regions.

SIGNIFICANCE

Technology in Stalin's Russia always had a political purpose. In the 1930's, for example, high-speed aircraft were viewed as the means by which the Soviet Union could demonstrate the superiority of communism to the rest of the world; the preoccupation with specific types of fast aircraft led scientists to ignore other important design characteristics in its aircraft, which resulted in their inferiority against German aircraft in World War II. In the case of nuclear power, the Soviet Union wanted to demonstrate that it could use atomic material not only for making weapons but also for improving the lives of its citizens.

State preoccupation with easily directed centralized projects made nuclear power plant construction an obvious choice for the communist system. Unlike a small electric generating system that in a market country could be built and maintained by a few private entrepreneurs, a nuclear plant virtually demanded large-scale state support. Moreover, atomic energy would exacerbate the contradictions inherent in the capitalist system by expanding the Soviet economy and serving military interests. Atomic energy soon became subject to proletarian science, which placed nuclear energy in the service of socialism. Some scientists advocated peaceful nuclear explosions for such purposes as rapid strip mining, canal construction, or filling deserts with water; one plan called for an explosion to divert Siberian rivers.

Nuclear plants also symbolized the Soviet image of size and power—imposing facilities under the control of the state. In constructing many of those facilities, however, the state ignored safety and environmental issues. Western observers who eventually examined data from the Chernobyl accident discovered total disregard of some of the most common safety features found in Western nuclear reactors.

There were also problems in the Soviet Union with the storage of nuclear wastes. In 1957, when wastes at the Mayak nuclear complex in the Ural Mountains exploded, contamination extended for miles and necessitated the evacuation of several villages.

The many safety and environmental problems occurred mainly because the Soviet Union had originally not planned to use nuclear power extensively—relying instead on oil and coal—but then expanded the program too rapidly. There would be an increasing number of news articles advocating nuclear plant construction in the 1960's.

Larry Schweikart

FURTHER READING

Josephson, Paul R. *Red Atom: Russia's Nuclear Power Program from Stalin to Today.* New York: W. H. Freeman, 2000. An excellent scholarly history of the Soviet nuclear program. Highly recommended.

Kramish, Arnold. *Atomic Energy in the Soviet Union.* Stanford, Calif.: Stanford University Press, 1959. An early assessment of the first reactor program in the Soviet Union.

LaFeber, Walter. *America, Russia, and the Cold War: 1945-2006.* New York: McGraw-Hill. 2008. Detailed analysis of relations between the United States and the Soviet Union, highlighting causes and effects of the conflict. Contains illustrations and maps.

Marples, David R. *Chernobyl and Nuclear Power in the USSR.* New York: St. Martin's Press, 1986. Focuses on developments in the Soviet Union and Eastern Europe since 1970. Notes the peculiar dynamics of the energy needs of the Ukraine, which led to rapid construction of reactors in that state with insufficient attention paid to safety.

Pringle, Peter, and James Spigelman. *The Nuclear Barons.* New York: Holt, Rinehart and Winston, 1981. Written before Chernobyl, this book reviews the history of the peacetime nuclear-power industry throughout the world.

Wilpert, Bernhard, and Naosuke Itoigawa, eds. *Safety Culture in Nuclear Power Operations.* New York: Taylor & Francis, 2001. Examines the safety concerns and issues surrounding nuclear power plants. Discusses how employees deal with the safety concerns of the industry, and discusses the management of safe work environments.

SEE ALSO: Aug. 1, 1946: Atomic Energy Commission Is Established; July 9, 1955-early 1960's: Scientists Campaign Against Nuclear Testing; June 20, 1963: Hotline Is Adopted Between the United States and the Soviet Union; Aug. 5, 1963: Nuclear Powers Sign the Limited Test Ban Treaty; Mar. 5, 1970: Nuclear Non-Proliferation Treaty Goes into Effect.

■ **JULY 10, 1954**

EISENHOWER BEGINS THE FOOD FOR PEACE PROGRAM

President Dwight D. Eisenhower signed Public Law 480, allowing the U.S. Department of Agriculture to buy surplus agricultural commodities and use them for donation abroad, for barter, or for sale for native currency.

ALSO KNOWN AS: Public Law 480, 83d Congress; Agricultural Trade Development and Assistance Act of 1954

LOCALE: Washington, D.C.

CATEGORIES: Laws, acts, and legal history; agriculture; diplomacy and international relations; trade and commerce

KEY FIGURES

Dwight D. Eisenhower (1890-1969), president of the United States, 1953-1961

Ezra Taft Benson (1899-1994), U.S. secretary of agriculture, 1953-1961

Don Paarlberg (1911-2006), U.S. assistant secretary of agriculture

Clarence Francis (1888-1985), special adviser to President Eisenhower on the disposal of agricultural surpluses

Clarence Randall (1891-1967), special assistant to President Eisenhower on foreign economic policy

William S. Hill (1886-1972), U.S. representative from Colorado, 1941-1959

SUMMARY OF EVENT

The Agricultural Trade Development and Assistance Act of 1954, commonly known as Public Law 480 or the "Food for Peace" program, provides for surplus U.S. farm commodities to be sold for foreign currencies and used as donations and barter goods. The objectives of PL 480, as stated by Congress, are to promote economic stability for American agriculture, to expand international trade in agricultural commodities, to encourage the economic development of friendly countries, and to promote the collective strength of the free world, in light of the Cold War contest for hearts and minds.

A variety of factors led to the passage of this legislation. Food and peace have long been closely linked in the minds of Americans. Many times in the aftermath of war, food from U.S. farms has aided in the rehabilitation of ravaged areas. In addition, from a political standpoint food has often been used as a lever to achieve political goals and objectives.

In the 1940's and 1950's, a domestic agricultural problem developed. Incomes from food production in the United States did not permit American farmers to live on a scale comparable to that of people in other occupations. In order to boost farm incomes, the government agreed to buy certain products that could not be sold on the open market above a specified price. Between February, 1952, and February, 1956, the stocks of the Commodity Credit Corporation (the governmental agency charged with stockpiling surplus agricultural goods) in inventory as well as pledged against outstanding loans and purchase agreements increased almost fivefold, from less than $2 billion to $9.1 billion.

Most of this buildup took place during 1952 and 1953, when annual increases in the stockpiles of 70 and 100 percent were registered. This problem of surplus government stocks was exacerbated by scientific technology. Farm productivity during this same period had increased significantly as a result of better products to control weeds, plant diseases, insects, and para-

President Dwight D. Eisenhower. (National Archives)

sites, combined with developments in plant and livestock genetics and improved farm machinery.

An additional factor was important in the subsequent passage of PL 480. American farm exports had been declining during the early 1950's. Factors in this decline included a reduction in American economic aid to Western Europe (which had been quite high under the Marshall Plan following World War II), the fact that agricultural production and protectionism were recovering in Western Europe, scarcity of the dollar in importing countries, domestic price supports that set American commodity prices above world levels, and American export controls that limited trade with the Soviet Union and its allies. As the repercussions of the decline in exports and the growth of surplus stocks rolled across the farm economy, farm spokespeople began demanding that the government act to stabilize farm income. President Dwight D. Eisenhower's administration was faced with the task of dealing with these multiple problems.

In the summer and fall of 1953, three groups began wrestling with program proposals for agricultural policy: the U.S. Department of Agriculture, the Commission on Foreign Economic Policy, and an interdepartmental committee on the surplus. In the summer of 1953, the U.S. Department of Agriculture surveyed three national farm groups—the American Farm Bureau, the Grange, and the National Farmers Union—regarding farm income stability and trade versus aid, among other things. Overwhelming support was shown for a "two-price" plan for agricultural commodities. Such a scheme would support a high domestic price for the percentage of a commodity normally marketed in the United States and would allow the remainder (ostensibly exported) to be sold at the world price. Thus, the mood in the country was to continue farm income support.

The Commission on Foreign Economic Policy was chaired by Clarence Randall, special assistant to President Eisenhower on foreign economic policy. The seventeen-member group was composed of agribusiness representatives, prominent agricultural economists, five U.S. senators, and five U.S. representatives. Agricultural policy was only part of the foreign economic policy reviewed by the commission. The commission issued a report on January 23, 1954, that included a five-page section on agricultural policy. The section on agriculture elicited written dissents from eight of the seventeen members. The report argued that "a dynamic foreign economic policy as it relates to agriculture cannot be built out of a maze of restrictive devices such as inflexible price-support programs which result in fixed prices, open or concealed export subsidies, . . . and state trading." It recommended the complete "elimination of such devices as a part of, or supplement to, our own agricultural policy."

This obviously went against the wishes of American farmers. The Department of Agriculture was effective in nullifying the report's agricultural recommendations by insisting that any inconsistencies between the report and President Eisenhower's January state of the union message be resolved in favor of the latter, in which Eisenhower had supported price supports on farm commodities.

Meanwhile, the interdepartmental committee on the surplus had been working on legislation. This study group had been Secretary of Agriculture Ezra Taft Benson's idea. He had persuaded President Eisenhower to establish it at the subcabinet level. After several meetings, on December 14, 1953, this committee had in hand the first draft of an administration surplus disposal bill. Despite President Eisenhower's call for fast action, the committee could not agree on a final draft bill. Stumbling blocks included disputes concerning which commodities to include, who would have administrative authority, and to what extent the private sector should be involved.

While the administration squabbled, the House of Representatives began considering various surplus disposal bills. As the spring of 1954 wore on, some sixty bills were introduced into Congress. This flurry of activity spurred the interdepartmental committee to compromise. A compromise draft was introduced by Representative William S. Hill of Colorado. It was discussed by the House Committee on Agriculture on June 3, reported out, debated for two days by the House as a Committee of the Whole, and passed on June 16. Following rapid Senate action, the conference committee made some adjustments. The bill was agreed to by both houses, and Eisenhower signed it into law on July 10.

SIGNIFICANCE

As passed, Public Law 480 had three titles. Title I authorized sales of surplus agricultural commodities for foreign currency to "friendly" nations, identified as any countries other than the Soviet Union and those under the influence of the world communist movement. Commodities were to move through private channels to the extent possible. Foreign currencies acquired in trade were to be used for market development, stockpile purchases, military procurement, debt payments, educational exchanges, new loans, and aid to friendly countries not part of the trades.

Title II provided for grants of surplus agricultural commodities to friendly nations to meet emergency situations. Title III authorized the donation of surplus food for domestic distribution and for distribution to needy persons overseas through nonprofit relief agencies. In addition, Title III allowed for the barter of surplus agricultural commodities for strategic and other materials produced abroad.

As written, the legislation did not assign administrative responsibility. Thus, President Eisenhower still had to decide which agency or agencies would administer the various titles. After considerable bureaucratic wrangling, Eisenhower issued Executive Order 10560 on September 9, 1954. This order gave the Department of Agriculture Title I authority, the Foreign Operations Administration (FOA) authority for Title II, and the Department of State the function of negotiating and entering into agreements. The budget office received allocation authority for foreign currencies, and the Treasury Department was to regulate the purchase, custody, deposit, transfer, and sale of currencies. The Office of Defense Mobilization received authority for stockpile purchases, the Department of Defense the military procurement authority, and other various agencies authority for other foreign currency uses.

The executive order and accompanying documents also formalized the position of the interdepartmental committee that had been working for nearly a year. Known now as the Interagency Committee on Agricultural Surplus Disposal (ICASD), it was to continue to formulate policy under the chairmanship of Clarence Francis. Francis was brought into this position from the chairmanship of General Foods. Actual direction of the surplus disposal operation was to be handled by an Interagency Staff Committee on Agricultural Surplus Disposal (ISC), composed of one representative from each agency in the ICASD. William Lodwick, a Foreign Agriculture Service (FAS) official, was appointed as both administrator of FAS and chairman of the ISC.

During the first two years of operation, PL 480 was broadened to include feed grains and to authorize the use of federal funds to pay the costs of ocean transportation and consumer packaging. During late 1958, the Department of Agriculture developed a message that the president sent to Congress on January 29, 1959. As part of this communication, Secretary Benson inserted a "Food for Peace" section in which Eisenhower announced that he was setting steps in motion to explore, with other surplus-producing nations, means of utilizing agricultural surpluses in the interest of reinforcing peace and the well-being of friendly peoples throughout the world.

Title IV of PL 480 was enacted on September 21, 1959. It provides for long-term supply of U.S. agricultural commodities and sales on a credit basis to assist in the development of the economies of friendly nations. The program is of particular help to countries that "graduate" from Title I foreign currency purchasing to dollar purchasing.

By early 1960, the original PL 480 program had been modified and extended several times. The Eisenhower administration wanted to heighten public awareness of accomplishments under the program. On April 13, 1960, Eisenhower designated Don Paarlberg as the Food for Peace coordinator. Previously, Paarlberg had been an assistant secretary of agriculture and had worked with the PL 480 program as a member of the White House staff.

The first, and least controversial, consequence of PL 480 has been the effect on food consumption in recipient countries. The diets of many thousands of people have been improved as a result of this program. There is some concern that the program has not facilitated economic development to the extent hoped for.

The effect around which there exists the most controversy and the most confusion regards the impact of PL 480 on producers and production in the recipient countries. One view holds that the surplus disposal operations of the United States have generally hurt producers in the recipient countries and, more important, have acted to remove the incentive to increase total production in those countries. In this view, the program has acted to perpetuate food shortages. An opposing view holds that PL 480 shipments have been administered in such a way as not to hurt the producers involved; through the beneficial effects on capital formation, they have acted to increase agricultural production above what it could have been without the program.

Two titles were added to the program, which became known as "Food for Progress." Title V is the "Farmer to Farmer Program." It provides for a minimum of 0.2 percent of total PL 480 funds to assist farmers and agribusiness operations in developing countries by transferring knowledge of farming methods from U.S. farmers, agriculturalists, land-grant universities, private agribusinesses, and nonprofit farm organizations to farms and agribusinesses in developing and middle-income countries and emerging democracies. Title VI authorizes certain activities for the reduction of debts of Latin American and Caribbean countries.

John C. Foltz

FURTHER READING

Baldwin, David A. *Economic Development and American Foreign Policy: 1943-62.* Chicago: University of Chicago Press, 1966. Discusses a variety of approaches the United States has taken to economic development in foreign countries. Contains numerous references to PL 480 but no in-depth discussion.

_____. *Foreign Aid and American Foreign Policy.* New York: Frederick A. Praeger, 1966. Documentary analysis of American foreign policy and aid. Presents the facts in a straightforward manner with little editorializing. Much of the book is dedicated to congressional hearings. One chapter is devoted to agriculture and foreign aid.

National Agricultural Statistics Service. *Agricultural Statistics Data Base.* Washington, D.C.: Author, 2003. Contains statistics on exports of agricultural commodities under specified government-financed programs, including PL 480. Produced in print and online; updated semi-regularly.

Peterson, Trudy Huskamp. *Agricultural Exports, Farm Income, and the Eisenhower Administration.* Lincoln: University of Nebraska Press, 1979. This is an excellent source on the background and implementation of PL 480. The author painstakingly researched the subject. Well documented with notes and bibliographic material. Quite detailed.

Tontz, Robert L., ed. *Foreign Agricultural Trade: Selected Readings.* Ames: Iowa State University Press, 1966. Has an entire section on trade programs, including Food for Peace shipments. The majority of the sections were written by well-known agricultural economists and are short and to the point.

SEE ALSO: Nov. 4, 1952: Eisenhower Is Elected President; Jan. 5, 1957: Eisenhower Doctrine; July 29, 1958: Congress Creates the National Aeronautics and Space Administration; 1959-1961: Famine Devastates China; Jan.
17, 1961: Eisenhower Warns of the Military-Industrial Complex.

■ AUGUST, 1954-MAY, 1955

OPERATION PASSAGE TO FREEDOM EVACUATES REFUGEES FROM NORTH VIETNAM

*The U.S. Navy's transport of 310,000 North Vietnamese refugees from communist
North Vietnam to South Vietnam after the Geneva Conference of 1954 was a significant Cold War triumph for the West. It temporarily strengthened the South Vietnamese
government and placed Vietnam in the American public eye, but deepened American
involvement in Vietnam.*

ALSO KNOWN AS: Operation Exodus
LOCALE: North and South Vietnam
CATEGORIES: Immigration, emigration, and relocation; Vietnam War;
    Wars, uprisings, and civil unrest; independence movements

KEY FIGURES
Ngo Dinh Diem (1901-1963), prime minister of Vietnam, 1954-1955, and
    president of the Republic of Vietnam, 1955-1963
Lorenzo S. Sabin (1899-1978), U.S. rear admiral in charge of Task Force 90,
    1954-1955
Edward Lansdale (1908-1987), U.S. Air Force colonel and head of the
    Saigon Military Mission, 1954-1956
Dwight D. Eisenhower (1890-1969), thirty-fourth president of the United
    States, 1953-1961
Bao Dai (1913-1997), emperor of Vietnam, r. 1925-1945, nationalist head
    of Vietnam, 1949-1954, emperor of the Republic of Vietnam, 1954-1955

SUMMARY OF EVENT
On July 21, 1954, the Geneva Conference concluded with accords to end
French colonial authority and military presence in Vietnam. Because of the
Cold War, Vietnam was to be partitioned temporarily along the seventeenth
northern parallel. In the communist North, the Democratic Republic of

Vietnam was led by Ho Chi Minh. In the noncommunist South, Emperor Bao Dai and his new prime minister, Ngo Dinh Diem, ruled the Republic of Vietnam. National elections and reunification were planned for 1956. To separate French and allied Vietnamese forces from the communist Viet Minh, article 14 of the Geneva Accords provided that military forces should regroup in their respective areas in the North or South. For a grace period of ten months, civilians could also move to the part of Vietnam of their choice. Because the Viet Minh violently harassed Vietnamese (especially the Vietnamese Catholic minority) whom they perceived to be aiding the French in areas of communist control, the number of Vietnamese willing to flee the communist North was significant.

In Saigon, U.S. Air Force colonel Edward Lansdale realized the propaganda and material value of evacuating as many anticommunist refugees from North to South Vietnam as possible. Lansdale was head of the Central Intelligence Agency's Saigon Military Mission and quickly became the friend of Prime Minister Diem. Diem shared Lansdale's vision of a successful population transfer to shore up the power of his government and state. With South Vietnam openly welcoming northern refugees, their numbers swelled. However, despite the safe passage assured by the Geneva Accords, the Viet Minh harassed and killed refugees on the roads to the South. Evacuation by air or by ship was necessary, yet the French lacked sufficient airplanes and ships.

On August 5, 1954, Prime Minister Diem asked for American help. U.S. president Dwight D. Eisenhower agreed with Diem and Lansdale on the value of a successful evacuation mission and authorized American support. That day, the U.S. Foreign Operations Administration issued a declaration of aid. On August 7, the U.S. Navy launched Operation Passage to Freedom. The commander of the Seventh (Pacific) Fleet, Admiral Felix Stump, created Task Force 90, which was charged with implementing the operation. The command of Task Force 90 was assigned to Rear Admiral Lorenzo Sabin.

Landing in the North Vietnamese port city of Haiphong on August 10, Rear Admiral Sabin started to coordinate the evacuation process with the French, who were airlifting and shipping out their own troops and matériel and as many refugees as they could handle. Because the Geneva Accords forbade the landing of foreign troops and equipment in Vietnam, the Americans were circumspect. Initially, American sailors went ashore in civilian clothing, and American equipment, such as bulldozers to clear refugee camp sites in South Vietnam, were stripped of military markings.

On August 16, the U.S. Navy transport ship *Menard* began taking aboard the first North Vietnamese refugees. For political reasons, boarding was done not in Haiphong but on Do Son Beach to its south, where by August 18 nineteen hundred refugees had boarded the ship. Four more American ships arrived there, two transporters and two attack cargo ships.

On August 21, the *Menard* landed in South Vietnam at Vung Tau, then known as Cape St. Jacques. The refugees were met by Ho Quan Phuoc, the officer in charge from the Saigon government, and were guided into a tent city awaiting them. The arrival on August 22 of the next American ship, the *Montrose*, was filmed by U.S. journalists, and President Eisenhower publicly praised the operation.

Admiral Sabin quickly set up a successful and efficient naval evacuation system. North Vietnamese refugees, Vietnamese soldiers who had fought the Viet Minh, and military vehicles and cargo were shipped from Haiphong and Do Son Beach to either Vung Tau or Saigon. At the height of the operations, Admiral Sabin commanded seventy-four ships, including large tank-landing ships, transport vessels, attack cargo ships, and dock-landing ships. Sabin's operations were aided by the Navy's Military Sea Transporta-

Vietnamese refugees waiting to board an American naval vessel at Haiphong in August, 1954. (National Archives)

tion Service, which contributed thirty-nine transport vessels. At Danang, the U.S. Navy based a Logistic Support Force.

To generate an impressive flow of refugees, Lansdale and his team used covert and overt anticommunist propaganda. However, this propaganda would not have been as effective if many North Vietnamese, especially Catholics, were not already suffering genuine Viet Minh persecution. September and October, 1954, were peak months for Operation Passage to Freedom. By October 2, aboard American and French ships and French planes, 400,000 people had left North Vietnam. On October 22, meeting with the National Security Council, President Eisenhower expressed his satisfaction with the operation.

Colonel Lansdale and Prime Minister Diem worked closely together to motivate the refugees and to process them upon their arrival. The United States allocated some forty million dollars to the operation, including initial donations to refugees. American sailors were genuinely welcomed by people fleeing communism. Aboard the ships, refugees gave birth and a few died. The U.S. Navy set up medical centers both in Haiphong and near Saigon to help sick refugees. One of the physicians operating in Haiphong since August, 1954, was Thomas Dooley, who later wrote a best seller about his experience, *Deliver Us from Evil* (1956).

By January, 1955, the majority of the refugees were evacuated. Operation Passage to Freedom continued to its legal deadline of May 20, 1955, but with fewer and fewer vessels allocated. In all, from August, 1954, to May, 1955, American vessels had transported 310,800 Vietnamese from the North to the South. Of those, 293,000 were civilians and 17,800 Vietnamese soldiers who had fought the Viet Minh. The American ships had also carried 8,135 military vehicles and 68,757 tons of cargo.

Dubbed Operation Exodus by Prime Minister Diem and encouraged by Emperor Bao Dai, the full southward evacuation consisted of about 860,000-900,000 people. The U.S. Navy transported about one-third of these. The total includes 190,000 French and Vietnamese soldiers, about 65,000 Nung people and ethnic Chinese, and some 30,000 French citizens. Approximately 45,000 North Vietnamese went South by land. From the South, 90,000 Viet Minh troops and 40,000 communist civilians were transported North on Polish and French ships, and 12,000 civilians went North by road.

SIGNIFICANCE

For almost 6 percent of the Vietnamese—a people traditionally tied closely to their ancestral lands—the flight from the North showed the world in 1954 that communism was indeed feared. The substantial American involvement in the evacuation not only enabled a large number of refugees to leave but also significantly increased U.S. involvement in the Vietnamese conflict. After its huge public support for South Vietnam, the United States would find it difficult to leave the South to the communists.

The success of relocating refugees in cities like Saigon and Da Lat and in 300 new villages, due also to generous American aid, gave the South an initial advantage. Because 80 percent of the refugees (including Prime Minister Diem) were Roman Catholics, the proportion of Catholics rose to a significant 10 percent in an otherwise Buddhist country. Of the 300 new villages, 267 were considered Catholic and 3 Protestant.

Diem used the Catholics immediately. After a national referendum, Bao Dai abdicated, and on October 26, 1955, Diem became president of the new Republic of Vietnam. Diem felt strong enough in the South to oppose the planned 1956 common elections. Diem's autocratic leadership, his reliance on his family, and his favoring of Catholics at the expense of Buddhists— together with missteps in handling the growing communist insurrection— soured his relationship with the Americans, as evidenced by the fact that the United States did not oppose a coup that assassinated him on October 2, 1963. After the fall of Saigon to the North on April 30, 1975, many of the earlier refugees and their descendants would flee again, this time out of Vietnam.

R. C. Lutz

FURTHER READING

Dooley, Tom. *Deliver Us from Evil: The Story of Vietnam's Flight to Freedom.* New York: Farrar, Straus and Cudahy, 1956. An eyewitness account by a U.S. naval physician who treated Vietnamese refugees, credited for familiarizing Americans with Vietnam when first published in 1956; the book was later blamed for some propagandistic language and Cold War exaggerations.

Frankum, Ronald B., Jr. *Operation Passage to Freedom.* Lubbock: Texas Tech University Press, 2007. The best and most detailed account from the American perspective. Built on archival research and more than forty interviews with members of the U.S. Navy who took part in the event. Illustrated, maps.

Karnow, Stanley. *Vietnam: A History.* 2d ed. New York: Penguin Books, 1997. Most widely available English-language book on Vietnam; chapters 5, 6, and 7 deal with Operation Passage to Freedom and its significance. Illustrated.

Lansdale, Edward. *In the Midst of War.* 1972. 2d ed. Bronx, N.Y.: Fordham University Press, 1991. The second half of this memoir by an American officer covers the event from an eyewitness perspective.

Nguyen, Thi Lien Hang. "The Double Diaspora of Vietnam's Catholics." *Orbis* (Philadelphia) 39 (Fall, 1995): 491-501. A Vietnamese perspective by the daughter and niece of three refugees; she includes their oral histories.

SEE ALSO: Nov. 29, 1947-July, 1949: Arab-Israeli War Creates Refugee Crisis; Dec. 14, 1950: United Nations High Commissioner for Refugees Statute Is Approved; Nov., 1946-July, 1954: Nationalist Vietnamese Fight French Control of Indochina; Nov. 14, 1961: Kennedy Expands U.S. Involvement in Vietnam; Aug. 7, 1964-Jan. 27, 1973: United States Enters the Vietnam War; Mar., 1973: U.S. Troops Leave Vietnam; May, 1975: Indo-Chinese Boat People Begin Fleeing Vietnam; Feb. 17-Mar. 16, 1979: China Invades Vietnam; Sept., 1989: Vietnamese Troops Withdraw from Cambodia.

■ SEPTEMBER 8, 1954

SEATO IS FOUNDED

The United States entered into a multilateral defensive alliance with the United Kingdom, France, Australia, New Zealand, the Philippines, Thailand, and Pakistan in order to protect Southeast Asia and the western Pacific from external aggression or internal subversion.

ALSO KNOWN AS: Southeast Asia Treaty Organization; Southeast Asia Collective Defense Treaty; SEACDT; Manila Pact
LOCALE: Manila, Philippines
CATEGORIES: Diplomacy and international relations; organizations and institutions

KEY FIGURES
John Foster Dulles (1888-1959), U.S. secretary of state, 1953-1959
Ho Chi Minh (1890-1969), president of the Democratic Republic of Vietnam, 1945-1969
Dwight D. Eisenhower (1890-1969), president of the United States, 1953-1961

SUMMARY OF EVENT
Delegates from the United States, the United Kingdom, France, Australia, New Zealand, the Philippines, Thailand, and Pakistan signed the Southeast Asia Collective Defense Treaty (SEACDT) in Manila on September 8, 1954. This treaty created the Southeast Asia Treaty Organization (SEATO). The

stated purpose of SEATO was the collective defense of member nations in Southeast Asia and the western Pacific. Specifically, it protected states south of 21 degrees 30 minutes north latitude. By design, the northern boundary prohibited the Nationalist Chinese on Formosa (Taiwan), the Republic of Korea, and Japan from joining the organization. A protocol was attached to the treaty that extended the benefits of membership to Cambodia, Laos, and Vietnam, even though these former French colonies were not permitted to join officially.

The creation of SEATO came about as a result of the collapse of the French colonial empire in 1954. Prior to World War II, the United States and several European powers had maintained colonial control over much of Southeast Asia. The Japanese took control of these colonies during World War II, and after Japan's defeat, many states in the region expected that they would finally receive independence. However, the French sought to maintain control of Indochina (Cambodia, Laos, and Vietnam) and refused to grant their colonies full independence. As a result, Ho Chi Minh led a rebellion in Vietnam and fought a bitter war against French forces. France fared poorly in the war, and Vietnamese forces defeated the French at the Battle of Dien Bien Phu in May, 1954.

During the spring and summer of 1954, Geneva hosted an international peace conference in the hopes of generating a peace treaty officially to end the Korean War. The timing of the French defeat allowed the nations meeting at Geneva to include discussion of a peace settlement for Indochina at the conference. The Vietnamese victory at Dien Bien Phu ensured that the French would have to make major concessions, which U.S. secretary of state John Foster Dulles feared would make any outcome at Geneva unacceptable. As a result, Dulles sought an alternative means of guaranteeing political stability in Southeast Asia in a climate of Cold War competition.

Dulles hoped the Geneva Conference would produce fruitful results, but he believed in the necessity of a separate course of action, because he accepted what has come to be called the "domino theory." This theory posited that if any Asian nation within Indochina became communist, then the rest of Asia would also adopt communism: Revolution would spread from nation to nation like a row of falling dominoes. To prevent this possibility, Dulles came to believe that a coordinated regional defense system could be utilized to halt further communist expansion without directly committing American troops. This idea built on existing mutual-security treaties with friendly nations such as Australia, New Zealand, and the Philippines. President Dwight D. Eisenhower concurred with Dulles, and his administration soon began making plans to create a regional alliance in Southeast Asia.

By the end of June, 1954, plans for a regional security pact had advanced

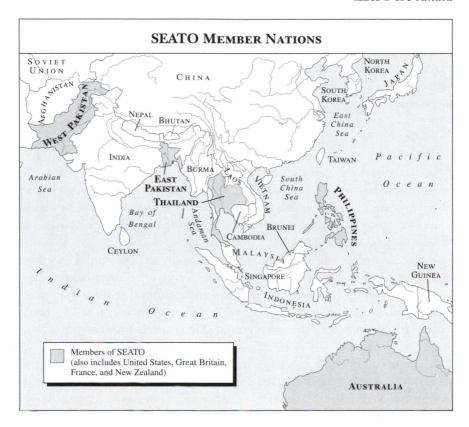

SEATO MEMBER NATIONS

Members of SEATO
(also includes United States, Great Britain,
France, and New Zealand)

enough to allow the United Kingdom to take part in the creation process alongside the United States. The British agreed that the region needed a collective defense system, and the two nations began a joint study group that produced the basic alliance treaty. During the planning sessions, they agreed that the treaty should contain provisions to help guard against overt or subversive communist activity in the region. Neither the United States nor the United Kingdom wished to participate in a noncommunist-related fight.

The British and the Americans also decided that Japan, Nationalist China, the Republic of Korea, and Hong Kong, along with any other colonial possessions, should not be allowed to join the treaty in order to obtain the largest possible body of neutral Asian membership. They agreed that the new alliance would not be a strong military organization like the North Atlantic Treaty Organization (NATO), because they believed that they already had sufficient strength to deal with the Soviets and the Chinese in the event of war with the communist powers. Therefore, rather than military strength, they wanted to increase the amount of territory they were committed to defending in order to prevent the spread of communism.

While meeting with the British, the U.S. State Department also consulted with Australia, New Zealand, Thailand, and the Philippines to ensure that these nations found elements of the proposed treaty acceptable, but these nations did not have as much influence over the treaty wording as did the United States and the United Kingdom. The United States did not initially confer with France in order to avoid disrupting the Geneva peace conference, but with the end of the Geneva Conference in early August, 1954, the French were belatedly consulted. Planning concluded by mid-August, and with the presentation of a draft treaty, the involved nations invited other nations who wished to join an Asian collective security arrangement to meet in Manila on September 6, 1954.

Pakistan was the only additional nation to attend the Manila meeting, and the eight nations debated the proposed treaty from September 6 to September 8. During the brief Manila conference, several nations expressed concerns that the United States wanted the alliance to target only communist aggression, and even the British questioned the legality of including the word "communism" in the treaty. As a result, references to communism were removed, but Dulles attached a clause to the American signature that stated the United States intended to honor the treaty only in the event of communist aggression. Since the United States had the strongest military of all the treaty's signatories, the U.S. stipulation made it unlikely that the treaty would ever be activated, except in the event of attack by a communist nation.

Another point of debate at the Manila conference was the fate of Vietnam and the rest of Indochina. The United States had initially intended these nations to join, but the Geneva peace accords specifically prohibited the former French colonies from joining a military alliance. As a result, they could not be allowed to join, but the SEACDT included a separate protocol that extended protection to Vietnam, Laos, and Cambodia even though they were not signatories. With these issues settled, the attendees signed the treaty on September 8.

SIGNIFICANCE

Once the treaty was in place, the SEATO powers set up a headquarters in Bangkok, Thailand, to oversee management of the organization. Although it was generally considered a military alliance, SEATO improved cultural and economic relationships between its members. Particularly important was the creation of the SEATO Graduate School of Engineering in 1959, which provided a quality technical education to students from the member nations in an effort to improve the level of technology in Asia. The school was privatized in 1967 and was renamed the Asian Institute of Technology.

SEATO also increased medical training and technology in the region and funded research designed to eradicate malaria. Despite these accomplishments, SEATO primarily remained a military organization, and the United States invoked the treaty in 1964, when it passed the Tonkin Gulf Resolution and entered the Vietnam War. Not all of the organization's members supported the U.S. action. Pakistan withdrew from the organization in 1968, and Great Britain and France contributed very little to the war effort. With the ultimate victory of Ho Chi Minh and the communists in 1975, the organization began to dissolve, and it ceased to exist in 1977.

John K. Franklin

FURTHER READING

Buckley, Roger. *The United States in the Asia-Pacific Since 1945*. New York: Cambridge University Press, 2002. An overview of American relations with East Asia since the end of World War II that puts the creation of SEATO into context and examines such themes as Asian concerns about colonialism and the American fear of communism.

Buszynski, Leszek. *SEATO: The Failure of an Alliance Strategy*. Kent Ridge, Singapore: Singapore University Press, 1983. Describes SEATO as a military alliance that failed to provide a significant deterrent to communist aggression in Southeast Asia.

Judge, Edward H., and John Langdon. *The Cold War: A History through Documents*. Upper Saddle River, N.J.: Prentice Hall, 1999. The text of the SEATO agreement is included in this collection of more than 130 primary sources including speeches, treaties, and declarations, arranged chronologically.

McMahon, Robert J. *The Limits of Empire: The United States and Southeast Asia Since World War II*. New York: Columbia University Press, 1999. Brief examination of U.S. relations with Southeast Asia that shows SEATO as part of a policy designed to contain communism while maintaining near imperial control of the region.

Marks, Frederick W. *Power and Peace: The Diplomacy of John Foster Dulles*. Westport, Conn.: Praeger, 1995. Biography of Dulles that describes the creation of SEATO as his most important accomplishment.

Westad, Odd Arne. *The Global Cold War: Third World Interventions and the Makings of Our Times*. Cambridge, U.K.: Cambridge University Press, 2007. Frames the outcome of the Cold War in terms of globalization and American interventionism in developing nations. Illustrated.

SEE ALSO: Nov., 1946-July, 1954: Nationalist Vietnamese Fight French Control of Indochina; Sept. 1, 1951: Security Pact Is Signed by Three Pacific Nations Against Communist Encroachment; Nov. 9, 1953: Cambodia Gains Independence from France; Aug., 1954-May, 1955: Operation Passage to Freedom Evacuates Refugees from North Vietnam; Aug. 7, 1964-Jan. 27, 1973: United States Enters the Vietnam War; Mar., 1973: U.S. Troops Leave Vietnam; Feb. 17-Mar. 16, 1979: China Invades Vietnam; Sept., 1989: Vietnamese Troops Withdraw from Cambodia.

◼ OCTOBER 23, 1954

WESTERN EUROPEAN UNION IS ESTABLISHED

The Western European Union was one of a series of institutions created in the wake of World War II to provide a framework for military collaboration among the nations of Western Europe. It originated in a series of mutual defense agreements signed between 1947 and 1949, directed initially against a potentially resurgent Germany. With the advent of the Cold War, however, its focus changed to containment of the Soviet Union and communism.

LOCALE: Western Europe
CATEGORIES: Diplomacy and international relations; organizations and institutions

KEY FIGURES

Konrad Adenauer (1876-1967), chancellor of the Federal Republic of Germany, 1949-1963
Charles de Gaulle (1890-1970), president of France, 1959-1969
René Pleven (1901-1993), premier of France, 1950-1951 and 1951-1952
Paul-Henri Spaak (1899-1972), first chairman of the WEU Assembly

SUMMARY OF EVENT

The end of World War II, with its widespread destruction and loss of life, left the nations of Western Europe with one common bond: a determination to prevent anything like it from ever occurring again. In particular, they were determined to prevent the resurgence of German military power, as had occurred after World War I. They determined, therefore, to sign treaties of mutual defense in which each would come to the aid of another signatory who was the victim of German aggression.

The earliest manifestation of this commitment to mutual defense was the Treaty of Dunkirk, signed by Great Britain and France in March, 1947. But the Dunkirk agreement soon morphed into a broader coalition that was formally initialed in the Treaty of Brussels (March 17, 1948). The Brussels Treaty had five signatories: Britain, France, Belgium, Luxembourg, and the Netherlands. The Western Union Defense Organization was created to draw up plans for mutual defense, envisaging the creation of a joint army, navy, and air force. Headquarters were established in London and Fontainebleau, France (echoing the collaboration of World War II), and a hero of World War II, Bernard Law Montgomery, was appointed to head this defense organization. It never became more than a planning organization, however: World events overtook the inchoate organization.

The risk of German resurgence was fading in the early 1950's. Meanwhile, the Soviet Union was emerging as the major threat to future European peace. The Soviet Union's threat manifested itself in the tightening of Soviet control over Eastern Europe, where its army was the dominant force; in the blockade of Berlin; and in the attempt to convert the government of Greece to a communist government, which provoked the United States into action. Under the leadership of President Harry S. Truman and his visionary secretary of state, George C. Marshall, the United States began to put together another "allied" force to protect Western Europe. This new alignment was embodied in the North Atlantic Treaty Organization (NATO), formally inaugurated on April 4, 1949. As part of NATO, the United States continued to dominate the defense of Western Europe, but it demanded the active participation of the other countries that had signed the Brussels Treaty.

The defense activities of the Brussels signatories were grouped together as the European Defense Community (EDC), proposed by the French prime minister, René Pleven. As Pleven envisaged it, the EDC would be, collectively, a part of NATO, but it would have its own internal organization. In particular, it would incorporate a revived German military organization, because the French believed that by establishing defense units as part of a collaborative system, any tendency of the Germans to pursue objectives of their own would be contained. The Americans favored such a scheme, mainly because they wanted to include a new, democratic German army in the mutual defense arrangements that were emerging as part of NATO.

Pleven's EDC concept, had it ever been carried out, would have created institutions similar to those of the European Coal and Steel Community. However, the French parliament was unable to agree to French participation in an organization that also included German military men, and it voted down the EDC. Accordingly, the Germans were invited by the United

States to become part of NATO, and this decision was accepted by the other Western European nations. (French intransigence reached its height in 1966, when France withdrew from NATO at the behest of Charles de Gaulle, its charismatic president: NATO headquarters, hitherto in Paris, was forced to move to Brussels.)

Deprived of its role as a vehicle for mutual defense of Western Europe, and shortly preempted by the European Common Market as a coordinator of economic policy, the union created by the Brussels Treaty might have just faded away. Instead, on October 23, 1954, West Germany and Italy joined

COLD WAR EUROPE, 1955

= NATO countries
= Warsaw Pact countries
= Neutral countries

the signatories of the original Treaty of Brussels to form the Western European Union (WEU). The chancellor of West Germany, Konrad Adenauer, was particularly pleased at the chance to join with Western Europe against the communist threat he perceived not only from the Soviet Union but also from his East German counterparts.

The reinvention of the EDC as the WEU began to have practical effects in 1955, when European leaders masterminded a referendum in the Saarland, a border community between France and Germany that had been contested for centuries. The inhabitants appeared to be predominantly culturally German, and, under the supervision of the Western European Union, the referendum confirmed that cultural alignment. The inhabitants voted to be politically incorporated into western Germany. That adhesion took place, formally, on January 1, 1957.

On May 6, 1955, what had previously been called the Western Union was formally renamed the Western European Union. It had a structure similar to the Council of Europe: a council of ministers consisting of the foreign ministers of all the member governments met twice each year. The WEU had a parliamentary assembly, though this body had basically only advisory powers, because all the operative decisions were made by the council of ministers, whose decisions in turn were determined by the governments of those ministers' nations. The members of the parliamentary assembly were chosen by the parliaments of the individual member countries as well; to avoid duplication, the members of the WEU parliamentary assembly were the same as the parliamentary representatives in the assembly of the Council of Europe.

The WEU was designed to coordinate defense activities of the various European nations that belonged to the union, including Great Britain. It existed alongside NATO but was separate from it, as NATO included the United States and Canada, neither of which were members of the Western European Union. When the union was established in 1955, military power in Europe was divided between the Soviet Union and the NATO countries (overwhelmingly dominated by the United States). Under the aegis of the Western European Union, the defense establishments of the various members were gradually expanded so that defense was increasingly a collective responsibility. This development was encouraged by the United States, as it entailed other countries taking on some of the obligations that, through NATO, had been almost entirely American but partly relieved by the much smaller defense establishment of Great Britain.

The Western European Union was given a headquarters in London and a permanent council that functioned when the Council of Ministers was not in session. The permanent council was composed of ambassadors of the various countries accredited to the United Kingdom, except for the representative of Great Britain, who was a senior official of the British Foreign Office. A small bureaucracy carried out security studies for the use of the council as well.

The Western European Union, through its Council of Ministers, monitored the armaments of the different members. In its earliest stages, this involved the gradual buildup of new armaments, especially those of West Germany, which was a WEU member, as were Portugal and Spain, not then members of the Common Market. As the years passed, one of the most contentious issues became the extent of nuclear armament of the various WEU defense establishments.

SIGNIFICANCE

The Western European Union, a scaled-back version of the European Defense Community rejected by France, operated largely behind the scenes. It collaborated closely with the officials of NATO, but its basic purpose remained that behind the Brussels Treaty: reintegrating German armed forces into the European defense establishment under conditions prevailing in the Cold War. Its precise effects are difficult to gauge, given the more obvious role of NATO in the Cold War-era defense of Western Europe. However, the existence of a counterpart to NATO that comprised only European nations helped set the stage for the emergence of the European Union as a significant political and economic entity with separate interests from those of the United States in the post-Cold War world.

Nancy M. Gordon

FURTHER READING

Godson, Joseph, ed. *Thirty-Five Years of NATO: A Transatlantic Symposium on the Changing Political, Economic, and Military Setting.* New York: Dodd, Mead, 1984. A collection of essays by political leaders of the various members of NATO on its changing mission.

Levering, Ralph B. *The Cold War: A Post-Cold War History.* 2d ed. Arlington Heights, Ill.: Harlan Davidson, 2005. Reexamines the Cold War in light of sources from archives that opened after the collapse of the Soviet Union. Includes detailed analysis of the wars in Korea and Vietnam and the Cuban Missile Crisis.

Lewis, David W. P. *The Road to Europe: History, Institutions, and Prospects of European Integration, 1945-1993.* New York: Peter Lang, 1993. A comprehensive account of the various European organizations that have moved the notion of European integration forward since World War II.

Rees, G. Wyn. *The Western European Union at the Crossroads: Between Trans-*

Atlantic Solidarity and European Integration. Boulder, Colo.: Westview Press, 1998. Focuses primarily on developments in the 1990's but has an introductory chapter summarizing the history of the Western European Union.

Urwin, Derek W. *The Community of Europe: A History of European Integration Since 1945*. New York: Longman, 1995. A compact, yet detailed history of the various organizations carrying out European integration after World War II.

SEE ALSO: Apr. 3, 1948: Marshall Plan Provides Aid to Europe; Apr. 4, 1949: North Atlantic Treaty Organization Is Formed; July 1, 1950: European Payments Union Is Formed; May 14, 1955: Warsaw Pact Is Signed.

■ 1955-1964

BREZHNEV RISES IN COMMUNIST RANKS

In the late 1950's, Leonid Brezhnev received a series of promotions within the Soviet Communist Party, becoming a key ally of Soviet premier Nikita S. Khrushchev. His fortunes declined along with Khrushchev's in the early 1960's, but he recovered and ultimately replaced his political patron as the head of the party and the leader of the Soviet Union.

LOCALE: Soviet Union
CATEGORY: Government and politics

KEY FIGURES

Leonid Brezhnev (1906-1982), Soviet Communist Party official, chairman of the Presidium of the Supreme Soviet, 1960-1964 and 1977-1982, party first secretary, 1964-1966, and party general secretary, 1966-1982

Nikita S. Khrushchev (1894-1971), first secretary of the Communist Party of the Soviet Union, 1953-1964, and premier, 1958-1964

Joseph Stalin (Joseph Vissarionovich Dzhugashvili; 1878-1953), general secretary of the Central Committee of the Communist Party of the Soviet Union, 1922-1953, and premier, 1941-1953

Kliment Voroshilov (1881-1969), chairman of the Presidium of the Supreme Soviet, 1953-1960

SUMMARY OF EVENT

Leonid Brezhnev, an ethnic Russian born in the Ukraine, came from a working-class background. Trained as an industrial engineer, he joined the Communist Party in 1931 at age twenty-five. He gradually assumed local and regional party responsibilities, eventually becoming party head of the Moldavian Republic in 1950. Significant promotions in the early 1950's placed him in key positions on the ruling Communist Party Presidium (later known as the Politburo) and also made him a member of the important Central Committee and Secretariat of the party.

These promotions occurred during the last years of Joseph Stalin, but Stalin's death in 1953 resulted in Brezhnev's removal from the party Presidium. The new party leader, Nikita S. Khrushchev, however, soon realized that Brezhnev could be useful to his administration. Therefore, in 1955, Brezhnev was appointed as the party head in Kazakhstan. He was given the responsibility for implementing sweeping economic programs in Soviet Central Asia, including the famous "Virgin Lands" project.

The next year, Brezhnev became a nonvoting member of the Communist Party Presidium. He held other key assignments in the late 1950's primarily related to defense and space issues. He was named a full voting member of the party Presidium in 1957 after supporting Khrushchev in blocking an effort to remove him from power. Brezhnev added to his party responsibilities as a secretary of the Central Committee in 1959. As these promotions show, Brezhnev was being cultivated by Khrushchev as a strategic ally, placed at the highest political levels to bolster Khrushchev's own position.

By 1960, however, both Brezhnev and Khrushchev had experienced a reversal of fortunes. In the aftermath of the U-2 spy plane incident, in which an American surveillance plane was shot down over Soviet territory in May of 1960, the party's Central Committee sought to limit Khrushchev's authority. The committee added several new members of the party Presidium and changed the size and leadership of the party's important administrative body, the Secretariat. Frol Kozlov assumed the direction of that significant and powerful part of the institutional apparatus. Soon after, in July, the Central Committee removed Brezhnev from the Secretariat, a step widely interpreted as a demotion.

In May, 1960, the party leaders selected Brezhnev to be the new chairman of the Presidium of the Supreme Soviet, the national legislature (not to be confused with the party Presidium). He replaced the elderly Kliment Voroshilov, then nearly eighty. This position, without requiring a national election to determine the winner, is sometimes referred to as the "president of the Soviet Union." Despite its impressive-sounding title, however, the office had limited authority since the Supreme Soviet historically had minimal political influence or independence in national policy making. The Communist Party always provided the guiding authority. This assignment further revealed a decline in Brezhnev's political status, but he remained on the party Presidium, still a member of the inner leadership core of the Communist Party. This gave him a voice at the center of power and time to hope for a future improvement in his career.

As the Soviet Union's head of state, Brezhnev's primary responsibility was to perform ceremonial duties and to attend public functions. He made numerous state visits to nations in Asia, Europe, and Africa, allowing him for the first time to see other countries firsthand and meet many foreign leaders. His skill as a diplomat added to Brezhnev's public image and stature, revealing a gregarious personality and a businesslike manner that impressed many. He also traveled throughout the Soviet Union, gaining more knowledge about the nation and making useful contacts with public officials.

During Brezhnev's tenure as president, the Soviet Union made impressive and important progress in its space programs. This included placing the first human (Yuri Gagarin) in Earth orbit in 1961, followed by succeeding cosmonaut missions. Brezhnev received a major award, Hero of Socialist Labor, for his connection with the Soviet space program.

However, these years also revealed serious problems facing the Soviet Union. The nation's economic performance was uneven at best and poor at worst. Khrushchev's scheme to reorganize the Communist Party's structure created ill will and opposition among party members. The authorities imposed controversial controls on intellectuals and cultural life.

These domestic conditions were compounded by three major Cold War crises in Soviet foreign policy during the period: the Sino-Soviet split, in which the ideological differences between Soviet Russia and communist China became apparent (1960-1961), the erection of the Berlin Wall (1961), and the Cuban Missile Crisis (1962), in which nuclear brinkmanship between the Soviet Union and the United States threatened to escalate into military conflict. These challenges, intensified by Khrushchev's erratic and blustering leadership after a decade in power, motivated several of his closest associates to discuss removing him from power in late 1963. They were not yet well enough organized, however, and feared the consequences of Khrushchev's wrath should the bid to replace him fail. They knew that the unsuccessful 1957 attempt had not only resulted in Brezhnev's placement on the party Presidium as a reward for his loyalty but also in Khrushchev's elimination from power of all those who had sought to remove him.

Brezhnev's precise role in the developing opposition to Khrushchev in 1963 is still debated by scholars. However, several incidents suggest that Brezhnev gradually gained more authority as both he and the party moved toward the final break with Khrushchev. Kozlov, widely believed to be Khrushchev's intended successor as party head, became seriously ill in the spring of 1963. His departure from the political scene led to Brezhnev's election in June, 1963, to a new assignment in the party's Secretariat, this time with the vitally important responsibility to oversee party personnel matters. This put him at the center of power once again and in a stronger position to turn against Khrushchev. His position as Soviet president was officially terminated on July 15, 1964. In September, the party leadership assigned him to oversee the Soviet Union's defense industry, another key appointment. Brezhnev clearly was on the move again.

During 1964, the anti-Khrushchev conspirators prepared carefully before openly confronting the premier. The dramatic moment came on October 13, 1964, following Khrushchev's return to Moscow from his vacation on the Black Sea coast. At a meeting of the party Presidium, the plotters cited Khrushchev's numerous failures and inadequacies, and they demanded his immediate resignation. Brezhnev actively participated in the meeting. Khrushchev put up a fight, but he could not overcome those determined to oust him from power. On October 14, the party's Central Committee confirmed the decision and Khrushchev was removed as first secretary.

Two days later, the Soviet media announced that Khrushchev had voluntarily asked to be relieved of his duties because of his age and poor health, an explanation that virtually no one believed, either at the time or since. The media also named the new leaders who assumed the positions that Khrushchev had held jointly: Aleksey Kosygin became premier and Brezhnev became first secretary of the Communist Party (the title would be changed to general secretary two years later). This transfer of power was immediate and complete, without the involvement or approval of the Soviet people.

Significance

Leonid Brezhnev was an important example of a new generation of Communist Party leaders in the Soviet Union after Lenin, Stalin, and Khrushchev. A steady personality and competent administrator who usually succeeded in his efforts, Brezhnev gained valuable experience at nearly all levels of the nation's political life and party bureaucracy prior to October, 1964, when he took power as first secretary.

During this period of political apprenticeship and ascendancy, Brezhnev astutely balanced his ambition with caution in seeking to advance his own career. He carefully developed good relations with most of the party's most powerful figures, gaining their confidence and avoiding antagonizing those who might later oppose his political aspirations. He accepted demotions, as in 1960 when he became president, without outward complaint. He usually supported Khrushchev as party leader but by 1963-1964 realized that the country needed new leadership and direction. This realization led him to abandon his loyalty to his mentor, showing little mercy in the rough world of Soviet politics.

Brezhnev was a logical consensus choice to lead the party after Khrushchev's ouster, but only time would tell if he had the intellect and ability to effectively guide his nation in future decades. He was the only Soviet president eventually to become the head of the Communist Party (although later party heads Yuri Andropov, Konstantin Chernenko, and Mikhail Gorbachev would all become president after first assuming control of the party). Brezhnev's assumption of the position of first secretary, then, was a remarkable transition from a figurehead position to one of real power in the Soviet Union.

Taylor Stults

FURTHER READING

Dornberg, John. *Brezhnev: The Masks of Power.* New York: Basic Books, 1974. Comprehensive biography covers Brezhnev's life and party career from the 1940's to the early 1970's.

Gaddis, John Lewis. *The Cold War: A New History.* New York: Penguin, 2005. Concise overview of the Cold War, covering its origins, ideologies, and technologies, written by a noted historian.

Hyland, William. *The Fall of Khrushchev.* New York: Funk and Wagnalls, 1968. Detailed presentation of Khrushchev's ouster in 1964, portraying Brezhnev as one of the three primary plotters.

Khrushchev, Sergei. *Khrushchev on Khrushchev.* Boston: Little, Brown, 1990. Revealing account, by Khrushchev's son, of the October, 1964, conspiracy to oust his father in which Brezhnev participated as a central player.

Tatu, Michael. *Power in the Kremlin: From Khrushchev to Kosygin.* New York: Viking, 1969. Lengthy account of Communist Party leadership; traces Brezhnev's rise to taking power as first secretary of the Communist Party.

Taubman, William. *Khrushchev: The Man and His Era.* New York: Norton, 2003. Scholarly assessment of Khrushchev includes Brezhnev's career during the 1950's to 1964, as he moved into higher party leadership positions.

Volkogonov, Dmitri. *Autopsy for an Empire: The Seven Leaders Who Built the Soviet Regime.* New York: Free Press, 1998. Provides a significant personality profile and detailed political assessment of Brezhnev, by a Russian historian who was a Soviet general during the Brezhnev era.

See also: Mar. 5, 1953: Death of Stalin; Feb. 25, 1956: Khrushchev Denounces Stalinist Regime; Aug. 13, 1961: Communists Raise the Berlin Wall; Oct. 22-28, 1962: Cuban Missile Crisis; Oct. 13-14, 1964: Khrushchev Falls from Power; Nov. 12, 1968-Dec., 1989: Brezhnev Doctrine Mandates Soviet Control of Satellite Nations; May 26, 1973-Dec. 26, 1991: Détente with the Soviet Union; Dec. 24-27, 1979: Soviet Union Invades Afghanistan; Mar. 11, 1985: Gorbachev Initiates a Policy of Glasnost.

■ **January 29, 1955**

Formosa Resolution Is Signed into Law

Passage of a joint resolution affirmed U.S. presidential power to defend Taiwan from attack by communist China and demonstrated the willingness of the United States to wage an active Cold War.

Locale: Washington, D.C.
Categories: Diplomacy and international relations; government and politics

Key Figures
Chiang Kai-shek (1887-1975), president of the Republic of China
John Foster Dulles (1888-1959), U.S. secretary of state
Dwight D. Eisenhower (1890-1969), president of the United States, 1953-1961
Walter F. George (1878-1957), senator from Georgia
William F. Knowland (1908-1974), senator from California
James P. Richards (1894-1979), representative from South Carolina
Zhou Enlai (Chou En-lai; 1898-1976), premier of the People's Republic of China

Summary of Event
In 1949, as the communists took over mainland China at the end of the Chinese civil war, Chiang Kai-shek, president of the Republic of China, or Nationalist China, withdrew with part of his government and army to the island of Formosa and the nearby Pescadores Islands. Formosa, a Portuguese name meaning "beautiful," was still used in the 1950's to describe the island in the West; as Asian nomenclature began to replace colonial-era names, the island's Chinese name, Taiwan, was used exclusively and the name Formosa

DEFENDING FORMOSA

U.S. president Dwight D. Eisenhower wrote a letter to British prime minister Winston Churchill (dated February 10, 1955), thanking him for supporting U.S. efforts to stop the advance of communism in Asia:

Dear Winston:

I have heard how earnestly you supported throughout the Conference of Prime Ministers the proposition that nothing must create a serious rift in British-American relationships. Not only do I applaud that sentiment, but I am most deeply grateful to you for your successful efforts.

I realize that it has been difficult, at times, for you to back us up in the Formosa question and, for this reason, I want to give you a very brief account of our general attitude toward the various factors that have dictated the course we have taken. You understand, of course, that we have certain groups that are violent in their efforts to get us to take a much stronger, even a truculent position. The number that would like to see us clear out of Formosa is negligible. I know that on your side of the water you have the exact opposite of this situation.

Because the Communists know these facts, there is no question in my mind that one of the principal reasons for their constant pressing on the Asian frontier is the hope of dividing our two countries. I am sure that we, on both sides of the water, can make quite clear that, no matter what may be our differences in approach or even sometimes our differences in important convictions, nothing is ever going to separate us or destroy our unity in opposing Communist aggression.

We believe that if international Communism should penetrate the island barrier in the Western Pacific and thus be in a position to threaten the Philippines and Indonesia immediately and directly, all of us, including the free countries of Europe, would soon be in far worse trouble than we are now. Certainly that whole region would soon go.

To defend Formosa the United States has been engaged in a long and costly program of arming and sustaining the Nationalist troops on that island. Those troops, however, and Chiang himself, are not content, now, to accept irrevocably and permanently the status of "prisoners" on the island. They are held together by a conviction that some day they will go back to the mainland.

passed into history. Formosa and the Pescadores had been held by the Japanese from 1895 until their return to China in 1945, at the end of World War II. Chiang claimed that his was still the legitimate government of China and announced his intention to return to the mainland and to power. His troops also held other islands off the China coast, notably Quemoy, a short distance from the port of Amoy; Matsu, off Foochow; and the Tachens, located about 200 miles to the north of Matsu.

Both Chiang and the Chinese communists held that Formosa was a province of China, and Quemoy and Matsu were part of the mainland province of Fukien. Though Quemoy and Matsu were small, both sides saw them as stepping-stones. In Chiang's view, they were strategic for a return to the mainland; to the communists, they were a step toward the inclusion of Formosa in their regime. The islands were staging points for occasional raids on the mainland and came under air attack from the communists.

The United States had supported Chiang in the civil war and recognized his regime as the legitimate government for all China. The Korean War (1950-1953) and the Chinese communist role in it strengthened U.S. antipa-

Chiang Kai-shek inspecting Nationalist Chinese troops on Taiwan in 1952. (National Archives)

thy toward the communists. Military and economic aid went to Formosa, and the Seventh Fleet patrolled the Formosa Strait to prevent invasion. Chiang increased the armament and garrisons on Quemoy and Matsu against the advice of many individuals in the U.S. military establishment. The mainland regime placed even larger forces on the shore facing the islands. In August and September, 1954, the communists began a bombardment of the islands, killing two U.S. military advisers.

Throughout the autumn, debate over policy continued, both within the United States and between the United States and its allies. Some of the Joint Chiefs of Staff and some members of Congress (such as Senator William F. Knowland of California) were willing to encourage Chiang in a return to the mainland and to give U.S. support to his forces on Quemoy and Matsu. This policy was popularly known as "unleashing Chiang Kai-shek." Others saw in such steps either continued defeat for Chiang or involvement in a major Asian war (World War III in some predictions), or both. Secretary of State John Foster Dulles viewed the question of Formosa and the offshore islands within the context of the Cold War, then at its height. To him, the maintenance of a strong Nationalist presence off the coast of mainland China would keep the Chinese communist regime off balance, while offering some hope to those who wanted it overthrown.

As a result of these debates within the government, a somewhat more definite policy toward Nationalist China began to emerge. On December 2, 1954, the United States and Nationalist China concluded a mutual defense treaty. No specific mention was made in the treaty about offshore islands, however. Consequently, a month later, the Chinese communists launched bombardment and air attacks on these islands. On January 24, 1955, as the attacks continued, President Dwight D. Eisenhower sent a special message to Congress in which he asked for authority to use the U.S. Armed Forces to protect Formosa, the Pescadores, and what he vaguely referred to as certain "closely related localities." This authority, like the mutual defense treaty, would not commit the United States in advance to the defense of the offshore islands, nor would it limit U.S. action in advance.

Eisenhower pointed out that the measure was not a constitutional necessity; he already had the requisite authority both as commander in chief and under the terms of the mutual security treaty already signed but not as yet ratified by the Senate. He wanted a demonstration of the unity of the United States and its resolve, while making thoroughly clear the authority of the president. In communist China, Premier Zhou Enlai called the message a war message.

The message went to the new Congress, which had a Democratic majority in both houses. In response, the chairs of the respective committees, Democrats Walter F. George in the Senate and James P. Richards in the House, introduced the joint resolution that became known as the Formosa Resolution. The resolution took as its premise the vital interest of the United States in peace in the western Pacific and the danger to peace from communist attacks in the area. It took note of the statement of mutual interest in the treaty submitted to the Senate.

There was strong bipartisan support among U.S. politicians for aggressive anticommunist positions. The House passed the resolution on January 25, 1955, by a vote of 410-3. In the Senate committee, an amendment to turn Formosa and the Pescadores over to the authority of the United Nations, and giving authorization to the president only until the United Nations acted, was defeated. Another amendment to limit the authority to Formosa and the Pescadores also lost. A similar amendment to draw a line back of Quemoy and Matsu, limiting the president's authority to Formosa and the Pescadores, was introduced on the Senate floor by Senator Herbert Lehman of New York. It was defeated 74-13. The Senate passed the resolution 85-3, on January 28, and Eisenhower signed it the next day.

The mutual security treaty with Nationalist China was ratified in February. Efforts to persuade Chiang Kai-shek to reduce his forces on Quemoy and Matsu and make them mere outposts failed. That same month, however, Chiang did evacuate the Tachens, which the communists promptly occupied. Communist premier Zhou Enlai, in an attempt to strike a conciliatory note, told the Afro-Asian Conference meeting in Bandung, Indonesia, in April, that his country did not want war with the United States. He further expressed his willingness to negotiate on Far Eastern issues, including that of Formosa. As a result, by May, without formal statement or agreement, there was an effective cease-fire in the Formosa Straits.

In the wake of the passage of the Formosa Resolution and the ratification of the mutual defense treaty with Nationalist China, Eisenhower addressed a letter to British prime minister Winston Churchill on February 10, in which he set forth his ideas on the importance of defending Formosa and the offshore islands. The United States depended on an island (Formosa) and a peninsula (Korea) as its defense line in Southeast Asia. The loss of Formosa would be a serious break in that line. The weakening of Chiang Kai-shek's forces could mean the loss of Formosa. The denial of their expectation to return to mainland China would be destructive of their morale. Therefore, it was important to the United States not only to aid in the defense of Formosa but also not to accept, or seem to accept, the loss of the offshore islands, which were of strategic importance in launching a return to the mainland. These ideas helped set the posture of U.S. policy in the Far East for some time to come.

SIGNIFICANCE

Judgments of the Formosa Resolution at the time of its passage and in historical perspective must depend greatly on attitudes toward the larger question of policy toward China. The overwhelming vote in Congress in favor of the Formosa Resolution may be taken as clear evidence of opinion there, and presumably of opinion throughout the country, that communist expansion must be resisted, but that the United States ought not be involved in further war. From another, but related, perspective, the Formosa Resolution was a reflection of the Cold War mentality that saw no possibility for diplomatic recognition of the communist regime on the Chinese mainland.

Even after this Cold War mentality had waned, the legacy of the Formosa Resolution ensured that the United States maintained residual ties with the Nationalist regime in Taiwan even after it afforded diplomatic recognition to mainland China in 1979. U.S.-China tensions began to increase in the mid-1990's and into the early twenty-first century, as Taiwan, now ruled by democratically elected indigenous leaders (rather than remnants of the Chinese Nationalist Party), mulled over the possibility of declaring independence. The consensus among U.S. policy makers remained that something should be done if China were to invade Taiwan. Thus, the impact of the Formosa Resolution was not confined to its immediate aftermath.

George J. Fleming and Nicholas Birns

FURTHER READING

Beeson, Mark. "U.S. Hegemony and Southeast Asia." *Critical Asian Studies* 36, no. 3 (2004): 445-462. Details U.S.-Southeast Asia relations since the end of World War II, focusing on "how U.S. foreign policy has impacted the region in the economic, political, and security spheres."

Bueler, William M. *U.S. China Policy and the Problem of Taiwan.* Boulder: Colorado Associated University Press, 1971. Covers the Formosa Resolution and its aftermath in detail.

Copper, John Franklin. *China Diplomacy: The Washington-Taipei-Beijing Triangle.* Boulder, Colo.: Westview Press, 1992. Examines how much actual communist threat there was to Taiwan in the 1950's.

Eisenhower, Dwight D. *Mandate for Change, 1953-1956.* Garden City, N.Y.: Doubleday, 1963. This memoir by the U.S. president at the time the resolution was enacted is still a valuable source for the American view of the Formosa situation.

Hickey, Dennis Van Vranken. *United States-Taiwan Security Ties: From Cold War to Beyond Containment.* Westport, Conn.: Praeger, 1994. Examines the complicated network of U.S. military guarantees to Taiwan through the years.

Hsieh, Chiao Chiao. *Strategy for Survival: The Foreign Policy and External Relations of the Republic of China on Taiwan, 1949-1979.* London: Sherwood Press, 1985. Illuminates the Taiwanese perspective.

Jian, Chen. *Mao's China and the Cold War.* Charlotte: University of North Carolina Press, 2001. Analyzes the strategies and motives of Mao Zedong and posits that China's allegiance shift from the Soviet Union to the United States turned the tide of the Cold War. Contains illustrations and maps.

McMahon, Robert J. *The Limits of Empire: The United States and Southeast Asia Since World War II.* New York: Columbia University Press, 1999. Brief examination of U.S. relations with Southeast Asia since the time of World War II.

SEE ALSO: Oct. 7, 1950: China Invades and Begins Rule of Tibet; Oct. 22, 1951: United States Inaugurates Mutual Security Program; Sept. 8, 1954: SEATO Is Founded; Jan. 5, 1957: Eisenhower Doctrine; Oct. 16, 1964: China Explodes Its First Nuclear Bomb; Oct. 25, 1971: People's Republic of China Is Seated at the United Nations; Feb. 21, 1972: Nixon Opens Trade with China; Sept. 9, 1976: Death of Mao Zedong Leads to Reforms in China.

■ **APRIL 18-24, 1955**

AFRO-ASIAN CONFERENCE CONSIDERS NONALIGNMENT

In an attempt to break free of the pervasive influence of the Cold War superpowers, the United States and the Soviet Union, representatives of African and Asian nations met in Bandung, Indonesia, to consider adopting formal positions of nonalignment. The Bandung Conference marked the birth of the "Third World" as a political entity and was a forum for developing nations seeking a greater voice in political, economic, and social affairs.

ALSO KNOWN AS: Asian-African Conference; Bandung Conference
LOCALE: Bandung, Indonesia
CATEGORIES: Diplomacy and international relations; United Nations

KEY FIGURES

Sukarno (1901-1970), president of Indonesia, 1945-1967

Ruslan Abdulgani (1914-2005), organizer of the Bandung Conference and future foreign minister of Indonesia, 1956-1957, 1959-1962

Zhou Enlai (Chou En-lai; 1898-1976), Chinese premier and head of the Chinese delegation to the conference

Jawaharlal Nehru (1889-1964), prime minister of India and head of the Indian delegation to the conference

Gamal Abdel Nasser (1918-1970), president of Egypt and head of the Egyptian delegation to the conference

U Thant (1909-1974), representative from Burma and future U.N. secretary-general, 1961-1971

Norodom Sihanouk (b. 1922), king of Cambodia, 1941-1955, and conference attendee

SUMMARY OF EVENT

By the mid-1950's, the two Cold War superpowers, the United States and the Soviet Union, had virtually forced most nations, including the poorer nations of the Third World, to align themselves politically, economically, and often militarily with one or the other. The existence of the Warsaw Pact bloc, the North Atlantic Treaty Organization (NATO), and the Southeast Asia Treaty Organization (SEATO) proved the attractiveness of aligning one's government with one of the superpowers. At the same time, however, the disbanding of the European colonial systems of Britain, France, the Netherlands, and Belgium saw the birth of numerous new countries, most of which were highly nationalistic, poor, and fiercely independent. These nations often felt that neither the United States nor the Soviet Union showed sufficient concern for their interests. They felt that the same attitude was displayed by the European powers, which were only now beginning to divest themselves of their colonial empires. Largely at the insistence of the "Colombo Group" (a group of Third World countries that had recently won independence), as well as the urging of Indonesia, Ceylon, Egypt, India, Pakistan, and Burma, the Asian-African, or Bandung, Conference was organized by Indonesian foreign minister Ruslan Abdulgani, with the backing of Indonesian president Sukarno.

From April 18 to 24, 1955, representatives of twenty-nine countries from Asia and Africa met in Bandung, Indonesia, to discuss their intentions to form a nonaligned movement of closely bonded member states, in the style of the Warsaw Pact and NATO. These newly developing nations expressed their desire to work with other nations in peace and to reject direct alignment with either the United States or the Soviet Union. Many of the most important political leaders of the twentieth century attended the Bandung Conference, including Indonesian president Sukarno, Indian prime minister Jawaharlal Nehru, Chinese premier Zhou Enlai, future secretary-general of the United Nations U Thant of Burma, Prince Norodom Sihanouk of Cambodia, and Egyptian president Gamal Abdel Nasser.

Among the most memorable discourses pronounced at the conference were those of President Sukarno, who first addressed the delegates, and the closing speech given by Indian prime minister Jawaharlal Nehru, which many believe to be his finest. Nehru sought to build on diplomatic advances that had already been achieved at a meeting in New Delhi in 1954 between representatives of India and the People's Republic in China, in which both

Chinese premier and foreign minister Zhou Enlai leaving a session of the Geneva Conference in 1954. (Library of Congress)

THE TEN PRINCIPLES

The Bandung Conference's final communiqué listed "Ten Principles" that have served as the basis of the Nonaligned Movement and the foreign policies of many Asian and African nations:

(1) Respect for fundamental human rights and for the purposes and principles of the charter of the United Nations.

(2) Respect for the sovereignty and territorial integrity of all nations.

(3) Recognition of the equality of all races and of the equality of all nations large and small.

(4) Abstention from intervention or interference in the internal affairs of another country.

(5) Respect for the right of each nation to defend itself, singly or collectively, in conformity with the charter of the United Nations.

(6a) Abstention from the use of arrangements of collective defence to serve any particular interests of the big powers.

(6b) Abstention by any country from exerting pressures on other countries.

(7) Refraining from acts or threats of aggression or the use of force against the territorial integrity or political independence of any country.

(8) Settlement of all international disputes by peaceful means, such as negotiation, conciliation, arbitration or judicial settlement as well as other peaceful means of the parties' own choice, in conformity with the Charter of the United Nations.

(9) Promotion of mutual interests and cooperation.

(10) Respect for justice and international obligations.

---

countries had agreed to the "Five Principles of Peaceful Coexistence," which included:

(1) mutual respect for each other's territorial integrity and sovereignty

(2) nonaggression

(3) noninterference in each other's internal affairs

(4) equality and mutual benefit

(5) peaceful coexistence and peaceful settlement of disputes

Prime Minister Zhou Enlai of the People's Republic of China (so-called communist China)—who had narrowly escaped an assassination attempt in Hong Kong on his way to Bandung—represented his nation in this, its first foray into international diplomacy. Zhou spoke so eloquently and performed so brilliantly that, as a result of this one gathering, communist China made significant inroads into the political landscape of the Third World. Zhou—for the first time meeting President Nasser and potentially hostile representatives from pro-Western nations such as India, Japan, Pakistan, and Thailand—adroitly persuaded them of the intention of the People's Republic of China to apply the Five Principles in affairs with all foreign governments, particularly with its Asian neighbors. Within two years of the conference, Egypt had established diplomatic relations with the People's Republic of China. President Nasser, a committed socialist, was so affected by his meeting with Zhou and the events at Bandung that he allowed the Chinese to use his nation as a base for their diplomatic and cultural operations on the African continent.

While attempting not to favor or antagonize either the United States or the Soviet Union, the nations assembled declared that "colonialism in all its manifestations is an evil which should be speedily brought to an end" and unanimously adopted a ten-point "Declaration on Promotion of World Peace and Cooperation," based on the Five Principles of Peaceful Coexistence and on the provisions of the United Nations Charter. The final communiqué of the attending nations expressed their desire to work for closer cultural, technical, and political cooperation and declared their intention to establish regional training and research facilities. The members proclaimed that membership in the United Nations should be universal, as should be nuclear disarmament. They also expressed their support for human rights and self-determination, and they resolved to meet again, as a group, in the near future.

SIGNIFICANCE

The Bandung Conference was the first international meeting in which the poor, developing nations gathered together as a political entity. Henceforth, all the world powers would have to consider the "Third World" when making international decisions. The Five Principles of Peaceful Coexistence established at New Delhi were expanded into the Ten Principles of the final Bandung communiqué and served into the twenty-first century as the basis of the foreign policies of many Asian and African countries.

As a direct result of the Bandung meeting, the gathered nations went on to establish the Nonaligned Movement in 1961. From the perspective of the Cold War, the People's Republic of China gained enormous international stature by playing a leading role in the formation of the Five Principles and then the Ten Principles. By distancing itself from the United States and the Soviet Union, and by defining itself as a "developing nation," the People's Republic of China positioned itself as an alternative leader for Third World countries seeking to extract themselves from the competition between the two superpowers for world hegemony. At the same time, the Chinese gained enormous influence in Asia and, especially, in Africa. The gathered nations spoke of following the "Bandung spirit," a policy of peaceful cooperation based on the Ten Principles. The People's Republic of China would continue to pursue a foreign policy known as the "Bandung Line," which sought to garner international favor through conciliation, understanding, and cooperation.

Mark DeStephano

FURTHER READING

Ampiah, Kweku. *The Political and Moral Imperatives of the Bandung Conference of 1955: The Reactions of the U.S., U.K. and Japan.* Honolulu: University of Hawaii Press, 2007. Making use of the primary sources available fifty years after the conference, Ampiah reevaluates the meetings, with particular attention paid to external geopolitical influences as seen through three case studies involving the United States, the United Kingdom, and Japan.

Brzezinski, Zbigniew. *Africa and the Communist World.* Stanford, Calif.: Hoover Institution/Stanford University Press, 1963. Incisive scholarly study of the great importance of the Bandung Conference to Third World diplomacy, showing how the Bandung agreements shaped the foreign policies of various nations. Thorough subject index with comprehensive notes.

Macfarquhar, Roderick, and John K. Fairbank, eds. *The People's Republic, Part I: Emergence of Revolutionary China, 1949-1965.* Vol. 14 in *The Cambridge History of China.* 1987. Reprint. New York: Cambridge University Press, 1995. Brief but complete study of the Asian-African meeting, with particular emphasis on its significance for Chinese international relations. Excellent bibliography and notes.

Mackie, J. A. C. *Bandung 1955: Non-alignment and Afro-Asian Solidarity.* Singapore: Éditions Didier Millet, 2005. A specialist in Indonesian politics and history describes the 1955 conference. Maps, bibliographical references, index.

Mullen, Bill V. *Afro-Orientalism.* Minneapolis: University of Minnesota Press, 2004. A study of the influence of the Asian-African meeting and the thought of various American scholars such as W. E. B. Du Bois, Robert F. Williams, Richard Wright, and Fred Ho. Thorough subject index and an ample bibliography.

Wright, Richard, et al. *The Color Curtain: A Report on the Bandung Conference.* 1956. Reprint. Jackson: University of Mississippi Press, 1995. An early scholarly examination of the work of the Bandung meeting, with insightful analysis of the relevance of race to Third World government and policy.

SEE ALSO: Apr. 25-June 26, 1945: United Nations Charter Convention; Dec. 14, 1955: United Nations Admits Sixteen New Members; Spring, 1957: Mao's Hundred Flowers Campaign Begins; Sept. 1-5, 1961: Nonaligned Movement Meets; Aug. 7, 1964-Jan. 27, 1973: United States Enters the Vietnam War; Sept. 30, 1965: Indonesia's Government Retaliates Against a Failed Communist Coup; Oct. 25, 1971: People's Republic of China Is Seated at the United Nations; Mar., 1973: U.S. Troops Leave Vietnam.

■ MAY 14, 1955

WARSAW PACT IS SIGNED

The Warsaw Pact, signed in response to the arming of West Germany, consolidated Soviet power in eastern and central Europe. The pact came to be seen as the opposing force to NATO, as the tensions between those two alliances would come to define the Cold War.

ALSO KNOWN AS: Warsaw Treaty; Treaty of Friendship, Cooperation, and Mutual Assistance
LOCALE: Warsaw, Poland
CATEGORY: Diplomacy and international relations

KEY FIGURES
Nikolai Aleksandrovich Bulganin (1895-1975), premier of the Soviet Union, 1955-1958
Ivan Konev (1897-1973), commander in chief of Warsaw Pact armed forces, 1956-1960
Nikita S. Khrushchev (1894-1971), first secretary of the Communist Party of the Soviet Union, 1953-1964, and premier, 1958-1964
Vyacheslav Mikhailovich Molotov (Vyacheslav Mikhailovich Skryabin; 1890-1986), Soviet commissar of foreign affairs, 1939-1949 and 1953-1956

SUMMARY OF EVENT
The Warsaw Pact—formally known as the Treaty of Friendship, Cooperation, and Mutual Assistance Between the People's Republic of Albania, the People's Republic of Bulgaria, the Hungarian People's Republic, the German Democratic Republic, the Polish People's Republic, the Romanian People's Republic, the Union of Soviet Socialist Republics, and the Czechoslovak Republic—was signed on May 14, 1955. To a large extent, this multi-

lateral alliance must be seen as an outgrowth of Soviet concerns over the re-arming of the Federal Republic of Germany (West Germany).

The Soviet Union formally protested the Western arrangements providing for the creation of West German armed forces and the entry of West Germany into the North Atlantic Treaty Organization (NATO). The Soviets

WARSAW PACT NATIONS, 1955

Soviet leaders overseeing the signing of the Warsaw Pact on May 14, 1955. From left to right: Soviet marshal Ivan Konev, the supreme commander of the alliance; foreign minister Vyache-slav M. Molotov; premier Nikolai Bulganin; and defense minister Georgy Zhukov. (AP/Wide World Photos)

served notice in November, 1954, that the remilitarization of West Germany would lead to new security measures in Eastern Europe. The actual signing of the Warsaw Pact was preceded by the Moscow Conference of the future members in November-December, 1954. At this time, Vyacheslav Mikhailovich Molotov, the Soviet foreign minister, presented a rather blunt statement regarding the revival of German militarism and the need for "special vigilance" and "practical measures."

Molotov's militant anti-Western stance was not entirely maintained by the subsequent Warsaw Conference. The new Soviet leaders, Nikita S. Khrushchev and Nikolai Aleksandrovich Bulganin, had only recently asserted themselves in a power struggle with Georgi M. Malenkov, who led a faction in the Soviet Politburo associated with the commitment to détente. The Khrushchev-Bulganin leadership, however, was similarly inclined to adopt a somewhat softer foreign policy posture than the one advocated by Molotov. Molotov saw the pact as an instrument of military preparedness and socialist consolidation, whereas Khrushchev viewed it as a Cold War political device. Thus, the language and terms of the Warsaw Pact reflected the new Soviet priorities in international affairs.

It is certainly appropriate to view the Warsaw Pact as the Soviet counterpart to NATO. Indeed, the Warsaw Pact's role as a military alliance opposing NATO continued to increase over the years. The Soviet Union maintained sizable combat-equipped forces in a forward deployment in the Warsaw Pact area, supported by tactical air and missile elements and reinforceable from the Soviet Union. Nevertheless, concern over the developments in NATO was not the sole reason for the Warsaw Pact. The period following Stalin's death in 1953 had seen considerable diversity and agitation for increased independence on the part of the Eastern European satellite states, a phenomenon known as polycentrism. The changing political environment in Eastern Europe required new approaches and methods in the continuing efforts to sustain Soviet control over the area. The creation of a formal treaty organization, together with invigoration of the Council for Mutual Economic Assistance (COMECON), established under Soviet auspices in 1949, appeared to be an excellent response to Soviet needs.

The eleven articles of the Warsaw Pact provided for consultation on all issues of common interest, the peaceful settlement of conflicts, and joint defense. The military convention was the most important part of the treaty; it allowed for the disposition of troops under the joint command for purposes of mutual defense. Soviet marshal Ivan Konev was appointed commander in chief, and the ministers of defense of the other member states became his deputies. Each of these deputy commanders was put in charge of the troops contributed by his own state. The headquarters, with a permanent staff of the joint armed forces and certain auxiliary bodies, were located in Moscow. For purposes of policy coordination, a political consultative committee was established.

Subsequent military integration efforts by the Soviet Union included the standardization of equipment and the development of a common infrastructure. Moreover, considerable effort was made to indoctrinate officers and men in loyalty to the "socialist camp." Key positions in the satellite armies were awarded, as a matter of course, to Soviet-trained officers. The German Democratic Republic was initially excluded from participation in the joint command; it was given equal status at the first meeting of the political consultative committee held in Prague in January, 1956. As a deliberate counter to the developments in NATO, the East German National People's Army was created and integrated into the joint command.

SIGNIFICANCE

In retrospect, it is important to note that at the time of its inception, the Warsaw Pact was primarily designed to strengthen the Soviet position at the Geneva Summit Conference held in July, 1955. The Soviet government envisioned a European collective security treaty, which, when achieved, would provide for the simultaneous termination of NATO, the supplementary Paris agreements, and the Warsaw Pact. As an alternative to this maximum goal, the Soviets proposed a nonaggression treaty between the members of each alliance. No steps were taken, however, on either proposal at that time.

In its initial stages, then, the Warsaw Pact served the Soviet Union essentially as a Cold War political device. Indeed, during the first years of the treaty's existence, the Soviet Union was not very intent on developing its potential as an integrated military alliance. The existing bilateral agreements with individual European states were sufficient with regard to the deployment of Soviet troops to counter American influence in Europe. Certain features of the pact, however, such as its "legitimizing" the presence of Soviet troops on Eastern European soil, gradually appreciated in value for the Soviet Union.

The Soviets came to regard the Warsaw Pact as a highly useful instrument in East-West relations and in furthering its hegemonic interests in Eastern Europe. The pact could be effectively used as a coordinating mechanism for foreign policy and the achievement of a uniform external posture. More important, it facilitated the achievement of general conformity to Moscow's policy line for the area itself. Moscow was able to promote what it called "fraternal bloc solidarity," and any member straying too far from the line could be subjected to disciplinary action behind the collective facade of the Warsaw Pact.

Riots and massive public demonstrations flared up in Poland and Hungary in the fall of 1956. The respective regimes attempted to respond to some of the demands and expectations, defying directives to the contrary from Moscow. Clearly, Soviet control over political developments in Eastern Europe was slipping. In October of 1956, the Soviets decided to intervene directly in Poland and Hungary. In the case of Poland, a Soviet delegation went to Warsaw and, backed by alerted Soviet troops stationed in the vicinity, was able to bring matters back under control.

In the case of Hungary, the great popular uprising ultimately led to the massive use of Soviet military force to crush the rebellion and to reestablish a regime subservient to Moscow. The Soviet use of armed might was justified under the Warsaw Pact's terms, although these terms referred only to aiding a member state threatened by aggression and did not state what to do in case of civil war. The Soviet action was presented as a response to "the sacred duty" to protect the "achievements of socialism." Reviewing the events in Hungary, there was no consultation within the context of the Warsaw Pact. The political consultative committee did not meet at all during this time of crisis.

The provisions of the treaty were reinterpreted to allow for "legitimate" intervention in the affairs of member states, including the use of force, under the doctrine of "proletarian internationalism." Such disciplinary and policing functions became a significant part of Soviet policy and practice over the years. The most extreme instances were the interventions in Hungary in 1956 and in Czechoslovakia in 1968. The resort to military force to bring these countries to heel did not truly depend on the Warsaw Pact. It was, however, politically and ideologically most expedient to give these operations a multilateral appearance.

Manfred Grote and Carl Rollyson

FURTHER READING

Brown, J. F. *The New Eastern Europe: The Khrushchev Era and After.* New York: Praeger, 1966. Early and highly acclaimed systematic study of the relations among communist states, containing useful information on the Warsaw Pact.

Clawson, Robert W., and Lawrence S. Kaplan, eds. *The Warsaw Pact: Political Purpose and Military Means.* Wilmington, Del.: Scholarly Resources, 1982. Chapters on the principal political relationships within the Warsaw Pact, on NATO and the Warsaw Pact, the pact's military strength and weaponry, and its doctrines and capabilities.

Epstein, Joshua M. *Conventional Force Reductions: A Dynamic Assessment.* Washington, D.C.: The Brookings Institution, 1990. See index for entries on the Warsaw Pact's combat power, its overall military significance, and its relationship to NATO. See also the section in chapter 5, "Soviet Perceptions."

Holloway, David, and Jane M. O. Sharp. *The Warsaw Pact: Alliance in Transition?* Ithaca, N.Y.: Cornell University Press, 1984. Chapters on the Warsaw Pact's history, defense capability, Soviet crisis management, foreign policy goals, the later policy of security through détente, and the Warsaw Pact in the context of the world system.

Judge, Edward H., and John Langdon. *The Cold War: A History through Documents.* Upper Saddle River, N.J.: Prentice Hall, 1999. The text of the Warsaw Pact is included in this collection of more than 130 primary sources including speeches, agreements, and declarations, arranged chronologically.

Kelleher, Catherine McArdle. *The Future of European Security: An Interim Assessment.* Washington, D.C.: The Brookings Institution, 1995. Chapters 3 and 4 discuss the politics of European security and the relationship between Eastern and Western Europe. An excellent study of how the Cold War alliance system broke down, with extensive notes and bibliography.

Mastny, Vojtech, and Malcolm Byrne, eds. *A Cardboard Castle? An Inside His-*

tory of the Warsaw Pact, 1955-1991. New York: Central European University Press, 2005. Massive, comprehensive history of the Warsaw Pact, reprinting many source documents written by officials of Warsaw Pact member nations. Bibliographic references and index.

Remington, Robin Alison. *The Warsaw Pact: Case Studies in Communist Conflict Resolution.* Cambridge, Mass.: MIT Press, 1971. Still among the best studies of the resolution of various conflicts between the Soviet Union and other member states. A detailed study of the origins of the Warsaw Pact and its relationship to the struggle for power in the Soviet Union.

SEE ALSO: Mar. 12, 1947: Truman Doctrine; Apr. 3, 1948: Marshall Plan Provides Aid to Europe; Jan. 25, 1949: Soviet Bloc States Establish Council for Mutual Economic Assistance; Sept. 21-Oct. 7, 1949: Germany Splits into Two Republics; Feb. 14, 1950: Stalin and Mao Pen a Defense Pact; Oct. 23, 1954: Western European Union Is Established; Nov. 12, 1968-Dec., 1989: Brezhnev Doctrine Mandates Soviet Control of Satellite Nations; June-Sept., 1989: Poland Forms a Noncommunist Government; Nov. 17-Dec. 29, 1989: Velvet Revolution in Czechoslovakia; July 1, 1991: Dissolution of the Warsaw Pact.

■ MAY 15, 1955

AUSTRIA REGAINS ITS INDEPENDENCE

The signing of the Austrian State Treaty marked the end of the four-power Allied occupation of Austria by the United States, the United Kingdom, France, and the Soviet Union and signaled the restoration of Austrian sovereignty. Conditions of the treaty included Austria's "permanent neutrality" and the departure of Allied troops from the newly independent nation by the end of September, 1955.

ALSO KNOWN AS: Austrian State Treaty

LOCALE: Vienna, Austria

CATEGORIES: Diplomacy and international relations; government and politics; military history; geography

KEY FIGURES

John Foster Dulles (1888-1959), U.S. secretary of state, 1953-1959

Vyacheslav Mikhailovich Molotov (Vyacheslav Mikhailovich Skryabin; 1890-1986), Soviet foreign minister, 1939-1949, 1953-1956

Ivan Ivanovich Ilyichev (fl. mid-twentieth century), Soviet ambassador to
  Austria
Llewellyn Thompson (1904-1972), U.S. ambassador to Austria
Julius Raab (1891-1964), federal chancellor of the Republic of Austria
Leopold Figl (1902-1965), foreign minister of the Republic of Austria
Harold Macmillan (1894-1986), British foreign minister
Antoine Pinay (1891-1994), French foreign minister
Roger Lalouette (fl. mid-twentieth century), acting French ambassador to
  Austria
Sir Geoffrey Arnold Wallinger (1903-1979), British ambassador to Austria

SUMMARY OF EVENT

The Austrian State Treaty is firmly rooted in Allied plans for the reconstruction of central Europe following the end of World War II and in the Cold
War between the United States and the Soviet Union. Generally, it can be
said that the first governing principle for the handling of Austria following
its liberation from National Socialist rule in April, 1945, was the Moscow
Declaration of October, 1943, which deemed Austria the "first victim of fascist aggression." The declaration also declared that Austria had a special responsibility to atone for crimes committed under Nazi rule, and that Austrian citizens would have to atone for their part in Nazi crimes. Still,
Austria's politicians for years portrayed their country as a victim of the Nazis
while forgetting the complicity of many Austrians in Nazi Germany's wartime conquests.

Austria's path to the state treaty was a twisting one with all sorts of dead
ends that mirrored the ups and downs of the Cold War. This course was fit-
tingly compared on one U.S. poster to a carousel spiraling upward, with Austria as a horse and a Russian "Nyet" ("No") at the top of the poster, representing Soviet reluctance to support the conclusion of an agreement.

On one hand, Soviet stalling on the drafting of a treaty, which had begun
in 1947, prompted U.S. secretary of state John Foster Dulles to compare Soviet foreign minister Vyacheslav Mikhailovich Molotov to the evil power that
kept "pushing the stone back" on Sisyphus in the story from Greek mythol-
ogy. For Dulles, Austria was Sisyphus and the stone was Russia stalling on the
state treaty, embodied by Molotov. On the other hand, the Soviets saw in
the treaty a chance to get concessions from the other Allies and to get hefty
payments from Austria for Soviet cooperation. By using delaying tactics, the
Soviets turned the negotiations into stop-and-go proceedings for nearly
eight years.

The issue of neutrality was a sticking point in the treaty negotiations,
even though, according to information from a poll conducted in March,

1947, by the Information Service Branch of the U.S. forces in Austria, 78 percent of Austrians in the U.S. zone of occupation favored strict neutrality for Austria on the Swiss model. The call for neutrality was later amended by Austria's politicians, who made clear that they intended to be neutral militarily, not ideologically, meaning that Austria would participate in the international political sphere.

The breakthrough in negotiations came when Austria was permitted to participate in the Berlin Conference of January, 1954, on an equal par with the foreign ministers of France, Britain, the United States, and the Soviet Union. Failure to agree on the status of Germany, however, blocked talks, because the Soviets were not willing to remove their troops from Austria until Germany had been made neutral, something France, Britain, and the United States were not willing to allow.

In February, 1955, the Soviets invited the Austrians to Moscow for bilateral negotiations. The United States was worried that the Austrians would be tricked by Molotov, but the meeting was allowed to proceed. In April the Austrian delegation arrived in Moscow and signed the so-called "Moscow Memorandum," in which the Soviet Union declared itself willing to restore Austria's sovereignty and remove its occupation troops if Austria declared itself "permanently neutral." This was a major breakthrough, although when Austrian federal chancellor Julius Raab read a statement on April 15 that "the Austrian Government will declare its status of neutrality like that practiced by the Swiss Confederation . . . ," Molotov was less than enthusiastic.

On May 15 foreign ministers and ambassadors of the Allied occupying powers and the foreign minister of Austria met at the Belvedere Palace in Vienna to sign the treaty. It was a huge coup for the Austrians, who, unlike the Germans, were able to get the Soviet Union to agree to withdraw from Austrian territory in exchange for a promise of permanent neutrality as well as compensation for wartime German assets they believed Austria still held.

The treaty had nine signatories: Molotov, Dulles, U.S. ambassador to Austria Llewellyn Thompson, French foreign minister Antoine Pinay, Russian ambassador to Austria Ivan Ivanovich Ilyichev, French ambassador to Austria Roger Lalouette, British foreign minister Harold Macmillan, British ambassador to Austria Sir Geoffrey Arnold Wallinger, and Austrian foreign minister Leopold Figl. Yugoslavia and Czechoslovakia became parties to the treaty later by way of accession, but since the dissolution of these nations in the 1990's, they are no longer considered party to the treaty, while Russia is recognized as the successor state to the Soviet Union.

Following the signing, Austrian foreign minister Figl declared "Austria is free!" at the Belvedere Palace and stood on the balcony with the other foreign ministers and ambassadors to present the treaty to the Austrian people, who cheered loudly when they saw the signed document. Vienna's *Die Presse* newspaper reported on May 17 that Vienna's streets were full of celebrants. People rejoiced in the rain, dancing, singing, and playing music until the early hours of the morning. They waltzed and sang the Austrian national anthem, "Land der Berge, Land am Strome" (land of mountains, land on the river Danube).

The Austrian parliament affirmed the country's permanent neutrality on October 26, the date on which Austria's independence is celebrated every year. Austria was formally admitted to the United Nations on December 15, completing the country's full reintegration into the community of nations.

SIGNIFICANCE

The Austrian State Treaty reestablished Austria as a "sovereign, independent, and democratic state" in its boundaries before 1938, when the Nazis annexed Austria to Germany in what is known as the Anschluss, or political union. Further prohibited was a restoration of the Habsburg Dynasty. Austria was indeed a "special case" during Cold War negotiations, for the treaty of sovereignty marked the first and only time the Soviet Union had relinquished control over a nation under its influence.

Perhaps Dulles summarized best what the state treaty meant in a television appearance with U.S. president Dwight D. Eisenhower two days after the treaty was signed: nearly "16,000 square miles and 1.7 million people have been freed from Soviet control and economic exploitation. . . . [I]t marks the first time that the Red Armies will have turned their face in the other direction and gone back since 1945." In short, the treaty legally recognized and fully legitimized the Second Austrian Republic and freed it from foreign occupation.

Gregory Weeks

FURTHER READING

Allard, Sven. *Russia and the Austrian State Treaty: A Case Study of Soviet Policy in Europe.* University Park: Pennsylvania State University Press, 1970. Looks at Soviet delays and demands during the state treaty negotiations.

Bischof, Günter. *Austria in the First Cold War, 1945-1955: The Leverage of the Weak.* New York: St. Martin's Press, 1999. Examines the place of Austria between the East and the West during the Cold War and concludes that Austria exerted its leverage to the fullest in bringing about the signing of the treaty. Excellent bibliography.

Carafano, James J. *Waltzing into the Cold War: The Struggle for Occupied Austria.*

College Station: Texas A&M University Press, 2002. Provides an overview of the Allied and especially U.S. occupation of Austria and the trials and tribulations of occupation for the U.S. forces in Austria.

Düriegl, Günter, and Gerhard Frodl, eds. *The New Austria: The Exhibition to Commemorate the Fiftieth Anniversary of the State Treaty 1955-2005.* Vienna: Österreichische Galerie Belvedere, 2005. The catalog that accompanied the fiftieth anniversary exhibit on the Austrian State Treaty. Contains comprehensive essays by noted Austrian experts on the treaty and its continuing significance.

Larson, Deborah Welch. "Negotiating the Austrian State Treaty, 1953-1955." Washington, D.C.: Georgetown University Press, 1995. A concise fifteen-page overview of the winding path to the state treaty.

See also: June 24, 1948-May 11, 1949: Berlin Blockade and Airlift; Apr. 4, 1949: North Atlantic Treaty Organization Is Formed; Sept. 21-Oct. 7, 1949: Germany Splits into Two Republics; May 14, 1955: Warsaw Pact Is Signed; Oct. 23-Nov. 10, 1956: Soviets Crush Hungarian Uprising; Aug. 20-21, 1968: Soviet Union Invades Czechoslovakia; Nov. 12, 1968-Dec., 1989: Brezhnev Doctrine Mandates Soviet Control of Satellite Nations; 1989: Hungary Adopts a Multiparty System; Feb. 26, 1990: Soviet Troops Withdraw from Czechoslovakia; Dec., 1991: Dissolution of the Soviet Union.

■ July 9, 1955-early 1960's

Scientists Campaign Against Nuclear Testing

During the post-World War II period, Linus Pauling and other scientists spoke and wrote on the perils of nuclear testing and weaponry, leading the public to rethink the dangers not only of nuclear fallout and radiation poisoning but also the ultimate danger: nuclear annihilation.

Locale: United States
Categories: Social issues and reform; environmental issues; health and medicine

KEY FIGURES

Linus Pauling (1901-1994), physical chemist whose campaign against
   nuclear testing won for him a Nobel Peace Prize
Barry Commoner (b. 1917), plant physiologist and environmental activist
   who helped pioneer the public dissemination of information on
   nuclear testing
Hermann Joseph Muller (1890-1967), biologist and geneticist whose 1946
   Nobel Prize later led to his activism against nuclear testing

SUMMARY OF EVENT

On October 10, 1963, the Nobel Peace Prize committee of the Norwegian
parliament announced that the 1962 Nobel Peace Prize would be given to
Linus Pauling. It was not a coincidence that this was also the day that the
Limited Test Ban Treaty went into effect, because the committee used its
award to Pauling to call attention to the scientists who had aroused public
awareness of the dangers of nuclear testing. Even though the treaty did
not ban underground tests, it did end nearly two decades of aboveground
testing by the United States, the Soviet Union, and Great Britain. In the
years following the ban, this cessation of testing dramatically reduced atmospheric and ground contamination with dangerous and persistent radioactive isotopes.

From July, 1945, when Manhattan Project scientists and the U.S. military detonated the first atomic bomb in the desert of New Mexico, to August, 1963, when the United States completed its final series of atmospheric tests in the Pacific, the accumulated tonnage of nuclear explosions
had been doubling every three years. A similar expansion in the quantity
and power of nuclear tests characterized the Soviet Union's testing program from 1949, when Soviet scientists first detonated an atomic bomb,
until the summer of 1963, when the Soviet Union, too, ended its atmospheric testing.

Because of the many nuclear tests by these and other countries, fallout all over the earth kept escalating, as the longer-lived radioactive isotopes gradually settled back to the Earth with other debris from nuclear explosions. As time passed, these isotopes became part of various ecosystems
and thereby endangered all levels of life. Because such fallout isotopes as
strontium 90 concentrated in the tissues of highly developed organisms,
they posed a particularly acute danger for human beings. The growing environmental contamination alarmed many scientists, some of whom participated during the late 1940's and early 1950's in the campaign for the civilian control of atomic weapons through the United Nations (U.N.).

Pauling, whose many basic discoveries in structural chemistry and molec-

Future Nobel peace laureate Linus Pauling (right) at Caltech around 1952 with fellow professor George Beadle. (California Institute of Technology)

ular biology had made him a highly respected scientist by the late 1940's, was representative of a small but growing group in his profession who believed that scientists had a responsibility to appraise the peril posed by nuclear weapons and to alert the public. In a world deeply divided by the Cold War, Pauling wanted people to set aside partisan feelings and think in new ways; he argued that people had to see themselves as members of a biological species that could become extinct. A pivotal event on the road to such an understanding was the detonation of the most powerful bomb ever tested by the United States.

The fifteen-megaton hydrogen-bomb test on March 1, 1954, not only obliterated an island in the Bikini Atoll but also sucked the pulverized remains into a gigantic, highly radioactive plume that slowly drifted around the world. Downwind from the explosion, the crew members of the Japanese trawler *Lucky Dragon* were exposed to such heavy amounts of radioactive fallout that all developed radiation poisoning, and one fisherman died. Furthermore, radioactive isotopes that fell on the ocean became part of the food chain and concentrated in the tissues of fish, creating dangers hundreds of miles from the test site. In the aftermath of these events, worldwide concern about fallout from atmospheric testing grew rapidly.

Hermann Joseph Muller, widely regarded as the leading expert on radiation-induced genetic changes, became concerned that nuclear tests were seriously undermining the biological integrity of humanity. With Pauling and other prominent scientists, Muller signed the July 9, 1955, Russell-Einstein Manifesto, an appeal stating that nuclear weapons threatened the continued existence of the human species and urging that an international congress of scientists be convened to pass a resolution imploring the governments of the world to settle their differences peacefully. This manifesto led to the establishment of the Pugwash Conferences on Science and World Affairs, many of which became forums for debating fallout and other nuclear issues.

Muller, who attended some of the early meetings of the organization, became very critical of medical, industrial, and military indifference to radiation damage. He believed that radiation caused harmful mutations in direct proportion to total exposure; as studies made clear, no level, even that received from a diagnostic X ray, could be considered safe.

As these warnings about the dangers of radiation percolated to the public, the debate about nuclear testing and fallout became intensely political. Adlai E. Stevenson, the 1956 Democratic presidential candidate, called for a test ban as a helpful way to revive the disarmament negotiations, but Dwight D. Eisenhower, the Republican incumbent, argued that the tests were necessary to prevent the United States from being put at a military disadvantage. After Eisenhower's election, Pauling, who had been publishing both scientific and polemical papers demonstrating the dangers of fallout, learned to his dismay that the president's new secretary of health, education, and welfare had terminated the funding for one of his research projects.

On May 15, 1957, in the middle of this divisive ideological climate, Pauling gave an address on "Science in the Modern World" at Washington University in St. Louis, Missouri. He discussed how bomb tests were causing an increase in the number of bad genes, which would result in the deaths of many people from leukemia and other diseases. He then gave Albert Schweitzer's definition of a humanitarian as someone who believes that "no human being should be sacrificed to a project" and concluded by stating that no human being should be sacrificed to the project of perfecting nuclear weapons. So well received was his address that Pauling and some scientists in the audience decided that some action should be taken to stop the testing of nuclear weapons.

Barry Commoner and Edward Condon, professors at Washington University, composed statements that Pauling combined into a two-hundred-word Appeal of Scientists, calling for an international agreement to stop nuclear testing. Within a few weeks, more than two thousand American scientists, including Muller, had signed the appeal. Pauling sent it to Eisenhower and issued a statement to the press. The petition became news all over the world; soon, Pauling was receiving signatures to the appeal from scientists in other countries. On January 15, 1958, Pauling and his wife Ava Helen presented the petition, with a list of more than nine thousand signers, to U.N. general secretary Dag Hammarskjöld.

Pauling's petition generated controversy in both scholarly and popular venues. For example, in February, Pauling engaged in a debate with Edward Teller, often described as "the father of the hydrogen bomb," on the educational television station KQED in San Francisco, California. Pauling argued that fallout from the tests was causing the birth of thousands of disabled children and that radiation from isotopes in the environment was causing leukemia and bone cancers. Teller argued that fallout contributed only a small fraction to natural radiation and that human exposure to this fraction was as dangerous as being an ounce overweight.

One month after this television debate, Pauling and seventeen others, including Norman Thomas and Bertrand Russell, brought a lawsuit against the U.S. Department of Defense and the Atomic Energy Commission to stop nuclear tests. About the same time, Commoner and others founded the St. Louis Committee for Nuclear Information (later known as the Committee on Environmental Information). One of the committee's first projects was a survey of baby teeth that revealed high levels of strontium 90 in the teeth of children in St. Louis. In his 1958 book *No More War!* Pauling brought together many of the arguments against testing; he sent more than fifteen hundred copies to influential individuals, including every member of Congress.

The work of Pauling, Commoner, and others began to have an effect. In 1960, a Gallup poll showed that more than 60 percent of the American public favored a test ban (as opposed to only 20 percent three years earlier). Despite this growing public support, Pauling continued to be harassed by the government. In the summer of 1960, he was called by a congressional subcommittee and asked to furnish the names of the individuals who had helped him gather signatures for his U.N. petition. When he was called before the subcommittee a second time in the fall, he refused to reveal the names of these scientists, many of whom were in the early stages of their careers, and the committee ultimately backed down.

Because of the work of Pauling and others, public pressure on government officials to end nuclear tests increased to such an extent that the United States and the Soviet Union embarked on a series of test moratoriums, but these were often broken by one side or the other. The event that, more than any other, caused negotiations to succeed was the Cuban Missile Crisis of October, 1962. This flirtation with nuclear disaster had a sobering effect on U.S. president John F. Kennedy and Soviet leader Nikita S. Khrushchev. Both leaders thereupon became willing to compromise, and their negotiating teams worked out the Limited Test Ban Treaty in the summer of 1963. To secure ratification by the U.S. Senate, Kennedy had to make important concessions to the military, including the promise to pursue an aggressive underground testing program. Once these concessions were made, the treaty was ratified. It went into effect on October 10, the day that Pauling's Nobel Peace Prize was announced.

During the height of the Cold War, signs such as this were common in public buildings throughout American cities. (©John Wollwerth/Dreamstime.com)

SIGNIFICANCE

The nuclear test ban debate brought about a new relationship between scientists and the general public. Scientists discovered through this debate that all knowledge, even esoteric scientific knowledge, could be political. The public learned that a nuclear explosion was not merely a physical process but also a vast ecological experiment. Scientists were undertaking these devastating interventions into the biosphere without an adequate grasp of their possible dangers. They were discovering that these weapons of mass destruction were especially pernicious because their impact could not be confined to a particular place or time. Fallout could insidiously spread a test bomb's radioactive poisons all over the world, and these poisons became part of various ecosystems for decades.

Pauling, Commoner, and Muller were able to alert the public to these dangers. Pauling, the chemist, was able to show that radioactive isotopes in test fallout could cause genetic and somatic damage to adults, children, and fetuses. Commoner, the biologist, was able to communicate how these isotopes became part of nature's ecosystems. Muller, the geneticist, demonstrated that radiation from the isotopes had teratogenic effects and that no radiation level was really safe. Pauling, Commoner, Muller, and the scientists who supported them recognized that their views prevailed because they used arguments that had more popular emotional appeal than those of Teller and his supporters. When strontium 90 turned up in the milk of nursing mothers, concerned citizens had an issue they could understand.

The most immediate result of the Limited Test Ban Treaty was the halt of atmospheric nuclear tests by the Soviet Union, the United States, and Great Britain, its initial signatories. Eventually, more than one hundred nations signed the treaty. In the years after the ban, contamination of the environment by fallout isotopes steadily declined. For example, levels of strontium 90 in milk and in children's bones have decreased dramatically since the ban.

A less direct effect of the treaty was its influence on arms control. The test ban proved that meaningful disarmament steps were possible. It was the first treaty that explicitly limited nuclear competition among nations, and it was respected by its signatories.

The treaty, however, did not prohibit underground testing, nor did it permit on-site inspections. To get the treaty ratified, Kennedy had to compromise by agreeing that technology not prohibited by the test ban would be vigorously developed; in the case of underground testing, it was. Both the United States and the Soviet Union tested more after the treaty was signed than before. In the years between 1945 and 1963, these two countries carried out nearly five hundred nuclear tests, most of them aboveground; in the years between 1963 and 1981, the two nations exploded more than seven hundred nuclear weapons, all underground.

In short, the limited test ban did little to stop the arms race; it simply forced testing underground, where the pace actually accelerated. This did not concern most citizens, because their anger had been directed primarily at radioactive fallout rather than at nuclear testing itself. Consequently, few obstacles remained to prevent the creation and testing of new and more efficient nuclear weapons. Instead of leading to an era of arms agreements, the Limited Test Ban Treaty actually called forth a new arms race.

Nevertheless, the treaty represented a first step. It served as a model of activism for many scientists, some of whom played major roles in the environmental movement. Most analysts agreed that aroused public opinion had much to do with the treaty's evolution and ratification and that scientists such as Pauling and Commoner did much to shape that opinion. Kennedy was assassinated six weeks after the Senate ratified the treaty, and Khrushchev was deposed a year later, but the test ban survived through many changes of regimes and political parties.

Robert J. Paradowski

FURTHER READING

Commoner, Barry. *Making Peace with the Planet.* New York: Pantheon Books, 1990. Commoner discusses the environmental costs of technological developments. His experiences in the campaign against nuclear testing form a subtheme in this book. Includes extensive bibliographical references and an index.

Divine, Robert A. *Blowing on the Wind: The Nuclear Test Ban Debate, 1954-1960.* New York: Oxford University Press, 1978. Detailed analysis of the debate that followed the development of the hydrogen bomb by the United States and the Soviet Union. Emphasizes the potential dangers that nuclear fallout poses for human health and genetic stability, and documents how professional scientists, humanists, and concerned citizens became involved in the debate. Includes a useful chronology, 1950-1963, an extensive bibliography, and an index.

Hacker, Barton C. *Elements of Controversy: The Atomic Energy Commission and Radiation Safety in Nuclear Weapons Testing, 1947-1974.* Berkeley: University of California Press, 1994. A sequel to the author's earlier work, *The Dragon's Tail: Radiation Safety in the Manhattan Project, 1942-1946.* Draws on government and medical documents to show how American nuclear weapons tests in the 1950's and 1960's subjected many soldiers and ordinary Americans to large amounts of radiation. Discusses the controversy whether overexposure to radiation actually caused the cancers and birth abnormalities that were attributed to it. Includes seven maps, one table, and a good index.

Kendall, Henry W. *A Distant Light: Scientists and Public Policy.* New York: Springer-Verlag, 2000. Written by a former UCS board chair, this collection outlines the challenges faced by scientists who are politically active especially on issues of science and public policy.

Lochbaum, David. *Walking a Nuclear Tightrope: Unlearned Lessons of Year-plus Reactor Outages.* Cambridge, Mass.: Union of Concerned Scientists, 2006. A brief report that discusses "extended nuclear power reactor outages" and outlines how the Nuclear Regulatory Commission can avoid a catastrophic nuclear accident.

Nuclearfiles.org. An excellent resource for students studying the history of the atomic age. The site, a project of the Nuclear Age Peace Foundation, includes links to primary sources, study guides, suggested readings, and much more.

Oliver, Kendrick. *Kennedy, Macmillan, and the Nuclear Test-ban Debate, 1961-63.* New York: St. Martin's Press, Scholarly and Reference Division, 1998. A history of U.S. and British negotiations to ban the testing of nuclear weapons and to control the global arms race. Part of the Studies in Military and Strategic History series.

Pauling, Linus. *Linus Pauling, in His Own Words: Selected Writings, Speeches, and Interviews.* Edited by Barbara Marinacci. New York: Simon & Schuster, 1995. A collection of the words and talks of Pauling, organized in the following sections: The Path of Learning, 1901-1922; The Structure of Matter, 1922-1954; The Nuclear Age, 1945-1994; and Nutritional Medicine, 1954-1994.

_____. *Linus Pauling on Peace: A Scientist Speaks Out on Humanism and World Survival.* Edited and selected by Barbara Marinacci and Ramesh Krishnamurthy. Los Altos, Calif.: Rising Star Press, 1998. This collection presents selected writings and talks, organized into the following sections: Education and Science in a Democracy; War, Peace, and Dissent; In the Nuclear Age; Peace Through Humanism; The Scientist in Society; and Future Prophecies.

_____. *No More War!* New York: Dodd, Mead, 1983. The twenty-fifth anniversary edition of one of the earliest books to alert the public to the potential dangers of nuclear war and nuclear weapons testing in the atmosphere. Explains the nature of nuclear weapons and the effects of radiation. Unaltered reprint of the 1958 version with addenda to each chapter that discuss some of the intervening developments. Includes seven appendixes, a bibliography, and an index.

Seaborg, Glenn T. *Kennedy, Khrushchev, and the Test Ban.* Berkeley: University of California Press, 1981. The author, who was chair of the Atomic Energy Commission and actively involved in the test-ban negotiations, deals only peripherally with the movement against nuclear-weapons atmospheric tests. Discusses, rather, the delicate negotiations carried out by representatives from the United States, the Soviet Union, and the United Kingdom. Includes the text of the treaty in an appendix and a good index.

SEE ALSO: Aug. 6 and 9, 1945: Atomic Bombs Destroy Hiroshima and Nagasaki; 1951-1952: Teller and Ulam Develop the First Hydrogen Bomb; Mar. 1, 1954: Nuclear Bombing of Bikini Atoll; Aug. 5, 1963: Nuclear Powers Sign the Limited Test Ban Treaty; Oct. 16, 1964: China Explodes Its First Nuclear Bomb; Mar. 5, 1970: Nuclear Non-Proliferation Treaty Goes into Effect; Oct. 16, 1980: China Conducts Atmospheric Nuclear Test; Oct., 1983: Europeans Demonstrate Against Nuclear Weapons.

■ **DECEMBER 14, 1955**

UNITED NATIONS ADMITS SIXTEEN NEW MEMBERS

After five years of vetoes and controversy in the U.N. Security Council, the permanent members overcame their differences and agreed to admit to the United Nations sixteen countries whose applications had been held up by Cold War feuding.

ALSO KNOWN AS: United Nations resolution 995 (X)
LOCALE: New York, New York
CATEGORIES: United Nations; organizations and institutions; diplomacy and international relations

KEY FIGURES
Henry Cabot Lodge, Jr. (1902-1985), U.S. representative to the U.N. Security Council
Dag Hammarskjöld (1905-1961), Swedish secretary-general of the United Nations, 1953-1961
José Maza (1889-1964), Chilean president of the U.N. General Assembly in 1955

SUMMARY OF EVENT

At its 555th plenary meeting on December 14, 1955, under the leadership of Secretary-General Dag Hammarskjöld and Assembly President José Maza, the U.N. General Assembly adopted resolution 995 (X), admitting sixteen new members to the United Nations. They were Albania, Austria, Bulgaria, Cambodia, Finland, Hungary, Ireland, Italy, Jordan, Laos, Libya, Nepal, Portugal, Romania, Spain, and Ceylon (Sri Lanka).

The admission of these sixteen countries was a result of a recommendation made by the Security Council, which had the power to discuss membership applications and make recommendations to the General Assembly. Candidates for membership needed to secure a recommendation by gaining at least seven affirmative votes from the council. The Security Council's recommendation then had to be followed by a two-thirds vote of the General Assembly. In 1955, the Security Council was composed of the five permanent members (Nationalist China, France, the Soviet Union, the United Kingdom, and the United States) and six non-permanent members (New Zealand, Turkey, Brazil, Peru, Iran, and Belgium).

The Security Council's admission recommendation represented a compromise between the Soviet Union and Western powers on the council, as four Eastern European states and twelve noncommunist states were admitted. Since 1946, only a few states had been admitted to the United Nations. In the course of membership discussions during that period, the Soviet Union typically advocated membership for the Eastern European states that fell under its dominance, and the noncommunist Western nations, led by the United States, supported membership for pro-Western states, such as Germany, Italy, and Japan (the former Axis Powers of World War II). This situation frequently led to a deadlock, because each of the council's five permanent members had veto power: Any one of them could prevent a new nation's membership from being recommended. Between 1946 and 1955, then, few nations joined the organization, because few were acceptable to both the communist powers and the capitalist powers on the Security Council.

While the original U.N. Charter included the principle of "universality," its article 4 provided that members were to be admitted by a decision of the General Assembly upon recommendation of the Security Council. Because the Security Council was dominated by the major Cold War powers, considerations of universality gave way to the advantage each side might derive by admitting a particular nation, thereby granting it a vote in the General Assembly. This paved the way for power struggles in the Security Council, in which membership proposals were blocked by one side or the other. The tensions in the Security Council were evident even in the vote to recommend admission of the sixteen new states: eight council members voted in support of admission, and three members abstained (Belgium, China, and the United States).

SIGNIFICANCE

The wholesale admission of sixteen nations to the United Nations at the end of 1955 marked a change in the rate of growth of the organization. After 1955, the expansion of U.N. membership became much more rapid. During the prior decade, battles over admission of new states exposed the tensions between the two ideological blocs and the world's two superpowers: the communist states under the leadership of the Soviet Union, and the noncommunist states led by the United States.

By 1955, it was clear that the use of their veto power by the permanent Security Council members had quickly become a political tool. It was routinely employed for reasons of pure self-interest, despite the absence of any substantive legal justification in a given case. For example, the Soviet Union hindered the admission of Italy, which enjoyed the support of the Western council members, even though the Italian government had fulfilled all of the necessary conditions to be admitted. The United States did not use its veto during these proceedings, in part because it was initially able to secure a majority of countries on the Security Council to vote for pro-Western candidates.

This early Cold War stalemate—as each side blocked admission of new members who did not share its views and ideology—had led to stagnation in the growth of the United Nations. Between 1947 and 1955, only five new members were admitted: Yemen and Pakistan in 1947, Myanmar in 1948, Israel in 1949, and Indonesia in 1950. The sixteen-nation admission in 1955 thus represented a breakthrough. It was a result of efforts, especially in the 1950's, to overcome tensions among the superpowers and realize the ideal of universal membership. It set a precedent for an organization that would eventually grow to encompass practically all the nations of the world.

Kasia Polanska

FURTHER READING

Arce, José. *United Nations: Admission of New Members.* Madrid, Spain: n.p., 1952. Firsthand account of Arce's experience as an Argentine politician and diplomat working within the United Nations. Includes accounts of discussions regarding the admittance of new members.

Ask, Sten, and Anna Mark-Jungkvist, eds. *The Adventure of Peace: Dag Hammarskjöld and the Future of the United Nations.* New York: Palgrave Macmillan,

2005. Details the secretariat of Hammarskjöld, under whom the United Nations broke its Cold War deadlock to admit sixteen new nations.

Bailey, Sydney D. *The Procedure of the U.N. Security Council.* New York: Oxford University Press, 1975. Examines the procedure and practice of the United Nations Security Council. Contains procedures and examples of discussions about specific membership applications.

Bishop, William W., Jr. "Conditions of Admission of a State to Membership in the United Nations." *American Journal of International Law* 42, no. 4 (October, 1948): 927-934. The text of the Advisory Opinion by the International Court of Justice dated May 28, 1948.

Chamberlin, Waldo, Thomas Hovet, Jr., and Erica Hovet. *A Chronology and Fact Book of the United Nations: 1941-1976.* Dobbs Ferry, N.Y.: Oceana, 1976. Details events and activities in the United Nations, including those surrounding the 1955 membership debates. Includes members and presidents of U.N. bodies and dates of applications for U.N. membership along with dates of admission.

Heller, Peter B. *The United Nations Under Dag Hammarskjöld, 1953-1961.* Lanham, Md.: Scarecrow Press, 2001. Assays the U.N. secretary-general both as an individual and as a professional.

Lee, Roy S., ed. *Swords into Plowshares: Building Peace Through the United Nations.* Boston: Martinus Nijhoff, 2006. Anthology of essays evaluating the United Nations' history and progress from the point of view of the early twenty-first century.

Rudzinski, Aleksander W. *The Admission of New Members.* New York: Carnegie Endowment for International Peace, 1952. Discusses the procedures and issues in admission of new members.

_____. "The So-Called Double Veto." *American Journal of International Law* vol. 45, no. 3 (July, 1951): 443-461. Explores the application of the veto power in the Security Council. Gives examples of how the veto has been used in cases of application for membership.

SEE ALSO: Apr. 25-June 26, 1945: United Nations Charter Convention; July, 1960: United Nations Intervenes in the Congolese Civil War; 1963-1965: Crisis in U.N. Financing Emerges Over Peacekeeping Expenses; Oct. 25, 1971: People's Republic of China Is Seated at the United Nations; 1990-1994: United Nations Admits Many New Members; July 16, 1990: Gorbachev Agrees to Membership of a United Germany in NATO.